FASHION
THE MIRROR OF HISTORY

A Chanticleer Press Edition

FASHION
THE MIRROR OF HISTORY

Michael and Ariane Batterberry

GREENWICH HOUSE
Distributed by Crown Publishers, Inc., New York

This 1982 edition published by Greenwich House, a division of Arlington House, Inc., distributed by Crown Publishers, Inc.

Library of Congress Cataloging in Publication Data
Batterberry, Michael.
Fashion, the mirror of history.
Reprint. Originally published: Mirror, mirror. New York: Holt, Rinehart and Winston, ©1977.
Bibliography: p. 392
Includes index.
1. Costume—History.   2. Fashion—History.   3. Costume—Social aspects.   4. Fashion—Social aspects.   I. Batterberry, Ariane Ruskin.   II. Title
[GT511.B37 1982]   391′.009   82-6220
ISBN: 0-517-388812   AACR2

Second Edition

h g f e d

Prepared and produced by Chanticleer Press, Inc.
Printed and bound in Hong Kong.

Project editor and designer: Ellen Hsiao

For our nieces and nephews

The editors wish to thank the following publishers and persons for their kind permission to reprint in this volume excerpts from the following:
Harry N. Abrams, *American Denim* by Peter Beagle, 1975
Doubleday & Co., Inc., *Book of the Courtier*, translated by Charles S. Singleton, 1959; and
Good Behavior by Harold Nicolson, 1956
Duell, Sloan & Pierce-Little, Brown & Co., *The Listing Attic* by Edward Gorey, 1954
Harper & Row Publishers Inc., *Madame de Pompadour* by Nancy Mitford, 1954; and
The Romanovs by Virginia Cowles, 1971
Holt, Rinehart and Winston Inc., *The Wings of the Falcon* by Joseph Kaster, 1968
Alfred A. Knopf, *The First Great Civilizations* by Jacquetta Hawkes
New Directions, *Elegiac Feelings America* by Gregory Corso, 1970
Harold Ober Associates, "A Millionaire's Girl" by F. Scott Fitzgerald, 1930 Copyright 1957 by Frances Scott Fitzgerald Lanahan.
G. P. Putnam and Sons, *Life in Italy at the Time of the Medici*, by John Gage, 1968

The editors wish to thank the following people who have been most generous with their advice and help in the course of our picture research and compilation: Sally Kirkland; Robert Riley, John Touhey, and Marjorie Miller of the Fashion Institute of Technology; Robert Kaufman and Sheila Smith of the Cooper-Hewitt Picture Library; Milton Sonday, Gillian Moss, and Xenia Cage of the Cooper-Hewitt Museum; Gordon Stone of the Metropolitan Museum of Art; Dominik Keller of "Du" Magazine; Mrs. Adrian McCardell; Madame Poiret; John Lynch; Betty Terry of Trigère Inc.; A. H. Cundey of Henry Poole & Co., Ltd.

CONTENTS

Foreword

Each day as we prepare to meet our world we perform a very popular ritual: getting dressed. This may mean only adding a daub of war paint or freshening a grass girdle. Or it may be the painstaking ceremonious levee of a monarch. For most of us, however, it means the exchange of nightwear for day clothes.

Although nakedness does still exist in some isolated primitive communities, there appears to be no society that is entirely composed of totally unadorned human beings. The desire to alter or to add to the original natural state is so prevalent in the human species that we must assume it has become an inborn trait that contributes to our "humanness" and sets us apart from the rest of the animals.

When did it begin? It certainly precedes recorded history. Bodily covering was probably the first man-made shelter and the human skin the earliest canvas. Standing erect with his arms and hands free to function creatively, man must have soon discovered that his anatomical frame could accommodate a wide variety of physical self-improvements. His shoulders could support a mantle to protect him from the elements. Around his neck he could hang amulets to ward off evil spirits. And if he sought some measure of modesty, or to accentuate his sexuality, he could suspend from his waist an apron to cover or enhance his private parts. To stand out above his peers and indicate his superior position, he found his head could be an excellent foundation for adding stature and importance. Intertwined with these motivating factors and building on them is the human instinct for creative expression, an outlet for the aesthetic spirit. Eventually, no external part of the body at one time or another has escaped some sort of adornment.

Changes in needs and outlooks often blur the purposes that originally gave articles of human raiment a *raison d'être*. Vestiges are relegated to tradition; others undergo a kind of mutation. The sheltering mantle, for example, can become a magnificent but cumbersome robe of state. Amulets, their symbolism lost or forgotten, become objects of decoration to show off the wearer's wealth.

Concepts of modesty can grow so complex that the mere sight of a lady's ankle might produce sexual excitement. And the king's crown in another version can be a dunce cap.

Man is a gregarious creature. And although innovations and changes may be initiated by individuals, the inspiration that triggers them grows out of the innovator's environment, and their acceptance or rejection is determined by his society. While this applies to every human endeavor, nothing so graphically and consistently reflects social and cultural patterns as the manner in which individuals within a society alter their original appearance. It is, then, this special manner that groups of people agree is the way to dress and behave that sets them apart in a point of time and place and gives definition to the word "fashion."

Fashion, a social phenomenon, can be a powerful force. Societies evolve for themselves a set of rules, and most people, consciously or subconsciously, do their best to conform. It is their social security. The nonconformists, those who do not wish to join in this game, must either sever their relationship and go it alone or suffer the consequences.

These regulations are hardly capricious. Their roots are in the foundation of a society which, although composed of individuals, develops an identity of its own and an instinct for self-preservation. A homogeneity in dress is a manifest catalyst, a visible unifier of a social group. Because this is so, costume if read properly can give us an insight not only into the class structure of a social organization but also into its religion and aesthetics, its fears, hopes and goals.

Our clothes continue to reflect our anxieties and how we try to cope with them. Today our society is rapidly becoming global. The recent worldwide rage for jeans is an example of this new universality and the wholesale movement to break down past barriers—geographical, social and cultural. Contemporary sages claim that we are returning to basic realities. How we express this in what we choose to wear will provide future historians with clues as to what we considered were the basic realities and how we attempted to reclaim them.

Stella Blum
Curator of Costumes, Metropolitan
Museum of Art, New York City

Dressing to dance:
Below: The Clal-lam Indians
of Vancouver Island wear
totemic masks for their medicine dance. Painting by Paul
Kane, 1847.
Bottom: Members of the
American aristocracy dressed
in white tie, hunting pinks and

bustles for their hunt ball.
Hunt Ball, by Julius L. Stewart.
Late 19th century.

Introduction

"Fashion is the mirror of history," Louis XIV correctly observed. Taken out of historical context, however, few fashions make sense. How, for example, could an Amazonian Indian or a Roman senator rationalize a hoop skirt, a starched ruff, or a powdered wig? Yet scrutinized through the specialist's lens, such vagaries of Western dress can help chart the course of shifting political moods, social mores, religious climates and moral codes, the health of commerce, the march of science, and the progress of the arts. This would explain why the genealogy of clothes, once the exclusive province of the costume archivist, today receives the rapt attention of the psychologist, sociologist, economist, anthropologist, political scientist, and art historian, each posing the same question: "Why do people wear what they wear?"

Why, indeed, have human beings chosen to transform themselves in such astonishing ways? For the sake of the flesh or the spirit? For themselves or the eyes of beholders? What has driven them? Lust? Ambition? Fear? Piety? Shame? There is and can be no single adequate response. It is the intention of this book to examine transient dress in the light of history. But before stepping into the past through the looking glass of fashion, it might be helpful to pause briefly and ponder the most plausible reasons for adorning the naked person, whether with a scrap of loincloth and a daub of clay or a blaze of tiara and a twenty-foot train. To our minds, clothes have traditionally served four basic functions: to protect the body, to exalt the ego, to arouse emotions in others, and to communicate by means of symbols.

Dress as Protection
Despite the ostensible logic of the theory, no evidence exists to demonstrate that clothing was invented exclusively to fend off cold. Following Darwin's lead, modern anthropologists frequently cite the virtually naked natives of inclement Tierra del Fuego as proof positive of man's ability to adjust to freezing temperatures. The Fuegians simply fashioned wind shields and let it go at that. "Nature," Darwin decided, "by making habit omnipotent, and its effect hereditary, has fitted the Fuegian to the climate and the productions of his miserable country." Excessive use can be made of this argument, however, as it is also true that northern cave men, early in their development, covered themselves with stitched skins. That these crude garments provided protective warmth must certainly have guaranteed their continued use. The point is that in trying to identify the initial impulse that led to attaching objects and stuffs to the body, the need for warmth cannot be regarded as the sole or possibly even dominant cause. Nor did primitive people wear clothes to protect them from the rain. Visiting Tahiti in 1850, Dr. Charles Pickering, "exposed for some days to frequent and heavy rains . . . soon began to envy the naked condition of the natives, who became dry in a few minutes," while his proper Victorian attire remained soggy for hours. The Polynesians, he added, "never had colds until they began wearing clothes."

Nevertheless, the original wearing of "clothing" was no doubt prompted by other strong self-protective instincts—namely safeguarding the reproductive organs and evading insects, the sun, and hostile spirits. Primitive societies have been haunted eternally by the specter of extinction; hence their characteristic preoccupation with fertility. This, rather than an innate sense of modesty, would explain the universality of loincloths, penis sheaths, and other rudimentary pubic shields. They help prevent damage to the genitals when the wearer is darting through the underbrush, diving into rocky streams, or engaging in any other hazardous activity.

Insects, it was discovered, could be thwarted in a variety of ways: by lavish smearings of mud, which later might evolve into stylized patterns; by some form of string passed between the legs and secured to a waistband to protect highly sensitive areas; and by dangling, fringelike ornaments, the swishing motion of which would keep tormentors at bay. This last arrangement might be designated the earliest skirt in certain areas of the globe. The earliest hat was probably an improvised sun shade. In time, different techniques would be devised to combat overexposure to the sun. The Mesopotamians, for example, preferred protective clothing; the Egyptians, scented oils. The smudging of kohl and dark pigments about the eyes in all likelihood developed for protective as well as cosmetic effect—like the blacking on a football player's face, it reduced glare considerably. On the other hand certain peoples have adapted to the environment so well that they must adjust to dress rather than to the elements. The Australian aborigine literally should not wear clothing. It has been shown that when he does, the areas of his skin no longer exposed to the sun grow lighter in color, and when the clothing is discarded these areas are prone to severe sunburn.

From earliest times articles of clothing were worn to ward off demons. Primitive man, convinced that hostile forces lurked everywhere, took all possible precautions to avoid the dispensation of fresh calami-

Below left: American Indians, by John White, a Roanoke colony settler and governor, 1587.
A chieftain of Virginia. "Their hair is cut . . . in the form of a coxcomb. One long bird's feather is stuck into the crest. . . . They hang large pearls in

their ears . . . their foreheads, cheeks, chins, bodies, arms and legs are painted . . ."
Thomas Hariot, 1588.
A woman of Florida. "The queen and her maidens were adorned with belts worn either at the shoulder or at the waist, made of a kind of moss that

grows on the trees. The moss is woven into slender threads of a bluish green color and is so delicate in texture as to be mistaken for filaments of silk."
Nicholas Le Challeux, 1565.
Below right: Trophyism: the tattooed head of a Maori chieftain. Engraving, 18th century.

The eye of the beholder: what one society interprets as disfigurement might be a sign of beauty, maturity, grooming and grace in another. African tribeswomen with pierced lower lips and plucked hairlines.

ties. Magic must be met with magic. The curse of sterility, for example, was universally feared. To combat it, cowrie shells, because of the close resemblance they bore to the "great life-giver," a woman's reproductive organs, were avidly collected in many parts of the world. In the primitive's wardrobe of amulets and other supernaturally endowed adornments we find the precursors of the charm bracelet and St. Christopher's medal. Superstitions die slowly. The original purpose of the European bridal veil was to protect its wearer from evil spirits on her way to the marriage ceremony. Swiss folklore asserts that the dress of a dead child will kill another child who wears it. The man who shod the Iron Duke with such distinction firmly believed, "If Lord Wellington had any other bootmaker than myself, he never would have had his great and constant successes; for my boots and my prayers bring His Lordship out of all his difficulties." Even today there are those who insist on investing articles of clothing with supernatural qualities. Why else "something old, something new, something borrowed, something blue"?

The Envelope of the Ego

There is every reason to believe that, protection notwithstanding, the human animal would dress himself for the sake of decoration alone. Scholars like to point with satisfaction to the observations of Professor Wolfgang Kohler, who found that chimpanzees like to frolic about ornamenting themselves with various vines and other "hanging things." Given ribbons,

they wind them about their bodies and seem, moreover, to enjoy the process immensely.

Certainly their human cousins appear to have devoted more attention to self-adornment than any other "material" interest, with the possible exception of hunting itself. Cave dwellers wore elaborate necklaces, bracelets, girdles, and anklets fashioned of animal teeth and shells. In fact, *fake* teeth and shells were carved of ivory as early as the Magdalenian period. Moreover, it may be that early metallurgy developed as a direct result of the search for colored ores, which were ground to fine powders and mixed with animal fat to provide a brilliant spectrum of body paints.

The relationship between early man and later "primitive" societies may be debatable, but the universality of the desire for self-adornment, its "life-enhancing quality, and power to arouse admiration is not." Darwin was amazed to find that when given a length of red cloth, the natives of Tierra del Fuego cut it into little strips for decorative purposes, and this despite their nakedness in the bitter Antarctic cold. Stanley describes Mwana Mgoy, a chief of the Manyeman: "I fancy I can see him now, strutting about his village with spectral staff, an amplitude of grass cloth about him which, when measured, gives exactly twenty-four yards . . . all tags, tassels and fringes and painted in various colors, bronze, and black and white and yellow, and on his head a plumy headdress." "The raiment of vain men," sniffs Stanley, with Victorian disapproval. He would have been even more upset to encounter a Mela-

Envelope of the Ego:
Below left: " ' Why isn't this
curl in place?' The lady
screams, and her rawhide/
Lash inflicts chastisement for
the offending ringlet./ ... See
the tall edifice rise up on her
head in serried tiers and
storeys! / See her heroic stature

—at least, that is, from the
front ..." Juvenal, Satire VI
(translated by Peter Green).
Bust of a lady of the Flavian
era. Marble, 1st century A.D.
Below right: The High Middle
Ages and Renaissance "envelope" drew heavily on the

East for inspiration—included
for women were depilation,
veils and sumptuous fabrics
which proved the foundation
of Western economies. A
Princess of the House of Este,
by Pisanello. c. 1433.

nesian wearing the feathers of a bird-of-paradise he had devoted weeks of his life to capturing. But even in his day an indisputable fact was recognized— namely, that vanity in personal adornment touched all men of all societies.

Perhaps most telling are the perceptions of "beauty" among children. Dr. Leo Spiegel, writing in *The Journal of Genetic Psychology*, reported on the responses of a controlled group of thirty-seven children of the average age of ten to a series of simple questions such as "If you had magic and could make the most beautiful woman in the world, how would you make her look?" The vast majority responded in terms of clothing and hair, with replies such as "Beautiful clothes on her, beautiful rings, buy her jewelry, buy her beautiful slacks." The children would appear entranced by the shimmering images of fairy tales, the heroines of the "collective unconscious" in their Rapunzel locks and dresses of spun gold. Dr. Spiegel arrived at the conclusion that "The emphasis on the *envelope of the body* is so overwhelming one has the impression that children consider beauty something one puts on and takes off with clothes and cosmetics, and not an *inherently intrinsic part* of the body."

If it is by means of dress that the child identifies others, it is also by means of dress, in many instances, that we define ourselves. Dress, our most enthralling gesture of self-elation, is also a means of self identification, and as if by divine law we identify ourselves as members of our society by assuming its "costume." The very words associated with dress give a clue to the human attitude. "Dress" itself, like the word "direct," is derived from the Latin word *dirigere*, meaning "to rule." "Apparel" derives from a term meaning "to prepare" or "to make ready" and "garment" from the French *garnir*, "to garnish." "Costume" itself is derived from the Latin word for "custom." It is clear that somewhere along the line we have been directed to garnish ourselves, as is the custom.

In the most simplistic sense, from the medieval maidens who embroidered poetic couplets on bodices to the modern monogrammed blouse or message-emblazoned tee shirt, our dress is our banner. Moreover, a drastic change in manner of dress appears capable of instantly changing an individual's spiritual attitude toward himself, whether it be a child "dressing up," a young woman assuming a nun's habit, or a man's assumption of the identity of a Black Muslim. Time and again "escape" from the self has been seen in terms of a romantic identification with

another era. The Pre-Raphaelites fled the stuffy and grubby constrictions of the nineteenth century by wearing the flowing locks and loose gowns they falsely assumed to be the fashion of the "pure" and "unspoilt" era before the birth of Raphael. But the romantic identification with an alien epoch is far less common than the habit of identification with a hero or heroine by wearing the key elements of his or her costume or mimicking his or her appearance, whether by wearing a Charlotte Corday cap or a Beatle wig. In its most extreme instance, the transvestite transforms himself in to the image of his favorite sultry female movie star. But in subtler ways such imitation seems almost a universal instinct, responsible for "fashion" itself. The fashion setters, the Pompadours and Brummels and thousands more, were merely eccentrics who expressed themselves within the dictates of the fashions of their age. A few, such as Evander Berry Wall, known in nineteenth-century America as King of the Dudes, placated a troubled ego by an obsession with clothing. Wall once changed his outfits forty times in one afternoon at a hotel in Saratoga Springs. But without their idolators, the trend setters would make no change in fashion whatsoever. To be fashionable is to "keep up," to dare to move ahead adventurously, but in good company.

It has often been noted that what we call "fashion" today dates from the Renaissance, depending as it does on two prerequisites: the financial ability of a large number of people to exchange old clothes for new with some regularity and a general style that invites change and evolution. But the human urge to be "fashionable" much predates that era. Portrait busts of Roman matrons of the second century have been found with wiglike detachable tresses that could be changed according to the elaborate fashions of the day. However, it is probably only in the last few centuries that the desire to be fashionable exceeded even the desire to survive. One Regency newspaper reported that by all counts "eighteen ladies caught fire and another eighteen thousand caught cold" in their thin muslin dresses. The instep strap of nineteenth-century trousers could bring about paralysis of the knee joint, and the extreme constriction of women's dress at the end of the century caused innumerable ills, including faintness due to insufficient aeration and numbness of the legs. Moreover, the extent of the mania in the Victorian era reached the hysterical proportions suggested in the lament (*Harper's New Monthly Magazine*, 1858)

> See that painted spectre,
>   The vampyre of the streets!
> What foul demon wrecked her
>   Hoard of youthful sweets?
> Made a crime of loveliness?
>   Oh! 'twas Dress—'twas Dress!

The Arousal of Emotions: Sex and Fear

"And the eyes of them both were opened, and they knew that they were naked; and they sewed fig leaves together and made themselves aprons." These words, from the Book of Genesis, more or less settled the matter of the origin of clothing in the minds of Western society for two millennia. Man and woman dressed to clothe their shame—more implicitly, their sexual shame. Until the publication of the findings of archaeologists and anthropologists in this century, the notion was never questioned.

It now appears that sexual attraction, rather than repulsion, has long served as one of the major purposes of clothing as decoration. It fulfills our instinctual desire for the equivalent of the luxurious plumage of the male bird—to populate the species. In many primitive societies, where little dress is worn, the genitalia are not only protected but accentuated. Australian aboriginal women perform a lascivious dance wearing an apron of floating feathers. The Bushwomen of South Africa wear an apron of thin strips of skins decorated with beads and eggshells. It could scarcely be claimed that the gold penis sheaths affected by the Cunas of Panama or the monumental three-foot structures of rolled leaves sported by the men of some Melanesian tribes are worn for the sake of protection alone. After the plague years of the Black Death, when the population of Europe had been decimated, people wore tight-fitting, parti-colored, and frankly "sexy" clothing as if by instinct. The Victorians may have been so prim that Mrs. Trollope was horrified to see a young lady embroidering a petticoat in the presence of a young gentleman, but the fact was that perhaps never in the history of Western dress had the inviting curves of the female breast and buttocks been more exaggerated in dress.

Clothing, when introduced to the naked members of primitive societies, did not seem to improve their "moral" state or reduce promiscuity, at least as far as the missionaries were able to ascertain. Rather, in the view of Arthur Grimbal, Research Commissioner of the Gilbert and Ellis Islands, clothing stimulated "a nasty curiosity which never before existed." It also stimulated the growth of vermin and every kind of parasite as well as dirt among the islanders.

A sweeping view of our own and other societies indicates that shame and a sense of modesty are emotions that are not necessarily associated with bodily nudity at all. The Indians of the Orinoco actually felt deep shame at the prospect of wearing clothes, and there are myriad other similar examples. Moreover, the notion of the location of the "shameful" part of the body varies from society to society and generation to generation. In China the female foot was never to be seen; in Japan, the back of a woman's neck. In eighteenth-century France the tip of the shoulder and elbow were always to be covered. A century later these were amply exposed by women in whose presence the word "leg" could not even be uttered. "Modesty" and "shame" would appear to be acquired emotions. We are reminded of the example of an unfortunate chimpanzee who

Below left: Dress as symbol: A group of 20th century Spanish penitents parade in an Easter Week religious ceremony, wearing uniforms appropriate to their spiritual state.
Below right: Motorcycles and leather garments spell liberation for a road-hungry genera- tion; Peter Fonda in a still from the movie Easy Rider, 1969.

was brought up to wear clothing. Finding himself naked in a room of fully clothed human beings, he became hysterical.

It has been observed that apes arouse fear by making faces. The effect of presenting a horrible aspect has seemingly always been known to man and has been practiced by many groups, from the Norse "berserkers" to the Ghost Societies of the Solomon Islands and New Britain. The following is a nineteenth-century description of a Melanesian devil dance:

> Some wore masks composed of skulls cut in half, and filled in with gum to represent a human face; . . . on their heads they wore long black wigs composed of coco-nut fibre, and their bodies are covered with dead leaves. Some had their faces painted an unearthly green colour, and on their shoulders were fastened a kind of wings. . . . On came these unearthly figures, creeping from the bush on every side, some with tailes and some with spikes all down their backs . . . and there begins a dance that defies all description . . . the fires are lighted and blaze up . . . demon faces showing here, toothless skulls there, the air above them seeming full of arms smeared with blood, and below legs apparently in the last stages of mortification, and above all this the moon sends a fitful light through the overhanging trees.

The devil dance was devised to create fear and awe, not only in the uninitiated audience but in the very spirits themselves. And the instilling of terror in this way often serves more than the purpose of warning. Among the Aranda, revenge killers wear "kurdaitcha" shoes trimmed with emu feathers. It

is believed that at the mere sight of the track of these shoes the culprit will drop dead with fear.

Certain tribesmen of Melanesia pick out the lines of their ribs with white clay. In fact the conversion of the living body to a skeletal specter as a means to arouse fear is found the world over. Boys are painted in this way for their initiation ceremonies among the tribes of the Mato Grosso. It is even believed that the horizontal braiding on a hussar's jacket, now found on the jackets of West Point cadets, has its origins in the representation of the skeletal ribs. Despite the black leather jackets of the Hell's Angels, however, modern man, fighting his wars at a distance, would seem to strive for subtler effects. In the words of Edward Gorey, a master of the evocation of evil:

> A dreary young bank clerk named Fennis
> Wished to foster an aura of menace
> To make people afraid
> He wore gloves of grey suede
> And white footgear intended for tennis.

Dress as Symbol

In *Sartor Resartus*, the darkly satiric parable of human dogmas, forms, and ceremonials in terms of dress, Thomas Carlyle teaches that "the beginning of all wisdom is to look fixedly on clothes . . . till they become transparent." Essentially he is saying that as man makes his life and work effective by symbols alone, whether visible or otherwise, one must penetrate these symbols in order to understand the true nature of human affairs. Without stretching the point, almost any form of dress can be given a symbolic interpretation. Dressing and adorning oneself is like filling in a census blank. Consider the scope of statistics possible to convey: one's sex, age group, nationality, religious affiliations, means of livelihood, social, economic, and marital status, political or military rank, personal achievements, loyalties and beliefs, family connections, state of mind (witness, respectively, red fingernails, rompers, lederhosen, wimple, fireman's helmet, club tie, sable coat, wedding ring, judge's robe, sergeant's stripes, cap and gown, political button, the tartan kilt, and widow's weeds).

Anthropologists tend to index symbolic dress under four principal categories: totemic, trophyism, hieratic, and emblematic. "Totemic" alludes to primitive man's impulse to imitate as closely as possible the animal the bird or, on rarer occasions, the plant he most wanted to influence. This is known

Below: Establishing status: The protective dress and martial accoutrements of these Roman legionnaires set them apart as members of the emperor's elite homeguard. 1st century A.D.
Lower left: Elaborately scarred warrior displays his indelible rank.
Lower right: Medals and sashes as decorative trophies. Albert Edward, Prince of Wales. 1889.

"Trophyism" refers to a less subtle concept, its express purpose being to advertise excellence if not downright superiority of character and deed. Trophyism's deepest roots inevitably tangle with those of totemism. Aside from their mystical overtones, the wearing of wild animal skins testifies to a man's courage and skill in the hunt. To festoon oneself with menacing claws, tusks, teeth, and fangs could only heighten the heroic impression. Scars and blood-stains bore further evidence of fearless encounters with man or beast. It is likely that certain forms of scarification, tattoos, and body paints evolved from such originally spontaneous marks of bravery. That trophies of this sort have continued to excite admiration until recently can be seen in the proudly slashed cheeks of the Prussian dueling societies and the leopard skins of the Scottish Guard.

In war, the capture of an enemy's weapons, augmented by the taking of his skull, skin, or other wearable bits of anatomy, suggested new styles of symbolic adornment. Belts, the scepter and mace, potent symbols of authority, trace their origins to weaponry. The killing of enemies in some societies is commemorated in dress, rather in the spirit of the notched gun. The Philippine Bagobo who has dispatched two men may broadcast the achievement by wearing a white-patterned brown costume; had he killed four, he would be allowed a pair of red trousers; if six, a red robe; if twenty-five, a shiny black costume and red flowers in his hair. While the sartorial celebration of killing others has not become a symbolic ritual in the West, the wearing of official decorations must not be overlooked as a lingering aspect of trophyism. Bloody battles, after all, are still spelled out in snippets of bright ribbon across the veteran's khaki breast.

as "sympathetic magic." To achieve the desired end, he would garb himself in the flayed skins of his prey—that is, if the hunt was of prime consideration—and perform the ceremonies which were in fact the earliest forms of ritual dance. He would have liked to enter the animal's head, too, as James Laver has pointed out, but being an inexpert taxidermist, he had to content himself with replicas carved in wood or bark. Here we find the earliest masks. What at first were presumably intended as literal, if clumsy, representations of animals or birds became increasingly stylized to the point at which they assumed a totally symbolic and mystical significance. Today the totemic principle is rapidly surrendering its last strongholds. To eradicate the purported evils of tribal society, at least one recently formed African nation has initiated a "demystification program" to oversee the burning of outmoded totemic artifacts. Pockets of resistance continue to survive, however. Australian aborigines of one clan periodically don tall headdresses of feathers and wooden plumes and stalk about with the jerky gait of their emu totem.

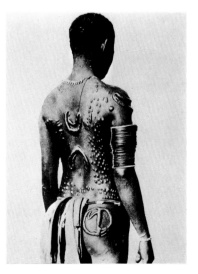

In the matter of decorations, trophyism spills over its boundaries into the anthropologist's third category, "hieratic" dress. As Sanche de Gramont once coolly observed, "There comes a time in the life of every Frenchman who has performed some small service to the state when he becomes preoccupied about the removal of his prostate and the acquisition of the Legion of Honor. The lapel of his jacket seems naked if that bit of red ribbon does not garnish it."

Here we sidle into the arena of exclusivity and rank, the hallmarks of "hieratic dress." Nowhere are the undemocratic principles of hieratic dress more clearly exposed than in the body of "sumptuary laws" which, since ancient times, have been inflicted with regularity on lesser mortals by those in power. Simply stated, the purpose of a sumptuary law is to limit the amount certain people or classes may display or consume. When pertaining to dress and adornment, as they usually do, they can be an effective means of keeping society visibly stratified. In the past not even the nobility has been exempt. Henry VIII demanded that a countess wear a train fastened to her girdle, but that a baroness have no train.

The wish literally to outshine others finds facile fulfillment in dress. As a consequence, the obsessive pursuit of wearable status symbols such as gold, jewels, furs, and silk has stretched human ingenuity with far-ranging results, from the opening up of sea lanes and uncharted continents to the chemist's conversion of air, water, and coal into artificial silk. By now, industrial mass production has erased many of the traditional dividing lines of hieratic dress. Ironically today's sumptuary laws are launched from the bottom rather than the top. Soaring crime statistics have led to high insurance rates, and the wealthy leave splendid jewels to languish in vaults when they might instead be radiating social and economic preeminence from fashionable fingers and throats.

The most common of the hieratic forms of dress that linger in our society are military uniforms and the formal robes of the clergy and judiciary. Whether they proclaim rank or not, all uniforms can be considered symbols in the emblematic sense. Emblematic attire embraces everything from occupational dress to athletic team uniforms to political buttons and badges. Interestingly, quite a few articles of dress have been assimilated into the language to express particular convictions, attitudes, and beliefs—"blue-stocking," "hardhat," "black shirt," "white collar,"

"blue collar," and more. The power of emblematic dress has been in some instances strong enough to make whole nations abandon their sartorial customs to demonstrate a change in social, political, or economic outlook. Both Peter the Great and Ataturk understood this power when they hauled the citizens of Russia and Turkey into the European community by outlawing certain traditional native garments. And what could be more emblematic of the worldwide craving for industrial progress than the wholesale adoption of the dreary "Western business suit"?

In any given era, many styles of clothing are worn. Not everyone is "in fashion," and this was particularly true when clothing represented a greater expense than it does today. The custom of dressing servants in "livery" of 18th-century cut even in the 20th devolved from the habit of dressing servants in cast-off and therefore out-of-fashion clothing. The Romantic painter Thomas Cole was amazed to find 19th-century Italian shepherds dressed in skins and resembling American Indians, at least to his eyes. But despite such incongruities, an individual and identifiable style has emerged in every age. Whatever the function that clothing fulfills, this style has always been formed, molded in every detail, by the society itself. In the words of Stella Blum, Director of the Costume Institute of the Metropolitan Museum of Art, "A fashion is no accident. It will always suit the situation, time and place. Fashion is really a matter of evolution. It has a natural life, unlike a fad, which is a stillbirth."

By his manner of dress an individual reveals not only his conception of society but also the role he plays in it. And while it is undeniable that a slave to fashion is, in the final analysis, a slave to society, an individual's appreciation of the mystical nature of dress can amount to a declaration of faith. Lucius Beebe, the journalist and indestructible dandy, describes a quintessential episode in the history of man, the clothed creature, the mirror of his society: "Because it was Sunday evening on the *Titanic* when not all passengers were dressed for dinner, a number of fastidious persons, who would have had it otherwise, faced eternity in business dress. Unwilling to make an exit on this note of informality, the aged Benjamin Guggenheim summoned his valet and retired to his stateroom, presently to reappear in full evening dress with tails and his best studs. 'Now we are dressed like gentlemen,' he said, 'and ready to go.'"

The Ancient Near East:

After the Fig Leaf

We have all been introduced to that primeval paradise, the first farming community, which existed in the Near East some eight thousand years ago. We are told that its inhabitants had learned to grow crops and breed animals, make pottery and build houses of sun-dried brick. Obediently, we summon to mind a scene in shades of parchment and dust, strangely devoid of animation. We cannot conceive of any color or decoration in such a tableau. Most disconcerting of all, we cannot imagine the people that inhabit this first of all man-made desolations. We soon realize that it is difficult for us to conjure up images of the denizens of these early communities because we do not know what they wore.

The Near East hardly suggests an appropriate setting for the stitched skins of cave dwellers. Nor can we suppose that the simple loincloth was the sole costume for a culture that had obviously far surpassed that of Cro-Magnon man. And yet neither remains of a loom nor any remnant of woven cloth from this period has been found. However, we know from the evidence of imprints found on clay pots and flooring that these early farmers did weave mats and baskets, and the presence of spindles and whorls prove that they also spun thread. So there is every reason to believe that they wove in some fashion and made clothing. How elaborate the material may have been we cannot know.

Soon enough in the continuum of history bits of clothing do appear. For example, a scrap of linen found in Turkey dates from about 5000 B.C. We also find what may be a hand loom depicted on a Predynastic Egyptian pottery dish of the fourth millennium B.C. It is extremely small, but early cloth was probably made in scanty sections and then pieced together. Only somewhat later would larger looms capable of producing cloth of a "drapable" breadth and length be devised. Precisely what garments were worn may have to be left to the imagination. Paleolithic buttons as well as the eyed needle have been found. We know from the evidence of cave paintings and Bronze Age burials that a basic repertoire was conceived at an early date: skirts (not necessarily for women), capes or shawls, and, very possibly, jackets or shirts and trousers (not necessarily for men).

It is time, now, to dispense with the hazily drab colorlessness of our vision. Man emerged from the cave already a dedicated dauber, with a passion for color. By the time of the earliest settled communities he probably applied yellow and red ocher as well as green and blue pigments (malachite

and azurite) as cosmetics. The latter are derived from ores of copper, and it is not impossible that man may have discovered his first usable metal while in search of eye shadow.

Flax and sheep were man's earliest source of thread and cloth, but it should not be facilely assumed that natural shades of linen and wool appealed to our primitive farmer. At the earliest opportunity he very likely dyed his cloth as well as himself. Even Stone Age man secured blue from wood, lilac from myrtle, yellow from pomegranate. Other substances produced red and white, and the ocher palette was certainly put to use. Moreover, the early plowman and his family very likely wore a great quantity of jewelry. He did not forsake the necklaces, pectorals, and bracelets of shells, colored stones, and animal teeth that his ancestors wore as cave-dwelling hunters, and he experimented with new baubles. At this period gold was first panned from stream sediment. Easy to work by hammering, its dazzling qualities were soon appreciated. These earliest farmers of the Near East were particularly attracted to lapis lazuli, the most brilliant of the colored stones then available, but lapis was in short supply. So some six thousand years ago, with more sophistication than is usually credited to them, these inventive souls were busy making the synthetic lapis called faience. They dis-

Opposite: Vanity far predates history: Prehistoric Saharan cave painting of a woman fishing. She is elaborately decorated with jewelry and body paint. Rock painting from Tassili n' Ajjer, Algeria. 10th–6th centuries B.C.

Below: Neolithic cave painting of members of a Saharan community, mounted on longhorn cattle, moving to a new campsite. Although "herdsmen" of a stone-age culture, these early inhabitants of the Sahara seemed to have known how to make cloth of fiber. The "women of high rank" in this painting wear elaborate capes and splendid turbans that remind us of those worn by the Tuareg today. Cave painting from Tassili n' Ajjer, Algeria. c. 4000–1500 B.C.

Left below: Procession of
figures in skirts of kaunakes
cloth. Plaque inlaid with lapis
and shell, from the royal tomb
at Ur. c. 2600 B.C.
Below: "They have eyes, but
they cannot see." Stone worshipers of the stone god at Ur.
These small figures, some

bearded and some clean-
shaven, wear skirts of flapped
kaunakes cloth, or saronglike
shawls. Group of figures from
Abu Temple, Tell Asmar, Iraq.
c. 2600 B.C.

covered that heat applied to azurite or malachite powder would cause it to form a kind of blue glass glaze which would adhere to soapstone. The first costume jewelry had been devised.

We can perhaps assume that early men and women stepped into recorded history literally bedizened with cosmetics, jewels (counterfeit and otherwise), and clothing of multiple tints. In fact, shortly after textiles were developed, dress in the Near East achieved a level of opulence not easily surpassed. Of course, the fact that luxuries of dress were known does not mean that all men and women wore them, but by 3000 B.C. our visual image of society begins to come into focus.

Mesopotamia

Ur of the Chaldees was merely one of many cities of the early Mesopotamian plain. There are others less known but no less important—Eridu, Lagash, Uruk, Mari, Nippur—some Sumerian, others belonging to the Semitic Akkadians of the north. All worshiped the same gods, although each had its special divinity. These gods did not reside in the ethers of the mind. They were palpable statues— stiff, upright figures with bulgy eyes—and they had

a taste for travel. In early spring, during the month of Nisan, they might journey in barges downriver to convene at another capital for the celebration of the New Year. At one point the son of a stone-cutter of Ur made a discovery about these godly figures: "They have eyes, but they cannot see." This is a pity, as they were lords of the terrain through which they passed, and it is worth seeing.

The plain between the Tigris and the Euphrates was originally desolate, but with a great deal of effort and ingenuity the settlers harnessed the erratic flooding of the river by means of a compli-cated series of dikes and ditches. The rich black soil then spread throughout the valley, creating a garden land of jade and emerald greens. Trees were planted to provide desperately needed shade, and patches of barley and other grains alternated with orchards of date palms and fig, apple, plum, and cherry trees. In open fields, flocks grazed by the tens of thousands.

But surprisingly, this is an urban not a rural society. Each city stands clearly visible from the surrounding plains, not because it was built on a natural promi-nence but rather because its inhabitants (perhaps a mountain people whose spirit ached for craggy peaks) have chosen to construct a man-made mountain, a towering prospect from which the unseeing eyes of their god could contemplate his domain. The "ziggurat" stands in the heart of each town, platform upon platform of sun-dried brick covered with a handsome facing of fired tiles. And at the top, a temple houses the chamber and the couch of the god. In solitude a priestess sleeps here, but she is joined by the god at night. Below is the temple precinct—where the god is cosseted and fed burnt offerings—and the palace of the king and, beyond these, the town. Even the formidable scholar Jacquetta Hawkes seems awed by the importance of these amazing structures: "Was not all this effort for surplus foodgrowing onwards and upwards to be devoted to the wildest of imaginative fancies—to the raising of artificial mountains for men-gods. . . ."

When we step into the town proper, we step into earthly reality with a jolt. Winding, brick-paved streets shaded by pleasant awnings meander through the leatherworkers' quarter, the smiths' quarter where hot air belches onto passersby, the stonecutters' quarter where eyes must be protected from the dust. Slave slums exist, but basically this is a middle-class city. Shopkeepers, merchants, master craftsmen, scribes and the like live in two- and three-story houses built with galleries around an open court and latrines out of sight. These homes are cool and comfortable, and gardens with songbirds blossom in every spare patch of earth. Outside the city walls, in the suburbs, homes are larger and are surrounded by beds of flowers and orchards. These people live with a certain grace. Their personality seems curiously split between the arduous irrationality of their religion and the crass practicality of their daily lives. In social matters they are easygoing, not dogmatic. Marriages are arranged, but love is an important element in the arrangement. The Laws of Hammurabi are of a later epoch, but they reflect long tradition. Divorce is easy and there is an equivalent of child support and alimony—that is, with the exception of the woman who leaves home to go into business on her own, "thus neglecting her house and humiliating her children." No support, then, for the liberated woman. But this suggests the possibility of "liberation" if that is what she wants.

The Sumerians dine well. Lamb and kid are milk- and barley-fed for the rich man's table, and so are beef and veal. The menu is varied by fish, pigeons, geese, cranes, and ducks, all washed down with ale, stout, lager, or date and grape wines. Cooking is done in sesame oil, and the dishes are sweetened with dates or bee's honey. Dancing to the music of flutes, lyres, timbrels, pipes, and drums is a frequent entertainment in the public squares, and in the palace the king's meals (perhaps the best of the sacrificial diet—scraps from the tables of the gods) are accompanied by the sounds of the lyre.

Above all, the Sumerians were a business-loving people, and wool represented "big business." Originally herdsmen from the mountains, they had always respected the shepherd and his flock. Their earliest script contained no fewer than thirty-one signs for sheep and goats, and they referred to their ruler as "the good shepherd." But this reverent posture did not stop them from turning the wool-making trade into a profitable industry employing thousands. Most such enterprises were owned by the temple, but as time passed they fell into private hands. Men and women, both slave and free, worked in what can only be called factories, producing several thousand tons of woven fabric a year. (Linen was also woven from flax, but on a far smaller scale.) Jobs were specialized: Spinners, weavers, dyers, and fullers are specified. Records tell of payment to women employees during sick and menstrual leave. (As so often in history a menstruating woman was considered unclean and therefore unfit for work.) The size of the industry in terms of employees can be judged by the time taken to weave one piece of cloth three and one half by four meters in size. Such a length would require the work of three women for eight days. Natural wool might be used for a white, brown, or black fabric, but other colors were achieved by dyes.

Wool was not woven for local consumption alone. As in Britain four thousand years later, it served as a basic export in return for which the Sumerians were able to import the raw materials they totally lacked—copper, stone, cedar, and other woods as well as the luxuries of dress and grooming, such as tortoise-shell and ivory for combs or antimony for eye shadow, and of course jewels: lapis lazuli, coral, carnelian, and even pearls. These came from as far afield as the Mediterranean, Armenia, Afghanistan, and the valley of the Indus.

With their wealth in textiles, the Sumerians were nothing if not well dressed. For the ancient Sumerian a new suit of clothing was a regular event. The garments themselves were often (but not always) made by the factory employees. In the following schoolboy's letter to his mother a familiar whine resounds through millennia:

> Gentlemen's clothes improve year by year. By cheapening and scrimping my clothes you have become rich. While wool was being consumed in our house like bread, you were making my clothes cheap. The son of Adadiddinam, whose father is only an underling of my father, has received two new garments; you keep getting upset over just one garment for me. Whereas you gave birth to me, his mother had him by adoption, but whereas his mother loves him, you do not love me.

We have a clear enough idea of the style of this clothing because the stony-eyed gods of the Sumerians and Akkadians were surrounded by equally stony-eyed statues of their worshipers,

Below: Gold wreaths of beech and willow leaves: headdress of Queen Shub-ad. From the royal cemetery of Ur. c. 2600 B.C.

Opposite left: Disposition of bodies in a death pit of Ur. In one such site the remains of sixty-eight women were found wearing short-sleeved red coats with cuffs of lapis, carnelian and gold beadwork. "It must have been a very gaily dressed crowd that

assembled ... for the royal obsequies ... which would in this belief be but a passing from one world to another ..." wrote Sir Leonard Woolley. Opposite right: Sumerian gold helmet from the tomb of "Meskalam-dug, Hero of the Good Land," showing curled

and pomaded locks and chignon of the wearer. Sir Leonard Woolley felt that for the workmanship of this prize alone the Sumerians should be accorded a "high rank in the roll of civilized races." From the royal cemetery of Ur. c. 2500 B.C.

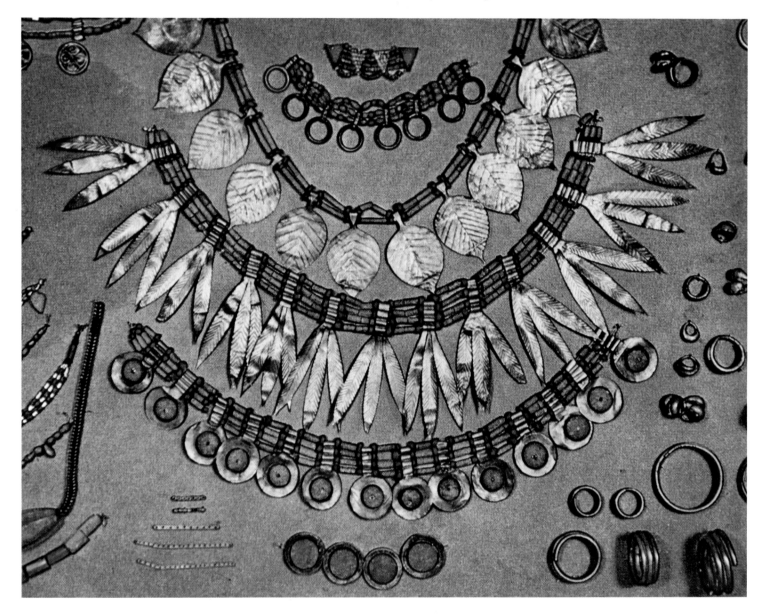

placed in the temples by wealthy individuals to do permanent homage to their deities, and wearing their very best. It is amazing that at this early date, the dawn of the third millennium before Christ, Sumerian dress was not simple, logical, and cool. Rather, it was elaborate, hot, and, frankly, outlandish. It would appear that before the early development of woven cloth these herding people lived in the cool mountain areas to the north of the two rivers. There they probably wore skirts made of rows of goatskin or sheepskin, forming flounces knotted in the back with sheep or goat tails. (This clothing was called *kaunakès* by the later Greeks.) When it became possible to substitute woven cloth for pelts, the Sumerians appear to have simply woven flaps of fabric that imitated tufts of sheepskin. Thus their earliest clothing may also have been

the earliest "fake fur." Woven wool appeared not as an improvement over hides but merely as a replacement. Capes and shawls were still made of skins, although these too were soon replaced by *kaunakès* cloth. At times a full-length garment, covering one shoulder and falling to the floor, was comprised of these flaps. At other times the flaps appeared as fringe at the bottom of a skirt. The devotion to this Stone Age style appears to have continued for centuries.

There is also evidence of another, more familiar garment worn by the ancient Sumerians: a long shawl that could be wrapped as a sarong around the hips or around the body beneath the arms, with the loose end covering the left shoulder. With its elaborate fringe or border, it suggests to our eyes the Hindu sari. As time went on, these borders, tassels,

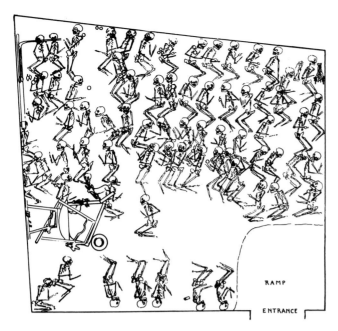

and fringes became more ornate. It may have been in Mesopotamia that embroidery was first practiced, and in later periods the shawl may have been embroidered with beads of gold or precious stones. The dress of men and women differed little, except that men no longer wore necklaces and bracelets.

Much attention was given to hair. It has long been thought that the figures of rotund little men with not only chins but heads clean-shaven represented Sumerians, whereas those with long beards and elaborately curled locks caught up in a bun at the nape of the neck were taken to be the Semitic Akkadians. It now appears, however, that these differences may not represent so much a racial distinction as a change of style. The reasons for such an alteration of appearance in a people so conservative are an intriguing mystery. Women's hair was pinned up in chignons of various forms, sometimes under a tall, urn-shaped headdress, creating an awe-inspiring and exotic effect. Moreover, nails were manicured, superfluous hair tweezed, and eyes heavily outlined (cosmetic cakes in shades of green, aqua, terra cotta, and charcoal have been found). To complete a well-groomed appearance, the Sumerian might go barefoot, or might wear sandals dyed or even decorated with powder of gold.

How did court or religious dress differ from everyday wear? Our information about court dress comes from a source so grisly and so out of keeping with the Sumerian's practical and businesslike conduct in daily life that its cause remains one of the unfathomables of archaeology. The Sumerians did not possess the Egyptians' detailed and refined concept of an afterlife, and the matter seems to have both frightened and confused them. Their concept of the "afterlife" was a shadowy underworld where ghosts flitted in the dust—shades so envious of the living that the "visitor" was advised to wear his oldest clothes and speak in low tones. Following prehistoric tradition, it might be expected that the dead would be buried with their earthly possessions for use beyond the grave, but nothing in the religious writings of the Sumerians, and little in their

tradition, could have prepared the archaeologist Sir Leonard Woolley for his discovery in 1927 when investigating a series of burials at Ur. Stone-lined tombs disclosed the splendidly dressed bodies of men and women, members of a royal family or of the priesthood, surrounded by lapis inlay and gold objects of extreme beauty. This in itself would be a precious if not extraordinary discovery. But other underground chambers disclosed scenes of calm but undeniable horror. In one, four soldiers were found; in another, two sleighs, complete with the skeletons of the oxen that pulled them, the riders that drove them, and the grooms that tended them. Finally, in one pit Woolley found the bodies of some sixty-eight women, all lying in a relaxed manner, side by side. Some were discovered carrying musical instruments, their fingers on the strings. These were not victims of a sudden plague. There can be no question that they entered the burial pit peacefully, perhaps even joyfully, and alive.

This grisly burial of a living court gives us a clearer picture of the dress of the nobility than we might otherwise have hoped to get. In the fine mother-of-pearl and lapis inlays of musical instruments, we see the king, naked to the waist in a many-tiered *kaunakès* skirt, drinking with his similarly dressed courtiers and intent on the music of a poet who chants lost ballads to the lyre. In another we see a troupe of tiny warriors wearing what appear to be capes of nail-studded leather and close-fitting, pointed leather caps, perhaps the first known military uniform. (Helmets of copper and even gold have also been found.) And the regalia itself is here, buried on the backs of the courtiers. Each of the sixty-eight women wore a robe of scarlet wool, perhaps the earliest example of court dress. Twenty were discovered wearing golden diadems. Were the others bare-headed? It was suspected that they may have worn diadems of less valuable silver, although no remains of such objects were found. Then an archaeologist inspecting the grave noticed a small blackened fragment caught up in one of the skeletons. On closer inspection it turned out to be

just such a silver diadem, preserved because it had been rolled up. Clearly its owner had forgotten in the excitement, joy, or terror of her last moments to unroll it and put it on.

The true sensitivity of Sumeria, often poorly reflected in the unyielding stone of its art, is perhaps best preserved in a headdress from this mass burial, probably worn by the queen. It consists of a wreath of the most delicate leaves and star-shaped flowers, created of paper-thin hammered gold, a re-creation in precious metal of the leafy beauties of nature that the Sumerians wrested from a forbidding, unyielding terrain.

Sumerian civilization formed the matrix for the many empires rooted in Mesopotamia. Rulers, governments, and even whole races passed through this changeless scene, although the basic culture—architecture, religion, written language, and even clothing—remained remarkably unchanged over a period of almost three thousand years. Sargon the Great of Akkad ruled an empire stretching from Asia Minor to the Mediterranean, and Babylon developed under the wisdom of Hammurabi in the 18th century B.C. In regard to clothing, it may be said merely that tunics and robes of varying length passed in and out of style, often the contribution of one or another of the constantly invading mountain tribes. Embroidery became more elaborate (whole scenes with human and animal figures were depicted) and color more brilliant. Costumes were of green, yellow, blue, brown, and most especially the precious purple that the Phoenicians obtained from a cyst found near the head of a mollusk. So expensive were these dyes that luxury came to be

identified with color, and to be "dressed in purple" meant more than wearing even the finest cloth.

The chief innovation over so long a period originated with the Assyrians, perhaps history's least appealing people, who first came into prominence around 1200 B.C. We have it on the unimpeachable authority of virtually all nations extant during the Assyrians' reign of terror that they were scholarly, artistic, efficient, fearless, endlessly bloodthirsty, and savagely cruel to man and beast. It was nothing for an Assyrian king to boast that he had flayed his enemies and exhibited their skins on the wall in which he had entombed them alive. The Assyrians were also inordinately cruel to women. The comparatively moderate laws of Hammurabi and the old Sumerian traditions of modest freedom and equality were effaced in favor of dicta whereby a woman could be "impaled on stakes" for self-abortion or have her ears cut off for harboring a runaway wife. If a "gentleman" raped a virgin his punishment would be the rape of his own wife and the father of the victim might then give her in marriage to the rapist, if he so chose. It comes as no surprise, then, that in all probability it was the Assyrians who invented the application of the veil peculiar to the Near East.

According to Assyrian law, wives, daughters, and widows of gentlemen were forbidden to go unveiled. Slave girls, temple prostitutes, and harlots, on the other hand, were not allowed to wear the veil on pain of flogging. Moreover, any man who recognized such a woman behind a veil and did not report her immediately was likewise to be flogged, humiliatingly mutilated, and obliged to do penal servitude.

Moreover, the Assyrian tyrants were vain. Perhaps never in history has such attention been given to the curling (with irons), plaiting, and arranging of long locks and beards. The kings themselves were heavily rouged, painted, and perfumed. However terrifying they were in pointed helmet and scaled cuirass, driving their war chariots into battle, the Assyrians were not always victorious.

In 612 B.C. Ninevah, the Assyrian capital, fell to a newly reawakened Babylon, the Biblical city of wonders. Its ziggurat, the Tower of Babel, rose to a height of almost three hundred feet. Its hanging gardens have teased the imagination since the captive Israelites first described them, and its temple of Marduk was plated with solid gold. In Revelations, the old Sumerian fascination with clothing is summoned up, and Babylon is seen in terms of dress, as a woman "clothed in new linen, and purple, and scarlet, and decked with gold, and precious stones, and pearls!"

Egypt

Eight hundred miles from the Valley of the Two Rivers, on the far side of an almost but not quite impenetrable desert, lay a totally different civilization, at more or less the same level of development. The Egyptians enjoyed a variety of advantages denied to the inhabitants of Mesopotamia. The more predictable flooding of the Nile was easier to channel into a complex irrigation system, and raw materials unavailable in Mesopotamia, such as stone and the ores of copper and gold, abounded in the cliffs and deserts bordering the valley. The protective girdle of deserts also provided the richest of all resources: long periods of peace. Moreover, the Egyptians, who never developed urban city-states comparable to those of Mesopotamia, remained one homogeneous political entity from the period of the unification of Upper Egypt (the Nile Valley) and Lower Egypt (the Nile Delta), early in the fourth millennium B.C.

Egyptian "cities," such as Memphis and Thebes, were largely administrative rather than commercial or manufacturing centers. The Egyptians therefore led a rural rather than an urban existence, but one of considerable charm. Important Egyptian officials enjoyed sprawling country estates rather than the impressive townhouses of their Mesopotamian equivalents. Their homes consisted of a series of courtyards and airy frescoed chambers. The amenities included comfortable bedrooms, bathrooms, and spacious gardens cooled by decorative pools. Existence was enlivened by pets, games (especially board games such as draughts), fishing and fowling expeditions, dinner parties with musical entertainment, vintage wines, and good food. A menu that has survived lists porridge, quail kidneys, pigeon stew, fish, ribs of beef, bread, cakes, stewed fruit, berries, cheese, and wine.

This particular dinner was intended to accompany a lady of the Second Dynasty into eternity. Because of the Egyptians' extraordinary optimism about death, their lives are well recorded. A corpse that had undergone seventy days of a dehydrating salt treatment and a wrapping of bandages was secure for eternity in the "Beautiful Roads of the West," the "Court of Re Across the Lily Lake," accompanied by all the appurtenances of life on earth. Not only were his possessions (or facsimiles thereof) sequestered in his tomb, but scenes of the occupations and pleasures of his household were painted on its walls. This custom and the extreme dryness of the Egyptian climate did in fact conspire to provide the dead Egyptian with a kind of eternal life, so that Egyptian dress and cosmetic habits, and much of the clothing itself, are more familiar to us and more readily available for scrutiny than much that was worn three hundred years ago.

The Egyptians were a linen-wearing people. Although they were capable of looming wool and used it for cloaks, it was officially abhorred, possibly because the Egyptians saw the nomadic shepherd peoples from beyond their desert borders as a force both inferior and threatening. We know that priests were not permitted to wear wool next to their skin or to enter the temple area wearing any garment of wool. Of course, wool was never included as any part of a tomb burial. Joseph warned his herdsmen brothers that "every shepherd is an abomination to the Egyptians."

every aspect of the visual world of Egypt: architecture, painting, sculpture, the design of furniture and small objects, such as mirrors and jars.

Women's dress was extremely uncomplicated, based as it was for many centuries on a simple sheath falling from beneath the arms to the ankle, attached by broad straps over one or both shoulders. This garment might or might not reveal the breasts. It also might be accompanied by a shawl for warmth or for ceremonial occasions. Men wore a simple knee-length loincloth or kilt (the *shenti*) attached at the waist by a belt, and they generally went bare from the waist up. The *shenti* could be folded in a great variety of ways. It was worn by all men, from workers in the field to the pharaoh, who was distinguished by the insignia of his rank. These included a combination of the white crown of Upper Egypt and the red crown of Lower Egypt and, curiously, a lion's tail attached at the back of his belt, reminiscent perhaps of the god-king's origins as shaman.

Garments were generally the natural white of flax (which took dye poorly), white being a sacred color among the Egyptians. Color and decoration were added to the costume by means of wide necklaces or collars of brilliantly colored beads of glass, green or blue faience, or precious stones (agate, onyx, carnelian, amethyst, garnet, malachite, jasper, lapis, and others) for those who could afford them. Bangle bracelets have been found in the earliest tombs. Egypt was rich in gold of both the alluvial and nugget variety, and Egyptian goldwork was of a very high order. Gold, so plentiful that it commanded only half the price of silver, was used solely for decorative purposes and never for trade.

Of course, over the millennia small variations on the basic theme occurred. Women occasionally wore a close-fitting, long-sleeved robe and men an absolutely simple short-sleeved shirt above their kilt, which might become longer and more elaborate. While white was the rule, it was not an unbroken one, and clothing might be dyed yellow, the color of gold and the flesh of the gods. Green represented life and youth; blue, the skin of Amon, god of air. Black was rarely worn. Woven patterns (and even interwoven beadwork) also appeared in fabric. But the simplicity of line was never lost. Mesopotamian dress appears fussy and shapeless by comparison. In Mesopotamia wealth was exhibited by the piling on of color, embroidery, and jewels; the Egyptians, with ultimate sophistication, chose always the refinement of simplicity.

The Egyptian love of pure line extended to hair wigs and headdresses. Wealthy men shaved daily with a copper razor, occasionally permitting themselves a small mustache. Only when in mourning or when journeying among barbarians might they grow a beard, although a small false ceremonial beard formed part of the pharaoh's paraphernalia of rank. Men usually wore their hair clipped short or

Linen was woven from earliest times, although flax may have been cultivated originally for the oil it produced. By the First Dynasty (c. 3000 B.C.) plain weaving as it is practiced today was known. An examination of fibers of the period shows that the flax used was finer than the finest of modern quality, and the fabric could be woven half again as fine as that of a modern handkerchief. The weave was the simple "one up, one down" known today as the "tabby." Many varieties of textures were produced, ranging from sacking to the equivalent of cambric.

Linen provided the solid basis of all Egyptian dress, and "dress" is the word we must use, for a style that changed little from the fourth to the first millennium B.C., cannot be called "fashion." In fact, this stability is the most notable quality of ancient Egyptian culture. For three thousand years taste was ruled by one aesthetic, developed early, and then scarcely changed. It was a lean, austere aesthetic based on what we today call "clean lines," one perhaps best described by the term "architectural," suited to massive form and in no way what might be expected of an "early" society. It pervaded

Opposite: The goddess Isis, "Great of Magic," leading Queen Nofretari. Isis, sister-wife of the god Osiris, wears the close-fitting sheath, full wig and heavy necklace typical of conservative Egyptian dress. The queen wears the "new" fashion popularized in the 18th

dynasty, a transparent, accordion-pleated robe, sashed beneath the breast. Wall painting from the Tomb of Nofretari, Valley of the Queens. Thebes. 19th dynasty.

Below: A cheerful family group, fowling and fishing in

the Nile. The master wears a long and elaborate shenti and a transparent shirt, while his wife has taken to the waves in the full regalia of 18th-dynasty fashion. The servant, repre-sented as smaller than his master, wears only the simple shenti. Wall painting from the

Tomb of Menena, "Scribe of the Fields of the Lord of the Two Lands." Thebes. 18th dynasty. c. 1415 B.C.

slightly longer and cut straight across; during later periods various short and long cuts were popu-lar. Women grew their hair longer and kept it black. The ideal cut for men's and women's hair was always thick and blunt. Moreover, it is in keeping with the Egyptian architectural sense of dress that members of the upper class, consisting largely of officials and court personages, frequently wore wigs, quite unnatural constructions of curled or plaited human hair giving the head an enlarged and often literally "pyramidal" shape. Such forms demon-strate the Egyptian preference for stylized "clean" lines to the loose freedom of naturally falling hair. This same triangular form was reflected in head-dresses, the commonest kind for men being a square of heavy material tied at the back of the head and falling, again along pyramidal lines, from head to shoulder.

Any society obsessed with the beauty of line, as we are in the 20th century, is also likely to be ob-sessed with maintaining the line of the human body. Whether the Egyptians engaged in rigorous diets we do not know, although Queen Nitocris did recommend daily massages for slimming. But one strong indication that the Egyptians were weight-conscious is the fact that, with very few exceptions, only foreigners are ever represented in Egyptian art as "fat." By and large, Egyptian art presents us with idealized figures rather than realistic portraits, and the idealized Egyptian figure is slender, even by today's standards. Men are portrayed with broad shoulders and seductively narrow hips. Women have long, lean arms and legs, slender hips, and handsomely rounded bosoms, an ideal more com-fortable to our eyes than that of our grandmothers. And so important was this ideal to the Egyptians that mummies of elderly women have been found in which the sagging breasts of old age have been plumped out with wax and sawdust so that the de-ceased will face eternity with a good figure. One female mummy presented to posterity a completely remolded body, constructed of bandages and resin-ous paste, like papier-mâché.

The elaborate construction of wigs and coiffures and the vast array of cosmetic pots, sticks and brushes, mirrors, combs, and manicuring equipment found in tombs reveals a mania for grooming. The importance of being "well groomed" found its way into love songs: "My heart can think of nothing but your love. . . . I run swiftly towards you, ne-

glecting my appearance. . . . But I will curl my hair and be ready at any moment." Women kept their "clean" body lines in pristine condition by the use of pumice stone to remove all bodily hair, as well as rough skin on knees and elbows. Prescriptions for face creams and preparations to nourish the scalp and prevent baldness had a prominent place in the Egyptian pharmacopoeia, along with hair dyes and a considerable variety of perfumes based on resins. Myrrh and stibid, extracted from acacia and teak seeds, were kept in delicate little glass bottles.

Cosmetics were of such ancient usage in Egypt that the palettes on which they were ground and spread evolved into ceremonial objects on which important historical events were memorialized. In earliest times black galena was used on the upper lid and green malachite on the lower, apparently to protect against insects and eye diseases. However, the aesthetic possibilities of body paint were known from Paleolithic times, and Egyptian paint pots multiplied soon enough. Contrasting shades of green malachite and blue copper ore on upper and lower lids were enhanced by a black line of kohl that elongated the eye, and brows were arched with the gray powder of antimony. The rest of the face was covered with the dangerous pale glow of lead paste. Red ocher was applied to lips and cheeks with a small brush. Veins in temples and breasts

were accentuated with blue pigment, and there is even some evidence that women occasionally painted their nipples gold. Men were often as heavily painted as women, and an orange ocher flesh tone, suggesting a rugged, sunburned masculinity, was reserved for them alone.

The Mesopotamians adopted an approach to clothing as protection against the scorching sun that is still common to the Bedouin tribesman: heavy garments shielding much of the body. The Egyptian solution of wearing little clothing, and that light and fine, appeals to us but suggests the necessity of some protection for the skin. The Egyptians were as clean as any people in history. Queen Nitocris recommended daily baths and a complete washing of hands, arms, and neck before and after each meal, using water with a natural calcium carbonate and a paste of clay and ashes as detergent. Such cleanliness would leave the skin lacking in even its natural oils. The problem was solved by lavish use of unguents, of which there were no fewer than thirty kinds, consisting of a base of animal fat, castor oil, or olive oil, scented with flowers, seeds, and wood essences. These unguents were so basic a part of Egyptian life that large quantities were supplied to workmen and soldiers in the field, along with necessities as basic as food.

The Egyptian style of dress remained almost changeless for three thousand years—almost but

not quite. During the Eighteenth Dynasty, called Egypt's Golden Age (1546 to 1319 B.C.) a new style appeared. It was at this time that Egypt, which had survived domination by the mysterious nomadic (and possibly Semitic) Hyksos, reemerged to become what might be called an international power. Lightly clad in leather, linen batting and possibly padded wigs, the armies of the great military pharaohs of the dynasty, Thutmose I and Thutmose III, penetrated as far as Palestine to the north, Nubia to the south, and east to Syria and the Euphrates (the "inverted" waters that, to the amazement of the Egyptians, flowed south). Considerable wealth poured into Egypt, which enjoyed a new prosperity. This was reflected in a new form of dress, a robe made of the sheerest linen, pressed into tiny "accordion" pleats and starched with gum, in the manner of a modern priest's surplice. It might possess bell-shaped sleeves, with pleats running horizontally, or it might be covered by a cape of the same pleated material, tied under the breast. A brightly ornamental sash was tied around the high

waist and fell to the floor. This garment opened right down the front. At times women wore it over the usual sheath, but it also seems to have been worn over the naked body. A similar robe of pleated gauzelike material was affected by men, as well as shirts with bell-shaped pleated sleeves.

On the walls of the Tomb of Neb-Amun (of the Eighteenth Dynasty) a party is shown in progress. It exemplifies the lavish entertaining of his time. Food is piled high on the tables, and wine sits in wreathed jars. The women are slender nymphs, their voluptuous bodies scarcely hidden by the yards of pleated and crimped gauze. Through their hair can be seen huge gold disks hanging from their ears, and they are weighed down with heavy gold necklaces and bracelets that band their arms from wrist to shoulder. It was literally as well as figuratively a golden age. The guests wear lotus-flower pendants over their foreheads. The cones of solid unguent that top their wigs will melt during the festivities, suffusing their hair with perfumes and causing their draped clothing to cling to their naked

27

skin. Priests as well as noblemen are attending the party, and as if in reaction to the spirit of their age, their heads are shaven. It was an era of ultimate sophistication:

Death is in my mind today
Like the perfume of lotus blossoms,
Like tarrying at the brim of the
    wine-bowl.

Death is in my mind today
Like the clearing of the sky
As when a man grasps what he has
    not understood.

Art historians rarely comment on the transparent or clinging clothing seen in Egyptian art. Nudity was, after all, common in ancient Egypt among the lower classes. Women working in the fields wore white kilts and nothing more, and the dancing girls at Neb-Amun's feast—dressed solely in belts about their hips—wore still less. And yet in these seemingly skin-tight shifts and transparent gauzes the seduction principle is clearly at work despite our puritanical notions of what should be displayed in tombs and associated with death. Poetry bears out our suspicions. Transparency of dress seems to have been the charming and innocent fetish of the era:

My god, my brother, my husband—
How sweet it is to go down to the lotus pond
    and do as you desire—
    to plunge into the waters, and bathe before
        you—
    to let you see my beauty in my tunic of
        sheerest royal linen,
    all wet and clinging and perfumed with
        balsam.

It might well be that Neb-Amun would have liked his wife and female guests to follow him, just so seductively, into eternity.

It would seem, then, that Egyptian society, most especially the society of the Eighteenth Dynasty, was a comparatively lax one. During this period the occasional adoption of a mannish, short haircut by women, and transparent pleated robes by men, has been considered a sign of moral degeneracy by scholars perhaps somewhat confused as to exactly what "morality" had "degenerated." In point of fact the women of ancient Egypt during most of its history seem to have been as liberated as any before the present century. As in Sumer, divorce was easy and a woman enjoyed property rights, a high degree of respect, and a share in most of her husband's activities. On tomb walls a wife might appear at her husband's side, fowling in the marshes or enjoying a dinner party, and this indicated she would be at his side "in the West." Law still condemned adulteresses to death, although this hardly seems in keeping with either the evidence of the wall paintings or Herodotus's claim that Egyptian women were the loosest in the world. He tells the story of the pharaoh who was obliged to find a single faithful wife in his entire realm as a cure for his blindness—and failed. Husbands countered by having as many concubines as they could afford. However, the power of the female goddesses such as Isis was paralleled in the earthly sphere by "Great Royal Wives" far more distinguished and powerful than the obscure consorts of Mesopotamian princes. Although Egypt was generally ruled by a king, descent frequently followed the female line.

One of the most brilliant rulers of the Eighteenth Dynasty was a woman, Hatshepsut, the Queen Elizabeth of Egypt, daughter of the powerful Thutmose I. She disposed of both her half-brother-husband and nephew-son-in-law to rule as pharaoh in her own right with her own Essex, a commoner called Senenmut, to advise her. Like Elizabeth, she consolidated her country's power and economic prosperity by means of diplomacy when war could be avoided. And, like Elizabeth, she was vain: "[I am] exceedingly good to look upon, with the form and spirit of a god, . . . a beautiful maiden fresh, serene of nature . . . altogether divine." It is interesting that although she was the royal heiress, there was no precedent for her seizure of power. So the "beautiful, fresh, serene of nature" was obliged to adopt a male persona in order to rule, dressing as a male pharaoh, complete with ceremonial beard.

The Eighteenth Dynasty ended in the fascinating mystery of the most flamboyant figure in Egyptian history, Amenhotep IV, known as Akhenaten or Ikhnaton, and his wife Nefertiti, a woman of such extraordinary appearance that what is known of her cannot be omitted from any history that touches on the subject of personal style. Akhenaten was born Amenhotep IV, and he has been called "the first individual in history." In a culture knowing only the most minute changes in customs, styles, and beliefs over periods of millennia, a total revolutionary such as Akhenaten may be seen only as a kind of miracle of nature. This fanatical mystic attempted to jettison the accrued religious beliefs of ages in favor of the worship of a single god, Aten, the "disc of the life-giving sun." Hence the conversion of Amenhotep IV's name to Akhenaten, "He who is Beneficial to Aten." Akhenaten built the sacred city Akhetaten, on the Plain of Amarna. By so doing he hoped to wrest power once and for all from the priests of Amun and their capital, Thebes. It was in this new capital, the "Brasilia" of ancient Egypt, that Akhenaten's other revolutionary tastes became plain. His search for ma'at, the truth, extended to the artistic decoration of the capital. The flattened and stylized representation of the human body that had controlled Egyptian art since its beginnings was to be replaced by a realism of physical appearance and gesture as meticulous as possible. The king himself was to appear no longer as a slim-hipped and indistinguishable ideal but as a living man. Egyptian artists responded so successfully to the new dicta that they proved beyond question that the

Below: Symbols of life radiate from the disk of Aten, the sun, on the elongated heads of Akhenaten and Nefertiti as they fondle their children. Relief from Tell el'Amarna. 18th dynasty. c. 1370 B.C.

Right: Bust of Akhenaten, wearing the composite crown of upper and lower Egypt, the false, pharaonic beard hanging from his pendulous jaw. 18th dynasty. c. 1360 B.C.

Far right: Bust of "the hereditary princess . . . the great royal wife, his beloved: Beauty is the beauty of Aten, Nefertiti." From Tell el'Amarna. 18th dynasty.

stylization of previous Egyptian art had had its basis solely in taste, belief, and superstition rather than in ignorance or inability. Some of the artists of Amarna seem actually to have made studies from masks of the living face.

At last, then, we might expect to see Egyptian rulers as they lived and breathed. But the vision that presents itself is startling: a man whose face and body are peculiarly distorted by disease, and his sister-wife, one of the great beauties of this or any time, also possibly suffering from the same disease. This unforgettable couple appear again and again on the walls and in the free-standing sculpture of Akhetaten, always together: Akhenaten, with his misshapen and elongated head, drooping jaw, pendulous stomach, and flabby hips; his wife, who may share some of these infirmities; and a bevy of daughters, six in all, displaying the elongated head of their father. Breaking with all precedent, the king's emotional life is also displayed. He is seen kissing his wife and children, playing with them, and grieving over a lost daughter.

But it is the famous Berlin Museum bust of Nefertiti, whose name suitably enough means "The Beautiful One Has Come," that epitomizes Egypt's brief age of *ma'at*. An inscription tells us she is "The heiress, great in favor, lady of grace, sweet of love, Mistress of the South and North, fair of face, gay with the two plumes, beloved of the Living Aten, the Chief Wife of the King, whom he loves, lady of the two Lands, great of love, Nefertiti, living for-

ever. . . ." The perfection of the nose and cheekbones, the arch of the brows, the tilt of the head, the languid neck, and the little smile that plays on her lips have made her an object "living forever." We assume that the crown that so accentuates these superb lines is merely the usual crown of the royal queen. In fact, it is not. It was chosen by the queen as her habitual headdress in preference to the heavy wigs or other forms that would almost certainly have destroyed her particular style, an early example of what we have come to call "personal taste" in dress. Again, however, we have the clean lines of the Egyptian aesthetic and again the pyramidal shape, this time inverted. The purpose of the crown might also have been to disguise an elongated head resembling her brother-husband's, for Akhenaten's malformation had actually become a fashion imitated in the representation of many of his courtiers.

The hedonistic and intimate life at Akhetaten came to a bizarre and murky end. Nefertiti seems to have been banished from the palace and to have gone north of the city. Akhenaten seems to have taken his half-brother and son-in-law, Smenkhkare, as co-regent, and then his daughter Ankhesenpaten as wife, although the final phases of the outré reign remain a mystery. With the death of Tutankhamen, Akhenaten's son-in-law and possibly his son, the Eighteenth Dynasty came to a close. In his tomb, by sheerest chance, the golden trappings of an era of curious profligacy and passion have been preserved for posterity.

The Draped Ideal

Crete

During the Golden Age, Egypt conducted a lively trade with the "Keftiu," the people of "the islands in the midst of the sea." These were the people we know as the inhabitants of Minoan Crete.

It has been said that to describe Minoan civilization one would have to have the vision of a poet. We have no texts, only paintings and objects to tell us of a people who rose to immense wealth during the second millennium B.C. and who controlled the entire eastern Mediterranean from the island that Homer so memorably described:

> Out in the deep, dark sea there lies a land called
> Crete,
> A rich and lovely land, washed by the waves on
> every side
> And boasting ninety cities.

The Cretans have left us no thoughts—no histories, stories, or poems, nor even the vaguest outline of the events of their existence. They possessed writing, but so preoccupied were they with commercial matters that it seems to have been used exclusively for accounting purposes. However, their palaces and their art are tantalizing suggestions of an intriguing and dramatic past. Side by side with the piles of tablets enumerating merchandise purchased and sold are found paintings of mystic rites in which scantily dressed youths and maidens catapult themselves over the horns of an onrushing bull (visual substantiation of the curious legend of Theseus and the Minotaur), as well as finely wrought figurines of autochthonous goddesses, snake-entwined earth mothers.

The great palaces also give evidence of a life filled with the most hedonistic delights. Gardens of blazing color, monkeys, sea gulls, flying fish, and the Cretans themselves—young, athletic, and beautiful even by the standards of our own day—are depicted in flat and almost abstract patterns of brilliant color on the walls. The Palace of Knossos itself, at once the home of rulers and an administrative and religious center, is labyrinthine in plan, containing between 1,300 and 1,400 rooms. With its broad staircases, shady courtyards, and chambers on many levels made airy by light shafts, it provided comforts that exceeded even those of Egypt. Here we are amazed to find hydraulic engineering, running water, and flush toilets. Moreover, the delights of Minoan life seem undiluted by hardship. There are no scenes of battle in Cretan art, and the fact that the palaces totally lack means of defense

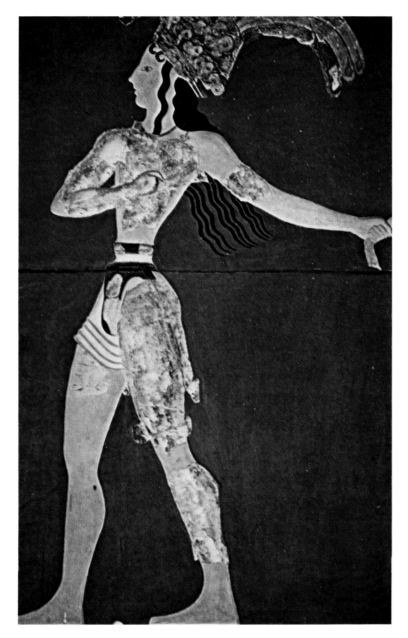

suggests that war was an unfamiliar terror. In fact, if we are to believe Thucydides, the fleets of the Cretan traders ruled the Mediterranean and served as the ultimate protection for their island home.

Because of the many representations in Cretan art, we have more detailed knowledge of Cretan clothing than we do of any other aspect of Minoan civilization. The Cretans would appear to have been among the most attractive people of antiquity, with huge dark eyes; long, straight, delicate noses; slender wasp waists; and ringlets of black hair. The Cretans depicted themselves with a kind of insistent prettiness and gaiety that has permanently "set" our visual image of them. We may fancy that their well-kept accounts produced a "good life."

Opposite: Fresco of a Cretan priest-king from the Palace at Knossos. Wearing only a kilt-like garment and a plumed crown, he epitomizes the Minoan ideal: wasp-waisted, broad-shouldered, muscular, and tanned. A restoration in which the crown, torso, and left leg are original. 1550–1450 B.C.

Below: This bare-breasted dancer with flying curls, straight nose, and dark eyes approximates the Cretan female ideal. Fresco fragment from the queen's megaron at the Palace of Knossos. c. 1550–1450 B.C.

Bottom: Even within the tiny confines of this seal ring, Mycenaean dress suggests almost irrepressible gaiety.

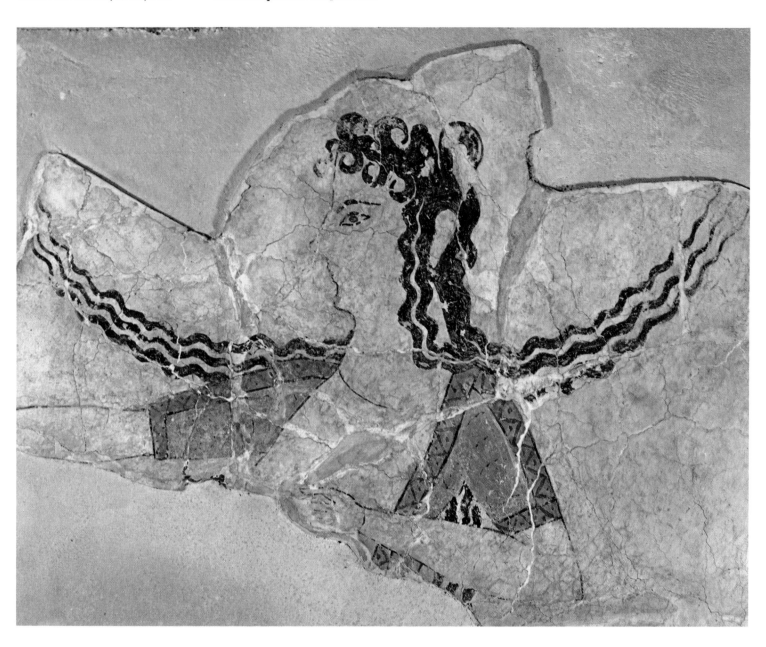

Cretan men, eternally ageless, dark-skinned, and muscular, wore a short, complicated kilt made of several layers of material, frequently coming to an elongated point at the front of the knee. They went naked above the waist, but wore a cloak for warmth and often high boots of a light or dyed leather, as befit men living in mountainous terrain. Like the Egyptians, however, the Cretans wore sandals or boots outside but rarely inside the house, so that the exterior palace steps are far more worn than those of the interior. Also as in Egypt, royal figures were distinguished chiefly by headdress, although in Crete these were elaborately feathered.

The dress of Cretan women, however, is most distinctive. Almost invariably they wore a wide,

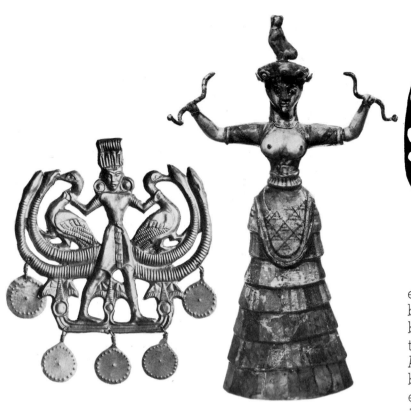

bell-shaped skirt, springing from a tight waist. These skirts, which might be made of either linen or wool, were splendidly decorated, quite in the spirit of the frescoed walls of the palaces, with brilliant and often abstract patterns of color: red, yellow, blue, and purple were favored. They might be banded in stripes, squares, or lozenges with braid or strips of embroidery, or entire scenes might be depicted on the skirt front—a garden of crocus blossoms, white, red, and yellow boughs, or swallows with outspread wings. The most usual decoration, however, consisted of a series of tiered "flounces." Moreover, such skirts may have been backed with horizontal hoops to make them stand out stiffly. Above the waist the Cretan woman wore a tight-fitting, short-sleeved bodice with a décolleté so wide and low that both pale breasts were completely exposed (women are always portrayed as lighter of skin than men). On her head this delicious figure might wear a coquettish hat; turbans, berets, tricorns, and pointed caps all appear. It is also interesting that men and women alike wore rolled belts apparently so tight that it has been suggested the Cretans were riveted into metal waist-cinchers in youth that they were obliged to wear all of their lives—certainly an enticement to diet as time progressed.

Cretan men and women wore their hair in serpentine coils, the women sometimes knotting theirs at the crown with pendant curls. They also braided pearls and ribbons into their locks, wore thin necklaces wound many times around their necks, and favored gold earrings and even gold belts. The effect was one of nipped waists, corkscrew curls, bright bows, ribbons, trinkets, and crinolines—rather in the style of a 19th-century "belle" were it not for the startling bare breasts.

What was the origin of the Cretans and their extraordinary costume? Elements can be traced to both Mesopotamia and Egypt. The pointed kilt worn by men is represented as far away as Libya, and the flounced skirt reminds us of the Sumerian *kaunakès* (the Cretan language also appears to have been of Semitic origin). Certain sacred symbols and emblems, on the other hand, seem to have originated in the Predynastic Nile delta. Despite such clues, no definite origins have been ascertained for Cretan civilization. However, Cretan dress, worn and possibly exported by one of the great trading nations of antiquity, did become the costume of much of the northern Mediterranean world for several centuries, and its spread is perhaps even more interesting than its origin.

Mycenae

In the early years of the second millennium B.C., when Cretan power was at its height, a tall, fair people who spoke Greek migrated from the north into mainland Greece, bringing with them their oxcarts, herds, and flocks. They are known variously by the name "Achaean," as they appear in the Homeric poems, and "Mycenaean," a reference to Mycenae ("rich in gold"), one of their greatest strongholds. These Mycenaean Greeks appear either to have conquered or infiltrated Crete. We know this because their language also appears on Cretan tablets and above all because they themselves became thoroughly Cretanized. The architecture of their mainland fortress settlements differs totally from the open, unprotected plan of Cretan structures, but the paintings that decorate their walls are almost identical in style. Only the spirit has changed. The bellicose Mycenaeans used the free-flowing patterns of Cretan art, created for a leisurely, civilized life, to portray their own favorite blood sports: hunting and fighting. The result is sometimes incongruous. A pack of dogs is depicted attacking a boar, their necks tied with big bows of ribbon.

In the matter of dress, the Mycenaeans went wholeheartedly "native," adopting Cretan "fashions" with other aspects of Cretan culture, although they did not adopt either the Cretan language or religion. They became "Cretanized" much as an Oriental

Left: Mycenaean fresco of a woman bearing votive gifts. Thebes. 1400–1350 B.C.
Above: Mycenaean fresco of a woman carrying a box. Cretan dress and the riot of Cretan pattern are to be found on the walls of the Mycenaean citadels. Many of these citadels are mentioned by Homer as the seats of his Achaean heroes. From Tiryns. 1400–1350 B.C.

businessman might become "Westernized" with respect to dress and technology. They retained their own male "sky" deity as opposed to the Cretan "earth" goddess, but they purloined the design for the Cretan drainpipe. They appear to have discarded their drapery in favor of tightly fitted and sewn Cretan dress, except that their men continued to wear beards and a short chiton covering their bare torso. The Mycenaean women also seem to have introduced a kind of bustle. Meanwhile, trade had carried Cretan costume as far as Syria to the east and Spain to the west. As the dress of the Mycenaean Greeks, it became the dress of most of the Aegean.

The world of the Mycenaean Greeks reminds us of feudal Europe. Tiny kingdoms, domains that were really little more than large estates, battled each other incessantly, and Vikinglike expeditions were undertaken against any coastal settlement where fortifications might be breached. Rivalries were fierce, offenses unforgotten, loyalties intense, and the mark of the man was valor in battle. The symbolism of the sword prevailed, and only the actual paraphernalia of knighthood was lacking. Women were almost as free—and as fierce—as their men.

And like the verbal traditions of feudal Europe, the tales of Mycenaean bravery, cunning, and battle became the "mythology" of a later, more settled and more civilized era. Homer's *Iliad* and *Odyssey* were its *Idylls of the King*, and the sophistication of these poems is sufficient evidence of the sheer genius that was to come.

Troy may well have been a Greek colony itself; it was certainly part of the Mycenaean world. And so we may perhaps imagine Helen as a fetching figure in tiered skirts, her superb breasts bare for Paris's admiration, and Cassandra, Andromache, and Hecuba similarly attired. Like the women of Crete, the women of Troy wore elaborate golden decorations in their hair. The head ornament that the 19th-century archaeologist Heinrich Schliemann romantically thought to be Helen's own (it belonged to an earlier princess) consisted of sixty-four delicate gold chains, some hanging over the brow and others falling to the shoulder, where they ended in small medallions that must have tinkled gaily as the wearer walked.

Moreover, the clusters of myths known as the Theban and other cycles suggest typical Mycenaean lays, so that we must alter the visual image so long cherished of the heroes and heroines of Greek mythology. We might do well to visualize the figures of Ariadne, Phaedra, Eurydice, Clytemnestra, Electra, Jocasta, Antigone, and others, not as the draped figures from the classical stage but as hoopskirted and wasp-waisted first cousins of the ladies of the Knossos paintings.

The Palace of Knossos was destroyed quite suddenly around the year 1400 B.C. on a spring day so windy that destructive fire spread quickly. The other palaces of Crete soon met a similar fate, although the cause of the destruction, whether earthquake, invasion, or internal dissension, remains elusive. The Mycenaeans continued to thrive on the Greek mainland, and it was during this period that Troy fell. At some point in the 12th century B.C., however, the Mycenaean citadels were also destroyed. Again the cause of the devastation is unclear, but most historians attribute the fall to the invasion of peoples who have been labeled the Dorians. As in Crete, archaeological evidence suggests social disorder, a breakdown in trade and communication, a loss of wealth, and the descent into a dark age.

It is a curious fact that a few centuries later, toward the end of the 8th century B.C., when Greece reemerged for us into the light thrown by art, the Greeks are differently dressed. Homer, whose poems took their final forms during this period, says little about dress. Of armor, of course, he speaks. His Achaeans were "bronze-clad," although iron was in use by Homer's day, and he describes them as well equipped, with greaves, cuirasses, and crested helmets giving protection for nose and cheeks. He also speaks of huge shields, "tall like a tower" and made of many bull skins, protecting the entire body. Such shields were depicted in works of Mycenaean art. Homer describes a helmet covered with boars' tusks, also unknown in his day, and yet just such a helmet has been found at Mycenae. Nevertheless, we do not know precisely what was to be done with the cloth that Penelope was weaving on her loom. This confusion may be caused by the fact, difficult to appreciate, that the people of whom Homer sang were dressed in a manner totally different from those around him—a difference that oral tradition may not have explained.

The Golden Age

In fact, the Greeks of the Archaic and later periods wore loose, draped, and often totally unsewn garments, as different as possible from the tightly fitted clothing of Crete and Mycenae. This change of style is perhaps one of the best proofs of the very existence as well as influence of the Dorian invaders of Mycenae.

The dress of Archaic and Classical Greece of the 5th century B.C. (the "Golden Age"), the superb and seemingly complicated draperies that play so important a role in Greek art, consisted of a very few basic garments. These required no cutting of fabric and little sewing. The Dorian *peplos*, worn by women, was nothing more than a rectangle or two rectangles of wool folded over at the top and draped about the body. A "dress length" usually measured a foot more than the height of the wearer and twice her width from elbow to elbow with arms outstretched. The front and back were attached by a *fibulae* (originally made of the leg bones of a small animal) on one or both shoulders. The voluminous cloth fell gracefully from these points to the wearer's ankles. The sides might or might not be sewn. The garment would then be belted on one or two levels—under the breast and around the waist —and pulled into a *blouson*. Men wore a similar garment, called the *chiton*. The Doric chiton, however, was shorter (just covering the knee), and men wore no overfold.

The Ionian chiton had its origin in the Ionian colonies settled on the coast of Asia Minor by Greeks fleeing the Dorian invasion and later overpopulation. It was made of fine linen, often tightly twisted for several hours to give a pleated effect, and was quite different in appearance from the Dorian wool chiton. Again, a length of material was held

around the body, but this time attachments were
made by means of *fibulae* or a seam not only at
the shoulder but all the way down the arm. When
a belt was added, the effect was a kind of sleeve.
The Ionian chiton was worn down to the ground by
women, to just below the knee by men, and short
by children. There were exceptions to this rule: Men
attending certain festivities, charioteers, or persons of
importance assumed the nobility of the long chiton.

The Ionian chiton, often made of a flimsy fabric,
was always regarded by the mainland Greeks
as a luxury, but this did not prevent it from being
adopted in the 6th century B.C. Thereafter the two
styles blended, so that the Ionian chiton appears with
an overfold, the peplos without it; at times the
Dorian peplos was worn over the thin Ionian chiton.

Over the chiton or peplos both men and women
wore the *himation*, another still larger rectangle of
wool, draped as a long cloak around one shoulder.
Women might wear it over both shoulders or
drawn up over the head. Horsemen, soldiers, and

young boys—in short, the more active males—wore
a shorter cloak, called the *chlamys*. No shoes were
worn in the house, but outdoors women and men
donned sandals, and men might wear high boots.

It is a tribute to the genius of both the wearers
of the chiton and the himation and that of the
sculptors who portrayed them that anything as
simple as these garments should produce the
variety and grace of drapery that we associate with
Greece. In fact, skill at draping one's own clothing
was taken as distinct evidence of education and
social standing. According to Plato, it was absolutely
necessary that a man should know "how to throw
his cloak from left to right as a gentleman should."

Diagrammatic drawings showing the construction and draping of the peplos and the chiton.
Top: Doric peplos before folding, together with a magnified fibula.
Center: Drape of the Doric peplos.
Above: Drape of the Ionic chiton.
Above center: Doric peplos, here shown loose, without waist banding, and open down the side in the Spartan manner. All from Ancient Greek, Roman and Byzantine Costume and Decoration by Mary Houston.
Above right: Hunter in chiton and chlamys, equipped with boots and a sun hat. Red-figure lekythos by the Pan painter. 470 B.C.
Right: Ionic chiton. The fall of the finely pleated, transparent material is here well illustrated, as is the "seductive" nature of this chiton. Red-figure kylix. Athenian. c. 490–480 B.C.

A certain grace, however, could be assured by the attachment of little weights at the hem.

Having no choice in what he wore, then, the Greek could exhibit what we call "good taste" by the way he wore his clothing. There were many caveats. Again according to Plato, a gentleman should never extend his arm outside his himation or wear a chiton so short that his knees protruded when he sat down. A woman might not leave her house unless both chiton and himation swathed her figure (hardly comfortable in hot weather). As a matter of eccentricity, however, there were men— and Socrates was among them—who went about wearing just the himation with nothing underneath, which was rather a blatant show of frugality combined with physical hardiness when done in winter. The soldiers serving King Agesilaus of Sparta knew it was bitterly cold when they espied their king wearing a chiton under his himation.

The sense of decorum was purely an aesthetic matter having nothing to do with prudishness regarding nudity—at least as far as men were concerned. The Greeks seem to have had a simple aversion to clothing of any sort whenever it was unnecessary or simply annoying. Both men and women bathed in the nude (although not together). The Athenian gentleman spent a good part of his life in the *gymnasia*, clubhouses comprising exercise rooms, baths, and lecture and discussion halls where philosophers, poets, and rhetoricians might hold forth. The word itself is derived from *gymnos*, meaning "naked." Certainly no clothing was worn during the many hours of athletic exercise regarded by the philosophers as necessary to the health of

both body and soul. According to Thucydides, a loincloth had been worn by contestants in the Olympic games and other athletic festivals until shortly before his time, when the Spartans were the first to appear naked and anointed with oil. In any case, during the historical period the contestants appeared nude and the genitals were regarded with a certain awe and respect; loincloths were considered ugly, a disruption of the beauty of the fluid line of the body and therefore not to be countenanced. Nude dancers and acrobats, both male and female, often provided the expected entertainment at those dinner parties that were the charm of Athenian social life. In fact, the open and hearty appreciation of the beauty of the nude has been recognized as an intrinsic element in Greek visual genius. The Greeks seem to have recognized it as such themselves. Their "barbarian" neighbors, most particularly the Persians, had a horror of nudity; and the Greeks regarded this as signal proof of Persian insensitivity.

This lack of prudery did not apply in any way to women. The Athenian citizen might enjoy the charms of a nude female flute player at dinner (which his wife could never attend), but any married woman caught in the audience of the Olympic games could be thrown from the Typaeum rock. This attitude, however, might not have been so much Greek as Attic. The good women of Athens had, in early times, learned to sew up the open side of their chitons. The women of Sparta simply left theirs open, a peculiarity that seems to have horrified the Athenians, particularly as Spartan women went about without the covering of a himation. They

were dubbed "thigh-showers," and to dress "in the Spartan manner" meant simply "indecently." The fact that Spartan girls also exercised and even wrestled in the nude and in the company of Spartan boys contributed to the Athenian sense that the Spartan's behavior was unseemly.

The Greek standard of propriety extended to hair and beard. During the Archaic period both men and women wore long curls, and men carefully crimped their beards, which may reflect an Oriental practice. The Spartans regarded their long hair as sacred; however, after the defeat of the Persians and possibly the rejection of all things Oriental, styles changed. Women began to pin up their hair in a knot or bun at the nape of the neck, sometimes supported by bands that wound around the head in various ways, and often enclosed in a net. It became traditional for a boy to cut his long locks upon becoming an adolescent, and thereafter he would wear his hair in "hyacynthine" curls. Styles varied: The *Kepos* was "cut like a garden," while the *Hectorean* was combed back in curls. The *Theseid* was short in front and long in back. Young men were generally clean-shaven, although it was a sign of distinction for older men to go bearded. In the fashion of his beard the Greek made a "statement," as we might say. The Epicurean wore his long and curly, the Stoic simply went unshaven. Blond hair, perhaps the trait of the early northern, Greek-speaking invaders, seems to have been more common in ancient than modern Greece, and it was much admired even in Homeric times. Both men and women bleached their hair with potash water, washed it with a dye made of yellow flowers, and dried it in the sun to achieve a blonder effect.

This bleaching of hair somehow strikes a wrong note in our perception of the Greeks. We think of them as being alien to artifice, and for the most part we are right in this. There was something obsessive in their search for absolute simplicity and purity of form. The Greeks would never have allowed the gewgaws of jewelry and embroidery to disrupt the pure lines of their clothing. Like the Egyptians, their taste was ruled by an all-powerful architectural aesthetic, and we know that they saw in the draperies they wore the austere fluting of the columnar supports of their temples. However, over and above aesthetic considerations, the Greeks had a flat moral objection to luxury of dress. Simplicity was the cornerstone of the Greek (typified by the Athenian) way of life after the defeat of the Persians, who represented to the Greeks all that was abominable in luxurious indulgence. It was the quintessential quality.

Demosthenes, writing in the 4th century B.C., gave a fair description of the attitudes toward personal wealth of 5th-century Athens: "The great men of old built splendid edifices for the use of the State, and set up noble works of art which later ages can never match. But in private life they were severe and simple, and the dwelling of an Aristides or a Miltiades was no more sumptuous than that of an ordinary Athenian citizen." The temples on the Acropolis might be of Parian marble, but the home of a Miltiades or an ordinary Athenian citizen would be a simple affair of sun-dried and plastered brick, a few rooms built around a courtyard, with a colonnaded porch for use in warm weather. Within, furnishings might consist of a few low chairs and couches that doubled as beds, a few stools, a wickerwork basket, and mirrors and such, along with the boxes, jars, and vases of the pottery ware for which Athens was famous. Clothing, those flat rectangles of cloth, would be stored in chests or hung on a nail. Windows were glassless, a small brazier provided warmth, and an olive-oil lamp gave light. In a setting of such austere simplicity, a painted and bejeweled citizen or his wife would be clearly out of place. This is not to say that the Athenians were not prosperous. They enjoyed an active trade in wine, olive oil, pottery, armor, and other products, and they controlled an empire of over two hundred cities, most of which paid tribute. However, this wealth was channeled into public expenditure. It is not surprising that Phidias's twenty-five-foot statue of Athena stood in the cella of the Parthenon wearing draperies of twenty-three-hundredweight solid gold, while even the wealthiest Athenian matron would not wear more than a linen chiton and a few trinkets, the dress of the first democracy.

This Athenian democracy, then, was not an acquisitive society. In his famous "Funeral Oration," Pericles claims: "We think it no disgrace to confess to poverty, but a disgrace to make no effort to overcome it." The educated Athenian devoted no more effort to business and the laying away of wealth than was necessary to get beyond poverty. Leisure time to devote to athletics, discussion at the gymnasium, debate in the councils of state, and conversation after dinner was far more highly prized than were material possessions. Moreover, in few societies has the type of material wealth a citizen might put on his back conveyed less status.

Color itself was regarded as a luxury. Greek statuary, washed clean by the ages, may give the impression that little color was worn, but in fact Greek dress appeared in a variety of shades: saffron (worn chiefly by women), indigo, scarlet, purple, green, black, and blue-gray, as well as the natural woolen shades of white, brown, and black. However, the man's himation was generally white, the color of purity, and when the populace took to dyeing their himations a reddish brown, the poor were forbidden to wear colored clothing at the theater or in public places. This rule was not meant to cause a social distinction but rather to prevent wasting money. The chief decoration of dress remained the border embroidered in a simple design such as the Greek "fret." Socrates disapproved even of this. To ornament a chiton or himation was, he

pronounced, "ignoble, illiberal and fraudulent." Alcibiades, the flower of Athenian nobility, was criticized for the extravagance of wearing a long chiton when it was not customary and for adopting the mode of a purple or scarlet loincloth.

Women of Greece

Frugality and social equalitarianism were not the sole reasons for the simplicity of Greek dress. Another may well have been the astonishingly low position of women. Socrates describes the life of a friend, one Isomachus, whom he regards as the perfect country gentleman, a sort of Greek Sir Roger de Coverley. He has found for himself a wife, just fifteen (the usual age of brides), knowing "no more than how, when given wool, to turn out a cloak, and had seen only how the spinning is given out to the maids." Isomachus is delighted to find that his wife is "docile and sufficiently domesticated to carry on conversations," and he sets about instructing her. Her education consists of lectures on how to save money and how to keep corn dry, wine cool and servants well. He assures her that her reward will be "to feel confident that with advancing years, the better partner you prove to me and the better housewife to our children, the greater will be the honor paid to you in our home."

This self-righteous declaration is followed by another to provoke cringes. One day Isomachus observed his wife and "noticed that her face was made up: she had rubbed in white lead to look even whiter than she was, and alkanet juice to heighten the rosy color of her cheeks, and she was wearing high-heeled shoes to increase her height." Surely one of history's most consummate prigs, he asks her if it would be honest for him to pretend to be richer than he was, and points out that such "tricks" may deceive strangers, but her husband is sure to recognize them for what they are. The wife, if we are to believe all this, then asks "how she might make herself really beautiful, instead of merely seeming so." The husband replies that true beauty lies in behaving as the mistress of the house, teaching those who know less, learning from those who know more, and seeing that everything is in its place. Moreover, good exercise in kneading dough and shaking and folding cloaks and bedclothes will improve her appetite and health and add *natural* color to her cheeks.

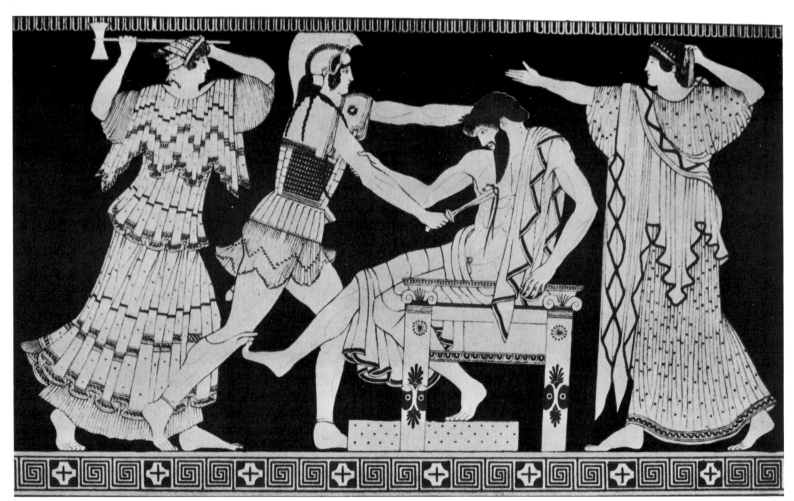

The Athenian wife, in fact, was kept in almost total seclusion in the women's quarters of her home, where her chief occupation was the making of clothing with the assistance of the female domestic slaves. The clothing she made for herself was unlikely ever to be seen, since women were not to appear out of the home. If she did venture forth, she was accompanied by a male relative and female slaves, until it was no longer asked whose wife she was but whose mother. Marketing was performed by a male slave, a wife gave up her male children at seven, and even the visits of other women were discouraged. In the words of Euripides, female visitors were "teachers of everything that was bad." Not only was the Athenian wife never present at the dinner parties and discussions, the *symposia*, that were the core of Athenian intellectual life; she was often not even thought fit to prepare the food. A special chef would be hired by her husband for that task. (Syracusians were considered particularly skilled.) The confining prejudice against women had infected even the greatest minds of the Golden Age, and women's inferiority seems

to have been one of the few human assumptions Socrates did not see fit to question.

It had not always been so. The Homeric epics are full of recollections of the power of Mycenaean women. Nausicaä, herself a bright and engaging figure, advises Odysseus to pass her father's throne and go directly to her mother, Queen Arete, famous for her skill at resolving dissension. Penelope's suitors decide to leave their fate in her capable hands. And the entire Trojan War was fought, theoretically, to reclaim an independent-minded adulteress whose husband does not, in the last analysis, presume to punish her. At some point after the Dorian invasion—possibly as a result of the need for physical strength engendered by the brutal chaos of the "dark age"—the position of women began to slide, and the golden and radiant vision of Homer's Penelope became the pathetic wife of Isomachus with her cautiously rouged cheeks.

Women still seem to have counted for something in Aeolia as late as the early 6th century B.C., at least enough for the girls of Lesbos to have received

an education in music, dancing, and poetry at the "home of the servants of the muses" under the tutelage of the poetess Sappho. She prepared her girls for marriage and taught them how to be women, then still an art. Charm, wit, and dress were of importance. The "tenth muse" described the preparation of a young woman's beauty:

> For with many a garland of violets and sweet roses mingled you have decked your flowing locks by my side, and with many a woven necklet made of a hundred blossoms your dainty throat; and with many a jar of myrrh, both of the precious and of the royal, have you anointed your fair skin. . . .

But this was an Aeolian attitude. Already the crabby Dorian farmer Hesiod had told how Zeus set the Olympians to create woman out of wet clay and grievous desire and guile and impudence, the "deep pitfall with steep sides and no means of escape."

Athenian intellectual life, then, was built on a rich subsoil of myth, legend, and quasi-history, inherited from the Mycenaean past in which powerful women played powerful roles. Sitting on the grassy slopes of the Theater of Dionysus, the Athenian was treated to the spectacle of the grand passions of a Clytemnestra or of an Antigone, women such as neither he nor the author had seen in life and who did not exist in their world.

The result of this unhinged view of life was a perhaps divine but also frightening confusion. The very appearance of the actors denied sexual identity. All roles were played by men, and to cope with the scale of the huge theaters, which attempted to accommodate the entire population, they wore thick-soled shoes, huge masks of stiffened linen on which basic emotions were traced, enormous wigs

and padding. The confusion of gender is reflected further in Greek art. Men and women were scarcely differentiated in their idealized beauty. Archaeologists have often found it impossible to identify the sex of a 5th-century figure in the absence of the genitalia if the hair also happens to be missing. The superb helmeted head of Myron's Athena might just as easily be that of a man. As we have seen, the dress of men and women differed little in its basic forms. However, it might be expected that with the passage of time differentiation would take place. In fact, the very reverse seems to have happened, as differentiation had been discarded and archaic female dress simplified and masculinized.

Plutarch in his life of Lycurgus tells of Spartan wedding customs that, if the tale has a grain of truth, reflect the ultimate annihilation of the female: After the wedding was arranged, the groom would carry out a mock rape of the bride. The so-called bridesmaid then received the girl, shaved her head, put her in men's clothing and shoes, and left her in the dark on a bed of straw. The bridegroom, who had taken dinner with his male table companions, then visited the bride in the dark, later returning to sleep with the other young men.

Whether or not the above effort to cope with the problems of habitual bisexuality and procreation were true in Sparta, it was not the custom in Athens. There the bride in particolored dress met her groom in white and was initiated into her theoretically uninteresting marriage by the strains of bridal hymns sung by friends. Before marriage, Athenian girls dedicated their dolls to Artemis. In a fragment from Sophocles a young wife laments: "Now I am nothing and left alone; I have often observed that such is the lot of womenkind—that we are a mere nothing."

Below: Athenian banqueting with a hetaera. She swings a kylix on her finger in the game of kottabas. *Red-figure kylix. c. 490–480 B.C.*

Opposite
Left: A hetaera, wearing an Ionic chiton, assists a gentle- man suffering from the aftereffects of overfeasting. *Red-figure kylix. 550–190 B.C. Center: Gold armband for upper arm in the form of snake spirals terminating in the figures of a Triton and Tritoness. Such jewelry became popular in the 4th and* 3rd centuries B.C.
Right: A girl playing a flute for Dionysus suggests a bejeweled hetaera of the late 5th century B.C. She wears armbands similar to the one shown at her left. Red-figure volute crater by the Karneia painter. Southern Italian. c. 400 B.C.

There were, however, women of Athens who whitened their faces with lead, rouged their lips and were applauded for doing so, women who escaped the chains of matrimony, who received something of an education, and on whom men lavished the luxuries denied to their wives—the *hetaerae.* The word is derived from the early Greek "comrade in arms," and these courtesans, or more specifically "geishas," of Classical Greece were precisely that. They were by no means to be confused with the common prostitute or *pornos.* Traditionally women of poor or questionable background, they set out with considerable spirit to charm even the more brilliant men of their era and to this end managed to gain for themselves a basic education in music, poetry, dancing, and, in the case of the most enterprising and serious, some grounding in politics and philosophy. For Athenians in flight from drab housewives they provided an appealing alternative to flirtations in the gymnasium.

The hetaerae were regarded with a certain sneering respect far more genuine than the more or less hypocritical "honor" paid the enslaved housewife. At Corinth, Greece's "city of sin," the Temple of Aphrodite perched on an elevation commanding the bay, serving as a beacon for sailors many miles out at sea. Within its precincts a thousand hetaerae, priestesses of love, plied their trade. It is useless to speculate on what they wore, since nudity appears to have been one of their attractions, but it is interesting that Pindar saw them as fit subject for an ode. Other individual hetaera enjoyed reputations that have come down to us. Aspasia was said to have been an accomplished sophist, and Pericles withstood considerable abuse when he divorced his wife to marry her, obviously having what to us would appear a modern view of marriage. Still he was author, in his "Funeral Oration," of the pronouncement to womenkind: "The best among you is she who is least spoken of among men for good or evil." Aspasia herself was the most discussed woman in Athens.

Phryne was famous for the beauty of her body and increased its allure by going about heavily

dressed. At the festival of Poseidon at Eleusinia, however, with consummate showmanship, she stripped and threw herself into the waves, thus suggesting to Apelles the subject for his painting of Aphrodite rising from the sea. She also seems to have served as model for Praxiteles' Venus of Cnidos, so we may judge for ourselves the perfection of the rounded breasts for which she was famous. They may have saved her life. it was said
that Phryne, the sort of "tempestuous" tart so favored in literature, was about to be condemned to death for a crime before a court of justice. She had been adjudged guilty, but just before sentence was pronounced her lover, the lawyer Hypereide, rushed up and tore off her chiton, exposing those matchless breasts. Obviously there could be no question about the verdict; such a form could not be dispatched to Hades. Beauty, in Greece, was above the law, and Phryne stood absolved. This is just as well, as she was one of Greece's most curious philanthropists in all senses. She presented the statue of Eros by Praxiteles to her native Thespiae and, with a characteristically wry sense of humor, offered to rebuild the walls of Thebes if the Thebans would agree to the inscription "Destroyed by Alexander, rebuilt by Phryne the hetaera."

Although we do not have the details of Phryne's wardrobe, we are told that a man liked to find his hetaera dressed in a special purple chiton, her hair well curled, nails neatly cut and polished, and doubtless powdered and rouged. Certainly they wore supporting garments under their flowing robes: a kind of bandage to reduce the waist and hips and another to support the bosom. Perhaps the hetaerae followed Hippocrates' advice and sang to develop their breasts. Aristophanes frequently based the characters in his comedies on well-known courtesans. He has left us with a fairly complete list of their aids to beauty, including "clippers, mirrors, grease-paint, soda, false hair, bands, ribbons, red paint, white lead, myrrh, pumice stones, veils, seaweed paint, chains for the neck, eye paint, gold ornaments for the hair, hair nets, girdles, mantillas, combs, ear-rings, ear-pendants, necklaces adorned with precious stones, bracelets, arm buckles, hair buckles, foot buckles, finger rings, beauty plasters and hair supports"—and a vast variety of other items for which we hardly know the translation.

Aristophanes wrote during the late 5th and early 4th centuries B.C. After the fall of Athens' hegemony, most especially after the conquests of Alexander the Great and perhaps under the dreaded Oriental influence, Greeks began to disregard the puritanical standards of 5th-century Athens and to indulge in a long-deferred taste for luxury. Men collected walking sticks with gold and silver handles; drapery became more voluminous, and ribbons were worn around ankles and even thighs. The jewelry for which Greece later became famous covered the arms and necks of "honorable" women, although this was the great age of the hetaerae. It was a period of feminization just as the 5th century had been one of masculinization. Fourth-century sculptors were such masters of soft flesh that the odd fragment of an unidentified statue that appeared to be of a woman might be of a man. The bisexuality and puritan ethic of the Athenian sense of "elitism" gave way to a more bourgeois heterosexuality and taste for material show, as Sophocles gave way to Menander. The eastern Mediterranean had fallen into a happy decadence and in voluptuous languor awaited the rise of Rome.

Rome:

An Empire of Togas

The Etruscans

The same movement that brought the Northern invaders into Mycenaean Greece brought a people speaking an Indo-European tongue into Italy. A traveler to the peninsula in the year 800 B.C., however, would have found straw huts, crude pottery, and barbarism—little, in short, to suggest a promising future. Then, quite suddenly, around 750 B.C., a high degree of civilization seemed to appear out of nowhere in the red hills of Tuscany. So completely developed was this culture, and so abrupt its appearance, that it might have simply descended from the heavens.

All at once forests were cleared, swamps drained, and sizable works established for the smelting of copper and iron. A chain of citadels was constructed, the first settlements that could be called towns in Western Europe. The Etruscans established an active trade in the ports and managed to export grain, wine, cheese, and linen. That all this happened almost within a single lifetime makes the Etruscan riddle all the more tantalizing. Usually when a civilization is transplanted its origin is fairly easy to pinpoint. Etruscan customs, arts, techniques, and tastes seemed to come, however, not from one locale but from everywhere in the then known world, except for those which seem to have come from nowhere at all. Their language, neither Semitic nor Indo-European, falls in the latter category.

Actually, the glorious hodgepodge of Etruscan civilization does suggest an Oriental origin, heavily overlaid with Greek influences and moved by a spirit quite different from anything we have yet encountered. The arid hills and marshy river basins of northern Italy underwent massive land reclamation along Near Eastern lines. A Mesopotamian system of channels and dams provided irrigation, and underground tunnels diverted excess water into towns in accordance with Phoenician drainage techniques. Spirits, demons, gorgons and nyads twisted and hissed from the eaves of Etruscan places of worship, which resembled Greek Doric temples in general form. Moreover, the major deities of the Etruscan religion roughly paralleled Greek divinities such as Zeus, Hera, and Athena. Their beliefs were fraught with the heroes, monsters, mythic beasts, and angel-like winged creatures common to all eastern Mediterranean cultures. The Etruscans' habit of foretelling the future by studying the entrails of a sacrificial animal and their concentration on divination by the interpretation of various astronomical signs were purely Oriental.

How did these many influences come to converge on the Etruscans? Some may have been remembered from an Oriental past, others picked up by the migrating tribe en route from its unknown home, and still others introduced by the teeming trade that brought produce into Etruscan ports from Egypt, Syria, Mesopotamia, Anatolia, Cyprus, Rhodes, mainland Greece, Phoenicia, Carthage, Africa, and even Tartessus in Spain. The Greek colonies of southern Italy were a constant source of inspiration, and Etruscan painting techniques were copied directly from those of Greek vase painting. Certainly the Etruscans must have been among the most receptive peoples of antiquity.

We might hope that Etruscan dress would give some key to the past, and in a way it does. Again the evidence is tantalizing. The tomb of one Princess Larthis, dating from the 7th century B.C., was found in the necropolis of Caere. Over her robe the lady wears a large gold breastplate with repoussé ornamentation so delicate that it resembles embroidery. Such a breastplate was a symbol of rank and authority, and it certainly originated in the

Opposite: Etruscan male and female votive statuettes from the period when the Etruscans were challenged by the Latin League led by Rome. The man wears no tunic but simply a tebenna around his waist and, significantly, over his left arm. The woman wears a fitted

dress with a suggestion of Greek-influenced drapery and a cloak. Bronze. c. 480 B.C.

Below: Carving of a husband and wife on an Etruscan sarcophagus. The female figure wears a dome-shaped hat and corkscrew curls.

Although the sculptural style suggests that of archaic Greece, the depiction of marital affection is purely Etruscan. Terracotta sarcophagus. c. 500 B.C.

Near East. It is to be seen on a statuette of Assyrian King Ashurnasirpal II and appears as an insignia of office, the *hoshen*, in the Bible, part of the "holy garments" made for Aaron according to the Lord's command. In another tomb of the same period, a noblewoman's necklace consisted of faience and silver figurines of Egyptian gods.

Certainly Etruscan dress of this period was "fitted and draped" in the Oriental manner. Women wore a long close-fitted dress, with sleeves of elbow length, belted at the waist, and opening with a slit down the back that might be attached by ribbons. Over the dress they wore a cloak of rectangular or circular cut that fell to the knees and could be pulled over the head. The material was the finest linen, often imported from Ionia, dyed in brilliant, harmonious shades. Such dresses and cloaks were often thickly embroidered in the Oriental manner or even painted, and bordered with fringe or braid. Men wore a more simple belted tunic and a circular cloak, its end thrown over the left shoulder. This cloak, the *tebenna*, was to evolve through many

forms and enjoy a long history as the Roman toga.

The Etruscans were the most luxuriously shod people of ancient times. The Etruscan cobbler produced a wide variety of shoes in many colors: fine gilded sandals, low-cut shoes with an upturned point of the Persian variety, high laced boots such as were worn by the mountain dwellers of the Near East. They even made overshoes, covered with finely hammered bronze, to be worn in the rain.

The Etruscans were also beautifully groomed. Women wore their hair sometimes simply plaited, sometimes drawn back, with the side locks braided and falling down in front of their shoulders. At other times they wore a bun or pendant corkscrew curls, and the effect might be completed by a round or pointed cap. They seem frequently to have been blond or to have bleached their hair. Moreover, the toothless smiles that must have been common in antiquity were not seen in Etruria. The miracles of Etruscan dentistry included goldwork, bridges to fasten loose or artificial teeth, and even dentures.

The Etruscans were not a belligerent people. The spread of their power over most of northern Italy seems to have been peaceful. The one quality of their character that emerges from fragmentary remains—their crumbled statuary, wall paintings eaten by damp decay, and the passing references to them in the works of later authors—was an ebullient, unembarrassed love of pleasure. They bred racehorses, played dice, and accompanied every act with the strains of the trumpet, the horn, the cithera, and the flute. Their devotion to music quite overshadowed any interest they might have had in producing a literature. According to Aristotle, the Etruscans boxed, whipped their slaves, and kneaded dough to the sound of flutes. Etruscan herdsmen trumpeted to their sheep, and hunters literally charmed the wild beasts out of their lairs by the tones of the Etruscan flute. The clatter of castanets accompanied their dancing.

The Etruscan love of music was matched only by their almost epicurean taste for luxuries and their extravagance. Their concept of kingly pomp was to influence the West for millennia to come. The golden diadem and eagle-adorned scepter, the gold-embroidered purple toga of office, the ivory throne, and the axes and bundle of rods known as fasces originated with them. Their priest-kings must have created an electrifying impression with their purple robes trailing and their faces painted a brilliant red.

To all this was added an appetite for gold. Etruscan goldwork is as much a mystery, and a miracle, as the extraordinary culture itself. The techniques must have been imported from Asia Minor, but they were infinitely refined. The Etruscans' repoussé work is so fine that it can be fully appreciated only with a magnifying glass. They were also masters of granulation, a technique whereby gold is melted into tiny globules that are then soldered with such minute care that the heat does not distort their shape. So complex was this process that it was later completely lost and not regained until the 19th century.

All this wealth was well exhibited. According to Diodorus Siculus, banquets were a favored Etruscan pastime: "Twice a day sumptuous tables are laid and everything brought that goes with exaggerated luxury—flowers, robes and numerous silver goblets; nor is the number of slaves in attendance small." Women joined their husbands at feasts, races, boxing matches, concerts, and in every aspect of daily life. They seemed to have enjoyed the right to a place at their husband's side that the women of Greece had lost. The banquet scene from the walls of the Tomb of the Triclinium at Tarquinii (5th century B.C.) could almost serve as an illustration to Diodorus's text. Dancers and musicians approach the revelers on light feet through groves of olive trees. The banqueters themselves—two women and four men—stretch out on upholstered couches covered with colored rugs and surrounded by shrubbery. Myrtle leaves wreathe the dark heads of the men and the blond hair of the women. For three hundred years the Etruscans had lived as neighbors of the Greeks of Magna Graecia; both their fashions and the style of the painting itself have a Greek quality. (By the 4th century B.C. Etruscan armor, for example, was identical with that worn by the troops of Alexander the Great.) The garments in this scene of golden-hued grace are diaphanous. The men wear luxurious full tebennas thrown over the left arm. Their chests and shoulders are bare. The women's dresses are almost transparent and richly decorated, as are their cloaks. The entire painting brings to mind the banquet scene from the Egyptian tomb of Neb-Amun, but the Etruscan scene is far calmer, more mysterious in the face of death.

Gay and insouciant as their world might seem, the Etruscans were, in fact, obsessed with death. They may also have had a streak of cruelty; gladiatorial combat seems to have originated with Etruscan funeral games. Like the Egyptians, they concentrated

Below: Etruscan girl dancing.
We must imagine the clatter of
castanets and the lively swirl
of skirts. Detail of a vase
painting. 4th century B.C.

Early Rome

The Romans, possibly the Etruscans' protégés and
certainly their conquerors and heirs, were left a rich
bequest: the vault; the gridiron plan for towns;
the atrium house; the reading of entrails and a
curious belief in fate; the habit of keeping ancestral
images; the royal insignia worn by Rome's first
Etruscan king, Tarquinius Priscus; and, of course,
the toga. The Etruscans also bequeathed a sensuous
appreciation of feasting, music, entertainment, and
luxury.

The early Romans, descendants of the settlers who
spoke an Indo-European tongue, did not immediately claim their inheritance. Their propensities
were dour. The virtues they prized most highly
give some idea of how the inhabitants of a few mud
huts precariously perched above a malarial swamp
to the south of the Etruscan empire came to rule
the known world. These virtues include *pietas*,
meaning the subordination of self to the require-
ments of the gods, parents, elders, children, friends,
and country; and *gravitas*, meaning a sense of seri-
ousness (as opposed to the despised *levitas*). They
also prized a series of more familiar traits: firmness
of purpose (*constantia*), tenacity (*firmitas*), good
humor (*comitas*), training (*disciplina*), hard work
(*industria*), manliness (*virtus*), and a stern attitude
toward oneself (*severitas*). Not the least of these hardy
virtues was *frugalitas*, meaning not only what we
generally call frugality but also simplicity of taste,
especially in dress and ornament.

Gold was despised, although this may have been
a matter of sour grapes. It happened to be very
scarce among the early Romans, who did not possess
the buying power of their Etruscan rivals. According to the Law of the Twelve Tables (about 450 B.C.),
penalties were imposed on those who possessed
gold or included it in a burial. Gold was permitted
for dentistry alone. According to Pliny, "The worst
crime against mankind was committed by him
who was the first to put a ring upon his fingers. . . .
It was a hand, and a sinister hand, too, in every
sense, that first brought gold into high repute: not
a Roman hand, however, for upon that it was the
practice to wear a ring of iron only, and solely as
an indication of warlike prowess. . . ." Romans,
even those of the senatorial order, wore rings of iron.
The state did equip its ambassadors with gold rings
as a symbol of status abroad, but these were never
worn in Rome proper. In Pliny's day an iron ring
was still the traditional token of betrothal.

The Romans set about paring Etruscan luxury
to suit their sense of *frugalitas*. The Roman consuls
adopted the insignia of their earlier Etruscan kings,
but they eschewed both the crown and the embroidered robe as "vulgar and invidious." A general
celebrating a public triumph wore no more than
an iron ring. The Etruscan crown of gold appeared
over his head, but symbolically it was supported
from behind. The early Roman toga was hardly more
than a woolen shawl, cut in the shape of a segment

their artistic efforts on monumental tombs—great
vaulted stone-lined tumuli that rose from their plains,
halls of the dead decorated with scenes from life.
The Etruscans, however, had a far weaker sense of
afterlife than the Egyptians and a far stronger sense
of inexorable fate. They believed that each man
and woman was allotted a life-span of seven cycles
of twelve years each in which to live. Any individual
over the age of eighty-four had survived beyond life.
The Etruscan husband and wife face death together,
often tenderly comforting each other in effigy on
their sarcophagi. Moreover, they face the reality
of their lives: Husband and wife are portrayed with
ruthless realism, gaunt or paunchy as the case might
be. It was an artistic attitude that did not bespeak
optimism.

The Etruscan race or "name," the "*nomen etrus-
cum*" itself, was fated to expire after ten cycles. The
tenth cycle ended, precisely as foretold, in the year
A.D. 54, on the death of the Emperor Claudius,
the historian of the Etruscans and the last Roman
scholar to speak their mysterious language. But the
soothsayers did not foresee that their end coincided
with another dawn.

of a circle, and worn by men and women alike. As we have seen, it appears to have been of Etruscan origin, although such shawls were general among European mountain peoples and may resemble the Greek himation because of a common origin among the Indo-European mountaineers. Men seem to have worn it over a simple loincloth and shirt. And yet it was already invested with an almost sacred significance. When the senators came to call Cincinnatus from his fields, he would not receive them until his wife had run to fetch his toga.

Grooming in these early times was thorough but rudimentary. The Romans washed their arms and legs daily, but Cato the Elder, who was regarded by Cicero as the very embodiment of *gravitas*, felt that boys should not be allowed to bathe daily. Steam baths were an attraction of market day, which occurred every ninth day.

It is interesting to note, in passing, something of the dress of Rome's enemy, Carthage. The Carthaginians, while repugnant to later sensibilities because of their practice of sacrificial infanticide, were in fact solid businessmen, little interested in the arts, and known for their courtesy. Like most aspects of Carthaginian culture, their courtesy was Oriental. The Carthaginians also manufactured the Oriental luxuries so despised in both Greece and early Rome: embroidered cushions, carpets, and fine muslins. Like their Phoenician forebears, they produced purple dye and also glassware. Moreover, they were internationally famous for their pastries, which they baked in the form of animals, fish, and even men on horseback. In matters of clothing they were thoroughly Oriental and their dress was of Mesopotamian origin, although women occasionally adopted the flowing garments of Greece. They regarded nudity with distaste; a long-sleeved, fitted but unbelted woolen robe trailed to the ankles. On their heads they wore a tall conical turban, and the image, totally alien to the Romans, was completed by heavy gold jewelry, which might include a ring through the nose.

The Republic

The period of Roman austerity quickly receded into the past and had largely disappeared even by Cato's day. Sumptuary laws, of which Rome enjoyed a long succession, were felt necessary by 215 B.C. According to the Lex Appia of that year, no woman was allowed to possess more than one half an ounce of gold, to wear clothing of different colors, or to ride in a carriage in the city under less than

ceremonial circumstances. In 184 B.C. Cato himself attempted to check the tendency toward luxury by craftily assessing luxury items at ten times their market value and taxing them accordingly, while the Fannian (161 B.C.) and Didian (143 B.C.) laws legislated against luxuries of the table (no more than a single hen *not fattened* to be served at a dinner party). Such laws were first initiated under the pressures of the Punic Wars, but *frugalitas* was not their sole object. They were, in fact, an attempt to stem a social revolution.

The Punic Wars had taken Rome's army out of Italy, and once abroad, Rome proceeded to implement a policy of imperial expansion not matched for millennia. The effect of its development during the first and second centuries B.C. amounted to a

Right: Livia, wife of Augustus, as priestess, wears the noble stola, attached at the shoulder by fibulae. She has drawn her enormous palla over her head. Marble statue, A.D. 14–29. Far right: Statue of an orator of the Golden Age of Latin oratory, his speech in hand. A statesman's rank depended on his ability to sway the Senate and the courts with his arguments. A great orator was the most highly respected of citizens. This speaker luxuriates in a full, intricately draped toga. 1st century B.C.

Opposite: Relief from the Ara Pacis, Augustus' Altar of Peace, depicting the members of the imperial family. Even the smallest boys wear the toga, with every fold in place. 13–9 B.C.

total transformation of Rome's simple agrarian society. As Rome expanded, particularly in the Orient, Romans made vast fortunes. The *nouveaux riches* were not members of the senatorial order, the old hereditary aristocracy that ruled Rome. However, wealthy citizens were able to buy their way into the lower nobility, the Equestrian order, consisting originally of those prosperous enough to supply themselves with a horse in battle and thus being literally the "order of knights." With time, a comfortable fortune and "honorable life" sufficed for membership. The *Equites*, basing their pride on fortune and doubtless infected by Oriental notions, tended to make a show of luxuries, and it was undoubtedly to control and frustrate them that the sumptuary laws were passed. Such repression of a class of *nouveaux riches* would prove to be the thinly veiled cause for sumptuary legislation.

But new wealth alone was not the sole or even the most profound social change that Rome underwent. The cancer of slavery, kept under control in 5th-century Athens, was growing throughout the Mediterranean world. In 200 B.C. ten thousand slaves were auctioned on the Greek island of Delos in a single day. Rome's victorious armies took a far greater fortune in slaves than in gold. Thus Rome slowly evolved into a slave holding society in which the wealthy Roman citizen could vie with Oriental princes, while the poorer citizens found

themselves without employment. Huge latifundia worked by slave labor replaced the small farmer, who was forced to migrate to the city. There he joined the urban unemployed to form that vast horde, the Roman *plebs*. These free but penniless citizens possessed only one thing of value—their vote under the Republic and, under the Empire, their menace as a street mob in a society in which the *coup d'état* had replaced the normal political process. By the first century B.C. 320,000 such freemen lived on the perpetual bribery of the dole and gifts of food and entertainment, the proverbial "bread and circuses," from vying magistrates. Some 650,000 of the city's inhabitants were slaves.

Meanwhile, Roman dress preserved the unhealthy social order in a kind of fossilized form. The toga was the standard uniform of all classes, from the senator to the lowest plebeian. It thus distinguished the Romans from the many visitors from Gaul in their leather leggings or barbarian slaves that thronged the streets, and it offered a false sense of the unity of all the citizens, already so disunited in financial terms. The significance of the toga was almost spiritual: A banished Roman was stripped of his toga, and all citizens were obliged to wear it for public ceremonies. A member of the noble orders could not appear without it in the street, and a poor citizen could not present himself in the chilly dawn as client in the atrium of a personage of power

unless he had his toga draped about his person. Tertullian's view of the toga must have been shared by most Romans: "It is not a garment, but a burden." If the vast majority of the citizens had not been discouraged from engaging in any physical activity, either by wealth or total unemployment, the toga would have prevented it in any case. Never again, until perhaps the Victorian era, did clothing in the West go further to induce a state of inactivity already sanctioned by society. The ellipse of fabric had to be draped with such pains that it was almost impossible for a man to put it on unassisted. Both shoulders were enveloped, and the left arm carried the weight of the cocoon of cloth, leaving only the right hand free for the rhetorical gesture that was one of the few activities it was likely to perform. The various ends and points of a proper citizen's toga were expected to fall to exactly the proper length, and the finished edifice was expected to stay in place without the assistance of

pins. The toga was a far more complicated drape than the Greek himation, and styles of drape varied. The "Gabinian cincture," for example, whereby the toga fell in a few deep folds, was customary for sacrificial occasions. It is not surprising, then, that those citizens who performed manual work wore only the undergarment, or tunica, and that the toga was eventually discarded by the mass of plebs in favor of a variety of simple capes.

The toga was generally made of dull white natural wool, often woven at the citizen's own hearth by his wife. It was well cared for and frequently sent to the cleaner. There it would be cleansed with fuller's meal, a kind of alkaline earth, although during the period of the Empire soap was imported from Gaul. The garment would be tread in vats, carded to bring up the nap, then smoothed in a large wooden press.

The poor man might be at pains to drape his toga so that the inevitable spots and moth holes did not

51

Below: A slave serves an elaborate dinner to a woman in a stola so diaphanous we suspect that its fabric is mixed with silk. She reclines in the Roman fashion, accompanied by her child and pet bird. Relief, 2nd century A.D.

Opposite: Portrait busts of a Roman couple fully draped as good Romans. 1st century A.D.

show, but the rich man luxuriated in what might be a large piece of the softest Milesian fabric. Further decoration was entirely a matter of rank, office, or age. Small boys wore the *toga praetexta*, with an embroidered purple border along the straight edge, which they exchanged for the white *toga virilis* upon coming of age (around sixteen). The *toga praetexta* was also assumed by certain magistrates. Moreover, the *toga picta*, dyed purple and decorated with gold embroidery, was allowed to the holders of high office when presiding at public games and was later worn by the emperor. A man seeking public office stressed his purity by bleaching his toga a brilliant white, thus becoming one of the *candidati*, which literally meant "those clothed in white." Togas dyed a dark color were permissible in times of grief caused by death or any public disgrace, ranging from military defeat to a lawsuit.

Beneath the toga the Roman citizen wore the tunica, and if he were a workman or a soldier he would usually wear the tunica alone. The tunica somewhat resembled the Greek chiton. It was a simple garment, rather like a long shirt, sewn along the shoulders and sides, with two holes for arms, or possibly short sleeves (long sleeves were considered effeminate). The tunica might reach to the ankle, but it was belted, and blousing above the waist made it considerably shorter. Several such tunics might be worn, one on top of the other, according to the weather.

The tunica, like the toga, indicated rank. A member of the senatorial order wore a broad purple stripe (lateclave) down the front and back of his tunic, while an Equestrian indicated his rank by a narrow stripe. If a member of the senatorial class wished to renounce his rank and go into business, he was said to have "narrowed his purple stripe." Footwear also indicated rank. Most Romans wore sandals at home and elaborately strapped shoes for the street. Senators, however, wore a red shoe, while Equestrians indicated the origin of their order by wearing tall boots.

Women also wore the tunica, although beneath it they might bind themselves with leather "foundation garments," as well as the loincloth, worn by both sexes. The woman's tunica, however, was generally of a light material and was covered by the female equivalent of the toga, the noble stola, a loose-draped robe attached by fibulae, belted below the breast and at the waist and falling in deep, loose folds to the feet. This, too, bore the mark of rank. In the case of a noblewoman, it would be banded with purple at neck and hem. Women also wore a large rectangular shawl, the palla, as a cloak. A wealthy matron might possess pallae in every weight and color, from coarse wool for rainy weather to flimsy gauzes for the purpose of seduction.

Until the very end of the Republic the Romans maintained a strong sense of propriety, of balance, along with a native suspicion of fripperies and a chronic yearning for the ancient virtues of agrarian Rome, even though they could not conceivably have been maintained in a cosmopolitan city with a population in the millions. Horace was able to write, "I loathe Persian panoply," and Cicero regarded with horror the young dandies who took to wearing huge togas: "They wrap themselves in sails, not in togas." The Romans maintained a prim virility in the face of what they regarded as Greek effeminacy. Cicero wrote: "We ought to regard physical beauty as an attribute of women, and dignity as an attribute of men." A gentleman, according to Cicero, maintained his dignity by refraining from dancing in public or singing in the street and by observing all proprieties in movement, gesture, and facial expression. He should never lose his poise by hurrying and becoming out of breath (thus distorting his features), or by "sauntering listlessly." And he should avoid the affectations inculcated by gymnasium instructors. Above all, his clothes should be neat but not fussy.

If the Romans did not share the Greek ideal of male beauty they also did not share the Greek reverence for the nude body. The word *nudus* in Latin means not only nude but also crude or uncouth, and it never wholly lost that meaning. The Romans, with their own blunt honesty and innocence of nuance, saw nudity flatly as a sexual stimulus. In the words of Lucilius, "Seeing others naked is the origin of vice." Their attitude toward nudity reflected their general ambivalence toward Greece and all things Greek, a mixture of groveling admiration for Greek culture of the 5th and 4th centuries B.C. (all educated Romans spoke Greek) and a total contempt for the Greeks of their day, whom they saw as crooked and untrustworthy businessmen or epicene actors. Gymnastics were considered suitable for a Greek but not for a Roman, whose proper exertion was warfare. Romans watched gladiatorial contests; they did not themselves perform. The Romans' admiration for nude Greek statuary was boundless. With greedy hands they confiscated every fragment of art that was movable, and

their own stonemasons busied themselves with thousands of copies of the finer works. But Roman sculptors, while they emulated Greek techniques and styles, rarely sculpted the nude figure themselves. Their particular genius was their ability to create striking portrait likenesses in the spirit of the Etruscans—identifiable men and women, fully draped as good Romans. In the words of Pliny: "The Greek habit is to conceal nothing. The Roman way and the warrior's way is to give the statues each a coat of armor."

Imperial Rome

It was said that Augustus's togas were woven by his wife, Livia, at the imperial hearth. The founder of the Empire, despite the ruthless carnage of his youth, set a stern tone for the duration of his reign and attempted various moral reforms. He even went so far as to banish his own daughter, Julia, as punishment for her glaring sexual misadventures. After his death, however, the descent into degeneracy seems to have been remarkably swift. The shocking grossness of Imperial Rome has not been dimmed by two millennia of human experience. The one unfattened hen of Republican banquets was replaced by costly turbot, plump swans, pâté, vintage wines, and tongues of parakeets, considered more delicious if the bird had been taught a few words of Latin. In the cuisine of Apicius, a dish was thought a failure if palate or eye could discern its true contents, and the guest whose capacity did not match the size of the feast repaired to the vomitorium to renew his capacity. At one feast Lucius Verus presented his guests with silver dishes, attractive slaves, and carriages complete with team and driver as "favors." If we are to believe Petronius, the rape of a child might cap the entertainment.

There is little reason to doubt his account since the known amusement of the plebs in the public arenas were even more savage: a prostitute ravished by a bull; young girls chanting in a boat that floats through the false seas of the flooded amphitheater until the waters are drained off and crocodiles emerge and devour them. The rot, naturally enough, began at the top, and our review of the Julio-Claudian dynasty is illuminated by such ingratiating scenes as that of the whore-empress Agrippina, fat and blond-wigged, staunchly swimming to shore after her son—and possibly her lover—Nero has arranged the sinking of her boat. Or we envision Heliogabalus, the strangely beautiful fourteen-year-old Syrian priestling who became Emperor, with his embroidered silken Phoenician gowns, his turbans, necklaces, bracelets, and face "painted more elaborately than any honest woman's."

Apologists have suggested various origins for the excesses of the Empire: an atavistic tendency toward cruelty and a taste for banqueting and over-eating inherited from the shadowy Etruscan past; the influence of a decaying and enslaved Orient; the fact that Rome was no longer Roman—the streets of the city teemed with foreigners of every race from every corner of the Empire, and the number of native Romans had dwindled. Finally, blame can be laid at the door of the Julio-Claudian clan, which isolated its court from the moderating forces of society. These moderating forces were potentially powerful. Between the mass of the plebs brutalized by the daily enjoyment of atrocities in the arena and a court sunk in degeneracy and madness, there remained a solid bulk of Romans and provincials of wealth, education, and standing who provided the bureaucratic machinery that made the *Pax Romana* possible.

Women of Rome

It is interesting to note the position of women in Rome. In earlier times they seemed no better off than their Greek counterparts. They were forbidden to drink wine or to attend banquets. Egnetius Mecenius

beat his wife to death for dipping into the wine vat and was absolved by Romulus. Another matron was starved to death by her family for having purloined the wine-vault keys. After this unpromising start, however, the status of Roman women seems to have improved immensely, and perhaps here Etruscan influence is responsible. By the 2nd century B.C., women such as Cornelia, the mother of the Gracchi, were accorded far more respect than that enjoyed by the obscure mothers of Greek notables. A century later the famous beauty Clodia was able to fill her salon with the most talented men of her day despite, or because of, her reputation for profligacy. Women administered their own fortunes and went freely to the forum and the public baths, attended dinner parties, and were prominent among the cheering spectators of the bloody events at the arena. But again, it is impossible to generalize. Cicero's educated and cultured daughter Tullia was clearly as different from a Clodia or an Agrippina as Cicero was different from a Nero. Pliny's touching letter to his wife, who has gone to the country to convalesce from an illness, puts Roman humanity back in perspective and reveals the position of women to be analogous to what it had been earlier.

For at this moment I particularly want to be with you; I want to believe the evidence of my eyes and see what you are doing to look after your strength and your little self, whether in fact you are enjoying to the full the peace and the pleasures and the richness of the place. Even if you were strong, your absence would still disquiet me. For, when you love people most passionately, it is a strain and a worry not to know anything about them even for a moment. But, as things are, the thought of your absence, together with your ill-health, terrifies me with vague and mixed anxieties. I imagine everything, my imaginings make me afraid of everything; and, as happens when you are afraid, I picture the very things I pray most may not happen. I beg you therefore all the more earnestly to be kind to my fears and to send me a letter, or even two letters, every day. While I am reading it, I shall worry less: when I have finished it, my fears will at once return.

To speak of the dress of Imperial Rome we must realize how very wealthy some Romans were. Never before in history had private individuals commanded so much personal influence or such vast fortunes. Certain Romans held the power of

life and death over as many as forty thousand slaves who worked estates the size of small but lucrative kingdoms. These magnates inhabited palaces that rivaled Nero's Golden House in size and ornate decoration. They were, in short, as wealthy as any Oriental prince, but they totally lacked the responsibility of state. The result was a condition in which any extreme was possible, in which an individual, no less than an emperor, might develop the noblest or most depraved qualities, the most exquisite or the most vile taste. In either case he was apt to indulge in every luxury of dress then known. Moreover, the thirst for ostentation extended even to those living on a modest income. In Rome, mused the threadbare Juvenal, "Everyone dresses above his means."

Women's dress was clearly differentiated from men's. The stola did not resemble the toga, and while the toga was almost always white, women wore many bright colors: shades of blues, yellows, and reds. Ovid recommends sea green or flesh

pink. Such colors would certainly have been worn by prostitutes. But color remained a luxury as in other early societies, and it might also be used to denote rank. At one point the peasantry were restricted to one color, officers of the legions to two, commanders to three, and members of the royal household to seven.

Women wore lighter, softer, more clinging clothes than men. The exception to this rule was the *synthesis*, a garment of Greek origin, made of light and brilliantly dyed cloth, which men wore at dinner parties in place of the heavy and uncomfortable toga. A wealthy host might change his synthesis several times during a meal, switching from shades of amethyst to azure with a change of course. The light materials used in this garment included linen, woven of yarns from Spain, Syria, and Egypt; cotton brought first from India by Alexander the Great; and, above all, silk.

Silk, actually worth more than its weight, ounce for ounce, in gold, was the great indulgence of the

Roman "millionaire's" wife—silk woven into a flimsy gauze, although in almost every instance, even for the wealthy, it was mixed with cotton. Silk was regarded as a most potent weapon of seduction. Basic Roman dress varied little; because the possibility of the décolleté did not present itself, fine, transparent, clinging materials replaced outright exposure as a means of arousing interest. It is pleasant to imagine the dresses from the island of Cos "finer than a cobweb" and the "colors of a meadow sown over with flowers." The effect of such silk, when it first became popular, may be judged by the vehemence of Seneca's outraged reaction: "There I see silken cloths, if they can be called cloths, which protect neither a woman's body nor her modesty, and in which she cannot truthfully declare that she is not naked. These are bought for huge sums from nations unknown to us in the usual course of trade—and why? So that our women may show as much of themselves to the world at large as they show to their lovers in the bedroom."

The reference to "nations unknown to us in the usual course of trade" constituted no small part of Seneca's outrage. The Roman Empire stretched from Spain to the borders of Persia, from Britain to the Sahara, and most Roman trade was of course internal. Seneca would have had only the vaguest notions of the origins of this "foreign" silk, supposedly from "Serica," and Virgil himself thought it grew on trees. In his natural history Pliny the Elder states knowingly: "The Seres [Chinese] are famous for the wool of their forests. They remove the down from leaves with the help of water, and the women have the double task of unraveling and weaving. . . ." This was the Roman explanation for the filament that surpassed all others in length, strength, and the ability to take dyes.

Silk was, in fact, first cultivated in China during the third millennium B.C. According to legend, a Chinese empress, investigating a parasite on her mulberry trees, found white worms eating the leaves and spinning cocoons. When she accidentally dropped one into hot water, over four thousand yards of thread unrolled. The culture of silk was a closely guarded secret, and the exportation of either the silkworm or the mulberry leaves on which it fed was punishable by death.

It was not until the Han Dynasty, when the Chinese Empire was as large as the Roman, that the Emperor Wu Ti sent emissaries in search of foreign trade and of allies against the Huns. In 138 B.C. his emissary, Chang Ch'ien, a charming and popular man of "strong physique," commenced a long trek west. Chang Ch'ien, like a landlocked Columbus, crossed a vast sea of nomadic barbarian tribes before arriving in Bactria, where Hellenistic civilization, left by the armies of Alexander the Great, still thrived. He returned to China bringing back news of a world in the West where silk was unknown. Within a few years a Silk Route some six thousand miles in length joined Rome and China. But the two empires remained largely ignorant of each other because the route consisted of a string of "middlemen," each of whom jealously guarded his source. At each change of hands the cargoes of thread and the bales of heavy brocades and taffetas became more costly, until they reached the astronomic prices paid by the rich of Rome. In Cos the heavier brocades were actually unraveled and rewoven into that scandalously sheer and drapable cloth. In their turn, the Chinese valued the purity of Roman gold as much as the Romans valued the purity of Chinese silk, and they also imported from Rome such unlikely commodities as the cure-all *theriaca* and the jugglers and acrobats of Roman Syria.

The Romans may have inherited from the Etruscans their penchant for jewelry of every sort—earrings, necklaces, bracelets, rings (often worn on every finger), toe rings, ankle rings, hair pins, buckles, and fibulae—from the more severe Classical designs of the Roman goldsmiths to the stone-encrusted filigrees of Antioch and Alexandria. Cameos, intaglios, and engraved gems were particularly popular. Among the stones considered precious were diamonds (worn only in rings, since the technique of cutting them had not yet been developed), opals, emeralds, and beryls. Onyx, rock crystal, aquamarine, jasper, and chalcedony were among the more popular semiprecious stones, along with amber from Germany. Most highly prized of all were pearls, brought over the great trade routes from Taprobane (Ceylon). These were especially popular as earrings, although they might be sprinkled everywhere—on dress, fingers, hair, or even sandals. Seneca tells us that women sometimes wore "two or three estates in each ear." Caligula's wife, Lollia Paulina, paraded a set of pearls and emeralds worth the equivalent of several million dollars. Pearls were the ultimate indication of status. One cynic wrote: "The sight of a big pearl in a woman's ear is better than a lictor at clearing the way for her." For sheer tastelessness we may remember Trimalchio's wife, weighted down by six-pound gold armlets. These were probably among her "winter jewels," since wealthy Roman matrons, like the *grandes dames* of the Victorian era, were assumed to have "lighter" jewels for summer wear.

The only jewelry men were expected to wear was a signet ring, used as a personal seal, or a simple gold band, bestowed in honor of rank. It may be assumed that this restriction was often broken, and the more outrageous figures, such as Caligula and Nero, covered themselves with bracelets and rings. Of course, some tales of the use of precious stones by powerful Romans are probably spurious. Antonia, the widow of Drusus, may or may not have fastened jewels to the fish in her aquarium to increase their glitter as they darted about, but Caligula may well have plaited the mane and tail of his favorite horse with gems.

What we call "grooming" cannot really be compared with the elaborate care for the body in which the Romans indulged. The bath, taken at the height of the afternoon after the long morning's exertions and before dinner, was the main feature of the day. The most costly appointments of each private mansion were installed in the bath: "Every man thinks he is poor and miserly unless he has Alexandrian marble set off by Numidian overlay, unless he has an elaborate frieze varied all around like a picture, unless the vault is concealed by a glass ceiling, unless Thasian stone (once a rare sight in a temple) lines the pool into which we lower our bodies exhausted by long sweating, unless the water flows from silver taps." However, no matter how wealthy or sophisticated the Roman, he would be just as likely to prefer the sociability of enormous public baths frequented by the mass of the free populace.

Like death, the public baths were the great leveler, and all freemen passed in undistinguished nakedness from the bracing pool of the *frigidarium* through the tropical warmth of the *tepidarium* to the bubbling heat of the *calidaria*, so fiery that Seneca blandly suggested that a criminal slave should be condemned "to be washed alive." The chief social distinction in the baths was that the wealthy senator was likely to be followed into the swim by a gaggle of fawning and equally naked clients and that he was more likely to have his toga filched in the process than were his less affluent fellow bathers. Because gymnastic contests were held in the gardens of the baths and because satirists depicted the baths as hotbeds of homosexuality, they have come to be equated with the Greek gymnasia. However, at least by the 1st century A.D., the baths were in theory open to women. It was expected that they would appear during the morning hours, they were required to wear a small apron, and separate chambers were set aside for them. In any case, women of substance preferred their private baths, and women of the street found the public baths an ideal habitat. The baths were therefore frequently closed to women by various imperial edicts—and just as frequently reopened.

Both men and women bathed daily. The bath was followed by a scraping with bronze strigils and a rubdown, first with towels and then with scented unguents. As among other early Mediterranean peoples, anointing with oil was a major part of grooming. Unguents and garlands were distributed by the host to his guests at dinner. In earliest times the Romans used simple olive oil, but later highly perfumed oils disguised all body odors, and pastilles freshened the breath.

Anointing with oil was considered sufficient for a man's grooming. Ovid's advice that a man is made attractive by simple cleanliness seems comfortingly reasonable. He suggests a wholesome appearance: tanned skin, a spotless and well-fitting toga, teeth clean, shoe straps not twisted, chin well shaven and hair neatly trimmed, nails clipped and cleaned, and nostril hairs plucked. "More than this is the business of strumpets and catamites." Juvenal has scant sympathy for the man who tries to improve his doubtlessly pimply complexion:

But tell me yet—this thing, thus
      daubed and oiled
Poulticed, plastered, baked by turns
      and boiled,
Thus with pomatums, ointments
      lacquered o'er,
Is it a face, Usidius, or a sore?

Theoretically, the cosmetic pots were for women.

The foundation of Roman cosmetology was the face pack, applied during the night, which might achieve a high stink by morning if it was made of sheep fat mixed with bread crumbs soaked in milk. It might also be made of crocodile excrement. Ovid's recipe for an ointment to give a "shining" white complexion was hardly more appetizing, although not very different from remedies used in

Europe and America in the last century: ten eggs, barley, vetch, powdered stag's antler, gum, twelve narcissus bulbs, and honey. Also basic to a woman's grooming was the removal of all bodily hair. Beyond this, there were various abrasives to polish the teeth, as well as pigments long in use in the Mediterranean to blacken lashes and brows and redden cheeks and lips. They seem also to have applied beauty spots, like 18th-century patches. Interestingly, the Roman ideal appearance was markedly different from ours. A white complexion and a low forehead and long eyebrows that met over the bridge of the nose were considered extremely beautiful, in Rome as in Greece. Petronius wrote: "The woman was more perfect than any statue in the world . . . her forehead was small with the roots of her hair turning back from it. Her brows ran into the line of her cheek, and they almost met beside the borders of her eyes."

The Etruscans had been known, even by the Greeks, for their barbering establishments, but it was not until Scipio Africanus arrived in Rome in the 2nd century B.C. with a troupe of Greek barbers from Sicily that it became fashionable for the Romans to be clean-shaven. The barbers of Rome invented the warm-water shave, and since respectable men were shaven daily, the barbering establishments, like the baths, ranked as major social institutions. The fashion of the clean-shaven chin continued for several centuries, until the Emperor Hadrian, in his admiration for all things Greek, took to wearing a beard. The custom was immediately adopted by gentlemen throughout the Empire. Slaves, who had formerly been distinguished from freemen by their beards, were now shaven. Men's hair was clipped short, and only dandies wore neatly arranged and pomaded curls until Hadrian also set the style for these. Not that men were wholly without artifice. A black dye was achieved by allowing a mixture of leeches and vinegar to sit for several months in a leaden vessel, and even men of senatorial rank touched up their hair. Moreover, a bald pate might be covered with a wig or paint.

For women, hair was both an obsession and a fetish. According to Apuleius, a woman's whole appearance depended on it: "The hair is such a noble thing that although a woman move in the beauty of gold, fine apparel, jewels and all adornments, if she has not cared for her hair, she is not really adorned." Such an "unadorned" woman would be an unlikely sight. Any matron of means possessed several slaves trained at hairdressing who would work on her with heated steel pincers and tongues. According to Ovid, an infinite number of hair styles appeared daily—as many as there were "honey bees in Habla, or wild animals in the Alpes." Women's portrait busts were sculpted with detachable hair that could be replaced when fashions changed. In the spirit of 20th century glossy magazines, Ovid further suggests that a woman should not be a slave to fashion but should choose a hairdo

to suit her face: "A long face requires a parting on the forehead; a light knot on top of the head, leaving the ears uncovered, is more suitable for a round face."

The Empress Messalina is credited with having started the vogue for enormous hairdos, padded out by wigs or switches of false hair, especially with the red or blond hair imported from Germany and Gaul. Martial wrote of Messalina: "Her toilet table contained a hundred lies, and while she was in Rome her hair was blushing by the Rhine." The fact that prostitutes were obliged by law to wear yellow hair did not, for some reason, make blond hair any less desirable. Red hair was equally popular, and Roman women dipped their hair in henna or Batavian caustic and bleached it in the sun. Nor were the imported tresses any more genuine in color. The Gauls themselves bleached their hair with a solution containing chalk. But no one could have achieved quite the radiant effect of certain very wealthy Roman women, who simply powdered their hair with pure gold. The Emperor Commodus's nimbus of snow-white hair, powdered with gold, represented for the Romans the ultimate in the superbly coiffed godhead.

Try to imagine Roman women of means as they must have looked in the 2nd century A.D.: butterfly creatures, their gossamer silks billowing in jewel-like shades of reds, purples, yellows and greens, gems twinkling from head to foot, skin radiantly pink and white, lips red, and on the head, piles of curls streaked blond. A trailing scarf or kerchief, a fan in hand and a sunshade carried by a slave who walked behind completed the effulgent image, which was seen always in the brilliant light of day. The Romans rose at sunrise and began their "evening" entertainments at four in the afternoon in order to avoid the dangers of returning home after dark.

Men were expected to affect a more sober, more conservative and less colorful image in simple signet ring and white toga, but it was useless to suppose that with their often vast wealth they would not attempt a show of luxury. Ovid complained that "husbands follow the fashions of their wives, and the bride can hardly find anything to add to this extravagance."

Most luxuries were associated with feminine dress, and although homosexuality might be taken for granted, the effeminate dandy was particularly a thorn in the side of those Romans who still remembered Cato. Seneca tells us that "in tricking themselves out men go beyond women. They wear tart's colors, and do not walk, but strut and dance, more like players, butterflies, baboons, apes, antics, than men." The dandy was frequently an object of legislation by those emperors who hoped to raise the swiftly sinking moral tone of their capital. Tiberius forbade men to wear silk, and under Aurelian, red, yellow, green, or white shoes, as well, were permitted only to women. Still the fop flourished as a natural concomitant to the society Rome had become. Martial's Cotilus was literally the man of the hour:

They tell me, Cotilus, that you're a beau:
What this is, Cotilus, I wish to know.
A beau is one who, with nicest care,
In parted locks divides his curling hair;
One who with balm and cinnamon smells sweet;
Whose humming lips some Spanish air repeat;
Whose naked arms are smoothed with pumice-
     stone,
And tossed about with graces all his own:
A beau is one who takes his constant seat.
From morn till evening, where the ladies meet. . . .
A beau is one who shrinks, if nearly prest
By the coarse garment of a neighboring guest.
Who knows who flirts with whom, and still is found
At each good table in successive round. . . .

We must not imagine Rome as a citadel of decadence run wild. It was simply a cosmopolitan capital in which citizens enjoyed a degree of freedom in their personal lives with which we are familiar. Much of the excess that was practiced was far from generally accepted. We must remember that if we have heard of Rome's decadence, we know it through the words of its critics, men like Seneca, Martial, and Juvenal, men of the era who were also thinkers of exemplary and enduring sanity. In a thousand towns and cities throughout the Empire men and women led quiet lives, adopting or rejecting Roman customs as they saw fit. The sturdy legionnaire, a prosaic figure in his thick-soled boots, rounded helmet, and cuirass of metal plates, served as both law enforcer and colonist. The rot of the Julio-Claudian court did not even pervade the city of Rome, much less the Empire, lulled into the great quiescence of the Pax Romana.

Byzantium:
Idolatrous Splendor

It should not surprise us that the reaction to Roman profligacy came from Judea. Like the boy in the tale of the emperor's new clothes, the Jews perceived the absurdity of deifying an emperor whose sanity—let alone probity—was in question. Moreover, the Jews rebelled against Rome on social grounds. Although scrupulously clean, they were nonetheless Oriental in their attitude toward the exposure of the human body, and the decadent nudity of the Roman baths filled them with as much horror as did the deification of the Roman emperor.

The Jewish people saw themselves as "The Daughter of Zion," and women were highly respected. They were also expected to be respectable. The rabbis taught that Eve was not taken from Adam's head for fear she would be proud, nor from his eye because she might be envious, nor from his ear for fear she would be curious, nor from his mouth lest she gossip, nor from his heart lest she be jealous, nor from his hand lest she be greedy. She was taken from his rib because that part of his body was always covered by clothing. Immodesty in public was held grounds for divorce. However, women were not only allowed but encouraged to indulge their aesthetic sensibilities. A woman could divorce her husband if he became repulsive in appearance or practiced a dirty trade like tanning or boilermaking. A husband could not oblige his wife to relinquish an attractive house for a dilapidated one, or force her to leave the beauties of Jerusalem if she did not want to go. Women, then, were clearly expected to be fussy and fastidious, and this doubtless extended to dress. Men and women alike wore robes that were long, fitted, and accompanied by shawls and turbans. Women also wore veils. However, the ancient Hebrews saw the injustice implicit in ostentatious dress. At the festival of Shevouth the wealthy were expected to provide poor girls with clothing like that of their own daughters, and all supplicants in a court of law had to dress identically lest appearances influence the jury. However, if the Hebrews had a bad conscience about overdressing, it was not, in the eyes of the prophets, bad enough. Jeremiah said: "Though thou rentest thy face with painting, in vain shalt thou make thyself fair. Thy loves will despise thee." And it would be difficult for any literature to produce an invective that could quite compete with Isaiah's denunciation of the "wanton" women of his day:

Opposite: Roman aesthetics, transported abroad, produced hybrid blossoms. Mummy portrait of a young girl of the Faiyum, a district forty miles from Cairo, 2nd century A.D. The naturalistic style of painting as well as her clothes and ornaments mirror Roman modes.

Below: An Early Christian manuscript drawing of "Mary and the Hebrew maidens dancing." Because of the ban on graven images, Jewish depictions of human beings had been extremely rare. The maidens' dress here combines Eastern fitted sleeves and Greco-Roman draperies; their hair is relatively loose and uncovered, testifying to their virginity.

Moreover, Jehovah said, Because the daughters of Zion are haughty, and walk with stretched forth necks and wanton eyes, walking and mincing as they go, and making a tinkling with their feet; therefore the Lord will smite with a scab the crown of the head of the daughters of Zion and the Lord will lay bare their secret parts. In that day the Lord will take away the bravery of their tinkling ornaments about their feet and their cauls and the crescents; the pendants and the bracelets and the mufflers; the headtires and the ankle chains, and the sashes and the perfume boxes, and the amulets; the rings and the nose jewels; the festival robes, and the mantles, and the shawls, and the satchels; the hand mirrors, and the fine linen, and the turbans and the veils. And it shall come to pass, that instead of a sweet smell there shall be stink; and instead of a girdle, a rent; and instead of well set hair, baldness; and instead of a robe, a girdling of sackcloth, and branding instead of beauty.

The sentiments of Isaiah were translated to the Rome of Messalina by the early Christians, and the message was not appreciated. Tertullian inveighed against women's coiffures: "All this wasted pain on arranging your hair—what contribution can this make to your salvation? Why can you not

61

Top: Colossal head of Constantine I, proportioned as if he were a deity. A.D. 324-330. Above: Early Christian marriage or betrothal scene. The East impinges on classical Roman dress. The woman wears patterned clothes, probably stiffly embroidered; the man's long sleeves would previously have been condemned as effeminate or barbarian. Bottom of a gold glass bowl. 4th century A.D. Roman.

give your hair a rest? One minute you are building it up, the next you are letting it down—raising it one moment, stretching it the next. . . ." Beyond that, he said, "All personal disguise is adultery before God. All perukes, paint, and powder are such disguises and inventions of the devil." He added a frightening warning: "The fake hair you wear may have come not only from a criminal but from a very dirty head, perhaps from one already damned." Clement of Alexandria had the final word, however, when he announced that if anyone was blessed while wearing a wig, the blessing remained on the wig.

It is small wonder, then, that when Christians first appeared in Rome they were flatly accused of "hatred of the human race" and "marring the felicity of the age" and were said to deserve the fate of common criminals—that is, to be devoured by wild beasts. They greeted their martyrdom in the simple tunic of the workingmen and slaves with whom they identified.

The Christians had gained considerable ground in Rome before the afternoon of October 28, in the year 312, when the Emperor Constantine and his army were seen marching toward the gates of the city for a confrontation with his foremost rival, Maxentius. Suddenly, as Constantine recalled years later for the benefit of Eusebius, his biographer, a fiery phenomenon, a "flaming cross," flared against the autumn skies. With uncharacteristic docility, he interpreted this as a sign from the Christian God. He encamped and went to bed. In a dream the flaming cross reappeared along with a message written in Greek, "By this sign conquer." The following day Constantine's forces overwhelmed the enemy. In recognition of divine intervention and support, he embraced the Christian religion, imposed it on his empire, and had himself consecrated as God's ruler on earth.

Officially speaking, Constantine's conversion marked the end of Roman paganism and the birth of the Christian era. Realistically speaking, his creation of a Christian Empire set into motion a complex cultural mechanism wherein the spare parts of old tastes and traditions were forcibly welded to the shiny hardware of new beliefs.

Radical changes did not stop with seismic shifts in political theology. For his glorious new empire, Constantine shrewdly decided to erect a new capital, a city whose splendor would complement his self-proclaimed omnipotence. Rome no longer lay at the crossroads of power. Moreover, the Italian peninsula was still cluttered with members of the landed *togati* who stubbornly clung to their privileged past. Constantine wanted his grandeur undiluted by dowdy aristocrats. Hence he moved to Byzantium, renamed Constantinople, a crumbling settlement on the Bosporus that overnight would reemerge as the shotgun wedding bed of the East and the West, a fertile spawning ground of sacerdotal tyrants and rigid pomp.

Byzantium

Just as the move to Constantinople had been engineered to unify the empire, so Constantine acted quickly to quell dissonant sectarian religious skirmishes, convoking the Nicean Council. For this meeting rancorous bishops were summoned from the breadth of the empire to settle their differences. None could have been prepared for the awesome apparition of the emperor himself. Constantine was proud of his broad bullock neck. Wide eyes glaring, he carried his head at a backward thrust that made the muscles and tendons of his throat strain with calculated sculptural drama. His approach heralded by raised torches, he swept into the council hall ablaze in gold-embroidered, jewel-encrusted purple robes, high-heeled blood-red buskins, and a spiked tiara. Alighting fiercely on a gilded wooden throne, he scintillated above the heads of the bishops like an Oriental idol posing for a Roman monument.

In regard to the future of dress, this tense scene was one of great significance, serving as an official prologue to a vivid tableau that would take many centuries to unfold. The players in this durable charade, performed in the cosmic arena of Church and State, would be formally distinguished by the increasingly hieratic elaboration of their costumes.

Over the years the relentless proliferation of caste systems would be forcefully illustrated by an individual's clothes. Now each member of society, whether from the most prestigious or most wretched rank, must not only know and accept his place in the divinely stratified order of life but must dress appropriately. Clothes might not necessarily make the man, but at all times they must identify him.

Matted beards and trousers for centuries had been considered the repulsive hallmarks of the barbarian by draped and blue-chinned Romans. Disagreements about the propriety of draped masculine silhouettes as opposed to trousered legs, coupled with controversy as to the merits of shaved or shaggy faces, would preoccupy different cultures for centuries. Far to the east, for example, civilized Persians would traditionally deem facial hair *de rigueur* for the virile; furthermore, Persian women would indicate their social rank by the layers of voluminous trousers they wore. When a European woman was ultimately presented to them wearing a skirt, they at first thought she had lost a leg. On the whole, Byzantine courtiers, while favoring the undelineated leg, were inclined to quibble less about shaving their beards—that is, until the last glorious phases of their empire, by which time razored jaws had come to represent the vulgarity of the West. But by then the gentlemen of Constantinople had also taken to tinting their lips and cheeks vermilion.

Byzantine culture reached dizzy heights under the reign of Justinian and his wife Theodora, two parvenus with a flair for opulence and an eye to the main chance. Their lives are worth examining

Top: More Eastern intrusions on Roman tradition: Beards may now signify either youthful virility or patriarchal dignity as opposed to outlandish scruffiness. 4th century A.D. Roman-Alexandrian ivory relief, detail.

Above: Aaron and representatives of the twelve states of Israel on Mount Sinai. Detail from Byzantine mosaics in the Church of San Vitale, Ravenna, enduring jewel of Justinian I's "overseas" building program and a remarkable fusion of Eastern and Western artistic styles. The stiff angularity of the draperies sheathing these Biblical figures probably reflects more than mere artistic convention. To Orientals, thick, stiff robes suggested both physical and spiritual grandeur.

because of their contribution to the development of ornate taste and ceremonial protocol. To this day they personify the essence of Byzantine style, a style we unconsciously associate with glittering mosaics, prostrate courtiers, ivories, intrigues, olive pallor, dangling gems and Oriental pearls, brocaded effigies gliding rigidly over patterned marble, agonizing poisons, glassy encrustations, miraculous levitating thrones, shrill jeweled birds, roaring wrought-gold lions, and icons gazing darkly through the flicker and smoke of pendant holy lamps.

Neither Justinian's nor Theodora's origins suggested the glories that lay ahead for them. They were loathed by the court historian Procopius, so the lurid gossip he has propagated down the centuries in the form of a memoir entitled *Secret*

History of Procopius must be read with many reservations. Nevertheless, this much is definitely known: The emperor was born a Balkan farm boy, and the empress's father had been a bear-feeder at the hippodrome.

Bread and circuses, as a political ploy, had been transplanted from Rome to the East with undiminished effectiveness. At Constantinople the populace regularly jammed the hippodrome to watch bear-baiting, acrobats, and lethal chariot races. Loyalties were divided between two major factions, the Blues and the Greens, dangerously inflammable groups more reminiscent of today's frenzied soccer-club fans than of political antagonists. Like the irrationally hostile Guelphs and Ghibellines of Renaissance Florence, or the Mods and Rockers of recent English social history, they adopted distinctive dress. The Greens, generally considered the more radical of the two, received their support from artisans and traders, many of them foreign-born. They wore the simple shiftlike tunics of workingmen. The activist Blues, the members of their more violent street gangs, who were protected by the Emperor Justinian as a form of political insurance in potentially difficult times, decked themselves out with bravado in Mongolian-derived "Hunnic fashion." According to Procopius, they "cut their hair short in front and grew it long in back, with a long moustache and beard, after the fashion of the Huns, and wore tunics with leg-of-mutton sleeves, riding breeches, and Hunnic capes. Their armed bands patrolled the streets at night, robbing wealthy passers-by of their cloaks and their gold, or silver buckles and brooches, sometimes finishing off their victims with their daggers."

Theodora's father had been employed by the Greens. Upon his death she, her mother, and her two sisters were abandoned by the party; the Blues, to embarrass their rivals, adopted the shaken little family group after they appeared in the hippodrome pathetically wreathed in flowers to appeal to the crowd for help. Throughout her life Theodora remembered the resolution of this traumatic moment with gratitude, despite the fact that the Blues' protection failed to save her from an early career as an "actress," a euphemism for a performing prostitute, when still a child. Striptease and bawdy improvised skits seem to have been her specialties; Procopius asserts that in one of her more original acts Theodora did unladylike things with live geese. His dubious anecdotes aside, it is almost certain that Theodora first came to Justinian's unwavering attention as a contestant in a hippodrome beauty contest, then as common a phenomenon in Constantinople as similar pageants are today in the West. Justinian himself awarded the prize, thereby launching an inseparable relationship that would endure until Theodora stoically succumbed to cancer many years later.

Theodora's seductive appeal, in her early days as an actress, was first manifested in a form of pre-

cocious piquancy that, under Justinian's adoring encouragement, would mature into the imperiously magnetic "star quality" shared by many of history's more dominating feminine forces. Her innate flair for the truly dramatic as well as the merely theatrical made Theodora recognize the crucial importance of spectacular clothes and self-glorifying protocol in maintaining her supreme position as empress, a flair that in later periods has also helped to enshrine such figures as Madame de Pompadour and Evita Perón. Women like these have understood fully the manipulative power of setting an unsurpassable personal style and have left their indelible imprints on the history of contrived appearance.

As empress, Theodora, who without a backward glance could order her enemies or unwanted rivals poisoned, drowned, tortured, butchered, or banished, reveled in the role of bedizened Lady Bountiful. Once, accompanied by an entourage of several thousand, she set out to take the mineral-water cure at Pythion and dispensed profligate amounts of gold to all the churches she passed en route. She also toyed with moral reform, buying the freedom of every inmate sold into the capital's brothels. The girls were summoned to the palace, where Theodora personally presented each with a change of pretty new clothes, a gold piece, and some knowledgeable advice about their futures.

Justinian, too, understood the mollifying effects of public works and charities. Earlier, his illiterate uncle Justin had introduced an ingratiating policy immediately on coming to power. Hoisted on a shield in the Romanized Old German manner and crowned with a golden chain, Justin had addressed the crowd through his brass-lunged herald, promising to endow every person present in the hippodrome with five gold pieces and a pound of silver. Justinian had ambitious plans to assure his own immortality and went on a binge of building monuments. One of them, Santa Sophia, with its vaulted mystery and glittering mosaic heavens, prompted Justinian, on first entering, to gloat, "Oh, Solomon, I have outdone thee!"

Justinian and Theodora are seen at the peak of their ornate hieratic form in mosaic murals of the

Church of San Vitale in Ravenna. The empress, a heavenly nimbus setting off her torrents of pearls, cascading emeralds, and hypnotized pride, wears lightly a Byzantine burden of jewels. A short-sleeved white tunic and gold shoes peep from the stiff folds of her purple cloak, itself deeply edged in gold-embroidered figures of the Magi. Justinian's tunic is also of white silk enriched with heavy gold embroidery, as is his semicircular purple chlamys, fastened at the shoulder with a stupendous jam tart of a fibula hung with giant tear-drop pearls.

The Greek chlamys, frequently decorated with a square of embroidery called the *tablion*, had by Justinian's reign usurped the classic toga of Imperial Rome. The long-sleeved tunic, which had been frowned on with Roman *gravitas* as being effeminate, fit only for musicians and actors, had become in the Byzantine world the most basic of garments; today it is usually known as the "dalmatic," a generic term derived from the tunic's Dalmatian origin. The archbishop and deacons flanking Justinian wear dalmatics identical to those of the laymen and eunuchs depicted in the mosaics. Here can be seen the fetal vestments of the clergy—a layman's dress to be appropriated and frozen in time for future generations of religious officiators and which is recognizable today in the raiments of the Greek and Russian Orthodox churches.

Imperial purple, as always, was the insignia of the mighty few. Even when a particularly grave political crisis threatened her life, Theodora refused to flee the palace, rhetorically invoking the supreme symbolic nature of the color. To an anxious Justinian and his cringing advisers she delivered a regal ultimatum: ". . . that one who has been emperor should become an exile I cannot bear. May I never be without the purple I wear, nor live to see the day when men do not call me 'Your Majesty.' If you wish safety, my Lord, that is an easy matter . . . as for me I like the old saying, that the purple is the noblest shroud!"

On another occasion the couple's insatiable lust for glory and revenge was gratified by the public desecration of the purple worn by the vanquished King of the Vandals, a shaming Roman custom that had fallen into disuse at least five hundred years before. Led into the hippodrome at the end of a creaking African wagon train of priceless booty, the royal prisoner was savagely stripped of his purple robes and forced to grovel in the dust before the imperial box, stammering, "Vanity of vanities, all is vanity." For Justinian and Theodora the spectacle must have been a thoroughly satisfying and exemplary one, although the Vandal's abject philosophic revelation appears to have fallen on flattery-deafened ears. This disquieting scene, typical of the couple's ruthless reign, epitomizes the cynical grandeur and cold-blooded malice that for centuries would glow like a smoky Oriental lamp, drawing countless artists and poets to its sinister flame.

Left: Justinian I hoped even to vanquish the past. At the consecration of his cathedral of Santa Sophia he gloated, "O, Solomon, I have outshone thee!" Here he appears shaven in the Western mode but orientally bedizened. Below: Areobindus, the Byzantine consul in the East in A.D. 506, dressed in a long-sleeved "dalmatic," presides over the festive carnage in the Hippodrome. Ivory diptych.

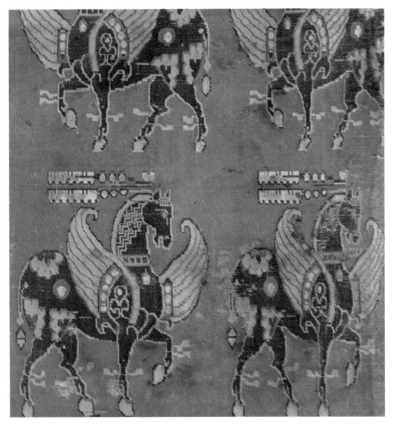

Magnificent Byzantine textiles emblazoned with fabulous beasts of the eastern Mediterranean. Top: Winged horses posture in quilted gold on the red background of an 8th-century fragment of silk serge. Above: Symmetrical griffons glare at each other on a printed 11th-century silk serge and wool fragment from a reliquary.

Silk, as well as purple, remained a primary symbol of exclusive rank. Unlike the Romans, who preferred to have heavy Eastern silks unraveled and rewoven into more gossamer and gracefully drapable fabrics, the Byzantines hoarded lustrous stiff brocades, the thicker the better. Constantinople had earlier shifted official taste; by the following generation the brocaded robe of Constantine II, designed for a triumphal entry into Rome, was like a jeweled carapace, so immobilizing that he could not move in his car of honor.

As official rewards or extravagant diplomatic gifts, silk fabrics and garments were constantly in demand. Occasionally, dragon-embroidered mandarin robes found their way from China, as did sable-trimmed "robes of honor" embroidered with imperial sentiments. Wise was the ruler who managed to maintain a source of supply along with stocks of silk to carry him through court emergencies. The Byzantines were constantly harassed by the prospect of Persia's wresting monopolistic control of the Asiatic Silk Road. Various sea routes to India and the East Indies were known, but as one Greek sea captain noted in the early 6th century, "The Indian philosophers called the Brahmins" were perhaps right when they said that if one stretched a cord from Tzinitza (Ceylon/Sri Lanka) and passed it through Persia toward the Roman dominions, "the middle of the earth would be quite correctly traced." For this reason, he went on to explain, there was always a great quantity of silk to be found in Persia, the overland route from Tzinitza being by far the most direct.

In all probability the secret of silk had remained a mystery for so many centuries because no one west of China would accept the absurdly simple truth that it was produced by worms. Not until two monks returned from the Orient to the court at Constantinople, bringing with them a hollow bamboo staff in which several hundred eggs of the silkworm moth *Bombyx mori* were housed, was the riddle solved and the Eastern middlemen's price-fixing stranglehold finally broken. Theodora has been given credit for commissioning this political and economic coup. If this is true, she was responsible for diverting the future course of much European trade and industry.

The Barbarians

Sophisticated Byzantine styles had been created in the Eastern Empire by the wedding of Greek and Roman sartorial traditions to Oriental opulence. In the West, however, Roman Imperial elegance, under barbarian duress, had been forced to mate beneath its station. Constantine's dream of a consolidated empire had not been realized. By the 5th century the schism between the empire's eastern and western factions had become a treacherous chasm. Marauding nomad hordes—Goths, Huns, Vandals, Arians, and others—trampled the West in

search of new lands to occupy. The Byzantines left their hapless Latin brethren to fend for themselves as best they could. Alaric, king of the Visigoths, sacked Rome in the year 410. By 475 the German Odoacer ejected Romulus Augustulus, the last of the Roman emperors; Gaul had been commandeered by the Franks and Goths; and at Bordeaux the Visigoths ruled. Sulking in the foyer of the Dark Ages, the Gallo-Roman Apollinaris Sidonius observed with distaste the barbaric gold jewelry and garish red mantles of the Visigoth elite. "How can I compose an ode to Venus," he complained, "when I live among long-haired hordes, being obliged to hear German spoken all around me, and having with a wry face to praise the songs of sottish Burgundians who spread rancid butter on their hair?"

The excitable Celts, who either by choice or unfriendly persuasion gradually emigrated from the vicinity of Hungary to the westernmost territories of Europe, had attracted the attention of the Greek geographer Strabo not long after the Teutons had first inflicted themselves on Roman consciousness. As a race, they cultivated a somewhat more gorgeous fashion image than other Barbarians. "To the frankness and high spiritedness of their temperament," Strabo notes, "must be added the traits of childish boastfulness and love of decoration. They wear ornaments of gold, torques on their necks, and bracelets on their arms and wrists, while people of high rank wear dyed garments, besprinkled with gold. It is this vanity which makes them unbearable in victory and so completely downcast in defeat." If this were not enough, "in addition to their witlessness they possess a trait of barbarous savagery which is especially peculiar to the northern peoples, for when they are leaving the battlefield, they fasten to the necks of their horses the heads of their enemies, and on arriving home they nail up this spectacle at the entrance of their houses." The Celts, aside from their weapons, raged naked into battle, wore handlebar mustaches, and, according to an early visitor to Gaul, "are terrifying in appearance with deep sounding and very harsh voices."

In the 5th century northern Gaul was invaded in turn by the Franks, a ferocious Germanic tribe who, believing themselves descendants of a water god, festooned their bodies with seaweed and clamped bison-horned headdresses over tangled

dyed red hair. Under their chieftain, Clovis, they set up the Merovingian dynasty in 481, their totemic insignia of a toad having been substituted by a primitive fleur-de-lis at the behest of Clovis' Christian wife, the omen-prone Princess Clothilde.

The Merovingians, over a period of nearly three centuries, dissipated their power through an injudicious policy of divide and let rule. On the death of a monarch, each of his sons would receive an equal parcel of the realm and the title of king. Eventually the title was about all that heirs could claim in terms of actual power, the reins of government having been snatched permanently from them by their "major-domos," or mayors of the palace, whose position, as chief officers at court, had become hereditary. Einhard, Charlemagne's biographer, ridiculed this dwindling race of royal puppets: "There was nothing left for the king to do but to be content with his name of king, his flowing hair and long beard. . . . When he had to go abroad he used to ride in a cart drawn by a yoke of oxen driven, peasant fashion, by a plowman; he rode in this way to the palace and general assembly of people." Einhard neglected to add

69

that streaming hair and jouncing in oxcarts were still admired in certain conservative quarters as divine aspects of the ancient tradition of Germanic priest-kings. Their clothes, weapons, and other personal paraphernalia were buried with them. Disinterred tombs reveal that they wore both short and long breeches, belted, knee-length, linen tunics called *gonelle* (the word for "skirt" in modern Italian is *gonna*), and heavy battle tunics, either cut from leather or sheathed in metal scales. Ultimately, one of the major-domos, Charles Martel (Charles "The Hammer"), deposed the last of the Merovingians. Charles extended the kingdom to encompass Aquitaine and on his death was succeeded by his son, Pepin the Short, father of Charlemagne.

Pepin, tiptoeing in the steps of Constantine, shrewdly dramatized his investiture as sovereign with a great show of panoply calculated to stun his subjects into an unfamiliar state of ceremonial devotion. Not that the former barbarians of his court were innocent of ostentation: Like all born plunderers, they still admired excess. Pepin's courtiers presented themselves in imported silks, exquisite linens, sea-green or sky-blue tunics, colorful Frisian embroidery, scarlet leather shoes shining with pearls and emeralds. Their strawberry-and-ash-blond braids were snared by garnet-studded diadems, and hairpins tipped with shapes of fabulous birds and beasts. The rich wore all the jewels, pearl necklaces, and heavy gold bracelets they could lay their hands on; the less affluent had to settle for mother-of-pearl, ivory, or lumps of colored glass. Each man and woman wore a wide girdle of heavy embroidered cloth or hammered leather fastened with ornate buckles.

From the neck up, all the Frankish warriors needed were metal-rimmed spectacles to pass for radical students of the 1960s. Their long hair was caught at the crown in lankly trailing pony tails, and mustaches drooped in straggly parentheses over beardless chins. Long hair, in fact, was a fetish with the Franks. A free man would be fined for cutting a slave woman's hair. If a slave cut a free woman's hair, the penalty was death.

The Franks appeared with their cherished weapons—leather-covered wooden shields, like the red-and-gold one mentioned in the *Nibelungenlied*. Shields were sublime; on them kings were elevated and the corpses of heroes were borne away from battle. A man's rank was measured by the magnificence of his sword. Like Siegfried's Balmung, swords were assigned heroic names. Saintly relics could be cached away within their hilts, and the finest scabbards flashed with gems. Even the clumsiest sword could be bartered for three cows.

As far as the Franks were concerned, however, the most arresting feature of Pepin's coronation was the anointing with holy oil of Pepin himself and his wife, a custom that had probably originated with the kings of Israel and that transformed Pepin into Europe's first monarch "by the Grace of God."

The tastes of the Visigothic elite ran to the aggressively ornate. Above left: Ancient Germanic tradition called for the burial of a man's martial effects along with his corpse. Domed helmet with ear flaps and mail reclaimed from a grave site. Above right: The dazzling crown of their King Reccesvinthus. 7th century A.D.

Opposite left: Equestrian bronze statue of Charlemagne in understated imperial regalia. Rarely a stickler for protocol, he began to receive early-morning visitors while still dressing in his bedchamber. This informal habit evolved into the suffocatingly strict grand levees of the Bourbon monarchs. 9th century A.D.
Opposite right: Transformed by a classical laurel wreath, Charlemagne appears on a coin in the guise of the Holy Roman Emperor.

Charlemagne and His Empire

At the time of his father's coronation Charlemagne was eight years old. If the spectacle of his parents receiving obeisance from ladies in tight-sleeved voluminous dresses and warriors in linen shorts, cross gaiters, and long fur mantles had any psychological effect on his character, it could be detected later in Charlemagne's passion for power rather than in any frivolous preoccupation with dressing up. Only twice in his life, and both times at the insistence of a pope, did he climb into the full regalia of Roman purple tunic, toga, and sandals; on the whole, he was happiest in a jerkin of otter pelts or, in bad weather, rain-resistant sheepskins.

Einhard, amused by Charlemagne's contempt for the extravagant finery of the courtiers, recorded one memorable episode to illustrate the point. At the tumultuous market fairs, foreign merchants—Jews, Venetians, Syrians, Spaniards—exhibited wares as wonderful, strange, and rare as the tales woven by itinerant storytellers. Among the booths of pet monkeys, spices, perfumes, intricate metal trinkets, and candies gleamed strands of pearls

and fantastic clothes made of powdered ermine, ethereal silks, and the lustrous feathered skins of flayed birds. Frankish nobles, never able to resist, splurged whenever possible. One cold, drizzly morning Charlemagne's courtiers, decked out in finery acquired at such a market fair in Pavia, met their sensibly clad sovereign after Mass. As Einhard reports, they were

> strutting in robes made of pheasant skins and silk; or of the necks, backs and tails of peacocks in their first plumage. Some were decorated with purple and lemon colored ribbons; some were draped round with blankets and some in ermine robes.
>
> The king, with a malicious twinkle in his eye, suddenly said, "Let us go hunting . . . dressed just as we are." The nobles had to obey. They scoured the thickets, were torn by branches of trees, thorns and briars; they were drenched with rain and defiled by the blood of wild beasts. . . . When they returned and began to take off their dresses of skins and slender belts, the creased and shrunken garments could be heard crackling like dry, broken sticks. . . .

Sardonically, the king then ordered, " 'Let no one take off his dress of skins before he goes to bed; they will dry better upon our bodies.' "

Next day Charlemagne directed his chamberlain: "Give my sheepskin a rub and bring it to me!" It came quite white and perfectly sound. Then, when his bedraggled courtiers appeared, the king said, "Most foolish of all men! Which of these furs is the most valuable and useful—mine, bought for a single shilling, or yours, bought for pounds?"

"Their eyes," concludes Einhard with satisfaction, "sank to the ground, for they could not bear his most terrible censure."

Nevertheless, throughout the Middle Ages, furs remained symbols of status. Only the elite, through rank or riches, were permitted the luxury of sable, ermine, miniver (squirrel), or vail, a gray-and-white-striped fur achieved by alternating strips of squirrel back and belly. With few exceptions, pelts were worn fur side in. Even the poor could obtain skins. Forest, river, cave, and stream teemed with predatory wildlife. Only England was relatively safe from wolves; on the Continent, ravening packs threatened people living in isolated communities. With the domestication of livestock, additional vigilance was needed to ward off smaller beasts of prey such as foxes and badgers. And if such pelts as these were to fall into short supply, there were always the ubiquitous skins of sheep and kid for protection against the cold. The Venerable Bede describes 8th-century English monks huddled in sheepskins, botching their lovely illuminations with fingers frozen stiff.

On august occasions Charlemagne appeared before his people in a majestic blue cape and other regalia suited, in a modified way, to the role of Holy Roman Emperor, a newly created office. Simultaneously attracted and repelled by Italian sensuality, however, he visited Rome only four times in his life and saw to it that his sons stayed clear of its corrupting sophistication. Yet a certain ambivalence was shown by this iron giant. From Roman architecture and decor, for example, he borrowed much for his capital at Aachen. But he drew the line at decadent clothes and flatly refused to dress in the Roman tradition except for the occasions of his investitures as king and emperor. At all times, however, Charlemagne wanted to see his subjects neatly and decently clad. In an attempt to promote cleanliness as an integral part of his Carolingian renaissance, the emperor not only set an example by swimming often and taking copious hot baths but went so far as to outlaw the customary barefooted treading of grapes.

Disastrously for the future in terms of a consolidated European empire, Charlemagne clung to the policy of disassemblement that was traditional with the Merovingians and divided his territories among his sons. Only one legitimate son, Louis "The Pious" of Aquitaine, survived him. The tale of Louis' entrance into his royal territories suggests the grotesque extremes to which society of the Middle Ages could go in regarding infants, let alone children, as miniature adults: "Accompanied by his *baiulus* Arnold, whose office was that of guardian and administrator, and by a retinue of nurses and soldiers, Louis was carried as far as Orléans in a cradle. There he was dressed in armor made specially to fit him, placed on a horse whose reins he clutched with his chubby baby hands, and so rode into his kingdom—a man on horseback."

If his sons were launched precipitously from the nursery, Charlemagne's daughters suffered an opposite fate, being permitted neither to marry nor to leave their jealous father's side. One in particular, Bertha, was praised for her "virility of mind," predating the much admired "virago" figure of the

Italian Renaissance. All were considered beautiful. Angilbert, Charlemagne's intimate adviser and chaplain and a distinguished poet, describes them and their latest stepmother arriving, like fairy-tale princesses, at a royal boar hunt: "The queen whom all await emerges from her royal apartments, the beauteous Liutgard. . . . Her gleaming throat has stolen the tender tints of the rose. The scarlet with which her hair is laced seems less dazzling than her locks. Bands of purple girdle her white temples. Gold thread bands the edges of her cloak. Her shoulders are hung with jeweled collars flashing in multicolored fires." The daughters appear; Rotrud, "her blond hair intertwined with ribands of violet and strings of pearls. A coronet of gold studded with precious stones circles her head. A brooch fastens her rich raiment"; then Bertha, in ermine, gems and shining belt of many colors; followed by Gisla, "lily-white, appareled in a purple gown shot through with tints of mauve, her face, her hair gleaming with many lights." Bringing up the rear is Rothaid, upon whose breast, throat, and hair "flash jewels of various sorts. A silk mantle drapes her white shoulders. Above her radiant forehead a coronet of pearls gleams. A gold pin mounted with a pearl crowns her coiffure." And lastly comes the adolescent Theotrade wearing "Sophoclean buskins, no less lovely than her older sisters. About her mild face her hair is of a brightness greater than gold. Rare emeralds adorn her lovely neck."

The king's mistresses are mentioned only in discreet haste by Angilbert and the poet-chaplain's own unseemly lust for the virile-minded Bertha not at all. However, it would seem his passion was returned by the frustrated princess, who found herself paternally and permanently denied the relief of marital consummation. Standing it no longer, Angilbert tapped on her window late one evening to whisper his affection; he was admitted readily and, one thing leading to another, spent the night, ecstatically oblivious to an unexpected snowfall. Awaking to a heavily blanketed ground, the panicky lovers decided that the only way in which Angilbert could escape undetected would be for the doughty princess to haul him away on her back, leaving only her staggered royal footprints in the telltale snow. They were duly observed in this disreputable position and reported. Charlemagne, who was neither monogamous nor a hypocrite, finally chose to overlook the matter, and Angilbert stayed on as the king's esteemed adviser and unofficial son-in-law.

Outside his family circle, a much stricter morality was imposed. Charlemagne was as indomitable a reformer as he was a general. The Church in particular felt the snap of his whip. The clergy was restricted as to the kinds of shoes and dress they might wear. Bishops, abbots, and abbesses must neither hunt nor keep falcons and hounds. Sunday, to the relief of an overworked peasantry, was reclaimed as a day of rest: "Women must not weave, cut garments, sew, embroider, spin wool, beat flax, wash clothes in public, or clean sheep," chores that along with farming, butchering, and tending barn kept them in perpetual motion.

At the palace, supplies and dispensation of clothing and food were supervised by the queen herself. The word "livery," which centuries later would come to mean the uniforms worn by household servants or retainers, originated with the medieval provision of clothing, food, and other necessities to underlings and derives from the Anglo-French livrer, "to deliver," in the sense of "to distribute."

Similarly, in England, the titles "lord" and "lady" would be compounded from phrases meaning "loaf ward" ("loaf keeper," hence "master of the house") and "loaf kneader." Here, essentially, we see the medieval feudal state in microcosm, the paternalistic lord-serf relationship that was to prevail for centuries to come.

The "Carolingian Renaissance" foundered after the death of its sponsor. Viewed from the present century, the daily lives of the nobles and serfs of ensuing generations blur into almost identical contours of lumpish discomfort. Even their dress, which served the elemental purpose of bodily protection, had a uniformity of silhouette, the chief difference being the length of the wearer's hemline. The peasant's usually ended somewhere about the knee, while those of the nobles, clergy, and women reached the ankle. Otherwise clothing differed little in form. The men wore simply cut tunics, cloaks, and hoods; the women preferred long roomy dresses girdled so that the skirts could be hitched up easily for active work. No distinction was drawn between summer and winter clothing; the rise and fall of the temperature simply dictated the number of layers of skins and pelts worn.

Plagued by smoke and drafts, mud and windowless quarters, aggressive wildlife, vermin, ghosts, and ghoulies, medieval society perforce lived in an ambience of what today are praised as "natural textures"—in a world of shingle, thatch, homespun and undyed linen, scratchy wools, axed lumber, daub and wattle, straw, bog, turf, tusk, horn, and rush-strewn earthen floors. People of that dim age responded to bright colors with unabashed delight. Zoë Oldenbourg writes that: "For lack of spacious halls and splendid palaces, even the greatest lords entertained their guests in 'flowery meadows' and voluntarily camped out in the open air, taking with them wherever they went what little they possessed in the way of carpets, plate, chests of clothes, and caskets of jewels. They were not above sitting on the grass and weaving themselves crowns of field flowers, or decorating their tents, banqueting halls, and lists with garlands of foliage."

The Middle Ages:

Flowers, Veils and Armor

The storybook aura that stubbornly clings to the image of medieval life was one perpetuated by 19th-century romantics. Thanks to them, we have been left with a lingering pageant set in a fantasy realm of romantic moated castles, tent-spangled fields, round tables, and jousts. To melodious fanfares, the players are introduced to animate this pretty scene: chivalrous knights; high-waisted, cone-coiffed virgins; flapping pennons; martial monks in tunics ablaze with fiery crimson crosses; troubadours suffering bland erotic transports in tight striped hose; wan, wimpled saints and tapestry unicorns.

In fact, monotony was the cornerstone of feudal life. Day followed day in dreary succession. Baronial pride of possession had yet to blossom into hotly competitive visual splendor. Wooden towers commandeering forlorn mounds were for long epochs considered the summit of noble residential architecture. The rank odors of the barnyard, stable and sty permeated the fortified households of even the tidiest feudal lords, ripening to full maturity in the summer heat.

For all walks of life, pilgrimages provided one of the paths of escape. Through pestilence, famine, and flood, it was the people's unshakable faith in God's infinite wisdom that helped them to endure. The Church rewarded them for their fidelity by condemning with mounting fervor life's few available pleasures. But making a pilgrimage to a holy shrine was by self-definition an act of faith. Who could be blamed if it turned into a convivial or possibly even profitable event? Small wonder, then, that when Pope Urban II preached the First Crusade against the infidel Turk in 1095, the people responded with hurricane force. The launching of the Crusades and the consequent birth of chivalry heralded the High Middle Ages, the realistic aspects of which modern man too frequently ignores.

Knighthood and the Church

The self-sacrificial aspects of chivalry or courtly love were an outcropping of feudal homage wherein the governing warrior class exacted fealty from its subordinates. The knight errant's avowed quest was for glorious bloodshed and death, including his own. Knighthood and the Church were considered the two most promising and admirable careers to pursue. The order of knighthood admitted boys to its rigorous training between the ages of seven and ten. After proceeding through the apprenticeship as page and squire, a candidate for knighthood

was expected to demonstrate formidable powers with weaponry. Only then would he officially be dubbed a knight.

A page most often was a noble-born son of one of his lord's good friends. This child exchange system functioned on several levels. For room, board, and training, a knight might augment his staff of lackeys with some aristocratic faces while at the same time demonstrating both his generosity and respect for the boys' family positions. A page was taught to revere ladies, to honor God, and to do as he was told. Much of his time was spent in attending the female members of the house. Frequently he was dressed in red with a colored girdle and had a horn hung around his neck. Upon his diligently combed hair perched a chaplet, and, in song and story, the

The flowering of chivalry and courtly love, fertilized by the Crusades to the East, where the concept of femininity was at once protective and sensuous, changed the image of Western woman. Having been treated like a minor, an enemy of the Church (had not Eve caused the Fall?) and a second-class man (Northern tradition had expected her to hunt with her brothers, pour her father's mead and bathe his hairy house guests) she was now hauled from the dung of the courtyard and set on a dainty pedestal. Accordingly, women of the upper classes began to dress less like drab, rumpled drudges and more like exquisite statuettes.

Opposite: A noblewoman, wearing ermine, presides over a loom and the wool-processing activities of her maids.

Below: These orientally plucked, veiled, and patterned ladies vie in splendor with their king and queen. Early 15th-century French manuscript.

75

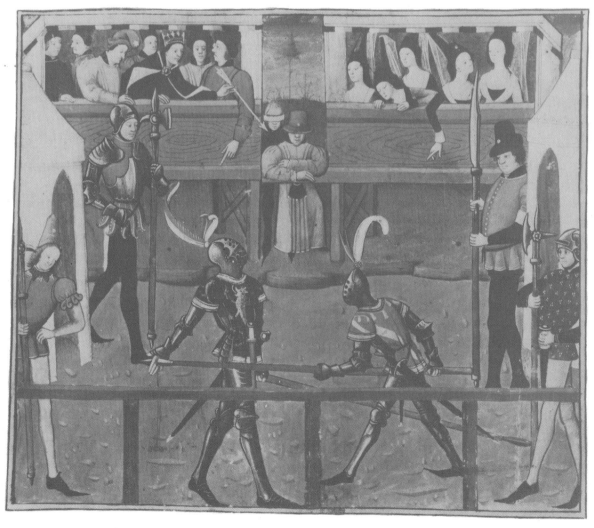

The hero who serves for love was an ancient literary motif that reappeared in shining armor in the medieval period. *Above:* An inspiringly ethereal lady receives a vow—"You or Death"—as the latter lurks ominously in the background. Flemish parade shield. 15th century.

Above right: Heroic joust attended by ladies and musicians. From *Composition de la Ste. Ecriture* for Philip the Good. 1462.

Right: Martial arts performed by magnificently sheathed knights at a royal tournament. Illumination from Réné of Anjou's *Traite de la Forme et Devis d'un Turnois.*

Opposite: Medieval rite of passage—the investiture of a knight. Sword and spurs are bestowed after an exhaustive initiation ceremony. English, 13th century, redrawn in 1775.

page was often seen carrying a white wand. Among other chores, a page was expected to pass the roast, tote the falcon, help his lord undress for bed, and sweetly sing the old heroic lays to put him to sleep. Upon entering squiredom in his teens, he dressed in everyday brown and white when called upon to oversee the stables or heave his lord into the stirrup. Abroad with his lord on pleasurable or bellicose missions—frequently one and the same—he changed into blue or gold and white to keep up baronial appearances.

Originally a youth's dubbing had been simply effected by kneeling before an older knight, who would hand the aspirant a heavy sword and then ceremoniously stun him with an open-handed clout to the head or neck. Reeling, the new knight was then expected to vault into the saddle and lambaste a quintain, a dangling suit of armor that was the medieval equivalent of a boot-camp sandbag dummy.

The medieval mania for symbolism, godliness, and pageantry soon elaborated this rough performance into a time-consuming ritual. As if the candidate were becoming a monk, he was first tonsured to symbolize his devotion to God. He might then be solicitously bathed (hence the Order of the Bath) and put to bed, thereby evoking the purification and rest waiting in Paradise for the spiritually worthy. Upon arising, he would be dressed in three layers of colored robes—white, red, and black. White signified the candidate's entrance into a state of pristine grace; red, the color of blood, indicated his willingness to die for the cause of God; black expressed his ready acceptance of death.

The secular celebration of a knighting next took place at the local lord's castle, where ceremonial robes, armor, and weapons were solemnly bestowed. On the final day of rituals the new knight took an active role in the tourney. Much has been made of chivalrous tournaments in which a love-smitten swain, entombed in armor, garnishes himself with his lady's colors. Weapons at the ready, he spurs his harlequin-robed horse into combat. Amorous triumph is his only aim, and in dainty response, pale-cheeked damsels swoon delicately on the sidelines. The true picture was decidedly more steamy.

"So violent and motley was life," muses J. Huizinga, "that it bore the mixed smell of blood and roses." Nowhere, he adds in his classic evocation *The Waning of the Middle Ages*, does the hot erotic element of the tournament reveal itself more frankly than in the knight's custom of wearing into the lists the veil or garments of his lady. Lady spectators were reduced to a form of striptease, shedding one article of finery after another, to fling them at the overheated, somewhat damaged knights. This scene suggests certain Latin American bullrings where aroused señoritas pelt blood-smeared matadors with whatever intimate lingerie they happen to be wearing. Medieval ladies thought it equally suggestive to toss their sleeves and veils.

A 13th-century minstrel's poem, "Of Three Knights and the Shirt," informs us in detail of the charms of the "service of love." The wife of a broad-minded noble has had her shirt delivered to the three knights who have sworn to serve her in love. It is her desire that they wear it instead of chain mail at a tournament given by her husband. The first two wisely demur, but the third takes the shirt to bed with him, kisses it frenziedly, and wears it in the tournament without the benefit of armor. Not surprisingly, he is messily wounded, the silken shirt is torn, the lady gives him her heart, and everyone applauds his mindless bravery. What can she possibly do, trills his benefactress, to reward him for his staunch devotion? Wear the bloody shirt over your gown, comes the dying knight's reply, and so she does, spoiling everyone's appetite at the bountiful feast her husband had planned to conclude the tourney on a festive note.

Splendid, articulated armor was the pride of the west until gunpowder, not used widely until the 16th century, rendered it a useless encumbrance. The fine art of armor-making reached its zenith during the so-called Maximilian Period, beginning roughly with the rise of that first great Hapsburg at the end of the 15th century, but it had evolved over the centuries through the ancient technique of trial and error.

Chain mail had been known since Biblical times. Goliath, according to the Book of Samuel, wore a helmet of brass on his head and was armed with a coat of mail "and the weight of the coat was five thousand shekels of brass. And he had greaves of brass upon his legs, and a target [shield] of brass between his shoulders." Until the 9th century A.D. Roman armor had still served as a loose model for many European warriors. This usually would include helmet, shield, leg greaves, and the "lorica," or breastplate, as it would later come to be known. Metal was the favored material until the Saxon King Harold of England brought to fashion the corietum, which sheathed the torso and upper leg in multiple pieces of overlapping leather. A rolling boil in oil,

Top: *Illumination from a 13th-century manuscript which shows that the weight of a knight's mail and accouterments separated the men from the boys.*
Above: *Medieval totemism. Flora and fauna translated into heraldic devices would become commonplace:* planta genesta, *the flowering plant known as yellow broom worn by Geoffrey IV of Anjou sire of the Plantagenet line of kings. From* Boutell's Heraldry.
Right: *Geoffrey is credited with introducing the first form of medieval crest—the sinuous lion rampant on his cap and shield. Enamel plaque from the tomb of Geoffrey Plantagenet. 12th century.*

called the *cuir boulli* method, transformed ordinary leather into a slithery material that could be easily stamped or molded on a form and which, when dry, assumed the nearly impregnable texture of thick horn.

Fully armed Normans and Saxons, clad in seven distinctly different types of body armor, populate the embroidered journalism of the Bayeux Tapestry. The armor is variously composed of patterned padded quilting, unshorn skins, iron, bronze, boiled leather, strips and disks, wool and tow, pointed scales, and, most importantly, rings. It may be that a truly interlinked chain mail existed by the time of William the Conqueror.

The hood so typical of medieval dress asserted itself in armorial fashions with the chain-metal coif that left only a small aperture for the face, falling in a sheet to the shoulders. To minimize painful chafing, quilting was worn beneath this clinking headgear and indeed proved necessary to all chain armor. It has been recorded that a crusading king paid a stiff sum to be stuffed like a tea cozy with pounds of insulating padding before venturing forth beneath the searing sun of Palestine.

During the period of the Crusades, the surcoat, sleeveless until a later date, was introduced to resist rust in rainy weather and, more to the point, to keep crusading knights from frying in the hellish glare of the infidel's wastelands. The surcoat followed the long flowing lines of the tunic worn earlier. Now, split either in front, back or sides to facilitate walking or riding, it was worn ankle-length over metal armor. Like ponchos, surcoats were slipped over the head; garments that opened down the front in the manner of Turkish caftans were not adopted in Europe until the 15th century.

Crests and similar heraldic devices evolved as a form of ready identification, much like labels on tin cans. Even at the battle of Hastings, well-meaning allies had slaughtered each other in armorial confusion. With the invention of the "heaume," a helmet that totally obscured the face, some sort of insignia became mandatory. The first form of medieval crest, a sinuous lion rampant upon his cap and shield, was worn by Geoffrey IV, Count of Anjou, father to Henry II of England, first of the Plantagenet kings. The family name derived from the sprays of yellow broom, called *planta genesta*, with which Geoffrey dashingly plumed his helmet.

Figurative devices came naturally to an age addicted to signs and symbols. Atavistic superstitions, inspired by the Church's aura of mystery and

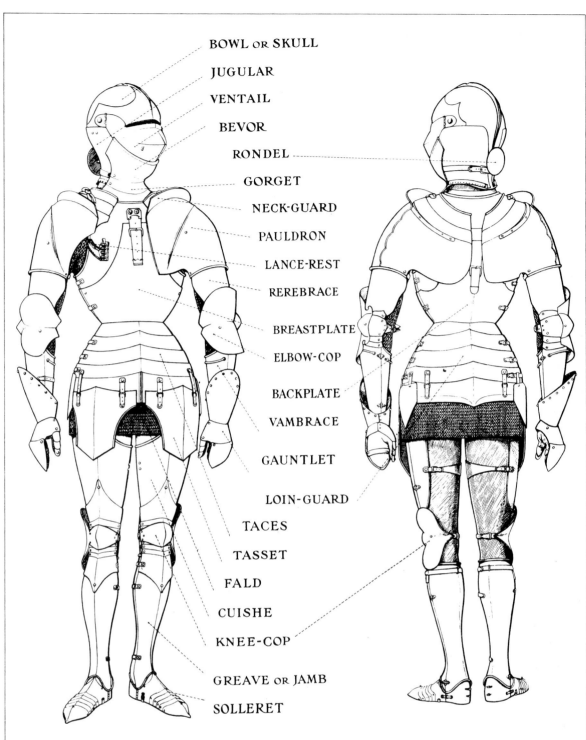

BOWL or SKULL
JUGULAR
VENTAIL
BEVOR
RONDEL
GORGET
NECK-GUARD
PAULDRON
LANCE-REST
REREBRACE
BREASTPLATE
ELBOW-COP
BACKPLATE
VAMBRACE
GAUNTLET
LOIN-GUARD
TACES
TASSET
FALD
CUISHE
KNEE-COP
GREAVE or JAMB
SOLLERET

Left: Chart of a complete suit of late-15th-century armor.
Below: Skull or "pig face" helmet, northern Italian. c. 13th century.
Bottom: Milanese helmet with engraved and repoussé decoration and traces of gilding, silvering and bluing. 1550.

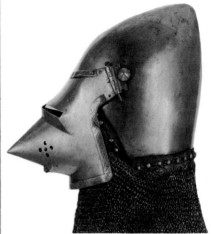

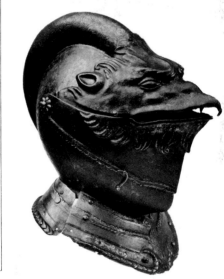

hidden meanings, motivated the medieval compulsion to give multiple significance to numbers, colors, days of the week, jewels, words, garments, weapons—indeed, almost anything with which one came into contact. The innate nobility of knightly weapons, for instance, made it out of the question for peasants to carry the lance and the sword. And if one knight committed an offense against another, he would be publicly disgraced by having his sword broken prior to his being cast out from his class.

The progress of a courtly love affair could be ascertained by the colors the knight successively wore. For both sexes, the two most common colors in the wardrobe of love were blue for fidelity and green for high passion. "You will have to dress in green," advises one 15th-century song. "It is the livery of lovers." The wearing of blue was not always an infallible indication of single-minded devotion. "To wear blue is no proof, nor to wear mottoes, of love for one's lady," pronounces the poetess Christine de Pisan. "But to serve her with a perfectly loyal heart / And no others and to keep her from blame. . . . Love lies in that, not in wearing blue. But it may be that many think to cover the offence of falsehood under a tombstone, / By wearing blue. . . ." Eventually, blue's symbolic meaning degenerated through too much falsehood covering, and in Holland and France it became the badge of both the adulteress and cuckold. Brown was despised, gray thought sad; yellow expressed open hostility. Knowing he would pass before Philip, Duke of Burgundy, Henry of Württemberg outfitted his entire retinue in yellow. The duke was apprised that "it was meant for him."

79

Religious orders: The body must be chastely obscured.
Top: Carmelite monks, French manuscript c. 1470.
Center: Beggars in cast-off clothes beseech alms from a symbolically cinctured monk. Detail from a French manuscript. 15th century.
Bottom: Monastic life and dress, as Chaucer well knew, did not necessarily breed incorruptible virtue. From Queen Mary's Psalter. c. 1300.

At the Synod of Arras in 1095, the bishops finally agreed that "simple illiterate souls," without jeopardizing their prospects of salvation, might be taught the scriptures through graven images on church walls and windows. For the benefit of the bishops themselves, as well as the lower clergy, symbolic references to scripture and holy tenets impregnated their every vestment. With few exceptions, the garments in the Catholic Church worn today to celebrate Mass are replicas, exact or slightly modified, of those worn by medieval popes, bishops, deacons, and priests. These had evolved from Roman and Byzantine prototypes. Of primary importance was the cassock, a long-sleeved, ankle-length garment, rather close-fitting and traditionally sewn with thirty-three buttons, one for each year of Christ's life. The cassock carries no rank. The alb, a white linen tunic touching the feet, alludes both to Herod's robe of mockery and to the virtue of chastity. In medieval times the alb was embroidered at hem, breast, and sleeves to recall the five wounds of Christ; its unblemished whiteness was also meant to remind a priest to keep his hands clean. The girdle, cord, or cincture cautions the wearer against lust; the amice, an oblong length of white linen, warns against lies. The chasuble, taking its name from the Latin for "little house" because it covers the other vestments, should suggest Christian charity and protection. The maniple, a band of silk that must match the chasuble, is carried over the left arm like the sweaty reaper's towel of early times, to impress upon the clergyman that he too is a reaper of souls. The two-horned headdress known as the miter alludes to the twin rays of light that shone from the head of Moses while recording the Ten Commandments, and it is worn only by high-ranking officials.

As in the symbolic breaking of a knight's sword, public disgrace and demotion could be brought down on a clergyman by a defrocking or other divestment of godly attire. A papal precedent was to be set by Pope Celestine at the Castel Nuovo in Naples; there, with his own hands, he "undid" himself, stripping from his body the insignia of divine dignity—ring, tiara, and purple.

The Chauceresque figure of the jolly, bibulous monk was clothed in a habit—a long, loose, wide-sleeved gown girdled by a knotted rope or leather belt and distinguishable by its color or weave. The habit's distinctive hood, known as a cowl, can be pulled over the monk's tonsure, the shape of which may also identify his order.

By Chaucer's time most pilgrims wore the clothing that designated their social station. Prior to this, however, an appropriately dressed pilgrim had worn penitential dress—a long, loose robe of crudely woven wool. From his shoulder a scrip, a small pouch for food, dangled from a strap, and he grasped a tall staff, the pilgrim's traditional walking stick. For penitential reasons, bare or roughly sandaled feet were *de rigueur*. The Cardinal of Lorraine

these little metal images, scallop shells, or whatever else franchised merchants peddled at popular shrines to his regal jewels. He distributed them liberally about his large royal person. The custom of wearing pilgrim hats, most typically round-crowned felt confections with brims turned up at the back and peaked in front, to which the wearer might pin an entire collection of pilgrim memorabilia, ultimately reached a point found ridiculous by Erasmus: "I pray you," gasps one of his characters, "what array is this that I see you in? Methinks your clothing is of cockle shells. On every side you are weighed down with brooches of lead and tin. How prettily garnished you are with straw coronets, and how full are your arms with snakes' eggs."

From earliest days northern Europeans had resorted to magical charms, talismans, and incantations to deal with the inexplicable. With the advent of holy shrines, they were now able to solicit favors from the Almighty by making a pilgrimage. One Crusader's wife, writing to her long-absent mate, inquires "how his sore doeth" and, pleading for a word from him, vows that she will make a local pilgrimage to keep him safe and that her mother, too, promises "another image of wax of the weight of you to Our Lady of Walsingham." For Christianized Europe, the ultimate pilgrimage was a trip to Jerusalem.

died of a chill after walking on sandaled feet carrying the Crucifix through sleet and snow in a procession at Avignon.

Truly repentant sinners might further mortify their erring flesh by wearing a hair shirt beneath the robe. This tormenting garment of bristly horsehair was designed so that each movement would inflict a fresh shock wave of unpleasant sensations on the skin. Thomas à Becket, something of a dandy in his youth, adopted the hair shirt in remorse for past sins as King Henry's carousing companion. After Becket's scandalous murder by Henry's associates in Canterbury Cathedral, the king was obliged by the pope to wear the hair shirt himself.

An examination of the clothing found on the corpse of the murdered saint tells us a good deal about both the dress and grooming of the period. The dead archbishop was found to be wearing, from outermost garment inward, a brown mantle, a white surplice, a fur coat of lambs' wool, two woolen pelisses, a black cowled Benedictine robe, and a shirt, all above his final suit of white linen, *lined* with coarse hair cloth. According to one account, "the innumerable vermin which had infested the dead prelate were stimulated to such activity by the cold, that his hair cloth, in the words of the chronicler, 'boiled over with them like water in a simmering cauldron.'" The martyr would seem to have had the saintly aversion to water and bathing deemed suitable for all Christians. Fleas and lice were regarded with something close to affection, and the wealthiest and most warmly dressed served as host to the greatest numbers.

Pilgrim badges and other similar souvenirs were to medieval man what hotel stickers on valises and jetliner flight bags are to status-conscious travelers today. France's saint-king, Louis the Pious, preferred

Left above: Philip the Good attends Mass in a private oratory, his piety accentuated by the somber blackness of his clothes. The Order of the Golden Fleece hangs from his neck. Before the altar a rug gleams with his coat of arms. 15th-century manuscript.
Left: St. James, patron saint of Spain, in pilgrim gear. 15th century.
Above: The scallop shell, symbol of Santiago de Compostela.

The Crusaders

With the Crusades initiated by Pope Urban II, kings and populace united to rid the Holy Land of the Muslim devil. This noble mission provided both a welcome means of escape from the ennui of grubby castle and hut and a sanctimonious excuse to butcher, pillage, and rape. In 1095 Urban had trumpeted his ultimatum. "God wills it!" shrieked the mob in reply, trampling each other to get at the red cloth crosses held out by the pope and his helpers. Stitched to their right shoulders, these would serve as the future badges of all Crusades.

After scaring Byzantine peasants out of their wits as they approached Constantinople, the first onslaught of Crusaders was received by the Emperor, Alexius Comnenus, whose daughter, the historian Anna Comnena, although then barely thirteen years old, shrewdly assessed the new arrivals in her journal. To the Crusaders, within whose ranks swarmed Franks, Germans, Anglo-Saxons, and even a contingent of bare-legged Scots, the Byzantines were nothing more than conniving, opportunistic Greeks. Worse, and this was monotonously underscored, they were small, dark, and effeminate. To Anna Comnena, one of the very few Byzantines to consider the Crusaders worthy of written comment, several of these Western giants were unbelievably handsome. Even back in Lorraine, tall, muscular Geoffrey of Bouillon was admired for the "broad shouldered and narrow hipped" physique idealized in the chansons de geste. Anna was equally drawn to Behemond, a Norman pirate chieftain. Tall and fair, with curly short-cropped hair and clean-shaven chin, unlike his hirsute Frankish colleagues, he answered exactly, she sighed, to the canons of beauty set down by Polycletes. Yet upon closer inspection his fixed blue gaze and taut smile were somehow frightening.

The scent of danger caught by Anna was hardly the figment of girlish reverie. Soon, treachery and vindictive fury would become the accepted code between marauding Crusaders and their presumed allies, the Greeks. The Crusaders wallowed in one atrocity after another. On a typical occasion they shipped back to Constantinople cases of the sliced-off noses and thumbs of Byzantium's secret allies.

In the light of such gruesome details, the Crusaders' almost instant capitulation to Eastern luxury and finesse comes as a surprise. Cities such as Antioch, Jerusalem, and Baghdad, exhibiting a civilization incontrovertibly superior to their own, threw even the least reflective European into what we now recognize as "culture shock." New sights, new sounds, new tastes and textures, new colors, aromas and rhythms of life were opiates wafting them into fantasies of unimagined pleasure. Most of the Crusaders were already familiar with Oriental objets d'art. Western churches, especially, liked to display collections of rare damasks, intricately wrought reliquaries and jeweled ornaments from the East. What the Europeans could not possibly have envisioned, however, was the sheer quantity of refinement awaiting them beneath the searing sun of Allah. Perfumes, spices, carpets and cushions, the echoing rain of fountain and pool, walled gardens melodious with birds, ornamental pavements, orchards heavy with fragrant fruit, the tinkling drift of bangled, silk-shrouded women, all lulled the Crusader into unfamiliar sensual repose. Those who managed to stay adopted native ways with alacrity. Some had brought out their wives, and they, too, rushed to adopt the local modes of jewelry and costume. Subsequent tides of Crusaders were appalled to find that their expatriated older brothers had degenerated into "effeminacy," meaning that they had adopted sleeping between sheets, frequent daily baths, sweet perfumes, pungent dishes served from exquisite vessels, and other odious practices. Their clothes, in which they were dressed by gaggles of slaves, seemed a disgrace—intolerably fine shirts, cloth-of-gold gowns, precious jewels, and, on occasion, even the turban.

East meets West: Islamic law prescribed ritual bathing four times a day, prompting Crusaders to reintroduce the public bathhouse to European cities. Northern citizens traipsed through the streets, towel over arm, wearing less than most bathers do today at public beaches.
Far left: Female bath attendants of the late 14th century.
Left: 15th-century bathhouse. Mixed bathing with lavish amenities on an oriental scale. French manuscript.
Below: Encampment of Moors and Europeans, from a manuscript of poems by King Alphonso the Wise of Castile and Leon. 14th century.

Nine Crusades were fought between the 11th and the 13th centuries. The first succeeded in establishing the Latin Kingdom of Jerusalem under the leadership of a Frankish nonentity called Baldwin of Boulogne, later named King of Jerusalem—a title that placed him on a footing with the proudest kings of Christendom. Receiving visitors at the Temple of Solomon, Baldwin had himself arrayed in a cloth-of-gold burnoose and a huge turban topped by a golden crown. Only ranking nobles were exempt from prostrating themselves before this swarthy, heavy-beaked, bearded potentate.

The Muslims felt the Crusaders unworthy of record. The only one who came into frequent contact with Franks and bothered to write about it was a nobleman, Usama ibn Munqidh, scholar, soldier, and diplomat. His opinion of the Crusaders must have been shared by many of his countrymen: "Anyone who has studied the Franks has seen in them wild beasts who have the merit of courage and ardor in battle, but no other." One benighted Frankish lord trod upon Usama's gold-embossed slippers by offering to take the scholar's son to Europe for a proper education. "He will see our knights there," explained the lord, "and will learn the science of chivalry." Usama declined the offer, privately noting that he would rather see his child rot in a dungeon.

Because of the language barrier, Western warriors could grasp only the externals of Eastern culture, its surface arts and technology. They might think that by changing their clothes they had changed their identities, but in this—at least to dark, derisive Oriental eyes—they were laughably wrong. The immediate future of European taste, none the less, would be directed by homeward-bound Crusaders. The West is more deeply indebted than we usually realize to Eastern culture and technical prowess. To architecture it brought two of the essential elements of the Gothic style, the cusped or pointed arch and stained glass, an art perfected over the centuries by Syrian jewelers. To music it brought the lute and the Muslims' exciting martial instruments —reed pipes, cymbals, bells, and kettledrums. To the table it brought ginger, rhubarb, aloes, cinnamon, pistachios, dates, and sugarcane; the last would inspire not only a wide range of sweets but an entirely new pharmacopoeia of soothing medicines. The Crusades also brought hospitals to Europe, although this would later prove slim compensation for the introduction of leprosy.

Among the most seminal of Eastern legacies, still greatly in evidence today, were the fashions, furnishings, and designs borne home by Crusaders. Upon their arrival, a craze for all things Arab swept across Europe, much like the chinoiserie epidemic of the 18th century: rugs and carpets—velvety to the touch—to stretch over drafty walls and floor; heavy hangings patterned with golden fleur-de-lis; and, for over the bed, the baldaquin, a brocaded canopy taking its name from a corruption of

"Baghdad." New colors and shades appeared: carmines, crimsons, and the lovely Arabic "laylak." New decorative motifs, particularly the Arabic letters of Kufic script, were gleefully appropriated. Giotto, Fra Angelico, and Fra Filippo Lippi, presuming that the lettering served only as elegant ornamentation, incorporated it into the costumes of Christ and the saints. This was the same script that would be combined with Roman characters to produce the typically "medieval looking" Gothic black letter.

For the improvement of personal appearance, the possibilities suggested by the East seemed limitless. For a while even the Arab custom of complete bodily depilation for women became fashionable with the aristocracy. Billowing gossamer veils would soon be draped before mirrors of Oriental glass rather than polished European steel. And certainly the allure of golden filigree, bells and bangles, glinting jewels, and shiny enameled cases of Cairo cosmetics was more potent than a troubadour's tenor.

The Church, as may be imagined, was outraged. Had Jesus not warned against laying up treasures upon earth "where moth and rust doth corrupt, and where thieves break through and steal"? Had He not specifically advised them to lay up treasures in heaven? "For where your treasure is, there will your heart be also"? Admittedly, the church had decreed that one of the techniques by which a man might save his soul and enter Paradise was to clothe the naked. On the other hand, as Saint Augustine so aptly put it, the act of charity itself was the essential clue to perfection, not the abhorrent "delight in beautiful or varied forms, in shining or agreeable colors."

Bernard of Clairvaux

A leading spokesman for drabness was Bernard of Clairvaux, future saint, rabid antifeminist, vilifier of sex, and hater of comfort. Wasted by fasts and clad in chaste white, he railed against his enemies with the fury of one possessed. In public he heaped sneering abuse on the cultivated Abbé Suger, who had announced that "It is only through symbols of beauty that our poor spirits can raise themselves from things temporal to things eternal." It was Bernard who disputed Abélard, the poet, philosopher, and scholar, at his trial for heresy. The tribunal presented a gorgeous panoply in blood-red robes and jeweled miters, nicely set off by the black starkness of the Benedictines. Bernard, eyes averted from the terrible glitter of the world, wore his customary virginal white. The King and his noble associates attended in their loudest spring finery, among them the enthralled young figure of Eleanor of Aquitaine.

Eleanor's love for Bernard was minimal. In the middle of celebrating Mass, he had hit her hostile father over the head with the nearest piece of religious equipment, inducing a fatal stroke. As Bernard called Eleanor the "counsel of the devil" and "Satan in the guise of fair-seeming woman," the feeling was plainly mutual. After a painful encounter with Eleanor and her retinue he scribbled a description, plagiarized from Isaiah, to his nuns:

The garments of court ladies are fashioned from the finest tissues of wool or silk. A costly fur between two layers of rich stuffs forms the lining and border of their cloaks. Their arms are loaded with bracelets; from their ears hang pendants enshrining precious stones. For head dress they have a kerchief of fine linen which they drape about their neck and shoulders, allowing one corner to fall over the left arm. This is their wimple, ordinarily fastened to their brows by a chaplet, a fillet, or a circle of wrought gold. Gotten up in this way, they walk with mincing steps, their necks thrust forward. . . . Some you see who are not so much adorned as laden down with gold, silver, precious stones, and indeed with everything that pertains to queenly splendor.

For a monk committed to war on luxury, Bernard made a first-rate fashion reporter. Had a lapsed nun wished to scale the social ramparts, there could be no doubt in her mind what sort of toilette she would have to assemble. "Fashion" in the modern sense of continuously revised modes of dress, as Bernard's bulletin suggests, was suddenly gathering steam. Little more pressure would be needed to set the mechanism of changing styles into motion.

Eleanor's flair for clothes could rise to any challenge. Her unusual interpretation of pilgrim's dress, for example, is legendary. Prodded by Bernard, Eleanor's callow first husband, Louis, led a major crusade to the Holy Land to expiate his sin of reducing to ashes the town of Vitry, its church, and most of its terrified inhabitants. Bernard, in turn, temporarily quit his beloved monastery, where he enjoyed sleeping in the crook of the staircase, to deliver an exhortatory address at the Cathedral of Vezelay. In his harangue he promised the crowds that the cross would keep them safe. At the close of the monk's performance Eleanor and her "ladies of quality," riding great white horses, pounded onto the scene, transformed into flabbergasting "warriors" complete with plumed crests, banners, and tall gilded buskins. After creating the desired sensation, they charged about, stirring listless lords from their lethargy and recruiting them to the ranks. Certain scholars have expressed their doubts about this episode; the historian Nicetus, however, records that on Louis's crusade "there were in the army women dressed as men. At the head of these was one in particular, richly dressed that went by the name of 'the lady of the golden boot.' The elegance of her bearing and the freedom of her movements recalled the celebrated leader of the Amazons." This was not an unprecedented phenomenon. Anna Comnena earlier describes Sigelgaita, wife of a Norman lord, who, dressed in armor and wielding a sword and lance like a man, led her troops into battle. "Obviously, a kind of monster and

Above left: Eleanor of Aquitaine. Engraving after a tomb relief from Fontevraud. According to Bernard of Clairvaux, above right, Eleanor was "Satan in the guise of fairseeming woman." Latin manuscript. 16th century.

Above: A prettified Victorian interpretation of Eleanor as the "Amazon" who claimed to have ridden bare-breasted into Jerusalem.

Below: Fanfare for fashion. A
decorative art form is born.
The new concept of "ele-
gance," in the sense of discrimination in matters of dress,
provided a means of exhibiting not only one's wealth but
one's superior taste. As beauty
now began to lie as much in

hateful to her sex," comments Anna. Presumably she would have passed the same judgment on Joan of Arc, whose appearance in male armor was not so great an eccentricity as it now seems.

To Bernard, a sweaty Templar was infinitely preferable to a vain, clothes-loving secular knight. The Templars, in fact, were his *beaux idéals*. Ever obedient, they wore only the clothes their commander gave them, "seeking neither other garments nor other food. They are wary of all excess in food or clothing desiring only what is needful. They live all together, without women or children." (Templars, incidentally, were the first military corps to wear what might be termed a uniform—cross-emblazoned surcoats of brown or red and white.) To complete the exemplary picture, Bernard applauds their coiffures: "They crop their hair close because the Gospels tell them that it is a shame for a man to tend his hair. They are never seen combed and rarely washed, their beards are matted, they reek of dust and bear the stains of the heat and harness."

With their curled hair and gay colors, the troubadours—itinerant singing bards—could not have presented a greater contrast. Decrying the use of force, they rejoiced in the arts, pressed for social reform, and, most significantly, elected the Virgin Mary their protectress. Until this time the mother of Christ had been relegated to the same oblivion to which woman generally was sentenced by medieval church and man. The Marian Cultists, as they came to be known, represented a revolutionary movement; their initial victory was achieved with the institution of the Feast of the Immaculate Conception, celebrated first at Lyons in 1140, to the distress of Bernard. The ceremony, he ranted, "was unknown to the custom of the Church, disapproved of by reason and without sanction from tradition." Despite his protestations, the Virgin was not to be dislodged from her new position as Queen of Heaven. Eleanor of Aquitaine named her first child Marie in allegiance to the troubadours and their patron. Later, both mother and daughter would help make courtly love fashionable internationally.

Like the Romanesque and Gothic styles in art and architecture, courtly dress and decor followed the same loosely circumscribed pattern in all principal European countries. At the time Aquitaine, a district of southeastern France, boasted broader boundaries than the kingdom of France itself. Together with the courts of Burgundy, Provence, and the Languedoc, this sunny realm would become the cradle of fashion.

The Court of Burgundy
In the 12th century the term "elegance" had first crept into the French vocabulary to signify aristocratic appreciation of refinement and beauty. "Elegance," in its original sense, suggested conscious "election" or "selectivity"—the selective interplay of texture, color, and pattern within an elon-

the eye of the wearer as the beholder, "fashion," in the modern sense of continually changing modes of dress, swung into a state of perpetual motion. In this scene of a marriage, the bride and groom appear twice, once dogged by a fashionable retinue attempting to impede the bride's progress by stepping on her train and next in the privacy of the nuptial chamber. From Renaud de Montauban. *Right: An April wedding, from the Duc de Berry's* Book of Hours *by the Limbourgs, 1413–1416.*

gated silhouette. The elite now transformed the princely weakness for showing off into a means of expressing one's superior taste. The medieval philosophy of Scholasticism, grounded on Aristotelian thought and expounded, at its heights, by Thomas Aquinas, drew up a rigid hierarchy of values among which beauty was defined as an ideal. Thus the ruling classes of a stratified feudal society found further encouragement in their competitive pursuit of sartorial splendor. The guiding aesthetic principle of International Gothic clothing and decoration was based on doting attention to delicate minutiae, as can be seen in the period's astonishing tapestries. This, coupled with a passion for jewelers' colors and attenuated shapes, produced the costumes so lovingly depicted in the Duc de Berry's *Book of Hours* and other contemporary masterpieces of illustrated manuscript. The height of Gothic fashion was seen as corresponding in form and spirit to the heights of Gothic architecture. The spire of the steeple suggested the hennin; pointed arches were echoed in pointed toes and pointed sleeves; the slim, soaring rib of a cathedral found a counterpart in the slender, molded shaft of the tightly covered human frame; the blazing symmetry of stained-glass windows was comparable to finely set Gothic jewels.

Milady's cloak now dragged the ground; a train indicated rank and was worn by all women of importance. Soon its length would be sternly regulated by the sumptuary laws. An Italian monk writes of Cardinal Latino's struggle to keep hemlines out of the mud and men's thoughts unsullied. A proclamation was read in the churches forbidding women to wear the trailing gown. Desolate, one confided to the monk "that her train was dearer to her than any other garment she had on." And she also complained that Cardinal Latino, in the same edict had bade all women—girls, young ladies, married women, matron-widows—wear veils of linen and silk. As a result, "they appeared ten times better looking, and drew the eyes of those that saw them still more towards wanton thoughts," clearly defeating his purpose.

Under Philip the Fair of Burgundy, who reigned from 1285 to 1314, the overall size of the robe or cloak, the width of its trimming, and the amount of fabric an individual was permitted to own was prescribed by law. The higher the rank, the greater the quantity of goods. Even the universal hood was scrutinized by watchdogs; commoners should wear only little sugar-loaf cowls to set them apart from nobles, whose capacious hoods could hang to their heels.

Footgear, too, gave measure to the man. One of the earliest French sumptuary laws dwelt on the extended toe. A prince, it stipulated, might wear points no longer than twenty-four inches. Twelve inches was permissible for gentlemen, whereas six inches was the limit for hoi polloi. In *The Romance of the Rose* the poet expresses his distaste for big boots pointed in front like a heron's bill and protruding in the back like a claw. Man, he reminds his readers, is not a bird. Why, then, should he try to resemble one? He reserved comment on shoes with points fashioned like a phallus.

Particolored hose and codpieces failed to delight Chaucer. Neither did he admire husbands who, to enhance their prestige and display their wealth, overdressed themselves and their wives. In *The Parson's Tale* padded shoulders and the infamous pointed shoes are passingly derided. Chaucer's purest scorn, as Phillipa Pullar has observed, was reserved for horrid clinging hose "so skin tight that 'the wretched swollen membres' departed their hosen in white and red so that it 'semeth that half hir shameful privee membres were flaine.' Sometimes they departed their hosen in other colours as well, white and blue, white and black, or black and red, in which case it seemeth that the privy membres were corrupted by St. Anthony's fire. As for the other side of their hosen, it was horrible to see 'eke the buttokkes' were as 'the hinder part of a she ape in the ful of the mone.'"

Outrageously exaggerated fashions frequently follow in the wake of disasters such as war or plague. In ancient Greece, after one decimating battle, women were instructed by the government to slit their clothing to the hip as an enticement to more frequent reproductive acts. More than one third of Europe's population perished between 1348 and 1350 in the Black Death, and one is led to ponder whether the blatantly seductive fashions adopted in the post-pestilential years did not spring from a subconscious fear of human extinction. Even the highest born women bought false hair, painted and powdered themselves (a leaden white complexion was still the fashion). They wore sleeves à *l'imbécile*, of such tightness that they had to be sewn on at each wearing, and fasted to keep their figures fashionably slim. Slipping in and out of décolletages so deep that frequently the nipple was exposed, they girded their breasts so high that "a candle could be stood upon them." Soon they would be found balancing the bovine double-horned hennin, veiled and curtained, above shaved hairlines and temples, or flirting beneath monster miter hats. Other cranial crazes included hair combed up over heart-shaped headdresses and puffy clouds of vaguely Turkish turbans.

Men wore both long hair and sleeves, the latter having to be tied in a knot to prevent tripping when out for a walk. Heavy gold chains and feather-trimmed cloth hats of fantastic shapes could not distract from their short coats that revealed the sexual parts in an explicit glove-like device known as a "braguette," an accessory that made the ornamental codpiece look prim by comparison. Under Edward IV the Commons petitioned to prohibit any knight under the rank of a lord, or any other person, from wearing "any Gowne, Jaket or Cloke" unless it be of sufficient length, on a man standing upright, "to cover his privy members and buttokkes." Nobles could reveal whatever they pleased—and did. Even the clergy caught the exhibitionistic fever and cut off their frocks at the knee.

Paradoxically, nudity in itself excited little comment. In Jerusalem, Usama ibn Muniqidh had been profoundly shocked when a Frankish knight allowed his wife to be served by a Muslim man-servant while she sat serene and naked in her bath. In Europe everybody slept naked in communal beds, except for those monks and nuns whose discipline it was to rise every three hours to say their prayers.

Islamic laws prescribed ritual bathing four times a day. The refreshing pools and steam baths of the East had prompted Crusaders to introduce the public bathhouse to European cities, unfamiliar with such a hygienic concept since Roman days. However, the arrival of the bath did not occasion a return to the cleanliness of ancient Rome, nor was the deadly effect of the common flea recognized. *The Secret of Secrets*, a helpful medieval manual, advised its readers upon arising to take a little exercise, rinse the hands and feet with cold water in warm months, scrub the teeth and gums with a leaf, oil the body, and cleanse the bile with a rhubarb purgative. With the advent of public baths (in the period before they became popular brothels), citizens traipsed innocently through the streets, towel over arm, wearing less than most bathers do today at family beaches. Neither Nordic nor Celtic codes of respectability had cast the onus of shame on nakedness. Here, atavism again came into conflict with churchly dogma, breeding the neurotic impulses which for centuries shunted the medieval consciousness between flights of inspired ecstasy and the abyss of sexual guilt.

Left above: International Gothic fashions displayed at a banquet. From Histoire du Charles Martel.

Left: Philip the Good, Duke of Burgundy, whose court might be labeled the "cradle of fashion," receives an illuminated manuscript from its "publisher."

Right above: Two men of fashion wear the cruciform insignia and pointed shoes. Detail from a manuscript.

Above: Marguerite of York, wife of Charles the Bold, with a fashionably high-domed forehead achieved by shaving or plucking. Late 15th century.

The Renaissance:

Urbanity in Bloom

Throughout the 11th and 12th centuries the towns of Europe, last glimpsed in the fading twilight of the Roman Empire, began once more to thrive as commercial centers for merchants, artisans, and craftsmen. The towns profited from an upward spiral of commercial success and growing prosperity in which dress played a central part. As we shall presently see, the demand for luxurious fabrics, among other products spurred by the Crusades, brought wealth and population to the towns. In turn, the social nature of town life and the growth of the trader class, the bourgeoisie, greatly increased the demand for clothing and fabric.

Social change ensued. The towns provided a haven for footloose hordes of landless men, at long last free from serfdom. "Towns breathe free air" became a popular saying, and to preserve its accuracy certain precautions were taken. Tall encircling walls were built, and, in Italy, *condottieri* (soldiers of fortune) were hired to command local militia.

Commercial discipline in the towns was imposed by the formation of guilds, whose regulations protected not only their members but also consumers by regulating prices and setting standards of quality. No product could be sold at market unless made by a member, and no one could work in a town unless he belonged to a guild; in time, even beggars and thieves would have their own. But from their inception the most powerful guilds were associated in one way or another with the textile trade, a business that increasingly enmeshed the West with the East. The Florentine Wool Guild grew to such importance that it was charged with the responsibility of raising funds for the construction of the city's cathedral.

Dress: The Token of Status

The various guilds kept a stern watch over their members to be sure they obeyed the association's rules of ethics, dress, and comportment. If, for example, a Florentine silk weaver or a Venetian glassblower revealed the secrets of his craft to outsiders, he was hunted down and killed, no matter where he might have emigrated. In all European countries the cap or hat of a craftsman varied in color and shape according to his trade or his rank within a guild. Certain guilds even regulated dress worn away from work; a German carpenters' guild insisted that a respectable member should not venture out in public unless attired in hat, cloak, collar, and gloves. Artisans should dress discreetly, never ostentatiously. It was suggested by a philosopher

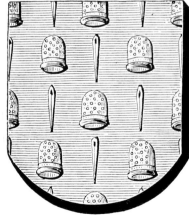

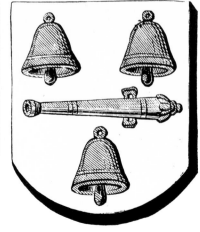

Booming commerce and burgeoning towns heralded the Renaissance. Escalating trade with the East called for a grander scale of international finance. Banks proliferated, and Italian coastal cities vied for contracts with foreign nations. Textiles were of primary interest; it could be said that the traffic in cloth paid for the Italian Renaissance. In England, as Harold Nicolson points out, "It was wool rather than individualism that first gave us our liberties." Within the new commercial structure guilds grew powerful and monopolistic.

to a merchant-banker that he dress in soberly dark and unadorned clothes to give the impression of being "safe and sound," advice which has apparently reverberated through banks and offices down to the present century.

The dress of townspeople gave a general indication of the local social pecking order, ranging from prosperous professionals to the destitute, who appeared, as in most periods, in hand-me-down rags, like the cobwebbed ghosts of vanished generations. In Florence cloaks of coarsely woven wool were distributed once a year to the poor (to cover their tattered shame) by tradesmen's guilds or religious fraternities. Ranking members of the community such as nobles, members of the city council, or the mayor, were of course permitted the greatest

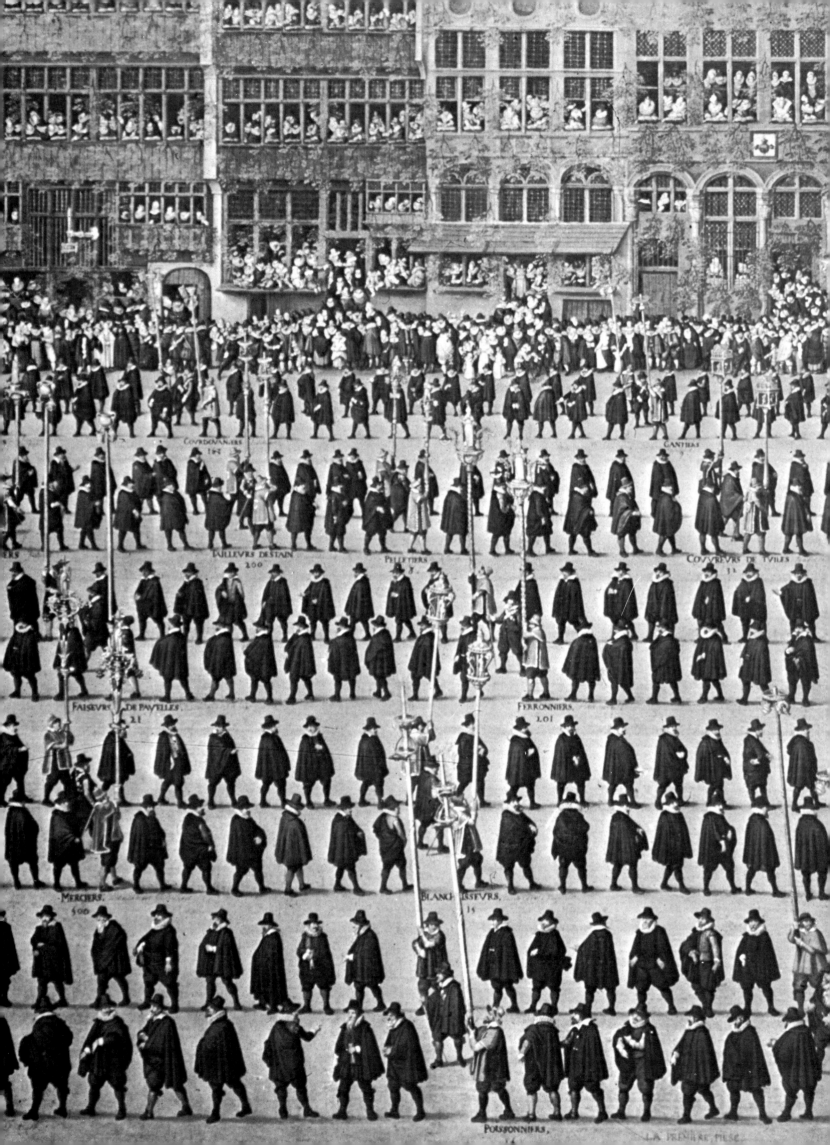

sumptuary license, while scholars and students had always to stress their dignity. To be entitled to wear the long robe of the doctor, a physician must be a graduate of an accredited medical school, such as those at Montpelier and Salerno. In times of epidemic, when a physician wore a great beaklike, bespectacled mask filled with medicines and aromatics to counteract evil fumes and protect his face, he resembled a weird humanoid bird, a creature escaped from the nightmares of Hieronymus Bosch.

The difference between peasant and townspeople's dress remained minimal until the 16th century, when the gulf suddenly widened. For everyday wear the peasant clung to the hoods, baggy tunics, loose smocks, rough cloaks, and leggings of the medieval past, while the townspeople, particularly women as far as they were financially able, now tried to ape the fashions of the gentry. In the countryside, kerchiefs, the most universal and ancient protection for the feminine head, were wrapped or coiled or even stiffened with wooden underpinnings to ease the carrying of loads and utilitarian objects. The particular draping and knotting of a kerchief might identify not only the wearer's country or state but her native hamlet as well. Local customs became inbred to an extreme degree as most peasants were forbidden to travel (one of the abuses leading to the Great Peasant Rebellion of 1524–1525, when forces rallied under the emblem of the peasant shoe demanded, among other things, the right to wear red clothes like their betters). For both women and men, their "Sunday" or "festival" clothes evolved into the patterns known as "local peasant costume," the peculiarities of which could become as much a part of a village's soul as its oral folklore. Lacing, tight bodices, and layered skirts, it must be admitted, were absorbed from the styles of city dwellers but hardly with alacrity.

Along with the wide-brimmed straw hats, the peasant contributed another important development to Western upper-class dress: the man's coat. This garment probably originated in the 15th century

when the smock was split down the front, donned from the back, and adjusted to size by a cord or belt. This garment was later adopted by soldiers in the Thirty Years' War and in the 17th and 18th centuries became the *justaucorps* ("fit-the-body"), precursor of today's coat.

The shirt, another essential of modern dress, particularly in the aesthetic sense of "clean linen," first began to peep out discreetly in the Renaissance. Heretofore the outward wearing of linen was unthinkable for a man of position. A medieval king strongly advised his son always to have his shirt cut appreciably shorter than his doublet so that the ignominious "flax and hemp" would be hidden from critical eyes. The Renaissance taste for lacing at shoulder, breast, and under the arm made total concealment impossible. The shirt's escaping sleeves and neckline were now deliberately emphasized; the neckline of the outer garment was cut increasingly lower and wide to show off the pristine edging, which itself was now occasionally bordered with a metallic embroidered band. Much in the same vein as the symbolic white collar of industrialized society, the white shirt conferred on its wearer an emblem of privileged rank in that a display of fresh linen immediately disassociated him from manual work. At the same time it proclaimed his affluence in that he could afford to keep his clothing clean.

In Renaissance dress the broadening effect created by widened, rectangular necklines and the padded shoulders of detachable sleeves, as well as the bulkier shapes of short cloaks, echoed the massed forms of the architecture, just as Gothic dress resembled the spired cathedral. Broad vaults were now needed for warehousing material gain; similarly, broadened shoulders, perhaps, would help bear the burden of an expanding material world.

The theatrical Renaissance fashion of slashing the outer garment with puffs of contrasting material pulled through the slashes originated not with the gradual exposure of undergarments but with what seems an unbelievable incident. When the Swiss managed to vanquish Charles the Bold, Duke of

Burgundy, in 1476, they gleefully attacked a windfall of spoils, hacking at bolts of superlative silks with their swords and using the brilliant patches to mend their own tattered clothes. German mercenaries, bowled over by the swagger of the new Swiss military fashions, which hardly constituted a uniform, each man slitting his clothes to suit his own taste, rushed to imitate them. Like the subsequent "rakish angle" of a hat, slashing permitted a man from the lower classes, the recruiting ground of most mercenaries, to express an attitude at once reckless and flamboyantly free. The imposition of one vivid color on a clashing hue exaggerated further an effect of virile panache. The Germans craved bright colors, especially fiery reds, and mixed them together wildly in a new garment of their own called *pluderhosen*—long, slashed, bloomerlike breeches as voluminous as those of a harem eunuch, with a ribbon bow enhancing the codpiece. Soon not only doublets and breeches fell to the razor's edge, but slashing and puffing began to appear on wide-brimmed caps, broad-toed shoes, stockings, and even gloves. Where tailors ventured to slit no more, for fear of a garment's complete disintegration, small round holes were burned into the cloth with a red-hot iron.

The first women to adopt slashing on their clothes were, not surprisingly, camp followers, a term embracing not only prostitutes but cooks, wives, and other female dependents. From the German mercenaries and their women the fashion of slashing spread to the French court, where a royal wedding

Slashing and puffing: a widely popular fashion unusual in that it worked its way up the social ladder rather than the reverse.
Left: Obsessively slashed soldiers' uniforms. Engraving from the Triumph of Maximilian. *c. 1512.*
Left above: Slashing and puffing influences even armor, as shown in this fine example of parade armor by Kolman Helmschmied. Austrian. c. 1530.
Above: Portrait of a young Farnese, wearing a slashed and quilted tunic with gold trimming. By Francesco Rossi, 1542. Detail.

in turn passed it on to England. In Venice, this northern craze, coupled with rising hemlines, caused concern in the Senate, where the expense incurred by changing fashions was proclaimed a danger to the state. In Florence the mounting tyranny of fashion was noted by a diarist:

> In 1529 they stopped wearing hoods, and in 1532 there was not one to be seen, for the usage had gone, and, instead of hoods, caps and hats are worn. At the same time they began to cut their hair short, where before everyone had worn it down to their shoulders without exception; and now beards began to be worn, where before no one could be found wearing a beard in Florence, except two men, Cobizo and one of the Martellis. Furthermore, at the same time, hose began to be made in two pieces, where before they were made in one, and without any slits; now they are slashed all over and they put taffeta underneath to come through all the slits.

Textiles

If one had elected a single feature of Early Renaissance dress as the most characteristic, it would be the display of magnificent textiles, whether gold and silver brocades, ornate patterned silks or velvets. (The origins of velvet are uncertain, but it is known that the cut silk pile of velvet was meant to imitate the sensuous texture of clipped fur.) The Roman passion for silk continued to course feverishly through Italy's bloodstream. In the Middle Ages, only the Church and the very rich could afford the superb fabrics imported from China and the Middle East. Pontiffs and princes alike preferred to go to the grave in brocaded Oriental splendor. At Perugia in 1304 Pope Benedict was buried in a stiff shroud of Chinese brocade. At Verona, in the same year, a lord with delusions of grandeur and a passion for Chinese silks took for himself the title of a Mongol emperor, Can Grande della Scalla—the Great Khan of the Staircase. Dante's impressions of a visit in the house of this megalomaniac can be deduced from a reference in the *Inferno* to his host's fixation: *drappi tartareschi*, or "tartar cloth." Needless to say, it is duly recorded that the Can Grande went to his final reward wound like a monstrous silkworm in a cocoon of his favorite stuffs.

The prohibitive expense of foreign silks led naturally to home-grown imitations. As early as the 12th century Sicilian workshops produced exquisite textiles based on Chinese, Islamic and Byzantine models. Most of these were intended for hangings in churches and secular buildings, ecclesiastic robes or princely costumes. In the first half of the 13th century, under the patronage of Emperor Frederick II, who reigned in Palermo, Sicilian weavers achieved even greater triumphs. They continued to look eastward for decorative motifs, among which the favorites remained the single- or double-headed eagle (the latter having its origins in Hittite

The Renaissance passion for opulent fabrics. Top: The megalomaniac Can Grande della Scala, whose horse was swathed in yards of his favorite "tartar cloth." Equestrian statue from his tomb. 1330. Eastern floral fantasies from Italian looms. Right: detail from a velvet brocade altar cloth. Milan. 1490s. Above: detail from an Italian textile. 15th century.

Opposite: From Le Costume Historique by M. A. Racinet, after a painting by Veronese.

monumental art), lions, mythological beasts, hunting animals, Kufic script, the pomegranate, lotus, palm leaf, and writhing arabesques. The seeds of Eastern design were scattered even more thickly over European soil with the introduction of printing and the publication of "pattern books" in which enchanting Oriental motifs were painstakingly catalogued.

On the Italian mainland, the textile industry soon burgeoned, and by the turn of the 14th century Venice, Florence, and her neighbor, Lucca, had commercial ties with Palermo, Aleppo, Alexandria, Byzantium, and cities on the Black Sea, buying both finished and raw silk products for trade in the West. When it was discovered that Italy's climate was ideal for the propagation of silkworms, local production began to skyrocket, showering gold and silver sparks all over Europe. By the following century Italian cloth merchants, like Italian bankers, had opened offices in Paris, Antwerp, Bruges, and other northern cities. Giovanni Arnolfini, a successful Luccese silk merchant settled in Bruges, not only was asked by Duke Philip the Good to act as his revenue adviser and moneylender, but saw his marriage commemorated by Jan Van Eyck, the Duke's court painter, as if he had been born a nobleman rather than a socially suspect merchant prince.

The Medici clan in their Florentine grandeur represented the height of mercantile power. Their name would literally be written in the stars when Galileo, on discovering that four moons revolved about Jupiter, baptized them the "Medicean planets." Under the guise of fellowship and fraternal protection, the Medici's manipulation of the working classes had swept the clan from the mean quarters of a shopkeeper into the palace of the governing Magnifico. There, behind rusticated walls, barred windows, and iron doors, they could take their ease, toy with their fabled collections, drain their own wines from gold goblets, and commission a palace, a painting, an intrigue, a war, or, the death or the advantageous marriage of a relative.

In the early years of the Renaissance, escalating trade with the East had called for a grander scale of international finance. Obligingly, banks proliferated. Italian coastal cities, especially Venice, vied with each other for exclusive contracts with foreign nations and dealers. Textiles were of primary interest to all concerned. It could in fact be said that the traffic in cloth, in all its aspects, paid for the Italian Renaissance. Even in England, as Harold Nicolson points out, "It was wool rather than individualism that first gave us our liberties."

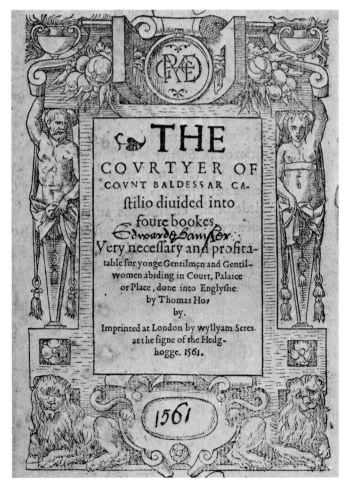

The Renaissance Man

If modern finance was the lifeblood of the Renaissance, creativity and the scholarly study of antiquity were its heart and brain. For the sculptor Donatello, the confrontation with ancient sculpture had an electrifying effect which inspired his ambiguous figure of David, portrayed by the artist as an adolescent voluptuary, booted, helmeted, but otherwise shockingly nude. It must be remembered that medieval statuary was expected to be chastely dressed, preferably from head to foot, and to unaccustomed eyes the image of a naked youth, albeit in bronze, was as disconcerting as the spectacle of an undressed person wandering down the aisle of a church would seem today. Yet Donatello had pried open another prison door, freeing artists once more to glorify the beauty of the human body. Inevitably this drastic shift in attitudes (with emphasis, as in ancient Greece, focused on the masculine rather than the feminine ideal) would influence the aesthetic concept of the clothed figure.

For the Greeks, male perfection had been epitomized by the philosopher-king, for the Romans by the dignified orator-cum-citizen, for the Age of Chivalry by the romantic knight. With the Renaissance came the concept of *l'uomo universale*, the "universal" or multifaceted man. Today, the threadbare cliché "Renaissance man" is trotted out to compare someone's creative diversity with the professional genius of a Leonardo da Vinci. As originally defined by Count Baldassare Castiglione in the early 16th century, however, the ideal Renaissance man had to appear professional only in the role of professional gentleman.

Two hundred years after its initial publication, Samuel Johnson advised: "The best book that was ever written upon good breeding, *Il Cortegiano*, by Castiglione, grew up at the little court of Urbino and you should read it." Penned during the same years as Machiavelli's bracing cynicisms, this eloquent manual, speedily translated into French, Spanish, and English (as *The Book of the Courtier*), became the definitive guidebook for generations of aspiring "gentlemen," fixing for posterity the standards of modern "courtesy."

Castiglione felt an obligation to preserve from oblivion the bright memory of the Duke Guidobaldo and his court at Urbino, which was superior, he insisted, to all others. At Urbino the qualities of the ideal courtier and his lady were assessed by a charming circle of nimble conversationalists.

According to Castiglione, the mastery of the arts of war took precedence above all other things. In battle the courtier must hound the enemy with ferocity. Physically he should be agile, courageous, and neither too big nor too small (if in this he must err, he should tend to shortness, for an overly large person might be taken for a dolt). As it was the "peculiar excellence" of the Italians to ride well, to subdue wild horses, to tilt and joust, the courtier

Top: Portrait by Raphael of Baldassare Castiglione, the delineator of the ideal Renaissance man. His instructive book Il Cortegiano *was so widely read and followed that before 1600 more than 100 editions had appeared in various languages. 1519.*
Above: The first English version, published in 1561, had as great a social impact on England as similar translations had on France and Spain.

should be a perfect horseman. In addition, he must know how to hunt, a noble pastime commended by the ancients for its close resemblance to war, as well as be able to wrestle, swim, run, jump, play tennis ("which shows off the quickness and lithe-ness of every member"), and throw sticks and stones, an exercise that could not only prove useful as a last resort in the heat of battle but also "impresses the crowd with whom, inescapably, one has to reckon." Finally, the courtier's most sticky problem was: how to make an elegant spectacle of himself without drawing undue attention.

Now the ambitions of successful city merchants rivaled those of kings. As the ineffectiveness of sumptuary laws made it impossible to assert one's superiority merely by wearing one's riches on one's back, new sartorial tactics were needed to distin-guish the aristocratic elite. Selectivity and refinement, the essential components of elegance, would fi-nally carry the day.

Convinced of their superior intelligence and grasp of aesthetics, the newly minted aristocrats worked with artists to raise fashion to the level of art. An-tiquity gave the Renaissance artist the example of uncluttered structural forms; this principle was now applied to clothing. In the paintings of Piero della Francesca and Fra Angelico, for instance, we see dress reduced to severely elegant shapes. Patri-cian costume was now dictated by the subtleties of texture and color, the perfection of form, and the studied settings of precious stones. In other words, the modern criteria of "good taste" were beginning to be defined.

The clothes of Castiglione's courtier could be considered "well in all respects if only they satisfy the wearer of them." Extremes in dress such as "overample" French or "overscanty" German styles, like affectations of any sort, must be shunned. For ordinary attire, the Spanish predilection for black was found pleasing, or, in a pinch, any somber shade that would attest to the sobriety of "inner things."

On the other hand, excessive solemnity could be a bore. Just as the Spaniard brightened his melan-choly with flashes of wit, so the Renaissance courtier

Right: Archers by Benozzo Gozzoli. In one of Gozzoli's tapestrylike paintings, Lorenzo the Magnificent is portrayed as the leading king of the three Magi. Gozzoli had served an apprenticeship to a goldsmith and so was particularly adept at depicting gilded, bejeweled, and other ornate surfaces and textures. Here fitted oriental fabric is cut to reveal the ideal Renaissance male physique, freed from concealment once Donatello's nude David had shattered moral restraints. c. 1460. Detail.

Opposite above: Peddlers fiddling to attract customers during carnival in Venice, from Mores Italicae, 1576. Peddler on left is dressed in a caricature of the Spanish fashion. *Opposite below:* Renaissance fashions of 1443 including particolored hose and knee-length sweeps of gathered brocades. Detail of a fresco by Domenico di Bartola.

should cultivate the manner of the supremely talented amateur, a form of nonchalance known as "*sprezzatura*—that art which does not seem art." Nonchalance, no matter how carefully cultivated, was preferable to any obvious self-consciousness such as stiffening of the neck for fear of spoiling one's coiffure, concealing a mirror in the fold of a cap or a comb up one's sleeve, or having a page follow one through the streets carrying a sponge and brush.

One should sing solos, play musical instruments, recite verse, speak foreign languages, laugh, frolic, and dance with *sprezzatura*. A young courtier named Roberto was singled out as a peerless dancer, chiefly because of his seeming lack of concern for what he was doing—"he lets his clothes fall from his back and his slippers from his feet, and goes right on dancing without picking them up." This performance was paralleled in England by a hulking ten-year-old, the future Henry VIII, who, at his brother's wedding, grabbed his sister Margaret, soon to be Queen of Scotland, and, to the applause of his parents, flung off his robe and in a thin silk shirt whirled through two jolly dances.

In Italy digressions from sobriety were appropriate for festive events; gala dress, Castiglione concedes, must be trimmed, showy, and dashing when designed for festivals, adding that bright and gay colors are particularly becoming to tournament armor, the finest of which was made in Germany and Italy. (By the 16th century the battle armor of some Italian knights was so intricately fitted that at the close of one skirmish those who had been unhorsed rolled helplessly on the ground like giant lobsters, much to the consternation of the enemy, who, unable to administer the *coup de grâce*, finally had to summon a party of woodsmen with axes.)

The suitable dress, movement, and speech for any occasion provided an inexhaustible topic to other people besides Castiglione. Della Casa minced no words: "Everyone should dress well, according to his age and his position in society. If he does not, it will be taken as a mark of contempt for other people."

Machiavelli, author of *The Prince*, always wore the sober dress suitable to a man of mature age, dress meant to enhance an impression of cultivation, gravity, and wealth. He wore such clothes on the street "to command respect" but also dressed with care to enter his study, where he felt somber attire gave evidence of his own respect for the Spirits of Great Men. (Later, Maurois, Mann, and a few other dignitaries of 20th-century letters were to do the same.)

It was suitable for youth, on the other hand, to strut and swagger in the bright colors and snug contours appropriate to its natural energy, beauty, and sexual drive. Castiglione defended the young against aging reactionaries who attacked new modes of attitude and dress simply because they had not been fashionable in previous generations:

Below: Two extravagantly dressed young Italian gentlemen of leisure. Their costumes reflect a society prosperous enough to employ armies of specialized craftsmen. Detail of an engraving. 1470–1485.

Bottom: A silver perfume flask or pomander with compartments for different fragrances. Suspended from a belt, this is the sort of "perfumed ball" Venetian dandies held to their noses to dispel unpleasant fumes from the canals. French. c. 1600.

Opposite: Venice and the art of sumptuously dressed spectacle. The city's close commercial ties with the East are evident in the trailing grandeur of the entourage's robes. Procession of the Doge through the Piazza San Marco. Copy of a woodcut after Titian, 1699.

They say it is not right for young men to ride about the city on horseback, or, especially, on mules, to wear leather scabbards, or long coats in winter, or caps, at least before they are eighteen, and other such things. And in this they are really deceiving themselves, because these customs, besides being convenient and useful, have been introduced by habit and common consent, just as in their day people generally liked to go about dressed up in tights and neat little shoes, and to be a gallant you had to carry a hawk on your wrist, for no purpose, dance without touching the lady's hand, and behave in many other ways, which were appreciated then, but would look very silly now.

In 15th-century Venice competitive clubs of young men, calling themselves "Companies of the Hose," vied to sponsor the grandest *festa* and to outdo each other in the magnificence of their emblazoned, hooded doublets and the revealing tightness of their expensive particolored hose. In their smooth, pale, tapered hands, long a noble ideal (it was suggested to Cesare Borgia by his father the pope that he wear gloves on a journey to preserve the delicacy of his murderous hands), the Venetian dandies carried perfumed balls, lifting them to their noses to offset the fumes of the canals. As the fashion for Companies of the Hose and their costumes mushroomed throughout Italy, Machiavelli sniffed that the prettified members were good for nothing but preening and backbiting.

Effeminacy of appearance was attacked by many. In 1462 a Venetian friar pressed the Doge to prohibit young men from growing their hair too long, "like women." Castiglione also deplored androgynous creatures, so tender and languid of limb that they seemed about to collapse and who uttered words as limply as did the dying. A man's face, he said, should ideally radiate an agreeable virility. With their curled hair and plucked eyebrows, these mincing visions should be driven from the society of noble men, "not as good women whom they clearly try to imitate, but as public harlots."

Renaissance Ladies

Blonds were universally admired by Italians, and to achieve the desired gilded effect hair was subjected to doses of henna, animal innards, prolonged sunbaths, and other more severe bleaching agents. Complexions were blanched and smoothed with sweet- or vile-smelling preparations, lips glistened

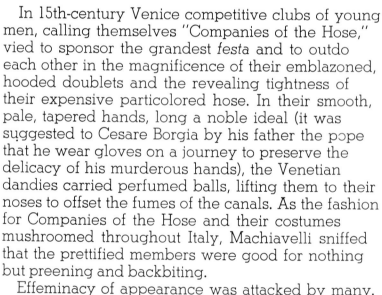

with honey, and teeth were enameled Della Robbia white. Even princes and mercenary soldiers were known to dip into the dye pot. In 1496 Isabella d'Este wrote asking for the recipe for a solvent used by the Duke of Milan, whom she had noticed "one day with black hair and the next with his own natural color." Ariosto, however, satirized old men who dyed their hair black or blond, tried to disguise their age

beneath yards of costly cloth, and daubed themselves with rouge and perfume. Some, he sniggered, went so far as to have themselves shaved twice a day.

The courtesan, a classical institution newly revived, with her beauty, intelligence, and cultivated manners, might easily be taken for a great lady. It was unwise for a great lady to be taken for a

courtesan—family disapproval could take a nasty turn. While it is true that romantic intrigues flourished among the nobility, the Duchess of Amalfi was strangled by her brothers for marrying beneath her station. In the relative calm of the Duchess of Urbino's drawing room, all agreed that it was easier to imagine the Queen of the World than the Perfect Court Lady. Nevertheless, put to the test, Giuliano de' Medici, likening himself to Pygmalion, drew up a roundly applauded list of appropriate qualities. Like her male counterpart, she must be untainted by affectation as well as prudent, magnanimous, continent, kind, and discreet. She must be witty, attractive but chaste, never revel in the character assassination of intimate female friends, nor cut an ungainly figure by blasting on trumpets or banging on drums. Contention arose as to the seemliness of certain physical exercises. If she must play tennis, handle weapons, ride, hunt, or take part in other activities of the cavalier, she must choose "garments that enhance her grace and are most appropriate to the exercises in which she intends to engage at a given time." In her choice of clothes and accessories, she must also recognize and accentuate her own individual type; if blessed with vivacious beauty, she should emphasize her assets with gay colors and cheerful movements and speech, just as one whose style is gentle and grave should swathe herself in melancholy mystery. Here we find possibly the first written directive for the attainment of one

Right: Beatrice d'Este, wife of Lodovico Sforza. In this portrait by Bernadino di Conti, 1494, we are confronted with the courage and implacable pride of a duchess who would come to blows with female passers-by when they insulted her rough cloth rain hood. Above: Her sister and rival, the ornately turbanned and equally unflinching Isabella d'Este, a celebrated intellectual and patroness of the arts, who would probably have set upon them with her knife. Detail of a portrait by Titian. 1536.

of the most highly regarded goals of modern dress —personal chic. Artful attire, it was furthermore suggested, should be used to counteract deficiencies in complexion or weight but always, naturally, with *sprezzatura*: "Thus, if she is a little stouter or thinner than normal, or fair or dark, let her help herself in dress, but in as hidden a way as possible; and all the while she keeps herself dainty and clean, let her appear to have no concern or care for this."

The minuscule annual laundry bill of the Este, one of the Italian Renaissance's leading and most populous ducal families, would suggest a somewhat less than pristine general standard of noble hygiene, despite de' Medici's pointed reference to habitual daintiness. Women painted, but so subtly that the fact was little noticed. Lodovico Sforza's insistence, however, that a lady of quality should comport herself with "a certain shyness bespeaking a noble shame that is the opposite of brazenness" does not jibe with the tenor of Milanese court life suggested in a letter he wrote to his wife's sister and rival, Isabella d'Este, in 1491:

> I cannot explain a thousandth part of the things that the Duchess of Milan and my wife do, and of the pleasure they take in horse riding at full gallop, coming up behind their ladies-in-waiting and making them fall off. Now they are in Milan, and as it was raining yesterday, they went with four or five ladies on a shopping expedition on foot about the city, with those rough cloth hoods on their heads to keep them dry. As it is not the fashion to go about with these here, it seems that some women were pleased to pass remarks, and my wife got angry and began to shower abuse on them, so that it would seem they would come to blows. They came home all spattered and torn, which was a beautiful sight. I believe that when your Ladyship is here, they will go about with greater spirit, because they will have you with them, and you are very high tempered so that if anyone dares to abuse them, your ladyship will defend them with your knife.

What, then, were the accepted norms of fashionable appearance that marked the transitions from the Middle Ages to the Early and High Renaissance and, eventually, to the Baroque?

Just as established schools of art invariably overlap, so Gothic fashions coexisted for a period with emerging styles of the Renaissance. In fact, the term "Gothic," originally one of disparagement, was coined by the 16th-century critic and painter Giorgio Vasari to deplore a disfiguring rash of steeples left on the landscape that could be dispelled only by the vaccine of the Renaissance. Renaissance perfection, wrote the architect Jean Battista Alberti, must now be achieved through the subordination of each structural or decorative element to the harmony of the whole, a principle ultimately to be reflected in Renaissance dress as it spread throughout Europe.

Left: François Ier, whose reputation for seductive dress and droop-lidded philandering was so vivid that as late as the 19th century he was supplying Romantics such as Victor Hugo and Rigoletto's librettist with a prototype for their frivolous and randy royal villains. Detail of a painting by Jean Clouet. 1525.

Above: The exquisite Agnès Sorel, the first royal mistress to be recognized officially as such by the king and, perforce, his court. Thus she opened the door for several of history's leading fashion arbiters. Immaculately plucked, she is here portrayed, rather astonishingly, as Christ's mother in Fouquet's Melun Diptych. c. 1480. Detail.

The Valois Court

For women, the early Renaissance had been a period of increasingly enhanced status, although they were encouraged to play an advisory rather than a participatory role in politics. In France, Charles VII's favorite, Agnès Sorel, the exquisite, high-breasted model for Fouquet's painting "La Vierge de Melun," was the first royal mistress to be recognized officially as such by the king and, perforce, his court. Now the equal of princesses, she opened the way for the Diane de Poitiers and Madame Pompadours of the future and also established herself as one of the great fashion arbiters of history. Agnès, at least in her portraits, if not in life, wore gowns that bared the bosom to the waist. With temples plucked and shaven, she encouraged

false hair and wigs, which eventually launched one of France's great industries, wigmaking, its raw materials supplied by peasants, nuns, and public hair auctions.

With the accession of François Ier, the "compleat" Prince, France began to assume the central position in culture and style that it still holds. The Magnifico Giuliano de' Medici claimed that although the rest of the French "recognized only the nobility of arms," François, even as a young prince, exhibited not only athletic prowess, beauty of face, noble manners, valor, and greatness of spirit but a deep respect for literature and men of letters. An impassioned admirer of Italian Renaissance artists, François brought to his court Il Rosso, Primaticcio, and the aged

Above: Leda and the swan, an eternally popular theme with voluptuaries, grace a brooch belonging to François Ier.
c. 1540.
Right: François listens to Antoine Macault reading his translation of the Greek historian, Diodorus of Sicily. Three of François's sons stand before Macault. The broad bulk of the king's costume is bespattered with decorative minutiae typical of earlier International Gothic fashions.
c. 1532.

Opposite left: Diane de Poitiers, lifelong mistress of François's son Henri II, a huge melancholic man who dressed in somber colors to honor Diane, two decades his senior, who was a widow. Her indestructible beauty endured through a strict regimen of icy baths and riding at a full gallop before dawn.
Opposite right: Eleanor of Austria, François's second wife, with the jutting Hapsburg lower lip, was described as "pretty enough" but with "the trunk of a giantess and legs of a dwarf". Detail of a painting by Joos van Cleve.

Leonardo da Vinci. Il Rosso's grafting of the French "cult of woman" onto Italian Renaissance roots bloomed into the "Fontainebleau" style in which the female figure was restored from heroic muscularity to inviting pliancy.

King François was an insatiable collector of women, paintings, tapestries, enamels, jewels, cameos, embossed leather hangings, antique weapons and statuary, prints, drawings, intaglios, coins, and medals. He kept a jewel room and a cabinet of curiosities that housed, among other esoterica,

a stuffed crocodile with seven heads, assumed to be the Hydra of Greek myth. He also showed a penchant for extravagant dress. In 1546 a Venetian ambassador reported with epic understatement that the king "likes a touch of elegance in his clothes." This referred to the fact that his garments were trimmed with braid or lace and embroidered with precious stones and ornaments. "This fastidiousness," he concludes, "doubtless contributes to the maintenance of his health," evidence of which was seen in the gargantuan amounts of food and drink

he consumed. As to dress, the king's fine shirt invariably protruded through the opening of his doublets, which, the Venetian observed, were sewn with threads of gold. Thirty-one years earlier, a predecessor of the ambassador had shown less enthusiasm for François' exhibitionism: "The king attended Mass for the obsequies of the late king attired in the purple mantle with a long train. He resembled the Devil." With a large sloping nose, small suggestive smirk, and little, lazy-lidded eyes, François did, in fact, present a saturnine appearance.

François Ier's Chateau at Fontainebleau, like Nero's Golden House and Louis XIV's palace of Versailles, was a form of "total environment" meant to vanquish nature and transform man into a finely crafted *objet d'art*. Fontainebleau's interiors of sculptured plaster and scintillating frescoes were like an architectural aviary about which bejeweled birds of paradise could preen and coo for weeks on end. The plumage of the French courtiers startled even the most blasé of their contemporaries.

Rabelais was familiar with the courtiers, devoting long passages in his fiction to the description of their apparel. The men, writes Rabelais, were outfitted with fine worsted or serge stockings, either black, white, scarlet or some other color, which were matched, or nearly so, by breeches embroidered and cut to individual fancy; doublets of cloth of gold,

cloth of silver, velvet, damask or satin, and taffetas of the same colors, embroidered, "suitably trimmed up in perfection," and sashed in matching silk; points (lacing tipped with ornamental tags or pendants) of matching silk, the tags enameled gold; coats and jerkins of cloth of gold or silver, gold tissue, or velvet, embroidered to taste; swords with gilded handle and hilt; velvet scabbards the same color as the breeches, banded in wrought gold; golden daggers, black velvet caps or bonnets adorned with jewels, golden buttons, and a white plume "most prettily and minion-like parted by so many rows of gold spangles, at the whereof hung dangling in a more sparkling resplendency fair rubies, emeralds, and diamonds."

To add to the harmony of their environment, gallants and their ladies appeared daily in apparel of corresponding textures and color. Rabelais is transported by the ladies who, like crystal prisms, flash every color of the rainbow: garters and velvet shoes of violet, or crimson; scarlet stockings, taffeta petticoats of red, white, tawny, gray; gowns of sunstruck cloth of gold or of velvet, satin, or damask in shades of crimson, white, orange, tawny, emerald, azure, yellow, and flame. With reverence, Rabelais in *The Inestimable Life of the Great Gargantua* (1534) describes the marvelous way in which, like trees, they also change their appearance with the seasons:

In the summer, some days, instead of gowns, they wore light handsome mantles, made either of the stuff of the aforesaid attire, or like Moresco rugs of violet velvet frizzled, with a raised work of gold upon silver purl, or with a knotted cord-work, of gold embroidery, everywhere garnished with little Indian pearls. . . .

In the winter time they had their taffaty gowns of all colors, as above named and those lined with the rich furrings of hind-wolves, or speckled linxes, black spotted weasels, marten skins of Calabria, sables and other costly furs of inestimable value. Their beads, rings, bracelets, collars, carcanets, and neck-chains were all of precious stones, such as carbuncles, rubies, diamonds, sapphires, emeralds, turquoises, garnets, agates, baryls, and excellent margarites.

Royal festivals, like many Renaissance forms of expression, turned to antiquity for inspiration. The Roman triumphal entry was revived (all work was suspended to cheer the passage of a prince), along with the mock water battle, horse ballet, and costumed dramatic allegory. Ancient myths were interwoven with medieval romances to emphasize the political implications of a court spectacle. Pomp and ceremony engraved the milestone for each major event in a prince or monarch's life—his birth and marriage, the birth of his children, his alliances, triumphs and treaties, his coronation, accession, his jubilees, and, ultimately, his death.

If Fontainebleau achieved the calculated effect of "total environment," court spectacles produced the art form of "total theater." Renaissance artists, poets, and writers believed that their primary professional responsibility was one of service to the state, and to this end, like devoted public-relations experts, they labored tirelessly for the splendor of their princes. Not only artists and men of letters but also composers, dancers, singers, musicians, choreographers, and armies of craftsmen cooperated to create stupendous pageants. This union of the arts, it was felt, reflected the harmony that governed the universe. Perhaps this view explains the repeated participation of such great artists and thinkers as Leonardo da Vinci, the Pollaiuolos, Holbein, Clouet, Tintoretto, Veronese, and, later, Ben Jonson, Rubens, and Inigo Jones. Even Descartes produced a ballet for Christina, Queen of Sweden. In time, the melodious *intermezzi*, introduced at Florentine fetes and composed by Monteverdi, would develop into modern opera. The French *ballet de cour* would blossom into classical ballet, and in England the court masque would be transmuted into the modern "fancy dress" party.

Although Castiglione favored solo musical performances, ladies and gentlemen of most Renaissance courts were expected to take active roles in spectacles as dancers, singers, actors, and declaimers of commemorative verse. Furthermore, the tournament still continued to represent a pivotal event with its three principal phases: "the tilt," in which knights charged at each other with lances; "the tourney," in which combative teams of knights, usually dressed in partisan livery, engaged in a melee; and, finally, the brutal "barrier," in which

gentlemen on foot bashed at each other across a decorative barricade. Their finely wrought gold and silver tournament armor has virtually disappeared over the years as the precious metals were melted down to meet financial exigencies.

The 16th century also saw the development of the indoor fete around a specific theme. Into transformed banquet halls rolled giant pageant carts, ancestors of the modern float, with horses and mules concealed beneath them. They bore costumed courtiers, angels blaring on trumpets, enormous ships embossed with frolicking nymphs and titans, illuminations, spangled grottoes, fountains of fire, caroling singers, turbaned Turks, shaggy "wild men of the woods," royal children clad in the antique mode, and "Americans with feathers in their hair." Clouds of perfume fogged the air—even the mules were generously doused.

The zenith of Renaissance splendor was reached at royal fetes and displays of diplomatic amity such as the Field of Cloth of Gold. This spectacular event, plotted by Cardinal Wolsey as a political summit meeting between France and England, was held in the open fields of Calais in the summer of 1520. For two dizzying weeks the courts of Henry VIII and France's François Ier feasted, jousted, and paraded in dazzling peacock fashions. Like an exquisite miniature in an ornate gilt frame, the meeting was literally encircled by cloth of gold. It was a stupefying show of woven wealth in an era when fabric was synonymous with prosperity and trade. Beneath floating tapestries and banners decorated by the painter Clouet, the French reconnoitered in a city of golden tents. The largest, sixty feet high, was striped in embroidered royal-blue velvet bands, lashed with violet taffeta and crowned by a six-foot statue of an angel in an azure mantle sewn with gold lilies. Queen Claude's tents were of violet satin and the ubiquitous cloth of gold and cloth of silver.

Not to be outdone, Henry and his entourage of five thousand pranced into view under banners painted by Holbein. At the center of their compound, before two allegorical fountains spouting red and white wines and hung with silver cups, the English had constructed a four-story wood-and-canvas crenellated castle, painted to resemble brick and stone. The apartments of the castle were hung with cloth-of-gold tapestries and with silk hangings of green and white, Henry's personal colors. Its central hall had a ceiling of ethereal green silk spangled with golden roses and a floor paved with yellow-and-white patterned taffeta sprigged with red roses.

Eclipsing all were the resplendent figures of the two young kings. At their first meeting François was attended by Swiss Guards, dramatic in black, white, and russet stripes, wearing tall plumes and brandishing sharp pikes—an outfit that, as worn today in the Vatican, is the oldest European military uniform extant. Henry appeared with archers in white-and-green liveries and the Yeomen of the Guard in gold and red with the emblem of the Tudors, a crowned

Below: Catherine de' Medici's water fete at Bayonne. Guests voyaged on a boat built to resemble a castle, past a mock whale attack, a tortoise bearing six musicians dressed as tritons, and Neptune in a car drawn by sea horses, to an island where they were awaited by dancing shepherds and shepherdesses, singing nymphs and a feast. According to Marguerite de Valois, depicted on the left with Charles II and Henri of Navarre, the beautiful ballet "so angered envious Fortune that a violent storm arose . . . the confusion in getting back by boat that night caused as much fun the next morning as had the festivity itself." Fetes de Catherine de' Medici. Valois tapestries. c. 1580.

rose, stitched to their breasts—today the second oldest uniform in the West, which, with the addition of an Elizabethan ruff, is still worn in England by "Beefeaters," the "Yeoman Warders" originally given their uniform by Henry VIII.

Both monarchs flaunted beards; Henry's was admired for its russet lushness. François' gave him an imperiously Mephistophelean air. Each had vowed to the other that he would not shave until the climactic day of fraternal meeting—a prospect, then, of many months. Catherine of Aragon soon expressed displeasure with her lord's cinnamon stubble— loudly, one presumes, for he quickly shaved it off. Diplomatic crises, courtly uproar, unhappy

days. What could this shaving mean? An affront, perhaps? No, now it was growing back. Gusts of diplomatic relief, serenity of princes. Later in life Henry's grudging respect for François' sense of style led him variously to copy Chambord and to crop his hair. The masculine craze for shorter hair was the result of an accident. It all began with François storming the house of the Count of Montgomery in a snowball fight; in retaliation, a torch was playfully thrown, striking the king on the head. Treatment of the wound necessitated clipping François' locks; tactful courtiers followed suit. In turn, Henry pondered the new style and finally decided to have his own head "polled"; in 1535 he commanded all his courtiers to do the same.

And so it followed for day upon night, this rondo of ostentation and outwardly gracious rivalry. In the end nothing was gained, despite the princely gifts, fraternal embraces, and sisterly kisses. The practiced eye of the Venetians pierced the gilded sham: "These sovereigns are not at peace. They adapt themselves to circumstances, but they hate each other cordially." While nothing had been gained, much had been lost. In England, nobles had been ordered by royal decree to have apparel created for the outing "as to your degree of honor to us and this our reame [realm] it apperteineth." The result was that, according to Du Bellay, the French ambassador, the Field of the Cloth of Gold destroyed more noble fortunes than any field of battle; "the great outlay that was made cannot be estimated; but many carried their mills, their forests, and their meadows on their backs."

It was still the universal belief that men had been put by God under princes, and in this not even Luther disagreed. But to bolster his position, a prince felt increasingly impelled to present a magnificent "public image," both to impress his power on his rivals and to set an example of grandeur for his own subjects. As in feudal times, the hierarchy must be visible, imposing itself on the people through symbols and ceremonies. Thus evolved the phenomenon described by a modern historian as the "politics of spectacle," typified by the Field of Cloth of Gold.

"palace" and wine-spouting fountain of the English, two of the wonders of the event. Since neither the castle nor "palace" could house the multitude, both the English and French pitched massed groups of tents (the English alone brought no less than 820), seen in the background. Despite such gargantuan preparations, it was reported that so many gathered that "both knightes and ladies that were come to see the noblenes were fayne to lye in hay and straw, and held theim thereof highly pleased." c. 1520.

The Court of Henry III

At the court of France in the late 16th century, Henri III was king, masque, and festival all in his own person. He was the most peculiar of the sons of Catherine de' Medici and of Henri II, a huge melancholic man who adopted the ruff to hide a scar on his neck, a disguise immediately copied by his courtiers.

Henri III was not the first of Catherine de' Medici's sons to sit on the throne of France, but he was the first monarch of France to appear before the Estates General in an outfit reputedly trimmed with six thousand yards of lace edging. Henri III was also the first important European ruler since the Roman Heliogabalus to imperil his reign by an effeminate appearance. He surrounded himself with "mignons" —his favorites, his "Darlings"—young men rouged, perfumed, and frizzed but also physically tough and courageous. The verse of one Protestant pamphleteer, wisely anonymous since the vengeance of the Darlings was never to be taken lightly, describes the "virtues and characteristics" of "Les Mignons":

Their speech and their attire
Are such that an honest woman
Would fear to be censured
For clothing so lascivious;
It is hard for them to turn their necks
In the long pleats of their ruffs,
White flour is not good enough
For the stiffening of their shirts;
To attain style more exquisite
They must have rice for starch

Their pates are clipped by compass
But not the same all over
For in front it is long
Over the ears, and in the back comes low.
It is held in place by artifice
For it is kept flat with gum
Or twisted into curls
And over their frivolous heads
A cap worn towards the back
Disguises them even further.

The verse goes on to suggest that the Darlings practice "the art of unchaste Gunnymede," paint themselves with makeup, and wear clothes far beyond their means. The cap to which the pamphleteer refers was a memento of Henri III's brief reign in Cracow as King of Poland, where his drunken courtiers tried to wed him to their forty-year-old princess. Upon the death of his brother, Charles X, Henri escaped, taking with him nothing but the Polish toque, which, with the addition of feathers and jeweled clips, he continued to wear over his thinning hair. By turns sensual and hysterically religious, he enjoyed the processions of flagellants, donning, for these occasions, a necklace of miniature skulls. At certain private gatherings he

dressed as a woman. On his flight from Poland he paused in Venice, where he was greeted with magnificence and went on a shopping spree for perfumes, lace handkerchiefs, jewels, colored breeches, and other extravagant clothes. Back in Paris, he remained a mystery not only to most of his subjects but even to the usually perceptive Venetians. "He has a noble enough bearing," writes one ambassador, "and the most beautiful hands of any other man in France," but everything about him

Joyeuse, poses at center with his bride. Whether as a direct result of Henri III's ambiguous sexuality or not, the clothes of the nobility, aside from the ladies' full skirts, have grown similar in their fluted ruff and swollen leg of mutton sleeve contours and precious little feather-trimmed hats. Even the men's pointed beards are mirrored in the deep V-shaped bodices worn by the women. School of Clouet. c. 1581. Detail.

seemed contradictory: his solemn manners, his shrill hysterics, his erratic affability, and—one could not help but return to the subject—his disturbingly equivocal dress. The ambassador continued: "In addition to the superb costumes ornamented with gold, gems, and pearls which he wears, he indulges in great luxury in the matter of his shirts and caps; on his neck he wears a double necklace of gold and ambergris, which gives out a most pleasant smell. But what in my opinion takes away much of his gravity is having his ears pierced in the way of a woman. Not content with wearing a single circlet in each ear, he has to have two, with pendants enriched with precious stones and pearls." In this not even a Dominican, Giordano Bruno, was able to set matters aright. Appointed by Henri III as His Majesty's Reader Extraordinary, the friar failed miserably in his attempts to exorcise the "Beast Triumphant of the vices from a royal heart tainted by bad education in a corrupt court."

115

Luther and Calvin

The possibility that infatuation with bright colored clothes, foreign fashions, glittering ornaments, and other similar frivolities could place one not only in earthly but posthumous peril had been pointed out to the Italians with some regularity over a period of several centuries. (St. Francis, after all, was the son of a wealthy merchant, and his exemplary renunciation of worldly goods began with his own dandified dress.) The monk Savonarola, Florence's splenetic 15th-century reformer, was by no means the first to organize bonfires of "vanities," although he set flame to an impressive quantity of masterpieces of Renaissance art and craftsmanship. Such was Savonarola's influence that a distraught and penitent Botticelli himself threw his paintings onto Savonarola's ornate slag heap of cosmetic pots, looking glasses, dice, masks, amulets, phials of perfume, songbooks, lutes, masses of false blond hair, and other loathsome devices of the devil. Before long Savonarola, rabid enemy of the Borgia and the Medici, was himself sacrificed in the same public square but not before predicting that the Church would be punished and renewed and that this Reformation "would happen soon."

Across the continent, the dress of the clergy on the whole had reached an enchanting degree of symbolic nitpicking and labored refinement. Certainly the disproportionate attention paid by some religious orders to outward appearance contributed heavily to the wrath of the Reformation. Erasmus, whose dream it was to see Europe governed by an educated, enlightened elite, its members elected solely on the basis of individual merit, threw up his hands in disgust at such orders:

> In church they bray like donkeys and from door to door they bellow for bread, to the loss of all other beggars, while their chief interest lies in being unlike each other, rather than striving to be like Christ. . . . But nothing could be more amusing than their practice of doing everything to rule, as if they were following mathematical calculations which it would be a sin to ignore. They work out the number of knots for a shoe-string, the colour of a girdle, the variations in colour of a

habit, the material and width to a hair's breadth of a girdle, the shape and capacity (in sacksful) of a cowl, the breadth (in fingers) of a tonsure, the number of hours prescribed for sleep. . . . These trivialities not only make them feel superior to other men but also contemptuous of each other, and these professors of apostolic charity will create extraordinary scenes and disturbances on account of a habit with a different girdle or one which is rather too dark in colour. Some you'll see are so strict in their observances that they will wear an outer garment which has to be made of Sicilian goat's hair and one of Milesian wool next to the skin, while others have linen on top and wool underneath. There are others again who shrink from the touch of money as if it were a deadly poison, but who are less restrained when it comes to contact with wine or women.

The absurd splitting of tonsure hairs was of less concern to Brother Martin Luther at this time than the Church's truly intolerable abuses, particularly the sale of papal indulgences or, more bluntly, the absolution of sins in exchange for cold cash. Echoing the cry of Savonarola, Luther in 1517 dared to hammer his theses against indulgences to the door of the Church of Wittenberg, an act that was to mark the end of a spiritually united Christendom.

Luther cloaked himself in the *Schaube*, a cassock-like overcoat owned by every prosperous German, often fur-lined and sleeveless. (If it did possess sleeves, they hung atrophied behind the sleeves of whatever garment was worn beneath it.) Luther's sanction of the *Schaube* ordained it the garb of Lutheran clergymen until the present day.

In France the Venetian ambassador noted the growing influence of Calvin, who, as principal minister of Geneva, maintained an active correspondence all over the kingdom and to whom incalculable sums of money were sent secretly by followers of his learned writings. Guerrilla forces of Protestant preachers were trained in Geneva before infiltrating French parishes, where, according to one dismayed priest, the hierarchy of the Catholic Church either resided at the court of the king or in the large cities, taking more delight in luxurious living than in relaying the true word of God to the parishioners. "This indifference," he complains, "gave the Lutheran heretics the occasion to speak evil of the Church of Jesus Christ and to lead Christians astray." The Field of the Cloth of Gold was the final regal flourish in the history of Christendom undivided. Now with self-mutilating fury, religious wars would tear Europe apart for more than one hundred and fifty years, draining the material reservoirs that had been filled by Renaissance commerce. As has been remarked by the British historian Hawkes, when pestilence and famine were ceasing to be necessities imposed by nature, the rulers of Europe, secular and ecclesiastical alike, reestablished them by political art.

Opposite left: Martin Luther in clothes fitting the solemnity of his earthly task. Portrait by Lucas Cranach the Elder. 1539. Opposite right: Portrait of Savonarola, Florence's splenetic reformer. By Fra Bartolommeo, 1514–17. Detail.

Below: Two daughters of Philip II of Spain, a glacial public figure but doting father. It was said that duty rather than blood ran through his veins. From his father, the Holy Roman Emperor, Charles V, Philip had inherited a vast empire, as well as a holy mission, and from these he never turned. Charles V, the "mightiest ruler since the Romans," had been the least exhibitionistic of monarchs. Upon the death of his wife, he adopted the black dress of mourning for the rest of his life, setting a somber precedent for the future of fashion throughout his empire. His son, Philip II, also dressed in this gloomily stark "Spanish habit." By Sanchez Coello.

Spain: Grandees and Heretics

While the Reformation and the court masques vied for the attention of northern Europe, in Spain the groans of the dying climaxed the Inquisition's relentless pageant of death, the auto-da-fé, or "act of faith." The burning of heretics in sulphurous yellow penitential dress celebrated, to the satisfaction of crowds of orderly fanatics, the triumph of the Catholic Church over forces of darkness. This performance was considered the choicest of spectacles at royal weddings and christenings.

Black-garbed Philip II of Spain loved his children dearly, and to amuse them he wrote letters telling about such trivia as the health of an alcoholic court dwarf, an elephant soon to arrive from India, and his presentation of the Order of the Fleece to the Duke of Braganza: "He helped me at Mass and we

HISPANISSCHE

both wore the Collar—mine was more elegant. . . . For the first time he had bootees on, which almost everyone here except myself is wearing." The king also ordered a growing daughter to be measured in silk ribbon and thread, casually adding that he and his nephew had yesterday attended an *auto:* "We watched it from a window and heard every thing very well. . . . First of all there was a sermon, as is customary. We stayed for the pronouncements of the sentences. Then we withdrew because they needed the house we were in for the civil power to condemn to the fire all those whom the inquisitor had handed over. It was eight o'clock when we arrived and we didn't dine till one. May God keep you as I pray He will, Your good father."

The *auto* was actually a religious ceremony preceding the human holocaust, a mass declaration of faith at which officialdom sat enthroned in boxes as if at the theater. Not since the heyday of Byzantium had Europe seen such observance of protocol as paralyzed Renaissance Spain. An obsession with orders of precedence, distinctions of title, and the position of each rank in a church pew or the tier of a grandstand clutched the Spanish in the same stranglehold as their religion. Obsequious servants scurried ahead of their masters to measure the height of a dais or bench so as not to imperil a hidalgo's dignity. An iron code of honor backed by etiquette, rampant superstition and bigotry burned into the Spanish soul, a chiaroscuro of passions. Like watchful spiders in a web of deadly lace, the spectators waited with patience for their victims. Pale and

immobile as moonlit effigies, stony as their sheepshorn plains, they waited, heads erect, as if to catch the shrieks of agony in the blackness of the Inquisitor's cell.

Not only the living were set afire for their crimes but also the dead and buried. To complete the grisly pageants, putrid corpses were torn from their graves and borne aloft along with the condemned themselves, exhumed bodies of suspected heretics, and painted effigies of fugitives, dressed alike in a travesty of a monk's robe, a yellow sack called the "San Benito," a corruption of "saco bendito," a name given before the 13th century to a penitent's dress. Upon the head of each—the quick, the dead, the hideous dolls—was jammed a yellow pasteboard parody of the bishop's miter decorated, as was the rough knee-length woolen sack, with red figures of devils, dancing flames, and other infernal symbols. These, if the condemned man were versed in the diabolic heraldry of the Holy Office, might reveal to him his final destination, purgatory or hell. Finally, as at the launching of a ship today, an honored guest would be singled out graciously to set a torch to bright paper, bone, and living flesh.

Having confined their intellects to the constraints of the Counter-Reformation, the Spanish now submitted their bodies to the constraints of the tailor. In their formalized garb of black and white, aristocrats resembled nothing so much as a morbidly elegant religious order, which in fact they were.

Essentially, the components of the widely adopted Spanish styles were these: for men, shorter, dis-

INQVISITION

tended "trunk-hose" from which by 1575 the cod-piece had virtually disappeared; the tight doublet, which had grown a skirt and was padded in front; stuffed epaulettes or shoulder wings ringing the armhole; squeezed waists; higher and narrower shoes (Philip II's "bootees"?); a stiff, high-crowned, scant-brimmed hat; and relatively wrinkle-free, knitted silk stockings, which replaced the customary cut-and-seamed leg covering. Swollen sleeves worn by both sexes as well as all other padding was achieved with bombast, a stuffing composed of animal hair, rags, or even bran (the least desirable since it had an embarrassing tendency to leak).

For women, a skirt supported by a farthingale—constructed of felt, horsehair, and, later, metal hoops—and a stiff corset emphasizing a long pointed waist transformed the upper torso into an inverted cone balanced on the tip of a pyramidal skirt. The darkness of the clothes of both sexes served, like the velvety void of a jeweler's case, to set off the nobles' fortunes in baubles, buttons, and other ornaments of silver and gold. Gloves came into their own. Charles V had a pair of pearl-encrusted cloth-of-gold gloves for court occasions, but for every-day wear the Spanish preferred supple, tightly fitting kid, perfumed with lavender or musk. As a status symbol, however, no other article of apparel could compete with the immobilizing Spanish ruff worn like a frothy, fallen halo to deify those who did not work.

The origins of the ruff, according to some scholars, may be traced back to India and Ceylon, where wide collars stiffened with rice water were worn by the natives to protect their clothes from long oily tresses—a kind of Oriental forerunner of the anti-macassar. In any case, the ruff was incorporated into the Spanish costume to the loud applause of all the courts of Europe. Its evolution most prob-ably began with the frilled edge produced by a drawstring at the neckline of the Renaissance shirt. Abruptly, in the dry Spanish soil, this frill began to blossom into such a giant bloom that inevitably it parted from its padded stem. Special hot irons were soon devised to create the delicate fluting, which was propped up with wire or pasteboard and starched into rigidity. Together with the padded dark parabolas of Spanish court dress, the ruff, in its ultimate pale and immobilizing state, gave its wear-ers a look as abstractly black and white as their spiritual codes.

Spanish dress did not remain at home. The in-fluence of Spain spread over much of Europe in the person of Emperor Charles V and his successor. As Italian society disintegrated it infected Italy, inspiring the bitter poetry of Campanella, tortured seven times for defending Galileo.

> Black robes befit our age. Once they were white;
> Next many-hued; now dark as Afric's Moor,
> Night-black, infernal, traitorous, obscure,
> Horrid with ignorance and sick with fright.
> For very shame we shun all colors bright,
> Who mourn our end—the tyrants we endure,
> The chains, the noose, the lead, the snares, the
>   lure—
> Our dismal heroes, our souls sunk in the night.

Opposite: 16th-century en-graving of an auto-da-fé. Effigies of heretics who had escaped and the bones of those who had died accom-pany the condemned to the stake. Dressed in a travesty of a bishop's miter and a painted woolen sack, each heretic is flanked by two men urging him to repent, as spectators await the grand finale. Above: Philip II of Spain in the characteristic black and white "Spanish habit." By Sanchez Coello.

119

At the Court of the Faerie Queene

The Spanish ruff came to its finest flowering in the court of one of Spain's most virulent enemies, the English "Faerie Queene" Elizabeth, a virgin goddess whose official artists were pleased to portray her not so much in human attire as in that of a mythical moth monarch; hovering in pearly painted suspension, gold-embroidered wings against the skies, it is Elizabeth I who still occupies the high throne of artifice in the pantheon of illustrated fashion.

"You may well have a greater prince," the queen announced to her subjects upon the defeat of the Spanish Armada, "but you shall never have a more loving one." Nor, she might have added, one more conspicuously regal. Like her father, Henry VIII, Elizabeth loved jewels and clothes and pompous display; in fact, they shared an almost childish passion for dressing up. In Henry's case this weak-

ness extended to antic masquerades, elaborate practical jokes for which he would disguise himself as Robin Hood and his intimates as the Merry Men and pounce from doorways on poor Catherine of Aragon and her squealing ladies.

With the passage of years the passion for dressing up became a mania for Elizabeth, the roots of which doubtless reached into the chill soil of her childhood. Elizabeth had suffered personal privation and terrors of imminent death constantly throughout her formative years despite the efforts of Mary Tudor, her sister, to protect her. That this gesture met with failure is revealed in a plea from the royal governess to Lord Thomas Cromwell that the three-and-a-half-year-old child Elizabeth should have some raiment, for "she hath neither gown, nor kirtall [underdress], nor petticoat, nor no manner of linnen, nor forsmocks [pinafores], nor kerchief, nor rails [nightgowns], nor mofelers [mob-caps], nor biggins [nightcaps]."

On the surface, this would appear an inauspicious period of incubation for one of history's most ornate figures of fashion. But on closer scrutiny of Elizabeth's sartorial progress we can see how childhood deprivation can produce in adult life a paradox—the prodigal miser, a neurotic driven to simultaneously squander and hoard. Thus at one point Elizabeth had accumulated more than three thousand

dresses, eighty wigs, and a dragon's cache of jewels.

Following the death of Mary, Elizabeth acceded to the throne at the age of twenty-five. Her coronation was celebrated in January 1559, and the ubiquitous Venetian ambassadors were moved to hyperbole: "The court so sparkled with jewels and gold collars that they cleared the air, though it snowed a little." Beneath triumphal arches Elizabeth passed in an open litter trimmed to the ground in gold brocade, surrounded by multitudes of officials and servitors clad in the new queen's liveries of scarlet damask. Bedecked like an idol in ermine and cloth of gold, with limp strands of lion-red hair cascading over her shoulders, Elizabeth paused to allow old ladies to press nosegays of winter rosemary into the smooth tapering hands of which she was so proud. Like Henry VIII before her, Elizabeth would be the sole arbiter of fashion in her kingdom. A one-woman pageant of contradiction, she could hoist England to unprecedented international prestige with one

hand while coyly extending the other to receive flattery's most unctuous kisses.

In the hothouse that was the court of Elizabeth, chivalry was forced to flower again; sometimes it was necessary to eke out the branches with artificial blooms. The sartorial tyranny of a domineering woman ruler, particularly one who disguised her strength behind doll dresses, could not but exert a dominant influence on the appearance of her male courtiers. In Elizabeth's circle we find two divergent physical types. One was the elegant, dashing, bearded gentleman-adventurer epitomized by Sir Walter Raleigh. The other was the tall, slender, flowerlike creature whose androgynous character is captured in a description of Lord Darnely's nodding marigold curls and long, lovely, disembodied hands "like satin gloves filled with damp sand." In boned and padded trunk hose, tight corsets, high heels, and, particularly, in the false pregnancy of the "peascod belly" (a silhouette reproduced even in dress armor), both types of men, however, tended to look like effeminate mannequins. Gone was the burly bulk of Henry VIII and the aggressive thrust of his padded codpiece. Long-legged, gartered grace replaced his bearish breadth, while at the throat and wrist appeared "triple quadruple Daedalian ruffles."

Earrings were permissible for men if worn in one pierced ear. This fashion was associated with navigators and explorers for whom it provided the safest means of transporting a valuable pearl or stone picked up on one's travels. A gentleman wore collars either so high and sharp that, like Dudley's, they could "cut his throat by sunlight," or lace-trimmed "falling bands," predecessors of today's soft shirt collar. Leg-of-mutton sleeves, padded to plumpness, were often richly embroidered, as were gauntlet gloves and the short cloak, which

now must be slung insouciantly over one shoulder. For a man of fashion, three cloaks were now desirable: one for morning, one for afternoon, and one for evening. It is a commentary on the times that Sir Walter Raleigh is more commonly remembered for spreading his cloak across a puddle than for his pivotal role in settling the New World. Incidentally, his cloak, if the anecdote is not totally apocryphal, was probably made of leather, hence salvageable. Like his beard, it would be highly perfumed.

Two further commentaries help sum up the increasing importance of a gentleman's toilette during the Elizabethan period. One, made by a chronicler during Her Majesty's reign, claims that forty years before, one could count no more than twelve haberdashers selling "fancy caps, sashes, swords, daggers, girdles; now, from the tower to Westminster, every street is full of them and their shops glitter and shine of glass." In the second, Shakespeare's Touchstone mordantly tabulates the qualifications for a courtier: "I have had a measure; I have flattered a lady; I have been politic with my friend, smooth with mine enemy; I have undone three tailors; I have had four quarrels and like to have fought one."

The ruff of court ladies, according to Stubbes in one of the passages in his puritanical antifashion journal, *The Anatomie of Abuses*, were "speckled and sparkling heer and there with the sunne, the moone, the starres and manye other antiquities

Under the dynamic domination of a self-enshrined virgin, Elizabeth's male subjects, at least in their dress, assumed two basic fashionable types—the elegant, dashing, bearded gentleman-adventurer à la Walter Raleigh and the languorous, slender, flowerlike figure epitomized by the adult Lord Darnley.
Opposite left: Portrait of Raleigh in lace-edged "Daedalian ruffles."
Opposite right: The future Henri III, androgynous king of France, who was forced to be a suitor to the aging Elizabeth.

Below left: The young Lord Darnley with his little brother. Detail of a painting by Hans Eworth. 1563.
Below right: Sir Philip Sidney, cropped and shaved, wearing the pregnant "peascod belly" armor. The debonair poet opposed puritanism with his Defense of Poesie *and was considered an ideal courtier.*

strange to behold." Starch, which filled him with disgust, came in a variety of colors; the favored three were white, a pale blue derived from rice powder, and a sunny yellow, the last the alleged invention of a certain Miss Turner. Her discovery enjoyed a tremendous vogue until the unfortunate woman was beheaded for poisoning a lord. Chic to the bitter finale, Miss Turner insisted on wearing her stylish innovation to the block, an excess which led other ladies of fashion to abandon the shade forever.

The court of Elizabeth introduced the "Tudor ruff," which fetchingly modified the Spanish, John-the-Baptist's-head-on-a-salver model by amputating much of its frontage to reveal the upper bosom. Along with this fashion the queen favored wide, wired-veil headdresses, frizzled real and false hair intertwined over wire frames, feather-tipped fans (until the introduction, via Italy, of the Chinese pleated fan), the wheel farthingale (later transformed into the "bum-roll," a sausagelike bolster tied around the hips beneath the skirt), iron-hinged corsets (later abandoned for flexible steel and rigid boned fabric), and embroidered high heels. Probably her most lasting contribution to fashion were long multiple strands of knotted pearls.

Unlike Bloody Mary, Elizabeth preferred women for close attendants. As decor for the queen bee, pretty young maids of honor were chosen with care,

usually from the Boleyn side of the family, and were made to swear an oath of service. But they must never outshine their mistress. Sir John Harington, the queen's godson, reports a disquieting scene in which the young Lady Mary Howard, to the envy of everyone and to her own great pleasure, flounced into Elizabeth's private apartments wearing a superb velvet dress powdered with pearls and gold: "Nor did it please the Queen, who thought it exceeded her own. One day the Queen did send privately and got the lady's rich vesture, which she put on herself and came forth the Chamber among the ladies. The kirtle and border were far too short for her suit. At length she asked the owner herself if it was not made too short and ill-becoming? Which the poor lady did presently [instantly] consent to. 'Why then,' the Queen observed icily, concluding the matter once and for all, 'if it become not me as being too short, I am minded it shall never become thee as being too fine: so it fitteth neither well.' "

At many great country houses the "progresses" of the queen and her entourage were as welcome as a visitation from assassins. The expense and worry

could ruin a man. Feasts, dancing (the Queen loved to dance), cannonades, and fireworks—all the allegorical diversions were observed to the limits of a family's resources. There must be new dresses for the lady to attract Her Majesty's attention, farthingales of stuffs—mackarelle, pomette, perpetuana, or grosgrain of hair or silk, mockado (a mock velvet) and, as Dame Edith Sitwell writes, "silks and satins falling like waterfalls, dripping like thick cream, drifting like the summer airs."

The names of colors, too, cling to ghosts in vanished gardens: popinjay blue, gingerline, mulberry and lustie gallant (a light red), pease porridge, Catherine pear and French russet (the bronze-violet of burning paper). Breaking the spell, we learn of gooseturd green and "couleur Isabelle," the dirty ecru white of the Spanish queen's petticoats, which, she had sworn rashly never to change until the Moors had been driven from her realm.

Embroidered flowers and animals began to bloom on Elizabethan clothes, not the stylized repetitions of Eastern designs but the fresh and natural flora and fauna beloved by the English. The importation of the steel needle, probably from India, and the Protestants' condemnation of elaborate altar cloths and other "Papist" embellishments freed ladies of

Above left: The farthingale, which needed piles of cushions to accommodate it. On the right, a woman attaches bolsters to the waist and hips to pad her silhouette. Caricature by an anonymous Dutch engraver of the early 17th century. Detail.
Above right: Lady Raleigh. Raleigh fell precipitously from

favor in 1592 when compelled by the queen to marry Elizabeth Throckmorton, one of Elizabeth's royal maids of honor, with whom he had been conducting an affair. Detail of a portrait by Gheeraerts. c. 1588.

Opposite: With age, Elizabeth abandoned the décolleté "Tudor ruff" for a throat-concealing round ruff. Portrait by Federigo Zuccaro.

Spenser, the author of The Faerie Queene, believed that "soul is form and doth the body make". Certainly this was true of Elizabeth I; she projected her soul through her body and into the extraordinary carapace of her clothes. To house the profusion of Her Majesty's wardrobe, suites of "clothes rooms" were required to accommodate elaborate dresses hung on wooden pegs, rather than folded away in traditional chests, a practice that anticipated the modern closet.

leisure to wander at will among bright new decorative motifs. Woolen "crewel" work evolved from the gaily printed fabrics that the English East India Company began to ship after 1600.

Elizabeth, like Catherine of Aragon and Mary Queen of Scots, loved needlework, just as she loved to play the lute, to annotate books in Latin, to converse flawlessly with ambassadors in their native tongues, and, especially, to dance. Later, to hold death at bay, the aged queen danced, leaped high in a narrow room to the accompaniment of a single pipe and a single drum, watched with dread by her faithful ladies-in-waiting. In a terrible dream she had seen herself engulfed in hell-like flames. An omen, it must be an omen! Bewigged in scalding red, the queen, from whose palaces mirrors, like fallen favorites, had been banished for twenty years, now called for a *true* mirror, not the opaque sham her conspirators in self-deception held up to her with noncommittal faces. With rage, she stared into unfamiliar eyes, embers in shadowy caves, but embers still fierce enough to melt the waxen skull from which they glared. Howls and curses. Damn the flatterers. Damn the smirking hypocrites. And still she refused to die, refused to go to bed. In a stupor she dragged herself around in restless circles. She would not change her clothes; she would not even sleep but propped her wasted body on cushions stacked about in piles for the accommodation of farthingales. Toward the very end, forced into bed, she whispered, "All my possessions for one moment of time."

Below: The Procession of the Queen to Blackfriars supported by knights wearing the Order of the Garter. By an unknown artist. c. 1600.
Left: A posthumous allegorical portrait of Elizabeth plagued by Time and Death.

The 17th Century:

Reformers, Burghers, and *Bons Vivants*

At first glance, the proscenium of 17th-century fashion is seen to shelter four distinct, broadly drawn stereotypes whose social incongruity begs for the satiric assaults of a Jonson or Molière. Accompanied by their female partners, the *dramatis personae* include the swaggering, amorous Cavalier; the grim and sexless Puritan; the complacent Bourgeois; and the vainglorious Baroque Courtier. But a stereotype by definition needs a prototype—an original model from which it can be reproduced. In turn, a social prototype and its visible insignia, dress, are achieved only through the survival of intensely felt beliefs.

Social attitudes of the 16th century were too often characterized by religious intolerance. Under the banners of religion, savage battles were fought, economies shattered, and atrocities performed. Queen Elizabeth of England, in the wake of her Catholic sister Mary's bloodbaths, restored relative Protestant peace to her country while avoiding the extremes that befell Scotland, where Knox inflicted the glacial codes of Calvinism. (In Geneva, the seat of Calvin's reign of spiritual terror, a child was beheaded for striking his father, bridesmaids were arrested for garnishing a bride too festively, and people were whipped for dancing.) With her usual genius for diplomacy, Elizabeth reached agreements with English Puritans on all major issues but one—the matter of dress. The question of what the clergy should or should not wear grew into an irreconcilable issue. For years the queen would insist that they retain the vestments and cap worn at the time of the Reformation, and with equal adamance the clergy would refuse. In the end, rather than conform to Her Majesty's obstinate theories on appropriate ecclesiastical costume, many pastors preferred to sacrifice their livelihoods.

At the court of the Valois the conciliatory gesture was an implement too bothersome to wield. In fact, it was Catherine herself, with her black clothes and pasta-colored face ("that abbess' mask," wrote Balzac, "wan yet full of depth"), who may have helped initiate the horrendous St. Bartholomew's Day Massacre of Huguenots. The religious conversion and the reign in France of Henri IV, her son-in-law, who had been a Protestant, served to undo much of the Valois–de' Medici internal damage to the nation. Constantly on the move, Henri kept in touch with his people and was sensitive to their needs and moods. With the Edict of Nantes, he gave freedom of worship and civil privileges to the Huguenots, among whom were many skilled

Below: "An earthly kingdom," declared Martin Luther, "cannot exist without inequality of persons. Some must be free, others serfs; some rulers, others subjects." In the eyes of this wedding party, visible prosperity is akin to godliness. A Wedding Celebration by Wolfgang Heimbach, detail. 1637.

weavers. The disruption of the textile industry and the dispersal of its skilled craftsmen, a recurrent aspect of European religious conflict, would continue through the Thirty Years War.

Henri IV's eccentric minister, the Protestant Sully shored up the country's sagging finances. For each Sunday dinner Henri's subjects were promised "a chicken in every pot," a gratifying prospect after the famines brought on by religious strife during which recipes were circulated for the most palatable preparation of leather jerkins and aprons, belts, and animal skins ("soak, scrape, boil, then fricasee like tripe or infuse with herbs and spices as a *ragoût*"). Importation of luxuries into France was now forbidden on pain of hanging. Foreign silks quickly disappeared from the wardrobes of the bourgeoisie, who were obliged to wear wool as a substitute. Courtiers stubbornly clung to silk clothing, but as a concession they subdued their sumptuousness by flaunting less gold and silver thread. Peasants were pleased by the encouragement of mulberry production, which in turn stimulated the silk industries at Lyons and Tours. The expensive finished stuffs, along with exquisite tapestries loomed in the Louvre's state workshops, were exported, teasing American gold from the pockets of spendthrift Spain. Spain's lower classes were also avid consumers of cheap French-made fans, artificial pearls, pins, and other gewgaws hawked in the streets.

Sully, born into the peasant class, was such a devout Protestant that he labored long hours beneath a portrait not of the king but of Calvin. To Sully's peasant distrust of the unfamiliar has been attributed the failure of France to grasp more fully the economic potential of the New World. In 1605, at the behest of the Rouen Company, a corporation exclusively interested in the fur trade, Samuel de Champlain established a base in Nova Scotia; in 1608 the company paid for the colonization of Quebec. Sully, hearing that these uncharted territories held no immediate promise of gold, dismissed the enterprise as singularly unpromising. As a result, by 1620 the residential population of Quebec had yet to surpass sixty persons. At the same time the canny Dutch, for a handful of dollars, glass beads, and bright cloth, had set up trading posts for furs at the mouth of the Hudson River on Manhattan Island.

Historically, the unstable health of the fur trade, has always reflected the relative prosperity of a Northern consumer society. Having depleted their own forests, the Europeans' craving for furs led directly to the penetration of the North American wilderness and increased trade with Russia. Russia was forced to push deeper and deeper into the unexplored vastness of Siberia in search of pelts.

Fur, in the lexicon of apparel, falls into two categories: "fancy" and "staple." The first is self-explanatory and includes sable, ermine, and mink. For countless centuries sables have been to animal

Top: Henry IV's minister, the Protestant Sully, ascetically cropped, in a chastely simple and clean white collar. Puritanical Protestants were taught to fear dirt as much as nudity.
Center: Choosing wolf pelts in a fur shop. 17th-century engraving.
Right: 17th-century Canadian on snowshoes on a fur hunt in the wilds. Engraving.

Left: Touché! *Almost any trifle could outrage honor, particularly the slighting of one's tastes, which, according to La Rochefoucauld, was less tolerable than the criticism of one's opinions. Engraving by Diedsrich Porath from the folio* Palaestra Suecena, 1693.

pelts what silk and gold have been to cloth and metal. They made impressive regal gifts. At the court of Queen Elizabeth of England the Spanish ambassador tried to pry information from the Lord Chamberlain with a bribe not only of a yearly pension but with the added lure of one valuable sable coat per annum. England's first purchase of Russian sables had been transacted by the navigator Chancellor, who "discovered" Russia while seeking a northward passage to Cathay. Edward VI was delighted, as was his immediate successor, Mary, who granted a special charter to the Company of Merchant Adventurers as added incentive to trade with Russia. In addition to sable, mink, ermine, fox, beaver, and seal, the Russians dealt in hemp, honey, flax, wax, salt, and oil; from the English, in return, they purchased large lots of wool.

The most sought-after "staple" fur in the 17th-century was beaver, used in the production of felt hats (to the point where "beaver" became the accepted slang term for "hat"). In the previous century the fashion for felt hats of fine Spanish wool had spread through the North. With the windfall of American gold, the Spanish found they could charge whatever sum they pleased for their exports. The consequent astronomic leap in prices forced disgruntled foreign customers to search elsewhere for new sources of felt. The mass slaughter of many North American animals for their fur was not limited to the beaver craze. Between 1699 and 1715 an average of 54,000 deerskins (160,000 in one peak year) were sent annually to England from South Carolina alone.

Despite his lack of colonial vision, at home in France the bureaucratic zealotry of Sully, a born accountant, helped to create some semblance of fiscal order out of chaos. To the rude snorts of the old landholding knightly class, bureaucracy itself was now elevated to a form of nobility with Henry IV's creation of the *Noblesse de la Robe,* a legal class named for its magisterial robes. To become a noble of the robe, a member of the *parlements* had only to pay a stiff tax.

At the turn of the century the possible extinction of the *noblesse d'épée,* the old nobility, was forecast not as a result of middle-class ambition but in the statistical light of their brutish duels. Much in the spirit of *The Three Musketeers,* these encounters tended to degenerate into microcosmic pitched battles, with the duelists' seconds heatedly joining the fray. During 1607 at least four thousand members of what might be termed the officer class were hacked to death in duels. In his compelling biography of Henri IV, Desmond Seward evokes the volatile ferocity of the *noblesse d'épée* in an account of the classic "duel of the hat" fought by Messieurs Bazanez and Lagarde Vallon:

> The former having sent the latter a fine hat and dared him to wear it, Lagarde Vallon donned it immediately, rushed out and, after finding Bazanez and giving him the lie, slashed his skull open with a broadsword before running him through and through, shouting each time "for the tassel!" "for the plumes!" Though weakened from loss of blood Bazanez suddenly rallied to cut his opponent down and then stab him fourteen times with a poignard as he lay on the ground while Lagarde Vallon managed to crack his skull with his sword pommel and bite off half his chin. At last they fainted but, amazingly, both survived, Lagarde Vallon continuing to challenge enemies with such insults as, "I have made ashes of your house, raped your wife, and hanged your children, and am at your service."

Had it not been for the ceaseless nagging of Sully, Henri IV would have continued benignly to ignore the scenes of carnage rather than sign the Edict of Blois, in which duelists were threatened with the death penalty.

The Cavalier Kings

In the short, knotty person of Henri IV we find embodied all the quintessential qualities of the 17th-century cavalier—courage, dash, swagger, honor, humor, amorous sentimentality, and unabashed carnality; in brief, as the quintessential cavalier, he managed to be at the same time both a man's and a lady's man. As was later the case of Napoleon, the chapters of his eventful life can be listed under the subheadings of significant changes in dress.

At his birth Henri's grandfather rubbed the baby's lips with garlic, flushed a swallow of old Gascon wine down his throat, and boasted, "My lamb has brought forth a lion." Hardy lion, hardy lamb. Henri's mother Jeanne d'Albret, Queen of Navarre, was a rabid Calvinist, a proud ascetic, and a pitiless enemy who, to preserve her son from the pollution of a courtly upbringing, had him raised by peasants on the craggy Gascon slopes. Barefoot and dressed in rough, shapeless peasant clothes, he was allowed to run wild through the countryside with the peasants' children, eat robust peasant foods, and speak the robust peasant dialect. The aroma of this earthy childhood marinade would never completely leave him. But the boy must have been adept at mimicry, at least of aristocratic manners. From Bordeaux a magistrate writes to the Duke de Nevers that Henri, now age thirteen, is a pretty youth, in appearance more like a boy of nineteen, who enters into conversation "like a polished gentleman." Already the ladies are attracted to his reddish hair, worn comparatively short and brushed upward from his face, brown skin, and expression of "uncommon vivacity."

A marriage between Henri de Navarre and Marguerite de Valois, daughter of Henri II and Catherine de' Medici, had long been contemplated by their parents. By the time the couple reached their late teens, both their mothers had been left widows—formidable widows—and tough opponents, one a steely Protestant heroine and the other a powerful Catholic matriarch. That her son had been invited to become the brother-in-law of Henri III, king of France, was too flattering an offer to renounce on grounds of religious scruples, although Jeanne wrote to Catherine with Calvinist rage that if she held her states and her son in her hand, she would rather throw them both into the sea than take them to Mass. And so, with well-founded forebodings, the Protestant queen journeyed to the French court to arrange the marriage. There her skepticism was amply rewarded: "Here the men do not solicit the women," she advises her son, "but the women the men. Were you here you would never escape without the great grace of God. I send you a bouquet to put in your ear, since you are for sale [i.e., his impending marriage to Marguerite] and some cockades for your hat. The men are now wearing many precious stones, but they cost as much as 100,000 ecus and they buy them every day." His betrothed, she adds, is beautiful,

Opposite above: Marguerite de Valois as a young girl. Later she would confess: "There is in us more of an appearance of sense and virtue than there is in reality." By François Clouet, 1561.

Opposite below: Jeanne d'Albret, uncharacteristically festooned with jewels, painted by François Clouet in 1570, the year of her son's momentous betrothal to Marguerite de Valois.

Left: Henri IV, first Bourbon King of France, in relentlessly amorous middle age—"aglitter with precious stones and pearls and a suit of utmost richness, dressed (so people say) as a lover."

Above: Equestrian portrait of Henri IV. French School. 17th century.

Below: Miniature portraits of the Valois, including François I, at upper right, Henri II and Catherine de' Medici, center, François II and Mary, Queen of Scots, as Dauphine, right, and Henri III in one of his notoriously flamboyant ruffs, left.

Opposite above: Gabrielle d'Estrées, the blond nymphet who turned a king into an overdressed figure of ridicule. Engraving after a painting by Pourbus the Younger.

Opposite below: Marie de' Medici and Henri IV are wed by proxy in Florence. Detail of a painting by Peter Paul Rubens, 1600.

very circumspect and graceful, but brought up in the worst possible company from which no one is free of infection. "This is why I desire you to marry and withdraw yourself and your wife from this corruption; for bad as I supposed it to be, I find it still worse than I thought."

Jeanne then addressed herself to the actual preparations for the marriage, visiting the ateliers of famous artists, choosing jewels, ornaments, and toilettes and permitting herself with uncharacteristic frivolity to be guided to Catherine's perfumer, René the Florentine, at the Pont Saint-Michel. There she purchased, among other fragrant items, a pair of scented gloves. On the following morning she was felled by frightful pains and five days later, at the age of forty-three, she died. Catherine made an expert show of weeping as Jeanne's body, clothed in silver-embroidered white satin and a mantle of royal violet velvet, was buried in a pauperlike coffin, devoid of all ornamentation, deemed proper by her austere faith. Pamphlets printed in Geneva proclaimed that the righteous queen of Navarre had been murdered by gloves poisoned by René on the express orders of the Catholic king of France and the queen mother. Probably Jeanne had succumbed to tuberculosis, but inevitably the accusation rose like a palpable wall between the two religious factions. Henri, on receiving the news, was seized by a violent fever; only his mother's confidant, Admiral Coligny, was able to persuade him to proceed to Paris, dressed in black and accompanied by an entourage of eight hundred gentlemen in deep mourning.

The wedding of the visibly unenthusiastic young couple was celebrated two months later. Marguerite has herself described her "very royal" costume complete with crown, long blue velvet mantle, and a speckled ermine *couet*, a piece of fur that wound about the figure from just below the breast to the waist. A Venetian ambassador, as usual, pressed forward to take a detailed inventory and count the carats. With the exception of the bridegroom, it was noted that all the Protestants affected sternly simple dress, while the Catholics flaunted a fortune in jewels and ostentatious clothes, their princes bedecked in "uniform coats of pale yellow satin, covered with raised embroideries and enriched with pearls and precious stones." The tight-lipped bride, whose head had to be shoved forcibly from behind to give some sign of assent in response to the ritual queries, was attended by one hundred and twenty ladies "in the most splendid stuffs."

Henri's marriage to "Margot" predated by more than a century the scandalous novel of extramarital sex by mutual consent, *Les Liaisons Dangereuses;* yet in this realm of activity it would appear that the king and queen of Navarre represented the promiscuous avant-garde. After the Peace of Nerac, the couple were able to set up a small but gay and glorious court, taken by Shakespeare as the setting

for *Love's Labour's Lost*, where, according to one account, "ease hatched vice as heat does serpents," and where the queen informed the king that "a cavalier without a mistress is without a soul."

She had not reckoned with the fair-haired Gabrielle d'Estrée (Margot, a brunette, achieved the late-Renaissance ideal only by wearing blond wigs), who, unlike herself, was able to bear the king children. Only on Gabrielle's death did she grant Henri, now king of France, a divorce so as to marry the fecund, foolish, and immensely rich Marie de' Medici.

Despite caustic criticism that the court continued to smell more of the stable than the study, Marie succeeded in reimporting Italian elegance. Henri, like his soldiers, rarely washed, and as a consequence the famous lover, the "Vert Galant," reeked

obvious relish in playing with the picturesque textures of lace, particularly when framing the face in ruffs, collars, and "falling bands." (The latter had originally been invented in the 16th century to separate the unlaunderable part of the garment from that which could be washed.) Henri IV's courtiers, both male and female, became infatuated with the luxury of lace.

At the court of Henri IV we begin to sense the blustering winds of competitive quantity in dress; a Venetian ambassador informs his readers that a man is no longer respected if he does not own at least "25 to 30 suits of different types which he changes every day." "A suit of clothes" is an expression that today we take completely for granted; in the 17th century, however, to order an outfit cut en suite, from the same cloth, was a novel concept. Separate articles of clothing of contrasting or harmonizing materials, such as detachable sleeves, had permitted the reshuffling of one's wardrobe into a mathematically expandable number of combinations. To be dressed en suite would clearly make greater demands on one's financial resources.

Henri recognized the political importance of pomp and when occasion demanded could appear either affable or terrifying at will. Forty ambassadors from the republican cantons of Switzerland were awed to find His Majesty sumptuously and magnificently dressed, "more so than anyone had ever seen him with an aigrette of diamonds of incalculable value in his hat, which was black and white, with a scarf [i.e., a diagonal, shoulder-to-waist decoration in the manner of a sword belt or ambassadorial ribbon] of the same colours completely covered with diamonds." But the wand that precipitously transformed the aging king, well into his fifties, into a laughable impostor of Prince Charming was wielded not by a fairy godmother but a fifteen-year-old nymphet brandishing a gilded spear at a ballet rehearsal. Henri allowed his disgraceful lust for the winsome child of the Constable de Montmorency to befuddle both his moral and sartorial judgment. Short, grizzle-haired, bleared eyes rimmed in clumsy silver-framed crystal spectacles, teeth veined with rich deposits of gold and lead, he suddenly emerged in "Chinese satin" sleeves and perfumed neckwear. He dissolved young Charlotte's engagement and married her off to the Prince de Conde, whom he mistakenly believed to be so taken up by hunting that he had lost his taste for women. At another wedding, that of a natural son, it was slyly noted that the king was "aglitter in precious stones and pearls with a suit of utmost richness and dressed (so people say) as a lover."

Like Margot, his former wife, Henri had visibly become one of society's traditional embarrassments —an elderly slave to passion, an old and amorous fool. The king, all dignity cast aside, behaved like the lovesick hero of one of the period's fashionable pastoral romances (it was reported that his

to the heavens. On their wedding night Marie had to douse herself torrentially with perfume to endure him at close quarters. Marie was silly and an inept schemer, but she had great personal style and was the patroness of Rubens. Henri IV forged the link between medieval France and the baroque preeminence of Louis XIV. This achievement can be laid not only to his progressive administrative expertise and passion for public building but also to Marie's Florentine persistence in keeping up a show of regal elegance.

Henri resisted the rigors of elegance with flagging energy but still tried to dress simply. "For he ordinarily wore gray cloaths," noted an Englishman, "with a Doublet of sattin or Taffeta, without slashing, Lace or Embroydery." Rubens, along with Veronese and other contemporary portraitists, took

always, traditions underwent lingering deaths. Marchesa Brigida Spinola Doria, *by Peter Paul Rubens, detail. c. 1606.*
Top: Infanta Maria Anna of Spain. *This portrait was carried back to England from Madrid by Charles, Prince of Wales, after negotiations for his marriage to the Infanta broke down in 1623. The following year England declared war on Spain.*
Center: Portrait of a conservative man. Rogier Clarisse *by Peter Paul Rubens, detail. c. 1611.*
Bottom: Portrait of a modern man *by Paulus Moreelse, detail.*

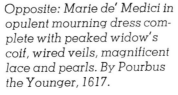

Opposite: Marie de' Medici in opulent mourning dress complete with peaked widow's coif, wired veils, magnificent lace and pearls. *By Pourbus the Younger, 1617.*

Above: The ruff, having reached the ultimate in breadth and intricacy, began to wane in Europe. By the 1620s it survived principally on the Iberian Peninsula, where, as

Le Blond excud/ anec Priuilege du Roy

condition had been aroused by having one of these novels read to him while lying in bed with gout rather than his lady love). His ex-wife's general performance, if possible, was worse. Variously addicted to piety, learning, and lechery, Margot kept a retinue of gigolos and a string of blond page boys, whose heads could be periodically shaved to provide her with glossy new wigs. Gaudily painted, monstrously obese, Margot made the error fatal to so many other aging ladies who down the centuries have tried to deny the evaporation of time by dressing in the fashions of their youthful prime. And so it was with Margot, known to Parisians as their lewd old "Queen Venus," a paralyzing apparition in huge, outmoded farthingales and shocking décolletages whose hungry bulk could now block a palace doorway.

If Henri IV represented the quintessential French

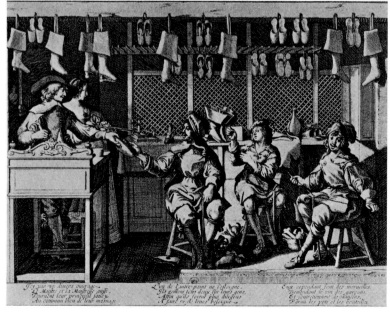

138

Left: Bravura, swagger and buxom curves: fashion hallmarks of the Cavalier era. From Le Costume Historique by M. A. Racinet.
Lower left: Charles I by Anthony Van Dyck. History identifies the beard with the artist rather than the king.
Lower right: The Rubenesque ideal: the painter's second wife, Hélène Fourment, detail. 1638.

chevalier, Charles I of England represented his quintessential English counterpart, the cavalier. Cavaliers and Roundheads: at no time in history had conflicting styles in dress created more visible evidence of civil dissension. Cavaliers and Roundheads: an association as opposite as light and dark, open and shut, gaiety and gloom.

The 17th century has been labeled the era of long locks, leather, and lace. Certainly this summons up the dashing vision of a Dumas bravo or the glamorous patina of an English cavalier. But only from the bright side of that distant world—from its shadows, from the melancholy midnight of Rembrandt's anguish, loom the pale avenging angels of the Puritans, close-cropped skulls of burly burghers, and the worn hands and homespun of the dim and hopeless poor.

The typical international cavalier was first and foremost a man of action, unsuited to the stiffly limned abstractions and padded parabolas of Spanish dress. Taut surfaces and immobile ruffs gave way to cascading folds and fluttering plumes, broad brims and drooping breeches. Heavy lace collars flopped, unstarched, and pliant "funnel-top" boots, made of soft oiled leather, slapped insolently with each step the wearer took. The boots could be pulled high over the knee for riding or folded down to exhibit, like frothing flagons of ale, the spilled white foam of lace-edged linen overhose. Opulent lashings of wide ribbon garters were tied in bow knots at the knee, and when shoes were worn, they hid beneath fluffy rosettes. Doublets, frequently slit and braided, shrank; waistlines rose as breeches tumbled; shirts were allowed to billow and blouse. Over the high waisted doublet a short swirl of a cloak either flapped from one shoulder or was flipped around the body like a bolt of fabric across a tailor's table. A look of elegant dishevelment seemed the sartorial goal; component parts of a costume were deliberately left undone, unstrung, unlaced, unhooked. Eventually the point was reached where a man of fashion would appear to have either dressed in the dark or in flight from a cuckold's bedchamber, or possibly both.

Correspondingly, women took on an enticingly billowy, buxom Rubenesque look with long frizzed hair worn loose or caught at the nape of the neck in a net. As metal superstructures vanished, the waist rose perceptibly beneath a bodice laced lightly in front; from this the full folds of the skirts fell naturally, creating a somewhat pregnant silhouette. (Considerable discussion had been aroused in 1628 by Harvey's discovery of the circulation of the blood. This revelation led to speculation as to whether stoppage caused by corsets explained everyone's minor aches and pains; as a plausible consequence, the demise of ironclad underpinnings was dramatically hastened.) Extremely wide collars of sculpturally textured unstarched lace, like the eaves of a roof, sheltered plumply puffed and frequently gartered and rosetted sleeves. Décolletages dipped, and soft hats, similar to those worn by men, hatched flights of feathers. All in all, to puritanical eyes, these women were a wantonly seductive disgrace.

Puritans and Burghers

From its very inception, Protestantism has consistently exerted a far deeper influence on Western dress than is generally recognized. To evaluate this influence properly, it is important to examine the "Protestant work ethic."

Lavorare est orare, "to labor is to pray," was the brisk motto of the Lutherans. Calvin, too, demanded that a person work as hard as possible at whatever job God had allocated him. If to work was holy, it therefore followed that a worker, whether a learned professional or ignorant shoemaker, became one of God's priests by dint of his labor. In this sense, work clothes became sacred vestments, the insignia of devoted industry and service—hence, blessings on thy business suit, thy laborer's smock, thy freshly laundered housewife's apron.

Nevertheless, the Puritan men affected the cropped hair of a wig wearer while spurning the wig—hence presenting a "round head." They also preferred dark colors, wool rather than silk stockings, and a minimum of lace.

Emboldened by the work-ethics sanction of commerce, the rising middle, trading classes for the first time were able to impose on a major part of society their cautious values of industry, honesty, public order, thrift, respect for property, and the avoidance of illegitimate birth; the latter could interrupt the system of family inheritance. The Protestants were bitterly opposed to aestheticism; in England, for example, Cromwell's contemptuous hatred of the arts and learning is well known. These hostile attitudes, produced rigid new standards of personal comportment and appearance. In the New World, children were taught by the Reverend Isaac Watts, author of *Divine Songs for Children*, to chirrup:

Why should our garments, made to hide
Our parents' shame, provoke our pride?
The art of dress did ne'er begin
Till Eve, our mother, learned to sin.

But just as Castiglione's courtier had been asked to solve the riddle of conspicuous inconspicuousness, Protestants had now to discover a sartorial technique that would simultaneously proclaim their sobriety and industriousness on one hand and God-given inequality on the other. The first attribute, of course, posed no problem. But if an enlightened believer was to work hard and exercise the self-discipline of thrift, as God expected him to do, it was only logical that he would be rewarded with the material evidence of his spiritual constancy —prosperity. Furthermore, some indication must be given of one's divinely ordained social rank. Without resorting to splendor, how then could a seemly impression of prosperous hieratic humility be registered by dress? Ultimately, in the Netherlands, the burgher's retention of outmoded styles was to supply the answer—moral conservatism expressed in fossilized fashions. That they should continue wearing black was not in itself remarkable; it well suited the austerity of Dutch Calvinism. However, the prolonged affectation of the elaborately pleated Spanish ruff, decades after it had disappeared elsewhere, introduces a perplexing new taste-making policy—one that might be called the "decorum of obsolescence."

The curly masculine wig, which would later erupt into the preposterous "full-bottom" periwig (an English corruption of the French *perruque*), expressed the very soul of the Restoration—a flat repudiation of the roundheads. It was first introduced at the court of France by the twenty-three-year-old King Louis XIII to hide his premature baldness. Respectful courtiers were quick to make fashionable their monarch's disfigurements and appeared in similar disguise. Louis XIII's nephew, Charles II, on his return from exile in France, popularized the periwig in England when his hair, we are told by Pepys, began to turn gray in his early thirties. Notorious for his many amours, Charles II had one particularly rare wig made up of the pubic hair of his numerous mistresses.

The insecurity and panic universally suffered by indecisive slaves to fashion are nowhere described more excruciatingly than by Pepys in his magpie's nest of a diary. An invaluable source of eyewitness accounts of the Plague and Great Fire of London, the diary, in its delightful human pettiness, also thoroughly acquaints us with the author as a frustrated Restoration fop, thwarted in his elegant aspirations by his own droll stinginess.

Beginning in 1663, Pepys scribbles repetitiously of his qualms about the wearing of periwigs. Should he or should he not buy one? What of the expense? The drama? The possible shame? Unconvinced, he tries on two or three at Mr. Jervas's, his old barber, "measuring to wear one; and yet I have no stomach for it but that the pains of keeping my hair clean is so great." Torn, he takes his leave, beneath a storm cloud of apprehension over "the trouble that I forsee will be in wearing them." The next morning, a Sunday, up early but still disturbed by a variety of personal dilemmas, not the least of which

Opposite: John Calvin in 1564, in sparsely trimmed garb, lifts a reformer's finger to make a moral point.

Above: With a servant hovering dimly in the background, these Dutch burghers are obviously well pleased with themselves. Six Regents of the New Almshouse for the Outdoor Relief of the Poor by Franz Bol. 1657.

Left: The sedate, pious, domestic Dutch cling conservatively to obsolescent styles. A Family in a Landscape by Frans Hals. c. 1650.

This unfortunate excursion set firmly behind him, Pepys is further consoled by the arrival of his brother's man bringing "me a new black baize waistecoate, faced with silk, which I put on from this day . . . also my new gown of purple shagg" (a kind of plush; this specific article of clothing, on which its owner doted, was gold buttoned and braided and worn in the privacy of the home rather in the manner of the Edwardian "smoking jacket") and a velvet hat, "very fine to ride in and the fashion." But the distressful specter of the periwig continues to haunt him: "to Jervas the barber's and there was trimmed and did deliver back a peri-wigg" (Pepys's spelling of this word is as susceptible to change as his attitude toward the object itself) "which he brought by my desire the other day to show me," but which, with deep irresolution, Pepys chooses to "put off for a while." At last the plunge is taken; after three months' soul-searching Pepys is persuaded to part with hard cash by a periwig-maker: "without more ado I went up, and there he cut off my haire, which went a little to my heart at present to part with it, but, it being over, and my periwigg on, I paid 3 pounds for it; and away he went with my owne haire to make up another of [it]."

Quickly Pepys summons his maids to inspect the momentous transformation and "they conclude it to become me, though Jane was mighty troubled for my parting with my own haire." Quickly, quickly, he scurries to a coffeehouse to galvanize the clientele; here "Sir W. Penn observed mightily and discoursed much upon the cutting of my haire, as he do of everything that concerns me," but, Pepys concludes with somewhat mixed sentiments, "it is over and so I perceive that after a day or two it will be of not great matter."

On Sunday the effect is one of hollow anticlimax, "for I thought that all the church would presently cast their eyes all upon me, but I found no such thing." Fresh blows fall: "my Periwigg," we read in portentous capitalization, which the maker swore would serve for two years, must be sent to the barber's to be cleaned of nits "which vexed me cruelly" (the ease with which one's own cropped natural locks could be kept vermin-free, on the other hand, was the periwig's noteworthy contribution to hygiene). Finally, an agreement is reached to maintain Pepys's swelling repertory of wigs in spruce condition for twenty pence a year, although one of them had nearly, but not quite, to be discarded by its miserly wearer in the interests of health: "Up and put on my coloured silk suit very fine, and my new periwigg, bought a good while hence, but durst not wear, because the plague was in Westminster when I bought it, and it is a wonder what will be the fashion after the plague is done, as to periwiggs, for nobody will dare buy any haire, for fear of the infection, that it had been cut off the heads of people dead of the plague."

concerns the tentative ordering of a wig, Pepys climbs into "a black cloth suit, with white lynings under all, as the fashion is to wear, to appear under the breeches" and, in his distraction, is "set upon by a great dogg, who got hold of my garters and might have done me hurt . . . but, Lord, to see what a maze I was in, that having a sword about me, I never thought of it."

Opposite above: Samuel Pepys, English diarist and fretful slave to fashion, adopts the full-bottomed "periwig." Opposite below: William II and Mary Stuart by Anthony Van Dyck, painted on the occasion of their marriage in 1641. Detail.

Below: Baroque French finery. Louis XIV sustained his power by keeping disruptive nobles busy with the expense and minutiae of such high fashions. Clothes became a national fixation: "In all professions one affects a particular look and exterior in order to appear what he wishes to be thought," observed La Rochefoucauld, "so that it may be said that the world is made up of appearance." From Le Costume Historique by M. A. Racinet.

The Baroque Courtier

Pepys's "coloured silk suit very fine" would reflect the palette of French fashions, introduced to the English upper class by Charles II on his triumphant return from exile at the court of his cousin, Louis XIV. The reign of Louis XIV once and for all had established the French as the international arbiters of fashion. For the French themselves, the sole paragon of style was their own Sun King, the radiant Louis XIV, who exalted in the "trade" of monarch and who, when analyzing his own passions, confessed that "The love of glory (la gloire) assuredly takes precedence over all others in my soul."

To assure his conquest of la gloire, Louis XIV doubled in the role of his own prime minister and hand-picked his assistants purely on the basis of personal merit and dogged devotion. Chief among these conspirators in the king's plot to capture immortality was the financial genius, Colbert. Colbert temporarily rescued the moribund French economy by imposing the mercantile system. The state,

he insisted, in its quest for greatness, should control everything, including the fine arts; this would ensure that "His Majesty will cultivate them with even greater care that may serve to immortalize his great and glorious actions." Colbert contended that France could dominate the European market through expanded production of luxury goods—refined sugar, precious metals, *objets d'art*, but particularly in the weaving of sumptuous silk fabrics. High fashion, he avowed with considerable prescience, must be to France what gold mines were to Peru. Furthermore, high fashion could not only help the king marshal his ambitious campaign of self-propaganda, but at the same time it could play a critical diversionary role in stifling political opposition and sustaining the power of the Crown. By overemphasizing the importance and expense of dress in the ritual of court life, Louis intended to keep his courtiers happily on the brink of bankruptcy and out of political mischief.

But high fashion, as we have previously seen, needs a stage on which to perform, and this dovetailed nicely with Louis' scheme to gather his cast of courtiers and keep them under close surveillance beneath one magnificent roof. Never has the world known a more opulent minimum-security facility than Versailles, with its incarcerating geometric vistas and its flat reflecting pools in which the drowning images of painted and beribboned inmates struggled silently for air against the mirror-gray façades of the classical Baroque.

The baroque style itself had originally been commissioned in 16th-century Italy as the bread and circuses of the Counter-Reformation. In its mystical exuberance and writhing motion, the harmony of the whole had frequently to be sacrificed to the theatrical focal point. In 17th-century France, under the patronage of Louis XIV and a growing taste for classical logic and dignity, the mystically voluptuous excesses of the Baroque were disciplined into a mathematical system of metronomic grandeur. At the French court this system of measured glory imposed itself everywhere: on ceremony, art and conversation, on dress, on thought, on manners.

The ideal French courtier was an *honnête homme*, as is summarized in Nicholas Faret's loose adapta-

tion of Castiglione's *Courtier*, now entitled for the edification of the French *l'honnête homme, ou l'art de plaire à la cour—The Honest Man, or the Art of Pleasing at Court*. Scholarship in an *honnête homme* is deplorable. First and foremost, it is the French courtier's function to be well bred, have the proper connections, and to ingratiate himself to superiors at any cost.

Other social influences had, to varying degrees, served to mold the ideal inhabitant of an apartment at Versailles. The phenomenon known as *préciosité*, "preciousness," made its debut in the 1640s in the blue-and-silver hall of the Hotel Rambouillet. At this private mansion the first of France's celebrated "salons," where society discoursed with the outstanding minds and talents of the day, were held on designated days. An effective civilizing force, the Marquise de Rambouillet's gracious gatherings also represented a feminist rebellion against the male-dominated social order of the time. Demanded in an unwritten manifesto were "a woman's rights to do freely as she pleases, to choose her life's companion, to cultivate, if it so pleases, before and during the marriage, art and *belles-lettres*, and to know the pleasures of the spirit." But just as they were burgeoning into a powerful cult of feminism, the Précieuses' energies were dissipated by a flock of imitative hostesses who suffocated their guests with affectation. In the name of "politeness," words like "breast" and "vomit" were primly banished and coy circumlocutions and euphemisms obstructed the flow of conversational speech—a candle became "the supplement of the sun," a brush "the instrument of propriety," and at a recital given by an Italian *castrato*, a Précieuse was heard to exclaim, "*Mon dieu*, how well this discommoded one sings!" Small wonder that Molière would satirize them in *Les Précieuses ridicules* and *Les Femmes savantes* and that Richelieu would found the all-male Académie Française chiefly to quell a threatened female appropriation of culture.

The genes of an additional social movement, an early-17th-century French development known as *libertinage*, must be mentioned to explain the code of human relations that evolved at the court of Versailles. Proclaimed by a group of rich

144

young noblemen and men of letters, the "free-thinking" philosophy of the "libertines" favored complete moral license and sensual indulgence. The Church finally silenced them, but not before they had left an indelible imprint.

And so it was that the court of Versailles came to be populated with the progeny of the Précieuse, *honnête homme*, and libertine. Extremely amorous in his youth, Louis XIV was nevertheless laden down with religious scruples; as a consequence, dalliance at court, while never outrightly forbidden, had to be camouflaged by an enameled appearance of stylized decorum. Along with sly flirtations and the exigencies of fashion, Louis offered at court dancing, gambling, hunting, and the acrobatics of genealogical recitations. Order of precedence now took on a ferocious Spanish intensity; the king alone might shine as the sun, but around him orbited satellites of calculably major and minor magnitude. Protocol must at all costs be kept straight. In the narrow streets of Paris, if two oncoming noble carriages could not scrape by each other, their occupants tumbled out onto the cobblestones to argue noisily the superiority of their genealogical charts before passage might be acceded. By the following century the French courtier's preoccupation with lineage would be seen at its grotesque apogee in the correspondence conducted between the Maréchale de Noailles and the Virgin Mary. In her dotage, humored by a sympathetic confessor, the Maréchale began to write letters to the Queen of Heaven, questioning her about the intricacies of precedence in the Kingdom of God. Her confessor took it upon himself to forge replies and in one of them committed a slight error in form, a blunder

immediately seized on by the Maréchale. "One cannot expect too much of her," she pronounced with steady condescension. "After all she was only a bourgeoise from Nazareth. It was through marriage that she became attached to the House of David. Her husband, Joseph, would have known better."

The minutiae of fashion were regarded at Versailles with equally monomaniacal fixation. "Fashion is the mirror of history," explained Louis XIV whenever the question was raised as to the disproportionate importance of clothes. In 1675 the guild of couturiers was established, more or less at the same time that the word "mode" came into currency.

Below: Louis XIV and His Heirs. Mme. de Maintenon, the prudish royal governess and later secret wife of the king, holds his extravagantly dressed grandson, the future Louis XV, in check with an ornate lead. Musing on regal opulence, La Bruyère, critic of his times, wrote in 1692: "In his devotion to splendor and luxury, a sovereign is like a shepherd bedecked in gold and precious jewels, golden crook in hand, a gold-collared, silk-leashed dog at his side. What use is all this to his flock? How does it protect them from the wolves?"

Detail of a painting attributed to Nicolas de Largillière. After 1715.

Right: Louis XIV at the Founding of the Observatory of the Academy of Science, 1667. Detail of a painting by Henri Testelin.

Below right: Queen Marie-Thérèse and the diminutive dauphin. By Pierre Migaud.

Fashion—that is to say, *French* fashion, as Colbert had predicted—was becoming big business. French workshops manufactured masses of fabrics, trimmings, accessories. French mastery of fashion, whether in dress, architecture, jewelry, furniture, glass, tapestries, metalwork, or textiles, was displayed most advantageously at the palace of Versailles, compared by Nancy Mitford to a dazzling shop window before which foreigners and dignitaries could stand and greedily gape.

The clothes of the French courtiers seemed almost too much to absorb at a single viewing. As Louis had intended, the nobility had been trapped in an intricate net of financially depleting trivia. Whereas in baroque art and architecture overall harmony of form had often been sacrificed to selectively highlighted detail, in the baroque dress of the French courtier, the form itself seems to be nothing more than an incoherent compendium of inessentials. Masculine costume, in particular, was an assemblage of jigsaw puzzle complexity: hundreds of yards of ribbon, lavishly looped or clustered into rosettes, festooned figures encumbered by broad ostrich-plumed hats, lacy cuffs and handkerchiefs, periwigs, canes, jeweled buckles and buttons, sword, sashes, embroidered gloves, knotted cravats, silk stockings, and square-toed high-heeled shoes. (As the king stood less than five and a half feet tall, the last were indispensable to regal stature.) Beneath all this, the basic elements of a nobleman's clothes included a large-collared, blousing shirt, over which was worn the doublet, now shrunken to a short-sleeved bolero, and *rhinegraves*, or open-bottomed "petticoat breeches." These breeches flared downward rather like a divided skirt. When worn over longer pantaloons and trimmed with massed loops of ribbon, an impression of deep horizontally tiered ruffles created a feminine overall effect. In time the cloak was discarded in favor of a collarless coat, the "justaucorps," at first somewhat tubular and later cut to skim the torso and jut out into a stiffened skirt. This was adapted from the military cassock coat, which itself, it will be recalled, evolved from the peasant's smock. At the court of Louis XIV, this coat, always worn open and with or without sleeves, blazed with jewels. The king owned four *parures*—coordinated sets of jewelry—two of diamonds, one of diamonds and pearls, and another, of many colored stones. The most important set comprised five hundred and eighty-six separate pieces, four hundred and forty-two of them for the ornamentation of his justaucorps alone. Yet this staggering inventory failed to include Louis' hatclasp, garters, cross belt, sword, shoe buckles, and the cross of the Holy Spirit. We can safely believe St. Simon's description of the king entering the gallery "bent under the weight" of his treasures. If fashion was to mirror the history of Louis's reign, it reflected precisely the refulgent image the monarch intended.

Louis XIV, who added many unique stones, including the Hope Diamond, to the crown collection, loved to see the female members of the family similarly ablaze, especially for the benefit of foreign ambassadors. In times of national economic distress the king preferred to have his extraordinary sets of silver furniture melted down for a fraction of their worth rather than see his ladies unadorned. In fact he loved all pretty women; even to ugly ones he showed assiduous politeness. But they must always look their best and appear punctually and *decollete* at Mass. Not to wear one's courtly ornaments constituted a gross breach of etiquette, although on occasions certain extenuating circumstances, such as sentimental hysteria, might be taken into consideration. St. Simon tells of loud and dolorous episodes caused by the virtuous Mademoiselle de Coetlogon, an unfortunately plain but usually amiable maid of honor to the queen, who had fallen madly in love with a notorious opportunist. When the object of her unrequited affection was called off on a military tour she "wept and raved and left off all ornaments while the campaign lasted." Upon his return, the gentleman acted as a second in a duel and as punishment was sent to the Bastille. Fresh outbursts of grief: "She discarded her jewels and dressed herself as badly as she could. Unable to persuade the King to release him, she called him names, became so furious she threatened him with her nails." At dinner she would never hand anything to Louis and "either evaded it, or said straight out that he did not deserve that she should wait upon him." The beloved one released at last, "Coetlogon resumed her ornaments, but it was only with difficulty that she consented to be reconciled with the King."

The stiffness of court etiquette, as might be expected, found an analogy in court dress—stiff boning returned to the multigored ladies' corset, which once again plunged in front to a pointed waistline. A gown, composed of a skirt and bodice, was worn over this; the neckline, edged in a lace or draped band, widened seductively until the shoulders were revealed. Madame de Montespan, a sparkling blonde who periodically had to take the water cures to regain her excellent figure, had been largely responsible for promoting Louis XIV's policy of incapacitating clutter—bows and laces, fans and ribbons, parasol, mitts, gold passementerie, busily patterned silks and embroidered, brocaded, bowed and buckled shoes with pointed toes and high curved heels. Sleeves, during the amorous reign of la Montespan, were full and often pleated.

An effect of added height, corresponding to that of the towering topiary forms of the male periwig, was achieved by elaborate coiffures and late in the century by the *fontange*, a stiff headdress that soared from a lady's curls like a row of organ pipes. Trains reappeared and lengthened, not only at the hem of the outer skirt but from another worn beneath it. To display this last ornamental garment, the

overskirt, like a stage curtain, might be swept back to either side and swagged over a supportive struc- ture of metal, whalebone, or basketwork (later known as "panniers") that artificially extended the hips. Respite from tedious hours spent at Versailles in the confines of the *grande toilette* came in the welcome form of "at home" or "undress" clothes— dressing gowns, sometimes of gaily painted Indian cotton fabric, short fur-trimmed jackets, and frothy little boudoir capes.

Confoundingly, however, even intelligent cour- tiers craved the repetitious rounds of protocol, spelled by bouts of idle boredom, that daily charac- terized life at Versailles. Elsewhere a new day might dawn with the rising of the sun; at Versailles it was heralded by the rising of the king. Each morn- ing a battalion of nobles and flunkies would observe the religious office of the *levée*, preparing their

master for his adorers by dabbing him with wine and water, combing, smoothing, straightening, sooth- ing. Similarly, the end of day would ritualistically be marked by the reverse process, the *couché*, which was climaxed with the drawing of the royal bed curtains. Much of these interminable perform- ances, we are told, took place before the eyes of an ever-thrilled elite. And La Bruyère, a usually clear- eyed observer of current events, could himself surpass Madame de Sévigné's incomprehensible gushing: "When you reflect how the happiness of a courtier depends upon the King's expression, how all his life he devotes his days to the ecstasy of seeing and being seen by His Majesty, then you will begin to understand how God can become the whole glory and the whole happiness of the Saints." In other words, dress correctly and strive to please, and you will find yourself on the side of the angels.

The 18th Century:

Rococo Dress

The 18th century was a period of profound economic and social change culminating in the charnel phantasmagoria of 1789. A preoccupation with dress, particularly at the French court, was both a cause and a symptom of the century's near fatal malady. The Industrial Revolution, associated in its abuses with the 19th century, in fact began in the 18th, and the root of its development was in textile production. Within fifty years a spate of new inventions mechanized the industry in Britain: the flying shuttle, Hargreave's spinning jenny, Arkwright's "water-twist frame," and finally Cartwright's weaving loom. Knitting machines were perfected and proliferated, and when, in 1785, James Watt installed his new steam engine in a cotton mill, the age of mass production commenced.

England enjoyed a unique position for the development of her textile trade. The American colonies provided a new market for her cloth, her growing interests in India supplied her with a source of cotton, and the Huguenots established silk mills in Britain after Louis XIV's mindless revocation of the Edict of Nantes. British woolens, broadcloth in particular, were already in wide use.

The new craze for cottons, the various fabrics called *indiennes*—lawns, batistes, muslins, and gauzes—was certain to have a decisive effect on fashions during the century. It also had a sinister influence on social institutions. The cotton ships out of Liverpool headed straight for Africa, where their cargo was exchanged for slaves. These were shipped to the southern colonies of North America, whence American cotton was shipped raw to England for processing. This demoralizing "triangle trade" was the unfortunate mainstay of much of the British textile development.

Along with new textiles came new methods for printing and dyeing. European technicians perfected the printing of cottons, and the superb *toile d'orange* and *toile de Jouy* were the result. The understanding of optics led to the development of new dyes achieving more subtle composite colors and halftones. The technique of bleaching was also transformed. Spain, Belgium, the Rhinelands, Saxony, and Switzerland developed their own textile industries, and General Washington was inaugurated President of the United States in a suit of American-loomed fabric.

We can well imagine the social as well as the aesthetic effect of these developments when we contemplate the gulf between the heavily constructed edifices sewn in the private workrooms of

Opposite: *During the 18th century, printed fabrics came into fashion. Lawns, batistes, muslins and gauzes for dresses, and heavier fabrics for furnishings, were inspired by printed cottons from India and called indiennes. Top: Alsatian indienne. c. 1795.*

Bottom: *French indienne. c. 1790.*
Below left: *Fabric production was a basic aim of the Industrial Revolution. Although the greatest changes came in Britain, the silk industry thrived in France as well, with Lyons as its center.*

French silks. 18th century.
Below right: *European technicians perfected the printing of cotton. The subtle and complicated repeating patterns of the toile de Jouy (top) were a special triumph of the art of fabric printing. Top: Toile de Jouy, 1793.*

Bottom: *English printed fabric. Late 18th century.*

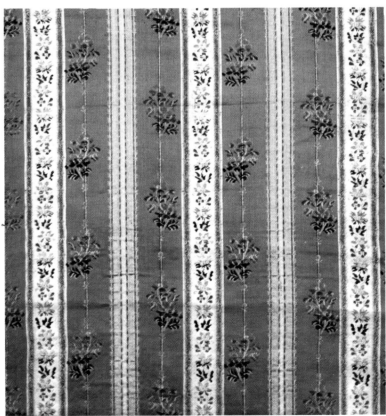

the noblesse of the era of Louis XIV and the simple ready-to-wear clothing that began to emerge at the time of the Revolution. By the early 19th century one writer observed, "Two centuries ago not one person in a thousand wore stockings; one century ago, not one person in five hundred wore them; now, not one person in a thousand is without them."

In the mid-18th century France suffered the severe reversals of the War of the Spanish Succession and the Seven Years' War, losing virtually all her empire and her sea power. Yet France remained, in all questions of taste, the arbiter of Europe, just as her rich agriculture made her the continent's economic core. If anything, her suzerainty of fashion expanded as her political power contracted. Despite setbacks, Lyons continued to produce rich silk velvets, a cotton industry developed around Rouen, cheap textiles were manufactured in the south, and Nantes became a major textile port of Europe.

Régence and Rococo

The booming 18th-century development of industry and trade led inevitably to one major social change: the rapid growth of the bourgeoisie. The nobility,

154

financially crippled by Louis XIV and further shackled by a repugnance for trade, soon found its economic power outweighed by that of the middle class. Class distinctions became blurred. Maintaining the lifestyle required at Versailles resulted in a tremendous burden of debt, which members of the nobility could often pay only by marrying a member of the class that made its fortune purveying this very style of life. The cycle was not broken but accelerated when, on the death of Louis XIV, the nobility breathed a sigh of relief and fled the drafty and imprisoning halls of Versailles to the greater freedom of the cozy hearths of the Paris salons. The sweep of the high Baroque appropriate for the palace gave way to the delicacy and miniaturization of forms found in the style of the Régence and eventually, in full-blown Rococo, an aesthetic well suited to the hôtels particuliers of Paris and more modest country estates. Once in Paris, the nobility mixed freely with the bourgeoisie and its fascinating offspring, the intelligentsia.

The new "looseness" of the Régence could not have been better expressed than in the new fashion for the "sacque gown." There was a sense of float-

erlands for the purpose of supplying whalebone.

The sacque dress has been called the Watteau gown, but the term is a misnomer. It is true that women in this gown, eyes averted and attentions elsewhere, drift through Watteau's *fêtes galantes*, and it is also true that Watteau executed fashion sketches. But although his paintings suggest the nobility at eternal play in the never-never land of a rococo dream, Watteau's figures wear many styles: Costumes of different eras and the fantasies of the stage, forms inspired by Rubens and Titian, mix freely with figures of the latest fashion in the spirit of that playful and sometimes melancholy madness that is the soul of the best of the Rococo.

Men's dress remained somewhat static for much of the 18th century. It consisted originally of the outer coat, or "justaucorps," the inner jacket and knee breeches. The justaucorps inherited its shape from the previous century. A collarless garment, it was tight in the body, flared out at the waist, and reached to the knee, as did the tight breeches. Buttons ran down the front, and sleeves were completed in a deep cuff. The underjacket was fronted with rich brocades and embroideries, although the back was of much simpler material. The cuffs of its long sleeves were also decorated where visible, and it was buttoned only at the waist so that the lace-trimmed scarf or jabot at the neck of the shirt that was worn beneath could be clearly seen. Silk stockings, buckled shoes, and the tricorn completed the familiar image.

ing freedom about this gown—as much as was possible in an era that invariably thought of aristocratic dress in terms of stays and brocades so stiff they stood by themselves. The sacque had loose sleeves to the elbow and a large, gently gathered skirt (inherited from the previous century), swathed by a voluminous overgown, flowing freely from the shoulders and enshrouding the rest of the dress. Beneath it only the pointed bodice was tightly fitted. The effect was of a conical structure, culminating in the head, which was kept deliberately small with a light coiffure of short curls and a lace-trimmed cap. The periodical *La Bagatelle* claimed in 1718, "At present comfort seems the only thing that the ladies of Paris care about when dressing." The sacque dress, in fact, was said to have been inspired by the actress Madame Dancourt, who dazzled the audience during a performance of Terence's *Andria* when she rose from childbed in a loosely fitted dressing gown.

However, as if in contradiction to the search for comfort, it was at this very period that "panniers"— or the hoop petticoat, as it was called in England— first appeared. This petticoat of gum-starched cloth stiffened with three tiers of whalebones made it possible to achieve skirts of a width of five feet and more. The very size of the figure cut by women of the period influenced both furniture design and architecture, resulting in the construction of chairs, settees, staircases, and doorways of a generous width. A whaling company was founded in the Neth-

Below: Arch conservative
Samuel Johnson wears a full-
bottom wig, while Boswell
and Goldsmith affect the
more fashionable Ramillie.
Johnson, Boswell, and Goldsmith at the Mitre Tavern by
Eyre Crowe. Late 18th century.

Bottom: Samuel Bernard in
all the glories of a full-bottom
wig. Bust by Guillaume
Coustou. c. 1720.

The strange artificiality and also the delicacy we associate with the Rococo owes much to the powdered head, which became the rule in the 18th century. The lady of fashion powdered her head with wheat meal, sprayed upward so that it fell evenly on the hair. Men powdered their wigs in a similar manner. The messy operation was carried out in a special chamber, or simply on the doorstep if space were lacking. Hairdressers were called "mackerels" because they looked like floured fish ready for the pan. The haze of powder that settled on four generations happily obliterated all but the most obvious distinctions of age. It was said that enough flour rested on the heads of Versailles to feed the poor of Paris.

Left: "The merchant, the man of business and of letters were distinguished by the grave full bottom ... the tradesman by the snug bob of natty scratch. All the conditions of men were distinguished by the cut of the wig, and none more so than the coachman, who wore his ... in imitation of the curled hair of a water dog." This observation by James Stewart in 1728 is confirmed in a portrait of Henry Fielding. Engraving by T. Roscoe, after painting by William Hogarth. Above: Gentlemen undergoing the discomfort of being powdered. Engraving by Collet. 1770.

In the early part of the century women wore short, neatly coiffed and curled heads of natural hair, delicately powdered, with the occasional enhancement of an added lock, while men's heads were still enlarged by the enormous "full-bottom" wig of the 17th century, now powdered white. The wigmaker in a contemporary Vanbrugh comedy assures his customer that his new wig is "so long and full of hair it may serve you as a hat and cloak in all weathers." However, the craze for the "full bottom" died with Louis XIV, and, needless to say, the delicacy of rococo taste dictated something lighter and easier to wear. The solution was found by men of the British Army in need of headwear more practical for maneuvering in action. They devised a wig with a sausage roll of curls over each ear and the remainder tied together with a ribbon at the back, called the "Ramillies" wig after Marlborough's victory in 1706.

Moreover, in the 18th century the price of wigs dropped. The full wig of a century earlier had been a very costly item, so expensive, in fact, that wig thievery was common. A tall man would saunter along the crowded streets of the city with a basket on his head containing a small boy. The lid would open, a tiny hand dart out, and by the time the victim realized it his wig (which might have cost him 140 pounds) was nowhere in sight. Or imagine the terror of the passenger in a hackney coach when he felt his wig being pulled from his head and turned to see a hand (and the wig) disappear through a hole bored into the back of the cab. By the time the coachman could be made to stop, all hope of retrieving his property would be gone.

By the middle of the century, however, such thievery was rare. The smaller wig was of cheaper construction, even when made of human hair. When made of goat's hair, horsehair, or vegetable fibers a wig could be afforded by almost anyone. A cheap wig could be had for less than a guinea, and wigs were now worn by all classes of men. Even an indentured apprentice was assured one good wig a year. In 1750 an English newspaper published an advertisement in which the wigmaker proposed "a wig of copper wire which will resist all weathers and last forever."

The word *rococo* is derived from the term *rocaille*, a form of intricate shellwork decoration. The expression was coined only when the 18th century was

157

at an end, and then it was used deprecatingly. The severity of the Empire style that followed was as forceful a reaction to the seemingly empty playfulness of Rococo as Rococo itself had been a reaction to the bombast of the Baroque. Rococo might be seen not only as a kind of miniaturization but also a kind of infantilization. The *putti*, bows and poseys of the Rococo might even seem an escape into childhood on the part of a society faced with the grimmest of socioeconomic problems. But Rococo is far more than this. As has often been pointed out, it is not a style of architecture but of decoration so overpowering that it necessitated new architectural settings to accommodate it. Flowers, butterflies, shells, palm fronds, and innumerable curling and twisting motifs ran riot over architectural forms, furniture, china, and silverware, obliterating their lines with asymmetrical fantasies of pure charm if little substance.

It is not the floating sacque gown of the Régence that one associates with Rococo and the middle years of the 1700s but the gown *à la française*: bodice tight-fitted with a lower, squarer décolleté and open down the front to reveal the "stomacher," a triangle of richly decorated material that might be a ladder of bows; sleeves tight to the elbow, where they burst forth in tiers of ruffles (it is interesting that exposure of the shoulder or elbow was considered indecent); enormous skirt opening in front to reveal the heavily decorated and flounced petticoat; at the back, loose pleats of fabric flowing from shoulder to hem. The gown is familiar to us from a thousand paintings by Boucher and his imitators. Over the years there were many variations along these general lines, and panniers altered in shape, becoming wider at the sides and narrower back to front.

Men's garments also changed imperceptibly: The underjacket shortened and lost its sleeves to become the "gilet," or waistcoat; the sleeves of the justaucorps became tighter, and its skirts, now narrower, no longer hung straight down in front but slanted away from the waist.

The riot of rococo decor that obliterated the lines of architecture also obliterated the lines of clothing. Quantities of lace, ribbons, ruffles, ruchings, and whole arbors of silken flowers, imported from Italy, embellished the gown, and these *garnissements* were often worth more than the dress itself. Their very names suggest the frivolous and flirtatious rococo soul: The gathered lace trimming the neckline was called the *tatez-y* (the "touch here"), while the bow at the center of the décolleté was called simply *parfait contentement* ("perfect contentment"). The image might be completed by a necklet of ruching, bows, or gathered lace. The men's gilets were often covered with hunting and battle scenes, and the very buttons themselves might carry portraits—of French kings, the Twelve Caesars, or even the wearers' mistress. The gown *à la française*, as well as its male counterpart, made the human figure nothing more than an extension of the decor in which it

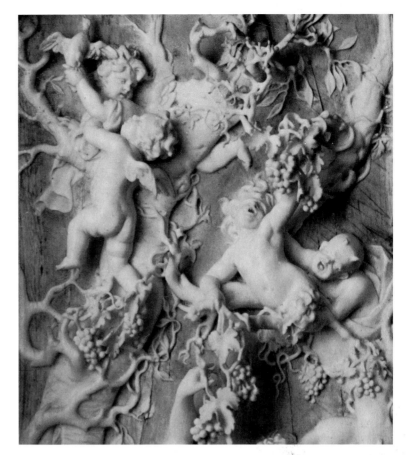

Opposite: Like most women of her era, the Marquise de Pompadour designed her own clothing. Here she wears a typical robe à la française. *Pastel by Quentin de la Tour. 1755.*

Top: Detail of a bacchanalian bas-relief in ivory belonging to Mme. de Pompadour exemplifies her rococo taste. Artist unknown. French. Mid-18th century.
Above: A carved wooden console bearing the arms of Mme. de Pompadour. French. Mid-18th century.

but moved, that movement did not jar the suspended perfection of the scene. On small silken or pale leather shoes the wearers of the gown à *la française* minced with such tiny steps beneath their huge panniers that the gown, occupant and all, would seem to be wafted from one side of the room to the other like a puff of thistledown in a breeze. Shoes were so fragile that when Madame Du Barry complained that hers did not last, her shoemaker protested, "But, Madam, you must have walked in them!" Fans of lace, silk, or parchment covered even the face with decoration. In such a setting the maxim "manners are essential, while morals optional" would seem the most natural conclusion.

A new and exotic element found its way into the energetic exhilaration of rococo decoration: the influence of chinoiserie. There is almost no explaining the "Chinese madness" that seized Europe in the 18th century. The first seeds of interest were sewn by the Jesuit missionaries over a hundred years earlier. By the end of the 17th century cargoes of Oriental porcelain, lacquerware, and textiles were bought by greedy customers the moment they reached port. Even pirates' treasure, such as that of Captain Kidd, contained bales of Oriental cloth. Many of these wares were manufactured to satisfy European tastes and usages. Tea itself had become a craze and with it the tea service. Even Chinese thought was enthusiastically championed, and Confucius became the model for Leibniz and, later, Voltaire.

It was inevitable that European craftsmen should attempt imitation. Augustus the Strong of Saxony suffered so violently from the Chinese madness that he exchanged a complete regiment of dragoons for a single forty-eight-piece set of China belonging to the King of Prussia. Two alchemists of Dresden in his employ discovered the secret of porcelain, and he established the Royal Porcelain Factory at Meissen. Lacquerwork from Japan was so readily imitated that young ladies were soon taught the art of "Japanning" as a basic "accomplishment." Chinese designs were adapted to rococo decor with alacrity, and airy vistas of a pagoda-strewn China of the imagination covered walls, furniture, and every available surface.

In 1685 no fewer than eight thousand bolts of Chinese silks arrived in France, the cargo of a single vessel, the *Amphitrite*. They were welcomed by Louis XIV and became immediately "the rage." By the turn of the century European textile manufacturers had discovered Chinese dyeing techniques, and a new range of colors was available, including a pale yellow-gold and the popular "Chinese green." European fabrics were soon printed with scenes of pagodas, parasols, temples, and other Chinese motifs as interpreted by artists like Watteau and Boucher. These visions were described as "fantastic without being grotesque, mysterious without any feeling of menace"—in short, ideal for adaptation into the *folie* of Rococo.

sat, so enfoliated by petals and ribbons that it would be difficult for the eye to disassociate the wearer from the delicate carvings of the sofa, the plasterwork fronds and *putti* of the walls and ceilings. The colors of dress, too—the delicate pinks and pale yellows, the misty blues and dove grays—merged into the rococo decor. And if the figure did not sit

Above: Court painter François Boucher, seized by the "Chinese madness" of the 18th century, created visions of an imaginary China that was a rococo paradise. Demoiselle Chinoise. Engraving by François Boucher.

Opposite: The Marquise de Pompadour was an accomplished artist. This series of engravings by her own hand includes: left, a self-portrait depicting her with a small, neatly coiffed head and patrician nose; right above, an elaborate frontispiece; and right below, a portrait of her lover, Louis XV. From the Suites d'Estampes Gravées by Mme. de Pompadour.

The Marquise de Pompadour

The most influential of all victims of the Chinese madness was none other than Madame de Pompadour herself, major shareholder in Compagnie des Indes and the first person in Europe to possess a goldfish. Jeanne Antoinette Poisson was born in Paris, a bourgeoise to the bottom of her soul, the daughter of a bourgeoise in the employ of the Pâris brothers, kings of French finance. Later biographers have spoken of her accomplishments, which seem to have been innumerable. She was adept at dancing, singing, acting, an excellent player of the clavichord, a botanist, gardener, and talented artist who painted, drew, and engraved. She also had that kind of personality that is now called charismatic and was then simply described as charming, and she possessed something then rarely allowed in women —a completely candid sense of humor. She was not one of those persons who would today be called "photogenic." None of her portraits give us any idea of the beauty that her contemporaries, even those who most loathed her, agreed she possessed. One famous description, that of Dufort de Cheverny, may

give us some notion of her appearance: "Not a man alive but would have been pleased to have her for his mistress, if he could. She was tall, not too tall, superb figure; round face with even features, dazzling complexion, hands and arms; eyes not so very large; but the most brilliant, witty and sparkling I ever saw. Everything about her was rounded, including her gestures."

People who knew the Marquise de Pompadour almost never mentioned her beauty without also mentioning the consummate elegance with which she dressed. She was famous, even before she met the king, for this particular talent, which in the early 18th century still consisted of more than merely choosing the best creations of talented designers. The extraordinary *robe à la française* was the product of dressmakers, and every woman designed her own, choosing her own stuffs, laces, *garnissements*, and the total effect she wished to achieve. In fact, it may have been her manner of dress that first attracted the eye of the king to the young Madame d'Etioles, as she then was, although she had felt

*Above: Marie Leczinska,
dowdy wife of Louis XV and
Queen of France, wearing
robes of state and the enormous Sancy diamond. Carle
Van Loo. 1747.
Right: This potpourri vase
is one of a pair from the
porcelain works at Sèvres,
founded by the Marquise de
Pompadour to compete with
those at Meissen established
by Augustus the Strong of
Saxony. Attributed to Jean-
Claude Duplessis. c. 1760.*

all her life destined for his embraces. Louis, long
estranged from his Polish wife, Marie Leczinska, and
brooding over the death of his most recent mistress,
devoted much of his time to hunting in the forest
of Sénart. Members of the bourgeoisie were not invited to attend the hunt, but neighbors were allowed
to follow in carriages. The enchanting vision of the
young Madame d'Etioles first appeared exquisitely
dressed in light blue, in a rose-colored phaeton.
Another day she would appear in a blue phaeton,
her dress *couleur de rose*. It was unlikely that the
searching eye of a deprived king would miss such
a vision.

A bourgeoise could not be presented at court, but
the king became closer acquainted with Madame
d'Etioles at the festivities celebrating the marriage of
the Dauphin to the Infanta Marie Thérèse Raphaèle.
It is probable that she attended the various balls
and festivities of the court by the arrangement of a
relative, one Sieur Binet, who was body-servant to
the Dauphin. It is certain that she attended the great
ball for the marriage itself.

There is one curious and often forgotten fact
regarding the great balls given in the state apartments of Versailles, the splendid *galerie des glaces*
and neighboring suites of rooms: They were open
to the public. Anyone in France could attend, provided only that one was properly *dressed*. In effect
the king entertained all those capable of begging,
borrowing, or stealing any clothing suitable for
his presence. Strangely, in a society so preoccupied
with the antecedents of every individual, anonymity
was not only allowed but actually sought. The
majority of those who attended went masked, often
in costume, and only one member of each party was
obliged to unmask and give his name. At this particular fete, one of the most splendid ever to be illuminated by the blazing candles of Versailles, it was
already late in the evening when the Queen appeared, wearing a dress covered with pearls as well
as two enormous diamonds, the Régent and the
Sancy. The Dauphin and his bride appeared ill-
disguised as a gardener and a flower seller. Search
for the king, however, proved fruitless. Finally the
doors to his apartments were thrown open, and
there emerged eight yew trees, clipped and potted,
exactly like those on the lawn in front of the palace.
Within the leaves of one of these ambulatory arbors
there lurked the king, determined to make the
acquaintance of Madame d'Etioles undiscovered.
Through his branches and needles he perceived a
familiar willowy and dazzling figure pointedly
dressed as the huntress Diana. Playing the forest to
her chase, he departed with her; the rest is history.

The extraordinary taste of the Marquise de Pompadour now imposed itself, not by force or influence
but simply by its excellence, on the court and on
French taste in general. She had the heart and soul
of perhaps history's greatest interior decorator.
She loved to reconstruct a house, cram it with furniture, paintings, objets d'art, bibelots, statuary, drap-

Below: The familiar portrait of Mme. de Pompadour by her favorite painter, François Boucher, gives some idea why Dufort de Cheverny said, "Not a man alive but would have been pleased to have her for his mistress if he could." She undoubtedly co-operated with the artist in choosing the garnissement for perhaps history's most famous robe à la française. 1758.

Below: The Yew Tree Ball,
at which Louis XV, dressed
as an ambulatory version of
the topiary yew trees on the
palace lawn, first approached
Mme. d'Etioles (later Pompa-
dour), who was pointedly
dressed as Diana. Detail of an
engraving by C. N. Cochin.
1745.

ery, china, linen, silver, and books, designed or chosen by herself, and then move on to another. She used Rococo itself as an art medium, almost as a painter uses paint, covering what surfaces she could and detesting what she could not handle, such as the vast and hollow vaults of Versailles. At the small and secluded Hermitage on the grounds of the palace, she arranged for the flowers of the garden to be changed daily. At Bellevue, which she commissioned Boucher to decorate, the garden was a mass of china flowers, so skillfully made and actually perfumed that they deceived the king himself. The Marquise founded the porcelain works at Sèvres to compete with those of Meissen.

Here, clearly, was a decisive arbiter of taste. Her clothing, of which we have a better notion from her many portraits than we have of her face, was usually of a pale and delicate shade that best complemented her pink-and-white complexion, and with her tall and graceful figure we may assume that she wore clothes well. Her dresses are elaborate, with exquisite detail that can be appreciated only in a Rococo context. She and the artists no doubt cooperated on the effect created. During the entire century painters such as Watteau, Boucher, and, later, Fragonard and even Chardin were more creators than copyists of fashion. The beauty of Pompadour's dress is easily communicated but not the sense of style we are often told that she demonstrated. Still, style and discrimination there were, the very qualities that the nobility felt set them apart from a bourgeoisie that could well afford the same silks and laces. The fact that Mademoiselle Poisson was born and educated a bourgeoise, a daughter of the salons of Paris that were also centers of fashion, galled them, and they never forgave her for it.

The Court of Louis XV

The Versailles of Louis XV resembled nothing so much as a combination of casino and grand hotel. As a hotel, it was conceived on a very grand scale indeed: Its library employed over forty persons; over fifty doctors were in attendance; 1500 worked in the stables; and the Department of the Mouth kept almost five hundred employees at work concocting dishes such as pigs' tongues stuffed with stag's-horn jelly and pheasant stuffed with carp and smothered in iris-root sauce to cover the huge buffets that fed the masses of courtiers. The king's wardrobe alone was maintained by over one hundred servants tailoring, pressing, washing, and starching. The fact that few of the staff were overworked must have lent a sense of ease and enjoyment to the establishment.

Unfortunately, boredom is an adjunct to the way of life of most grand hotels. At Versailles it was fought with a kind of desperation by courtiers who were there for purposes of advancement or because they had nothing better to do. It was fought by organized hunts during the day. Evenings were devoted to cards and gambling, so that the fortunes

Three decorative panels painted for Mme. de Pompadour by Boucher. Top: An overdoor panel entitled "Spring," painted in 1755. Above: The two vertical panels are from a series of eight commissioned by the Marquise for her boudoir in the Chateau de Crécy. The panel on the left depicts "Painting and Sculpture"; the right, "Architecture and Chemistry." c. 1750–53.

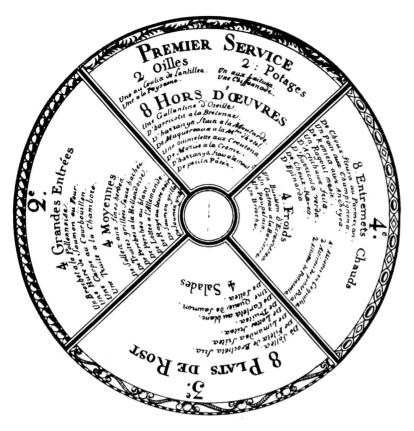

Within the menu wheel:

PREMIER SERVICE

2 Oilles
- Une à la Santilles
- Une à la Paysanne

2 Potages
- Un aux Laitues
- Une Chiffonnade

8 HORS D'ŒUVRES
- Une Gallantine D'Oseille
- D'haricota à la Brienne
- D'haricorya Stiux à la Moutarde
- De Maquereaux à la Maître d'Hôtel
- Une Omelette aux Croutons
- De Morüe à la Crême
- D'harranya Frais à la Maud
- De petits Pâtés

8 Entremets Chauds
- De Choux fleurs au Parmezan
- Un Pain aux Champignons
- Un Romica meule
- Un Ragoui au Anchoyra
- D'Artichauta verde
- D'harricota à verba
- D'haricaca à niere
- Choux Karea
- De Espinaca

4 Froids
- Un Buison d'Escrevisse
- Un Gateau à la Boviere
- Un poupelon à la
- Un Brioche

4 Salades

4 Grandes Entrées
- De Pollenmoide
- De Brochet de Saumon au Four
- D'une à la Courbouillon
- De Carpe à la Chambone

4 Moyennes
- Un Brochet à la
- Une Sallade aux fines herbes
- Une Truite au blanc

2ᵉ

5ᵉ — 8 PLATS DE ROST

4ᵉ

of France that did not change hands as a product of economic evolution changed hands on a throw of dice in the gambling chambers. Boredom was fought unofficially with a good deal of gossip, intrigue, and backbiting and officially by organized fêtes and balls ("come as a favorite proverb" or "come as a Chinese mandarin"). Above all, boredom was fought by an ardent concentration on fashion.

Fashion does not always succeed as an antidote to ennui, but it can be strong medicine. Where a group of men and women see each other daily, having much in their pockets and little on their minds, and, above all, when a show of wealth is a statement of status and even politically expedient, fashion is inevitable.

At the court of Louis XV fashion followed fashion in everything. There were fashions in dances ("The Feasts of Paphos," the "All Too Brief") and fashions in thought. Religion was more or less permanently out of fashion. Fashions in dress, of course, were paramount and were given voguish names. Even fashionable colors obtained curious nomenclature. A sickly off-white was known as "Carmelite's Stomach," a chichi brown as "Paris Mud" and another

Above: This menu for a supper party given by Louis and Mme. de Pompadour on November 4, 1757 enumerates four courses containing forty-five dishes.

Opposite: The courtiers of Versailles spent their evenings around the gaming tables, and fortunes which did not change hands as the result of economic evolution often did so on a throw of dice. Detail of an engraving by C. N. Cochin after Cochin fils. 1747.

"Queen's Hair," and a deep blue was known as "King's Eye." The theater inspired fashion too, and there were dresses à l'Harlequin and à la Figaro. However, a fashion might also be inspired by aeronautics (à la Montgolfière) or medicine (à l'Inoculation) or even a novel (ribbons à la coque, after the publication of Marguerite Marie Alacoque's biography). Politics also played a role. An inspector-general who wore tight suits inspired the fashion à la Silhouette, and a bonnet without a bottom was called a cap à la Caisse de'Escompte. At the time of the famous scandal of the Queen's necklace there was even a hat au Collier de la Reine.

Strangers who arrived at court and were not fashionably dressed were not even "seen" by the courtiers. Madame Roland visited Versailles as a drab young girl and was so outraged when the courtiers looked vacantly through her that she remained disgruntled and unforgiving until her violent end.

There were those who carried fashion to the point of foppery and eccentricity. The Princess of Taranto, for example, emphasized her relationship to every royal member of the Holy Roman Empire by going into full mourning with each passing. When Madame de Sévigné espied her in a bright silk dress she remarked cheerfully, "I am pleased to see, Madam, that Europe is in good health." Or, going to the other extreme, there was the young courtier who attempted to make fashion history by presenting himself to Marie Antoinette in a scarlet red coat, pink-and-green-striped gilet, pale-blue breeches, blue-and-red-striped stockings, a lemon-yellow overcoat with green stripes, and a huge wig.

Eccentricity of dress at Versailles might have political overtones. The strange tastes of the Austrian ambassador, Prince Wenzel Anton von Kaunitz, offer an example. He was known for his complicated coiffure, called "love laces," and he wore black silk coats, piled one on top of the other—nine if necessary, depending on the weather. In matters of grooming he was particularly peculiar. He invented ingenious instruments for picking the teeth, which he would produce at mealtimes, and he had four valets with bellows to blow powder off his wig, so that only the finest particles would remain. Madame de Pompadour humorously put these practices down as an elaborate plot to deflect attention from his true purposes; his manipulations to get France to enter an alliance with her old enemy, Austria, a move that drew her into the disastrous Seven Years War in which she lost her colonial empire.

There is the still more extraordinary case of the Chevalier d'Eon. Transvestism seems to have appeared more blatantly in the 18th century than it had since the fall of Rome. A possible explanation may be the fact that it was a period of sexual laxity in which the aristocracy still retained such power that its behavior went unquestioned. An English governor of New York, for example, a nobleman of high rank, was so unconcealed in his proclivities

that he reviewed his troups in the skirts and panniers of the latest Paris fashion. The Chevalier d'Eon himself, Charles-Geneviève d'Eon de Beaumont began life as just what his title would imply, an army officer and one known for his bravado. He was a clever lawyer and gifted writer. It also appears that he had uncommonly fresh pink cheeks and a high voice.

At one period prior to the Seven Years War the Empress Elizabeth of Russia concluded a treaty with England and refused to receive members of the French diplomatic corps. Louis XV, always prone to intrigue, hit upon a scheme that would appear brazen in any epoch. Since French women, known for their taste and charm, were welcome everywhere, Louis dispatched young d'Eon, outfitted with *robes à la française*, to the court of Elizabeth, bearing documents proving that "she" was one Lia de Beaumont. The ruse worked brilliantly. "Lia" put the Empress in touch with Louis, and the French king was presently invited to send an ambassador. Although the fact may strain our credulity, it appears that Louis redispatched d'Eon as secretary to the embassy, this time in knee breeches and posing as the captivating Lia's brother.

The Chevalier then proceeded to chalk up an admirable career as spy of both sexes. Unfortunately he ran up debts, and equally unfortunately he fell out of favor with the government upon the accession of Louis XVI. From a hiding place in England, to which he had been sent as spy, the Chevalier blackmailed the king with a threat to disclose his activities. A resolution was found, however, to the royal dilemma. The Chevalier was to be paid a sum to cover his debts, and he could expect to live freely in France, under one condition—that he remain, for life, a woman. As such, his prison sentence could be commuted without setting a dangerous precedent, and thus cut off from all possible positions

of power he could cause no further trouble to the king. The Chevalier assented, but the conditions proved a tiresome burden. Time and again the swashbuckling hero would appear at Versailles in breeches, only to be whisked away and forcibly re-apparelled in skirts and panniers by the palace guard. The confusion left so many doubts in the public mind, however, that when he finally died as a respected matron of considerable age, an autopsy was performed just to be sure. The Chevalier, the examiners found, was indeed and unquestionably a man.

As under Louis XIV, the expense of keeping up appearances at Versailles—for either sex—could cripple even the wealthy. A dress might easily cost in excess of one thousand pounds, and frequent changes were necessary. Men's clothing, of course, was not one whit less expensive. The Marquis de Stainville's suit of silver cloth embroidered in gold and lined with sable cost him almost twenty-five thousand pounds. It has been pointed out that the only consideration that prevented many of the bourgeoisie from a greater show of wealth was the tax inspector. The nobility was not taxed. For them the extravagance required for maintaining a position at court—the servants, houses, services, equipages, and clothing—was itself a tax. A sizable part of the French economy was actually sustained by "conspicuous waste" alone.

If rococo dress and grooming devoured large sums of money, it also devoured a great deal of time. The morning "toilet" consumed half the day. Madame de Pompadour may have actually died of the exhaustion of a regime whereby she retired at three in the morning and was obliged to appear for Mass at eight, as fully dressed as for a ball. Her attention to grooming was more than meticulous. It is said that her last act, having received the final sacrament,

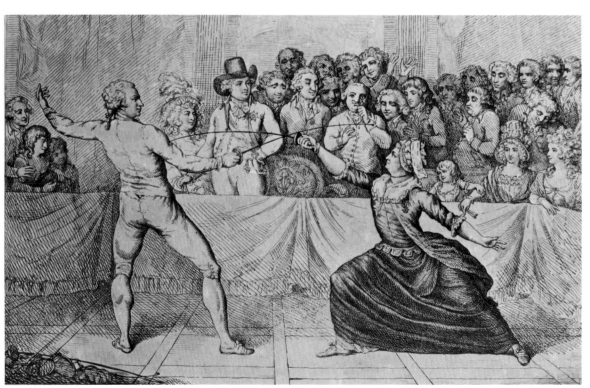

Although he enjoyed a long and dashing career, it was never clear whether the Chevalier d'Eon was a man or a woman. Upon his death he was discovered to be a man. Here, "Mademoiselle d'Eon" is shown engaged in a fencing match with Monsieur de Saint George at Carlton House, London, April 1787. Engraving.

was to call for her rouge pots. She carefully dabbed her cheeks, closed her eyes, and drifted into the sleep of death.

Although cosmetics were widely used everywhere in Europe in the 18th century, the French managed to set a flamboyant style. Early in the century Lady Mary Wortley Montagu described French women as "monstrously unnatural in their paint!" Compared to English women, who were subtle in their use of applied color, the effect was alarming. She discovered "on their cheeks to their Chins, unmercifully laid on, a shining red japan that glistens in a most flaming manner . . . they seem to have no resemblance to Human faces. . . ."

In fact, a battery of creams and lotions were used to impart a luminous white complexion (regularly protected from the sun by a velvet mask), while cheeks and lips were stained vermilion. And these cosmetics, often made at home, could be brutal indeed. The pigments employed included ground cinnabar, alkanet, and red and white lead. Many, most especially the latter, were poisonous, and women were exhorted to make use of "natural" coloring agents, such as red wine and macerated rose petals. Concoctions were also available claiming to remove wrinkles, freckles, excess hair, scurf, smallpox pits, and sunburn.

The vivid appearance of the 18th-century face was enhanced by the habit of "patching." Black patches of paper, silk, or velvet, small as they were, could be cut into a great variety of shapes. One source describes a patch in the form of a tree with lovebirds, and tiny silhouetted profiles of friends appeared on the faces of nearest and dearest. Glued on with

mastic, patches might be placed anywhere on the face (or even on the bosom), at whim, to cover a pimple or pock mark or to draw attention to an attractive feature. For some reason inexplicable to us, it was believed that patching made one appear younger.

One notion that jars our image of the 18th century is the undeniable fact that men also painted. They blackened their eyebrows, patched, and rouged both cheeks and lips. Admittedly, men who did so were regarded as fops and dandies, but the practice seems to have been common throughout Europe. However, it was especially stylish at the French court and considered especially suitable in the evening. Men had not been as brightly painted since the days of the Pharaohs, and the custom was certainly not the exclusive habit of the effeminate. In *Fashions in Makeup* Richard Corson points out that George Washington himself was probably both powdered and perfumed.

Only one item of grooming did not take up as much time as it should. As late as 1827 it was said that the use of a bath was "regarded rather as a means of curing certain diseases than as a means of cleanliness." Although some women of the court (and few men) appear to have bathed, the place of bath water was often taken in both cases by the scented waters prepared at Cologne by the Farina brothers, also taken as a medication for headaches and indigestion. The shortcomings of this kind of hygiene were all too evident; essences "to correct the ill scent of the arm pits" were advertised. Nails were polished and worn very long, although only in Turkey did women paint them red.

Big and Little Pandora

Of course, the fashions of France in everything from painting to the fluting of a rosette spread, like the French language, to every court in Europe and from there to every salon and private circle of the bourgeoisie. The means of this dispersion of style were two—the still familiar fashion publication and the continued use of the fashion doll.

The first fashion periodical, the *Mercure Galant*, was published in 1670. But it was not until the mid-18th century that numerous competing journals blossomed: the *Journal du Goût*, the *Courier de la Mode*, the *Gallerie des Modes*, the *Cabinet des Modes*, and in England *The Lady's Magazine*. Several eventually presented engravings, and the art of the fashion plate was founded with masters such as Gravelot and Moreau le Jeune.

The little jointed fashion mannequins were sent out monthly from Paris to merchants throughout Europe and America as well. "Little Pandora" had only an informal wardrobe, whereas "Big Pandora" wore evening and ceremonial clothes. The hair,

jewelry, and even the complexion of these mannequins were also in the very latest fashion. The eagerness with which the Pandoras were received was satirized in the London *Spectator*:

I was almost in despair of ever seeing a model from the dear country, when last Sunday I overheard a lady in the next pew to me whisper to another that at the Seven Stars in King Street, Covent Garden, there was a Mademoiselle completely dressed just come from Paris. I was in the utmost impatience during the remaining part of the service, and as soon as ever it was over, having learnt the milliner's address, I went directly to her house in King Street, but was told that the French lady was at a person of quality's in Pall Mall. . . . I was therefore obliged to renew my visit this morning and had then a full view of the dear puppet from head to foot. You cannot imagine how ridiculously I find we have been trussed up during the war and how infinitely French dress excells ours.

Illustrations from the Gallerie des Modes, an 18th-century fashion periodical. Opposite: "Coiffure of a lady of quality." Below, top to bottom; left to right: A frontispiece; a drawing of Marie Antoinette; a lady in a fur-trimmed winter court dress; a satirical view of the costume of a "comfortable bourgeoise."; a gentleman in riding costume; after getting fully dressed, a lady discovers she has not washed her feet, and does so with the help of her maid.

Fortunately, during the Napoleonic blockade the combatants arranged for the passage of Big and Little Pandora to London, Rome, and Vienna.

The Pandoras were not received with equal enthusiasm everywhere. In the American colonies their more exaggerated styles were modified. Scarcely a building in the whole of North America was constructed on a sufficiently large scale to accommodate five-foot panniers. In a land where even stockings were chronically rumpled because the rubber for garters was unavailable, "hoop skirts" were considered sinful. Upon arrival in New England, the Pandoras ran into the Puritan ethic. When the Bay Colony suffered an earthquake, women took it as a sign of "awful Providence" and generally laid aside their "hoop petticoats." Panniers were simply not in the spirit of the colonies, where physical activity was both a fashion and a necessity.

The Spanish stamped their own eccentric imprint on French fashion. In an era that admired Raphael, Spain was a nation that could accept the wilder fantasies of El Greco and was not drawn to the homogeneous European style. Spanish women wore, as ever, the Moorish black or white mantilla, supported by a tortoise-shell comb and enveloping the figure in cascades of lace to below the waist. Men added the cummerbund belt to the usual dress, and their gilet and coat became increasingly short as the century wore on. The cape was always preferred to the overcoat. Needless to say, the fashions of Spain dominated South America.

The Italians accepted French fashion with a certain reluctance. Black remained a popular color in the north, although Italy's reaction to the decline

of her power ranged from dourness to depravity. That delicious anonymity to be found at the great balls of Versailles was available on a day-to-day basis in 18th-century Venice. The mask was worn during carnival, which extended from Twelfth Night until Lent, and on so many other holidays that it became the common mode of dress for all classes of society. The city beloved of Casanova was more than the gambling house and brothel of Europe. It was also the city of romantic intrigue on a more elevated level. As such it had already established a thriving tourist trade, and the tourists were not disappointed. Figures in the black silk *tabarro*, the fancy-dress mask, or the *bautta*, the convenient half-mask, and all-encompassing cape, crowded the quays and piazzas. The women of the paintings of Longhi

Opposite: One aspect of the eccentric imprint the Spanish set on 18th-century dress was the black or white lace mantilla of the women, which cascaded to the panniers of their skirts. La Tienda *by Luis Paret, detail. 1772.*

Left: The bautta, *the small half-mask worn during the lengthy carnival, lent an air of piquant mystery to the women of Venice.* The Rhinoceros *by Pietro Longhi, detail. 1751.*

wore the three-corner hat over the *rochetto*, a little silk or lace capelet covering the head and falling to the waist. Figures of such piquancy must have been as much a part of the fascination of the city as its architectural fantasies, so well preserved by Canaletto and Guardi, and the art of Tiepolo, which managed to keep the gorgeous excesses of the Italian Renaissance alive in the thin air of rococo frivolity.

Goethe's experience with fashion in his youth exemplified Germany's unprogressive attitudes toward style. His father was a staunch conservative, one of those worthy enemies of fashion who keep their best clothes for "good wear":

My father kept whatever belonged to his clothing in very good and neat order, and preserved more than used it for many years. Thus he had a predilection for certain old cuts and trimmings, by which our dress sometimes acquired a strange appearance.

In this same way had the wardrobe which I took with me to the university been furnished: it was very complete and handsome, and there was even a lace suit among the rest. Already accustomed to this kind of attire I thought myself sufficiently well dressed, but it was not long before my female friends, by gentle raillery, then by sensible remonstrances, convinced me that I looked as if I had dropped down out of another world.

The conservative tastes of Goethe's father were reflected also by both Frederick William I of Prussia and his son, Frederick the Great, who condemned those wearing foreign silk or lace to corporal punishment, forbade the importation of cotton, and threw a courtier's muff into the fire. He acted, however, not so much out of moral disapproval as for economic reasons. Frederick imported sheep, introduced silkworms, and improved both cloth and dyeing techniques in Prussia, and he intended to protect these industries.

In other German principalities, however, the reign of French dress was absolute. The axis of power in the 18th century was moving steadily east, and while Spain, Portugal, and Italy lapsed into impo-

tence, the prosperity of Austria, Prussia, and Russia rose sharply. These countries, without great periods of supremacy behind them, were willing to look to France as arbiter in matters of taste, and the laces and stays of French fashion were provided by French tailors on permanent tour of the principalities. However, a more authoritarian note was introduced. Many of the small courts imposed court uniforms on guests: in Munich, green piped with white; in Hesse, a special costume for each residence; in Dresden, blue and gold for women, red and gold for men. One fop, Count Brühl, owned no fewer than five hundred suits and over one thousand wigs. As Frederick II saw it, "rather a lot to cover an empty head."

German ladies have "devilish hard bones," grumbled Peter the Great, mistaking whalebone for human when he made what may be called his first grab at "Western dress." During his Great Embassy to the West, Czar Peter disguised himself as everything from a ship's carpenter to the servant behind the chair of his own governor-general. Peter was most determined to remove from his populace (with the exception of the clergy and peasantry) their caftans, long coats, turbans, and the age-old fur jackets and trousers of the steppe and to impose on them the latest in Western dress. To this end, on the day of his return from his tour in Western Europe, he shaved the beard off every noble present with his own hands and proceeded to organize several entertainments, instructing the court barber to shave all those who passed out drunk, easily the majority of guests. Henceforth beards, which had been a sacred badge of wisdom and piety in Russia, were taxed and licensed, if not outlawed outright. The long Russian coat was forbidden. Coats of "Western" (knee) length were to be worn, and those who did not comply were forced to kneel on the ground while their coats were cut off at the proper length. The British Ambassador to Constantinople reported the effects of the not-quite-digested Westernization on the Russian delegation:

> The Muscovite Ambassador and his retinue have appeared here so different from what they always formerly wore that ye Turks cannot tell what to make of them. They are all coutred in French habit, with an abundance of gold and silver lace, long perruques and which the Turks most wonder at, without beards. Last Sunday being mass in Adrianople, ye Ambassador and all his company did not only keep all their hats off during ye whole ceremony, but at ye elevation, himself and all of them pulled off their wigs. It was much taken notice of, and thought an unusual act of devotion.

Peter's success, however, was enforced by his daughter, the Empress Elizabeth, an eccentric soul who instituted transvestite balls at court so that she could exhibit her shapely calves in men's knee britches. She took a liking to the robe à la française

and on her death was found to possess no fewer than fifteen thousand Paris gowns.

While Peter the Great was attempting to bring the elaborately "civilized" dress of the West to Russia, the thinkers of the Enlightenment wanted to reduce that dress to the ideal simplicity of a more primitive society. For Rousseau, seeking the "noble savage" of pre-history to arrive at the original social contract from which society sprang, this simplicity appeared desirable (if remotely so) in all things, including dress. We may wonder whether Rousseau would not have been disillusioned had he seen the painted and bejeweled farmers of the earliest agrarian societies struggling to imitate his lapis lazuli jewelry in faience. We wonder, too, whether he might have been disillusioned by Chateaubriand's encounter in the American wilderness, where, intoxicated with the unspoiled nature of the Mohawk Valley, he bumped into a wigwam and perceived the first noble savages he had ever seen:

> There were a score of them, men and women, all daubed with paint like sorcerers, with half-naked bodies, slit ears, crows' feathers on their heads and rings in their noses. A little Frenchman, his hair all curled and powdered, wearing an apple-green coat, a drugget jacket and a muslin jabot and ruffles, was scraping a pocket fiddle and making those Iroquois dance *Madelon Friquet*. M. Violet (for that was his name) was the savages' dancing-master. They paid him for his lessons in beaver skins and bears' hams.

In any case, the most palpably visible result of Rousseau's return to the primitive was Marie Antoinette in the dress of a Boucher shepherdess.

Children of the Enlightenment

In one less known respect, however, Rousseau and the thinkers of the Enlightenment had a direct and far-reaching effect on dress: Their theories influenced the design of children's clothing. Evidence from early periods and cultures is skimpy, but it would appear that Egyptian children wore little clothing at all, and the Greek child wore his small chiton. The unfortunate Roman boy, however, was obliged to wear a purple-bordered toga, and we are tempted to wonder how an active child would ever keep it on without pins. From Roman times European children were dressed as small adults, and this reflected society's general attitude toward childhood. It was a transition to be gotten through quickly, and the child was to assume the responsibilities of an adult as soon as he was able. Children do not appear in European art as anything but small-scale adult figures until the 13th century, and

then only the Christ child is portrayed as a recognizable infant. It is a poignant reflection that it may well be that children were little regarded because so few survived. It is perhaps shocking to realize that many portraits of children that we see in later European art were in fact posthumous remembrances. As late as the 18th century the American artist John Singleton Copley completed the famous painting of his own family when two of his children were already ghosts. Moreover, the expectation that those children who lived would function as adults was very real. The children of the poor were obliged to assist at earning their sustenance as soon as they could walk. For the ruling aristocracy it was sometimes necessary to put harrowing responsibilities on small backs. We have already seen Charlemagne's son in his suit of baby armor and tiny Mary Tudor's excellent comportment during the

Left: Later in the century, British and American parents, "enlightened" by the thinking of Rousseau, dressed their young children in looser, more comfortable clothing. Detail of The Copley Family *by John Singleton Copley. 1776.*

Opposite top: Maximilian and his sister Marie Antoinette (at age thirteen), children of Empress Maria Theresa of Austria, were typically dressed as small adults confined in tight clothing. Miniatures. Artist unknown. 1765.

Below left: Frederick the Great and his sister Wilhelmina, who at age eight observed that the Czarina of Russia dressed as if she bought her clothing secondhand. Frederick, like many very small boys of his day, wears a dress like a girl's.

Detail of a portrait by Antoine Pesne.
Below right: Although the dress of small children gradually changed, older children remained dressed as adults. Lloyd Heneage and his sister, by Thomas Gainsborough, detail. 1750.

ceremony of her engagement at the age of two. Boy kings were not unusual. Among them might be listed Alfonso, the little brother of Isabella of Spain; Baldwin IV, the Leper King of Jerusalem who defeated Saladin at the age of sixteen; and Henry de Bray, the son of Edward I, who had his own castle complete with herb garden, dove house, pigsties, sheepfolds, and bakehouse, occasionally visited by his parents. His large staff, including his cooks, butlers, nurses, retainers, and chamberlain, tried desperately to save him when he fell ill and died at the age of seven. Such children were suitably dressed in small trunk hose, doublets, codpieces, farthingales, ruffs, and stays.

The children themselves seem to have acquired a sophistication well beyond their years, especially in matters of dress. The following is believed to be an extract from the copybook of Wilhelmina,

sister of Frederick the Great and, at the time of writing, eight years old. She is describing Peter the Great's wife Catherine, the Lithuanian slave girl taken to Russia as part of the booty of Marienburg:

The Czarina has a stumpy little body, very brown, and has neither air nor grace. . . . With her huddle of cloths she looked for all the world like a German play actress; her dress you would have said had been bought at a second-hand shop; all was out of fashion, all was loaded with silver and greasy dirt. The front of her bodice she had ornamented with jewels in a very singular pattern: a double eagle in embroidery, and the plumes of it set with poor little diamonds of the smallest possible carat, and very ill mounted. All along the facings were Orders and little things of metal; a dozen orders and as many portraits of saints, relics

177

have been some backsliding, and he was forced to put on the robe again as punishment for conduct unbefitting a man of seven.

These clothes, thought suitable for children, were not adapted to their needs or build. What, then, was their origin? In *Centuries of Childhood*, Philippe Ariès discerns a deliberate archaizing of children's dress. The robe, he notes, closely resembles the long medieval robe, discarded at the time of the Renaissance. However, it was always regarded as highly respectable, and churchmen and the elderly continued to wear it. The ribbons may be remnants of the false sleeve of the 16th century rather than the "lead strings" they were thought to be. The bonnet itself was worn by men in the 13th century. The urge to put children in something "old-fashioned" is followed even in our own day, when children are often displayed in Victorian fashions and laces. In fact, when adults first began to choose a differentiated dress for children, they did not invent. Rather, they chose something familiar but completely out of fashion and therefore innocent and suitable to the young. The children in the paintings of Lancret and Boucher wear collars of the period of Louis XIII and the Renaissance. Children were still dressed as little adults, but adults of another era.

Erasmus recommended that children be dressed so that they could move with more freedom, but it was not until the Enlightenment, with the desire to return to a natural state, that the question of children's dress was reexamined. Locke in his *Thoughts Concerning Education* revived the theory of a "sound mind in a sound body," and a sound body could not develop unless it was free from restraints and able to exercise properly. But the decisive voice was Rousseau's. In "Emile," his essay on education, he wrote:

> The limbs of the growing child should be free to move easily; there should be nothing tight, nothing fitting closely to the body, no belts of any kind. The French style of dress, uncomfortable and unhealthy for a man, is especially bad for children. The best plan is to keep children in frocks for as long as possible, and then to provide them with loose clothing, without trying to define the shape which is only another way of deforming it. Their defects of body and mind may all be traced to the same source, the desire to make men of them before their time.

and the like, so that when she walked, it was with a jingling, as if you heard a mule with bells to its harness.

Suddenly, at the turn of the 17th century, male children began to acquire a dress of their own (although little girls continued to be dressed as women). Until the age of four or five boys now wore the same dresses as girls, which in effect meant that they too dressed as women. They then progressed into a long robe, under which they later wore breeches. Children of both sexes wore two ribbons attached at the shoulders and falling down the back, as well as a bonnet. The succession of outfits in the childhood of Louis XIII was taken very seriously. At four he was given breeches to wear under his robe. At five his bonnet was replaced with a man's hat and the pronouncement, "Now that your bonnet has been taken away, you have stopped being a child and you have begun to become a man." There may have been some trouble here, because a week later the Queen put him back in his bonnet. Finally, "he was dressed in a doublet and breeches, abandoning the clothing of childhood and took cloak and sword." Again there seems to

Above: Mary Queen of Scots holds James I, who is dressed in the long robe traditionally worn by small boys in the 16th century. Detail of the Duff-Ogilvie Portrait. 1567–8.

Children's clothing, then, changed with the attitude toward children and their education during the 18th century, when the first true interest in pedagogy appeared. It may be seen as a concomitant of the rise of a middle class having the wealth to keep their children alive (as far as possible), the leisure to indulge them in the luxury of a "childhood," and the desire to educate them in a tradition more practical than the aristocratic or clerical tutelage then available. It was an era when many new schools opened their doors—to a new kind of child.

Georgian England

The English had no need of the teachings of a Rousseau to simplify their style of dress. The nature of English society was quite a suffcient source of inspiration in itself. Of England one thing was certain: The Hanoverian court was not, by any stretch of the imagination, either the heart of "society" or the center of fashion. George III married Charlotte of Mecklenburg-Strelitz, a plain-faced seventeen-year-old German girl totally lacking in all sense of style but a perfect *hausfrau*, which pleased her husband well enough. They were both economy-minded, and to cut expenditures they reduced the size of their court, which has been described as "the most boring in the world, a kind of dreary family boardinghouse."

The aristocracy of England, never having known the bridle of a Louis XIV, had remained from time immemorial on the land. Over the centuries this

aristocracy had worked at perfecting the image of the "country gentleman," something quite specifically English, which was polished to a high shine by the 18th century. Harold Nicolson in his *Good Behavior* strikes at the heart of the matter:

> Being intelligent rather than intellectual, inarticulate rather than garrulous, they have always preferred the country to the town. . . . Although in France the courtier was always regarded as the social superior of the squire, in England gentility came to be associated with the possession of land. . . . It was a salutary incentive, in that ploughland and woodland possess their own humanism, rendering calm the temperament of man, and his mind, slow and gentle.

The rural squire or large landowner, his mind taken up with scientific farming and his body with

Left: Queen Charlotte and King George III of England, who were accused of keeping the most boring court in the world. Queen Charlotte by Alan Ramsay, detail. 1762. Engraving of George III after a portrait by Thomas Gainsborough, detail. 1764.
Above: Although they kept their skirts relatively narrow, English women of the 18th century affected large, wide-brimmed hats, worn coquettishly forward on the head. Silhouette of a family group by Francis Torond. c. 1785.

field sports, was the English ideal. At best he approached the Arcadian man, attuned to nature, a gracious master who brought both art and architecture to a rural setting and made of that setting a work of art. At worst he might well be illiterate or besotted or both. In any case, neither he nor his wife, whose time was devoted to riding to hounds and caring for the aged and ill of the village, would be likely candidates for the fashions of Versailles.

Early in the 17th century Sir Francis Bacon likened behavior to a garment and in so doing revealed the English ideal in both:

> Behavior is the garment of the mind and ought to have the conditions of a garment. For first, it ought to be made in fashion; secondly, it should not be too curious or costly; thirdly, it ought to be so framed as best to set forth any virtue of the mind and supply and hide any deformity; and lastly, and above all, it ought not to be straight, so as to confine the mind and interfere with its freedom in business and action.

This love of freedom in both dress and manner was not championed by all Englishmen. There were those, like the worldly and traveled Lord Chesterfield, whose image of the 18th-century gentleman is as close to an international concept as we are likely to encounter in that era. He conveyed his ideas of "air, manners, graces, style, elegance, and all those ornaments . . ." in persistent and nagging letters to his dutiful, put-upon, and awkward illegitimate son, Philip Stanhope. In the matter of dress Lord Chesterfield advised sobriety and a high respect for the customs of other countries:

A man of sense carefully avoids any particular character in his dress; he is accurately clean for his own sake; but all the rest is for other people's. He dresses as well, and in the same manner, as the people of sense and fashion of the place where he is. If he dresses better, as he thinks, that is, more than they, he is a fop; if he dresses worse, he is unpardonably negligent. But, of the two, I would rather have a young fellow too much than too little dressed; the excess on that side will wear off, with a little age and reflection; but if he is negligent at twenty, he will be a sloven at forty, and stink at fifty years old. Dress yourself fine, where others are fine; and plain where others are plain; but take care always that your clothes are well made, and fit you, for otherwise they will give you a very awkward air. When you are once well dressed for the day think no more of it afterward; and, without any stiffness for fear of discomposing that dress, let all your motions be as easy and natural as if you had no clothes on at all. So much for dress, which I maintain to be a thing of consequence in the polite world.

Opposite: The English country gentleman, who was "intelligent rather than intellectual," gave up lace and silk fripperies early in the 18th century. Sir Robert Walpole, Earl of Oxford by John Wootton. Before 1730.

Above left: A simply dressed English couple, Mr. and Mrs. William Atherton.

Detail of portrait by Arthur Devis. c. 1747.
Above right: The widely traveled Lord Chesterfield, who maintained that dress was "a thing of consequence in the polite world." Samuel Johnson charged that he had "the morals of a whore and the manners of a dancing master." Detail of portrait by Alan Ramsay. 1765.

181

easier. The sporting young men of the period began to take an interest in driving and even in hunting, and to dress more like their stud grooms."

The English evolved several characteristic garments. The frock coat, cut long and straight, was far more suitable for riding and sports than the tight-fitting justaucorps with its nipped waist and flared skirts. The greatcoat, an overcoat covering all garments, made perfect sense in the chilly damp of England. The round, flat-brimmed, high-crowned hat gradually replaced the tricorn.

Moreover, changes were going on under the hat. Wigs had become so common that they were passing out of fashion, and young bucks began to prefer the comfort of their own hair, unpowdered. The wigmakers of London took alarm and staged a protest march in 1765. They petitioned George III to enforce the wearing of wigs by law. The London crowd became so irate at the demonstration that they attacked the unhappy petitioners (many of whom were wigless) and cut off their hair.

English women were far less addicted to panniers than their French counterparts, although their skirts were occasionally quilted or padded. Moreover, the heavy decoration of their dresses, usually lace, stopped at the waist, as it would be foolish for a woman who actually moved through the rough foliage of the country to attach delicate valuables to a wide skirt. The riding coat (or "redingote"), a jacket tailored like a man's coat, fitting tight to the waist and flaring over a wide skirt, was a sportswoman's fashion and a completely English innovation. English women wore hats, usually with large brims, far more often than did their French contemporaries. Moreover, they painted less, although white lead was said to have caused the death of Maria, Lady Coventry, one of the famed Gunning sisters.

England's overseas colonies influenced dress at home. Successful colonials returned from India with a taste for cotton, as did planters from the West Indies, and these preferences were easily fulfilled by England's growing cotton industry. Queen Mary, the wife of William III, wore chintz and printed calico (the name itself is derived from Calcutta). Such simpler "Arcadian" dresses were championed by Gainsborough, who, like the French painters, created fashion more often than he copied it.

Of course, England's commercial community was immensely powerful, and we would expect it to have made London, to some extent, the center of fashion. But, in the words of Adam Smith, "merchants are commonly ambitious of becoming country gentlemen." Fashions in London seem to have differed from those in the country by only an occasional touch of lace. The rakes and harlots of Hogarth's paintings appear to be like country people tempted to evil by the seductions of the city, where clothing becomes disreputably disheveled, blown by the winds of urban decadence.

Lord Chesterfield's "foreign tastes" and views were not held by every Englishman. Samuel Johnson's sentiment regarding his precepts was succinct: Chesterfield taught "the morals of a whore and the manners of a dancing master."

Still, Lord Chesterfield put great weight on the fitness of dress, and the English gentleman evolved with considerable taste a wardrobe "fitting" to his sporting and outdoor manner of life, as independent of his lifelong enemy, the French, as was possible while remaining within the general outlines of fashion. English custom had from the beginning of the century been somewhat different from French. Waistcoats were shorter, and breeches in suede or buckskin were worn correspondingly tighter. By 1731 the newspapers proclaimed that "gentlemen did their best to resemble servants," and by 1776 lace ruffles and embroidery had totally disappeared from men's dress. At the end of the century broadcloth could be worn at any time, even at court. Among the leaders of the reversion to casual fashions was the bumptious Charles James Fox and his circle. According to William B. Boulton, "Mr. Charles Fox and his friends at Brooks's had made a fashion of an affected negligence in dress, and the gradual disappearance of the lace ruffle, powdered wig and embroidered waistcoat . . . made the change

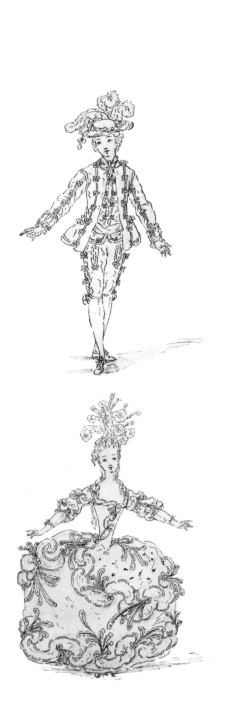

The Last Queen

France in 1770 saw the marriage (by proxy) of the grandson and eventual heir of Louis XV and Maria Antonia, the fifteen-year-old daughter of the Empress Maria Theresa of Austria. The child marked from birth by Kaunitz to become queen of France was in the words of the French ambassador, a "delicious little morsel," with that transparent pale skin so much admired, china-blue eyes, a long neck and regal bearing, soft even features, and fine blond hair. Her affectionate but strait-laced mother did not indulge her children, and the dauphine was brought up "lacking for everything." Moreover, Maria Theresa's court was hierarchic in the extreme. Not only was there a prescribed court dress (for men a red coat over gold-embroidered gilet and for women a red gown with gold and silver embroidery and lace trim), but the entire society was divided into five

classes and the clothing worn by each was prescribed. Tailors who espied nonconformists were instructed to report them. This severely structured setting seems to have been mitigated by a great deal of sentimentality. The girl who arrived at Versailles all uninstructed innocence was also a paragon of sticky sweetness, later to be reflected in the love knots, *putti*, nosegays and hearts she inflicted on the already overladen rococo style. She was a lover of animals, children, and sentiment.

Marie Antoinette also possessed an overriding desire to have a good time. It would be too facile to say that this represented a reaction to the stuffiness of her mother's court. Her doltish husband, who tinkered with clocks and retired to bed early, suited her well enough; in spite of later calumnies she was always a dutiful wife. But she developed a

passion for a kind of self-centered freedom—freedom from hated corsets, freedom to gamble, to go to parties, to take a hackney cab to the opera if her own coach broke down. But to generalize her own desire for freedom to a deeper understanding of mankind and the role of the state was quite beyond her capabilities. As a result she simply added new enmities to those she inherited with her position and reacted, with her lifelong tendency to flight, by seeking the comfort of a small circle of seemingly trustworthy favorites.

Marie Antoinette's greatest weakness was a possibly quite innocent but nonetheless impressive extravagance, again perhaps a reaction to the strictness of Maria Theresa. This extravagance expressed itself in reckless gambling debts, remunerations and gifts to her favorites, and the enormous expense of her toilette, said to be as high as 258,000 livres in one year. In this she was assisted by Mademoiselle Bertin, her "Minister of Fashion."

In 1776 the marchands et merchandes de modes, the haberdashers who provided the garnissements and headdresses that turned a simple gown into a work of art, broke away from the corporation of mercers

and founded their own. The *frivolistes*, fashionable haberdashers, became creative artists, and although they did not actually sew the dresses they decorated, they set the styles and served as the ancestors of the later French couturiers. Of these the most famous, or infamous, was Rose Bertin, who started life as an errand girl and whose shop on the rue St. Honoré became the bastion of French fashion. Introduced by the Princess de Lamball to Marie Antoinette, she became confidante, dressmaker, and the temptress who was blamed for the excessive expenses of the princess.

Marie Antoinette quickly became the unquestioned leader of French fashion. When her chestnut-colored dress was admired by the Prince, dressmakers were kept up all night so that the women of the court might be seen wearing that very color the next day. When *Athalie* was performed at the Théâtre Française, Marie Antoinette adopted the straight, loosely sashed gown à *la Lévite* to cover her pregnancy, and throughout the court men and women alike were to be seen dressed in the style of ancient Hebrew priests. When she found the various shapes of the handkerchief (a late Renaissance innovation) inconvenient, Louis XVI signed an edict commanding that all handkerchiefs be square, one of his few decrees to survive intact to the present.

Unfortunately, it was during the early reign of Marie Antoinette that the most grotesque and ridiculous hair fashions in all of the history of dress seized the imagination of the court. Enormous constructions were elevated on top of the head. Women combed up their powdered hair (natural and false)

Left: Benjamin Franklin, in the simple dress of a republican, enjoying the attention of the ladies of the French court, who are elegantly costumed in panniers and giant coiffures. Detail of an engraving by W. O. Geller, after a painting by Baron Jolly. c. 1778.

Above: Marie Antoinette seated at her harp. La Reine dans sa Chambre à Versailles by J. R. A. Gautier-Dagoty, detail. 1775.

Top: The notorious Rose Bertin, Marie Antoinette's dress designer and sometime confidante, who was said to be partly responsible for the Queen's downfall. Engraving. 1780.

Above: In the fashion of 1776, a lady of the court of Louis XVI sails an entire frigate on her head.

Right: Mesdames de Montesson, du Crest, and de Damas taking tea, their hair suitably dressed with ribbons, laces, gauzes and feathers. Stripes were obviously in style. Watercolor by Louis de Carmontelle. 1773.

to cover a horsehair pad worn on the crown of the head, with rows of curls at the back, the entire arrangement kept in place by pins and pomade. This edifice might also support an exaggerated version of the lace caps formerly worn on small coiffures, or decorations of ribbons, gauze, and flowers. Such two-foot-high creations often took on decoration of the most extraordinary variety. One Baroness Oberkirch covered hers with flowers standing in vases of water ("spring in the middle of snow").

Madame de Lauzun carried entire dramas on her head: a hunting scene, ducks in a lake, a mill and its active population, the miller's wife flirting with the local cleric while her husband pulls an ass by its reins. *Poufs* à *l'asiatique* were covered with Oriental drapery. Political events were, as ever, an inspiration of fashion rather than an incitement to thought at the French court. A coiffure à *la Belle Poule*, consisting of a frigate at full sail, celebrated a famous naval victory. A satirist depicted a woman's

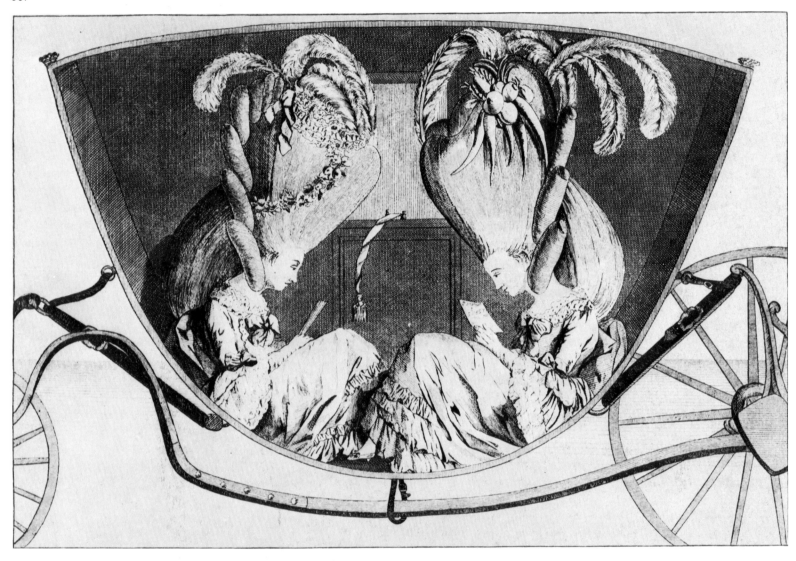

headdress on which was enacted the entire battle of Bunker Hill, a comment on what must be called the "radical chic" of the period.

One morning at her toilette Marie Antoinette seized some enormous ostrich feathers and implanted them in her coiffure. Louis XVI heartily approved, and within days the female part of the court had donned feathers. The queen arranged to have her portrait painted in this, her favorite headdress, and sent it to her mother. The empress's reaction was violent. She returned the painting with a note: "There has been, no doubt, some mistake. I received the portrait of an actress, not that of a queen. I am expecting the right one."

As a practical matter these coiffures presented a considerable number of problems. Women were forced to travel in a kneeling position, with their heads hanging out of the windows of their carriages. Even the very wealthy could afford the lengthy

attention of the hairdresser only once a week. The less fortunate might be obliged to maintain their hair in place for a month. In such cases the pomatum, based on beef marrow, often went rancid. One horrified gentleman witnessed the "opening up" of an elderly aunt's coiffure. Swarms of bugs appeared, but he was assured they could not scurry to other parts of the body because they were glued in place by the pomatum. Nests of mice were also reported, and the long-armed ivory "scratcher" became a necessary implement.

It must be said in defense of the huge coiffure that it was worn with voluminous panniers only in the evening or for ceremonial occasions. By day women were content to balance a larger head with a smaller body, wearing light dresses with small hooped petticoats rather than panniers and skirts so short that ankles and high-heel shoes were clearly visible.

Marie Antoinette did not remain oblivious to the intellectual atmosphere of her time. In her simplistic way she grossly misinterpreted it. She insisted that *The Marriage of Figaro* be performed at court, and she was among those to applaud and assist the American victories over France's enemy, England. But she mistook the winds of revolution for the soft breezes of Arcadia. The very notions of the Philosophes that led to the meeting of the Estates General and the public's predictable reaction could and did also lead, by another turn of argument, to the notion of Romantic escape, and Marie Antoinette followed the latter train of thought.

If *The Marriage of Figaro* was a splendid entertainment not to be missed, Rousseau's *Nouvelle Héloïse* and his vision of the bucolic past invited a change of decor and fashion. At her Petit Trianon Marie Antoinette created a Rousseauesque paradise: a little *hameau*, meadows with peeping wildflowers, a miniature manicured forest, artificial ponds. This was a world true to her own sense of sweetness, the setting for a heroine by Greuze. For this toy Arcadia Marie Antoinette and her favorites abandoned the court and its more adult problems. Here only children's games were permitted—hide-and-seek and blind-man's bluff.

The setting required a different style of costume. With the "English garden" Marie Antoinette and her court adopted the English dress of *indienne*, of percale or muslin. More nationalistically, these were known as *chemises à la Créole*, gowns such as

French women wore in America. Now the "village maiden" in virginal white was the fashion. Panniers and hoops were replaced with a kind of bustle, balanced by a "pigeon-breasted" bodice, effected by a padded triangle of wire. The low décolleté might be demurely covered by a pristine white fichu, or neckerchief, and modest sleeves covered the arm to the wrist. A girlish sash around the waist and a large Florentine straw hat tied with ribbons at the neck completed the image. Other English styles, such as the redingote for women and the frock coat for men, also became fashionable. The enormous constructions of hair were now replaced by soft curls falling artfully into the disorder of a windy day. Some attributed this change to the fact that Marie Antoinette was losing her hair after the birth of her last child and had to have it cut.

It is interesting to note that although these fashions did come from England, they need not have. Because of cheap cottons the French peasantry and city workers no longer dressed in the worn-out clothes of the wealthy, giving them a beggarly appearance. They had evolved their own fashion, and French peasant women had for several decades worn dresses with a simple bodice or fitted jacket and loosely pleated skirt in the printed calicos and cottons now available, garnished with a white fichu at the neck and a white apron. The little bustle at the back, the *confort*, may have developed as their more comfortable response to the hoop skirt. It was, therefore, an exquisite form of a fashion already

Marie Antoinette and Louis XVI attempt a life of Rousseauesque simplicity in the gardens of the Petite Trianon, where dress was in the English fashion, and only children's games were permitted. Engraving. Late 18th century.

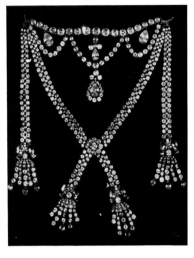

worn by the lower classes. Meanwhile, French laborers adopted the ankle-length trousers, the *matelots* worn by sailors, making them literally the *sans-culottes*, those "without knee breeches."

Marie Antoinette's reversion to simplicity had come too late, and the public sensed that its spirit was not fitting. By the mid-1780s France's problems, the problems of the rusty machinery of state inadequate in every detail for the structure and sophistication of the society that it controlled, had become intolerable. They were exacerbated by the insolvency of the state, inflation, and failing crops. All disasters were laid at the door of Marie Antoinette. The public mind converted her vast sins of omission to sins of commission, and the rather prudish queen was accused in scurrilous pamphlets of every sexual profligacy, as well as every extravagance imaginable. When her portrait by Vigée-Lebrun ap-

peared in the salon of 1783, showing Marie Antoinette in her simple and unadorned (and newly fashionable) white muslin, she was accused of "dressing like a chambermaid in order to humiliate France" and of deliberately ruining the French clothing industry to assist the cloth trade of her brother's Austrian Netherlands. The scandal of "The Queen's Necklace" delivered the *coup de grâce*. We shall probably never know whether in fact Marie Antoinette accepted a diamond necklace as a bribe from the Cardinal de Rohan or whether she was the innocent dupe of a complicated intrigue hatched by an adventuress and implicating a magician. What is certain now, however, and was so even then, is that the shabby imbroglio would never have taken place had the queen not been the sort of woman to be tempted to accept such a bauble at such a time. The view was clearer from Vienna than from the Petit Trianon. With maternal prescience Maria Theresa scolded her daughter once again: "Your luck can all too easily change and by your own fault you may well find yourself plunged into deepest misery. . . . One day you will recognize the truth of this, but it will be too late."

Above left: Marie Antoinette as she appeared during the last years of her life, confined to the Temple. It was said that her hair turned white from the shock of seeing the head of her friend the Princess de Lambal on a pike. Though only thirty-six, she seems much older in this portrait by Alexander Kucharski. 1793.

Above center: "The Queen's Necklace," a reproduction of the famed original made by Baszange. Paris. 1784.
Above right: Although a crude sketch, this picture by David of Marie Antoinette going to the guillotine in shorn locks and mobcap is a telling comment on human vanity and its consequences. 1793.

The French Revolution:

Fashion at the Barricades

Theatrically speaking, the French Revolution and its aftermath was a costume drama, with dress playing a significant role in each shattering act. The first rumblings caused by dress were felt at Versailles in May 1789, when Louis XVI called together the Estates General for the first time in nearly two centuries. An irreparable blunder was made by the King's Master of Ceremonies, Dreux de Breze. When convening the Assembly, he invoked the same sumptuary laws that had governed the last such gathering 175 years before. Nobles, clergy, and the Third Estate were required to wear "appropriate dress"—that is to say, appropriate to the year 1614. Nobles were expected to exercise their privilege of rank by displaying themselves in gold-embroidered brocades, white stockings, plumed hats, and swords. Brilliant red hats and the solemn rustle of purple robes would identify the religious hierarchy (although two hundred parish priests were restricted to wearing their traditional simple cassocks). The sumptuary laws were obviously directed at an indignant Third Estate, whose prescribed uniform, drearily dark and unobtrusive, was calculated to make them look like a convention of nameless shadows.

At the most, the nobles and clergy represented a minority of four hundred thousand people. The Deputies of the Third Estate, on the other hand, represented millions of commoners, indeed, almost 95 percent of the population of France. Outraged by de Breze's arcane form of sartorial humiliation, they banded together mutinously against all the class distinctions that had been crystallized in repressive rules of dress. The era of the sumptuary law and the legal division of men into uniformed classes had long passed, and it was a sad comment on the King's lack of awareness of social change that he should have thought otherwise.

Within six weeks the Third Estate had wrested power from their former superiors. At the top of the infant Assembly's agenda was an act abolishing all laws granting sartorial privilege. Ostentation suddenly became tantamount to suicide. Disconcerted nobles were quick to get the point. Within a few months the entire paraphernalia of rococo dress was cast off. Gone were the panniers and five-foot-wide skirts they supported, as well as the exquisite *garnissements* that so pleased Madame de Pompadour. Gone too were the scented powders, court rouge, diamond buckles, ornate vests, and *mouches*. Even good manners were considered "a weapon of the aristocracy" by the radical Jacobins,

192

Left: Dress for the Deputies attending the fateful meeting of the Estates General in Paris in 1789 was officially prescribed.
Top: The scarlet hat and purple robe of the clergy.
Center: An aristocrat in the costume, required by laws then 175 years old.
Bottom: The dark anonymity of the Third Estate.

and one was wise to cultivate an image of uncouth
gruffness.

Now sober little bonnets, caps, and turbans covered the heads that only recently had borne the
towering, elaborately powdered *coiffures à la flore*
and *poufs à l'asiatique*. Men and women alike
sported a tricolor cockade in case anyone should
question their political allegiance. The cockade itself had been designed by Lafayette, the white of
the King intermingling with the red and blue of
Paris. Unfortunately, this protective device could
not always be relied on, and heads began to roll.

193

The costume of the day was no longer established by idle courtiers but by a cautious bourgeoisie and by the implacable spirit of the Revolution. The fripperies of Versailles gave way to the uncluttered fashions of the rustic English gentry, who for years had fled the discomforts of court dress in favor of horsy understatement. As we have seen, these styles already enjoyed a certain vogue. Under the *ancien régime* French laborers, like sailors who wore *matelots*, had dressed in ankle-length trousers. This plainly plebeian fashion was now accepted, and silk knee breeches, although soon reintroduced, were gradually replaced by longer "pantaloons" for informal wear. The other principal features of the new garb for men, foreshadowing their modern dress, included somber wool frock coats, sensibly short waistcoats, stiff collars, folded stocks, and, in place of the tricorne, high-crowned round hats with rolled brims. Discretion dictated women's dress; skirts became narrow and colors dull. Bodices were modestly covered with a white fichu à *la citoyenne* (or à *la Charlotte Corday;* there was always a certain degree of gallows humor about the Revolution). Of course, women's dress would one day regain its brilliance. The dress of men never has, and they remain to this day in the habit of bourgeois worker drones.

Among the less fanatic political factions, the most notable outfits had been devised by the Republican Girondins, who complemented their relentlessly classical rhetoric with flowing black robes and muslin cravats, which for some reason were supposed to suggest Roman senatorial dress.

"My ugliness," gloated Mirabeau, an early leader of the Revolution, "is my strength." It is interesting to note how many of the Revolution's principal players seemed to draw power from the same source. Danton, the Revolutionary government's minister of justice, his features disfigured by smallpox, had two childhood encounters with rampaging bulls. Marat, the rabble-rousing pamphleteer with a repellent toadlike face, was covered with scabs and running sores. Even the painter Jacques Louis David, the movement's official portraitist, costumer, and set designer, had a mouth twisted into a sinister smirk by a tumorous growth on his upper lip. Danton continued to dress like a disheveled provincial lawyer and, but for his distinctively battered face, would have "blended instantly with the crowd." Marat, driven by insatiable hatred and paranoia, refused to change the stinking rags and greasy bandannas he had worn as a fugitive in the sewers. They had become his political badge, a terrorist campaign dress as fearsome as the gory massacres he loved to plot. In the Assembly not even his admirers could bear to sit less than three benches from him, so overpowering was the stench.

"David and Robespierre," observed the Goncourt brothers from the peaceful knoll of the Second Empire, "two icy geniuses in a volcano!" Frisking like a mountain goat from the peak of one regime to another, David was the Talleyrand of the arts. His career in neoclassic painting had been launched when the Académie Royale awarded him the prestigious Prix de Rome. In effect this made him a protégé of Louis XVI, a favor he would later repay by voting for the King's death. A three-year sojourn in Rome broadened his classical repertoire. This invaluable experience would later permit David to paint togas reflecting a diversity of political persuasions. For the Revolutionaries he could celebrate the no-nonsense austerity of the Roman Republic, while for Napoleon he could obligingly recreate the dazzling grandeur of the Roman Empire.

Throughout the Revolution David was an influential Jacobin and slavish follower of Robespierre, the asexual zealot who wore tiny guillotines embossed on his buttons and who described bloodbaths as "cleansings." David attended public executions gladly; he sketched from life both Marie Antoinette en route to Dr. Guillotine's "humanely" perfected machine and Danton's final agony. He was less interested in the unlucky members of the lower classes, the seamstresses, chefs, and similar innocents who, quaking in the tumbrels, rumbled to an ironic fate—decapitation, which until the Revolution had been a ritual form of execution exclusively reserved for the nobility.

Choreographed by Robespierre and designed by David, the Terror became a carnival, and the daily beheadings were enlivened by "patriotic and fraternal banquets" and "feasts of Virtue" in the streets.

The earliest phase of the Revolution had seen the heyday of atheism. The cathedral of Notre Dame, blithely renamed the "Temple of Liberty," was commandeered for one particularly memorable occasion: A nineteen-year-old chorus girl from the Opéra, Thérèse-Angélique Aubry, "a living model of antique perfection," was decked out as the Goddess of Reason and set upon an elevated Throne of Liberty. For the event, which was not a performance but a solemn ceremony of state attended by the President and representatives of the nation, she wore classical drapery and the ubiquitous red "Phrygian" cap, supposedly the hat of the ancient galley slave. In the spirit of the era she carried a pike

Above: A self-portrait of David, master painter, father of French neoclassicism, and costume designer for the Revolution. He created for France first a republic and then an empire of the classical model. 1794.
Left: A sans-culotte and his female counterpart: he is in the loose trousers, she in the narrow skirt, apron, and white fichu of the working classes of Paris, both armed to the teeth and sporting the tricolor cockade. Interestingly, working women felt free to exhibit their ankles. Engraving by Charbonneau after a drawing by Emil Walker. 1795.

Robespierre deplored such classical excesses. In June 1794, with David's technical assistance, he presented his own theological compromise at the Festival of the Supreme Being, a ceremony at which God's return to France was honored by lengthy hymns and sermons, automated effigies, and mountains of papier-mâché. Robespierre himself appeared in curiously counterrevolutionary daffodil knee breeches and a turquoise silk coat. Primly, he set a torch to allegorical figures of Atheism, Egotism, and Insincerity. A statue of Wisdom was meant to arise phoenixlike from their smoking ruins, but unfortunately it too caught fire. Following this inauspicious and cautionary episode, old men wearing crowns of vine leaves blessed adolescents, children tossed flowers into the air, and virgins swore "to marry only citizens who had served the fatherland."

That same spring, Robespierre's last, David was commissioned to design a national costume that would celebrate the revival of Republican Rome. He proposed breeches, a togalike tunic, a round plumed hat, and a blue cape for warmth in winter. Military students in the Ecole de Mars were to be toughened by a costume "half Roman and half Scotch," with a tunic and epaulettes worn above bare legs and accompanied by an "antique" sword thrust in a tigerskin belt for swagger. They were obliged to live on herb soups, "in the Spartan manner." The quest for total authenticity led the designer Wicker, David's pupil, to suggest that the women of Paris go about in true Spartan simplicity, naked to the waist.

Robespierre was executed on July 28, 1794, and with him ended the Terror in all its paralyzing aspects. Danton had once half seriously joked that, after all, the Revolution was a battle, and the spoils should go to the victors. As usual, however, they went to the speculators and profiteers. Fortunes were made and spent within a matter of months. Inflation roared into the stratosphere. By 1795 two hundred livres were demanded for a pair of shoes that would have cost five livres in 1790. Republican "virtue" was cheerfully abandoned for the licentiousness of the Directoire period.

Above: Costume for the members of the Directory, as conceived by David and satirized by Gillray in an engraving. 1798.

Right: Dress decorated with cross-binding à la victime, suggesting the trussed victims carried by the tumbrils to the guillotine. 1798.

Far right: Women in the fashions of Napoleon's Consulate. The spirit is still classical, as is shown by the high-waisted sheaths of fragile fabric. The furniture reflects the same politically inspired style. Engraving. 1800.

Opposite above: Three Incroyables of the Directory at the gambling table sport the frock coats and the exaggerated collars and stocks of the era. Engraving. c. 1798.

Opposite below: A Merveilleuse in outsize bonnet and frills. Engraving by Horace Vernet. c. 1798.

Directoire License

Meanwhile, emigrés trickled back from abroad, and even the newer social wounds began to heal. David, mildly chastened by two incarcerations following the downfall of the Jacobins, galvanized the public by charging admission to view his post-revolutionary paintings, in which the Sabine women were depicted in a conciliatory mood, trying to make peace between their irate male relatives and their Roman abductors. The gratuitous symbolism of the painting made a huge and happy impact—as did the skimpy costumes of its subjects. David's pupil Wicker, in his wildest dreams of feminine Sparta, could not have imagined the extremes to which Directoire women would soon go in their efforts to dress à la Grecque. High-heeled shoes, corsets, and all constricting garments were discarded, and classical dress was adopted (by women only) in the form of the chemise, a high-waisted sheath with a wide, low décolleté, scant sleeves, and, somewhat surprisingly, a train. The chemise was generally white and of a delicate fabric (it might be linen, cotton, muslin, or even tulle), sometimes almost transparent so that it revealed the natural shape of the body. (The fabric might be rendered still more revealing with a dash of water.) Or occasionally it might be slit from waist to ankle, exhibiting the new underclothing, a type of flesh-colored silk body stocking, called the *maillot*, which originated with the costume worn by ballerinas in the Opéra. The vision was completed by ankle bracelets, toe rings, open sandals, and gilded nails. To achieve the effect à la Vestale (or à la Diane), hair was caught up in a "Psyche knot" at the back of the head. Men cropped their hair in short curls à la Brutus.

The new fragile materials did not provide sufficient warmth in winter, so elaborately embroidered shawls were artfully draped over the figure. Accompanying the costume was a heavy tunic coat, usually in a bright contrasting color, that was full-length, high-waisted, and often trimmed with fur. Also popular were little Spencer jackets, which gave no protection below the waist.

A mania for dancing swept Paris onto its feet, and public balls were held night after night on the sites of recent carnage. The Empress Josephine's biographer, Ernest John Knapton, reports that "an especially popular entertainment was the *Bal à la Victime* to which only relatives of those who had been guillotined could be invited. As if in preparation for the guillotine, men cut their hair short and women wore theirs high on the head, leaving the nape of the neck bare. A narrow scarlet ribbon worn by the ladies seemed to make a blood-red line around the throat, while during the dance the head was jerked back and forth "as if ready to fall into the basket of the guillotine."

It was at this time that a most peculiar sartorial aberration burst into grotesque flower. Young Parisian dandies calling themselves Les Incroyables and their female counterparts, Les Merveilleuses, irrationally transformed themselves into startling caricatures of *la mode anglaise*—the latest London fashions. The Incroyables wore their collars so high that they almost covered their gold-ringed ears, and the tails of their frock coats were so long that they sometimes trailed on the ground. Further exaggerations included indecently tight trousers hiked to northerly waistlines just beneath the armpits. The Merveilleuses teetered about in enormous skirts and outsize bonnets ludicrously trimmed with yards of lace and ribbons. Both sexes took pains to dishevel their hair. The Merveilleuses and Incroyables were parvenus, but, in reaction to their parents' political views, they were Royalists. In the manner of their spiritual descendants, the zoot suiters of the 1940s, the Teddy Boys of the 1950s, and the even more recent Mods, they spent an inordinate amount of money on their clothes, and they evolved their own argot, including dropping their "r's" in imitation of the English.

In 1795 a frustrated young brigade commander, Napoleon Bonaparte, despaired of a nation that could mindlessly suffer the society of profiteers, adventuresses, Incroyables, and Merveilleuses. "I hardly care what happens to me," he wrote, ". . . such is the abyss to which I have been brought by the moral spectacle of this country and by my familiarity with danger." Certainly the Revolution had come full cycle, and when the last head had dropped into the executioner's basket and all was said and done, it would seem that the French had changed little but their clothes.

With the formation of the Directoire, David, ever ready to lend a hand, was called on to design an

Left: Fashions of the era of Napoleon's Consulate. Women varied their dress à la Grecque with a great variety of bonnets. Men adopted the new high-crowned hat and the Napoleonic bicorn. From Le Costume Historique by M. A. Racinet.

Post-Revolutionary Paris was overcome by a "dance madness," during which balls were held nightly. Right: Dancing Parisian couples. The men have exchanged their daytime "half-dress" for evening "full dress" with knee breeches. Engraving. 1805.

appropriate costume for the five powerful officials who together governed France. Blandly turning his back on the proletarian image of the *sans-culotte*, David poked about in the hateful wardrobe of the *ancien régime* and emerged brandishing knee breeches, silk stockings, and the aristocratically plumed hat. Other symbols of rank he preferred to confect himself, among them such items as a long, pompously embroidered mantle of magisterial red, a pretty lace collar, and a "Roman" sword.

Most durable of the Directors was the venal Paul Barras, an ex-nobleman and victor of Thermidor whose tastes epitomized the general tenor of post-revolutionary political life. La Revellière, in his description of Barras, provides us as well with a sketch of Directoire social circles:

> With a fine carriage and a manly figure, he always had something of that common and brash air found in low society. . . . He had a great, a tireless, capacity for intrigue. Falsehood and bottomless dissimulation, joined to other vices, grew stronger over the years. At the Luxembourg palace built by Marie de Medici he was surrounded by the most dissolute fomenters of anarchy, by lost women, ruined men, "fixers," speculators, mistresses and *mignons*. The most infamous debauchery was openly practised in his house. Though he always employed the language of a patriot, and even of the *sans-culotte*, he surrounded himself with an extraordinary luxury. He had all the tastes of an opulent, extravagant, magnificent, and dissipated prince.

Below: A society ball. "Paris adores, cherishes, worships, the dance—it is second only to money," wrote Sebastian Mercier in 1798. Engraving by Bosio.

Orbiting most brightly among his galaxy of hangers-on was the languid Creole widow, Josephine de Beauharnais.

Josephine adapted easily. She had to. Barely a year before she had had good cause to fear a rendezvous with the guillotine. Prior to this she had shuttled between Paris, Fontainebleau, and the countryside in an effort to elude Republican malice. In compliance with the convention's decree that all children should learn a trade, she packed off her daughter Hortense to a governess to learn the trade of seamstress and her son to the country as a carpenter's apprentice. Josephine composed a letter to the President of the Committee of General Security, professing that she was "a genuine *sans-culotte.*" Insisting that neither she nor her husband Alexander had ever deviated from the principles of Liberty and Equality, she hoped to tender irrefutable proof: "I am an American," wrote this stylish viscountess and daughter of a Martinique plantation holder, "my household is a republican household: before the Revolution my children were not distinguishable from the *sans-culottes,* and I hope they will be worthy of the Republic."

Not only was her letter never answered, but within three months she and her husband had been jailed. Josephine's charming manners never deserted her, although apparently, to the embarrassment of her noble fellow prisoners, her courage did. Bouts of sobbing and solitaire were only infre-

quently interrupted by visitations from her children, who, to cheer her up, dragged along on a stylish green ribbon leash their mother's fashionably stunted mongrel, a weasel-headed creature that would survive to bite Napoleon on his wedding night. Josephine herself would survive to become successively the mistress of Barras, one of the queens of fashion in the Directoire's inner circle, Napoleon's wife, and empress of the French.

An Empire of Fashion

The story of Napoleon and Josephine is that of two adventurers who shared their fortunes, up to a point, with equanimity. They understood, as adventurers should, the caprices of fate, and, like camels loping off into the unknown, they guzzled at the springs of glory whenever the opportunity arose. Yet to be a lazy adventuress can prove fatal; and Josephine, eventually, would be a case in point. But she had the requisite personal style and sexual flair, and while her luck held, favors had a way of fluttering into her indolent lap.

When Napoleon and Josephine first met, the lank-haired, pasty, underweight young general was shabbily dressed and wore ill-fitting boots; Josephine, in contrast, the jewel of Barras' circle, was at her radiant best. She paid him compliments, and he, possibly out of gratitude, proceeded to fall passionately in love. He pressed her to marry him, and she, having few other options, agreed. The couple's liberated marriage contract showed a curious prescience. There would be no community property, Josephine would have control of her two children, and if ever the union were to be dissolved, she would be permitted to keep all the clothes, jewels, silver, furniture, and other appurtenances purchased for her personal use. As Bonaparte was practically penniless, he and Josephine also contractually agreed to share the wedding costs. Riguideau, the bride's lawyer, advised her not to sign, commenting dryly that all the man was bringing her was his cloak and sword. According to reports, Napoleon, who had overheard the remark, waited eight years to respond. At his magnificent coronation, to which he had been careful to invite the lawyer, the new emperor in his jewels and splendid regalia paused to murmur, "Well, Riguideau, what do you think of my cloak and sword now?"

Rarely in history has the rise and fall of an overreaching titan been documented more tellingly than in the evolution of Napoleon's wardrobe. On his initial rise to power as First Consul, the stained and threadbare hero's garb was discarded in favor of a gold-embroidered red tunic, a suitably decorous official costume designed by Napoleon himself. Sartorially, Napoleon still followed Josephine's lead and dressed with elegant restraint at their receptions. At the Tuilleries, Josephine, conducted on the arm of Talleyrand, would waft through the gaudily jeweled and befeathered crowds in a simple costume usually consisting of a short-sleeved white muslin dress, a pearl necklace, and a handsome tortoise shell comb piercing her dark braided hair. Josephine chose her ladies-in-waiting from the old order. A favorite was the Marquise de Montesson, at whose resuscitated salon gentlemen guests, admitted by servants clad in the household liveries outlawed by the Revolution, were first to reappear in buckled shoes and silk stockings. At Josephine's receptions her husband would materialize unannounced, in a plain military coat, breeches of white wool bound at the waist by a fringed tricolor silk sash, gleaming top boots, and, in his hand, the Napoleonic trademark— a broad black bicorn hat.

Napoleon felt distinctly more at home with his men, whose long-buttoned gaiters were the only article of clothing to set the common soldier apart from civilians. Rousing dress uniforms would have been superfluous; the Corsican's genius for inflaming *esprit de corps* was enough to send them rejoicing to join enemy fire. It was Napoleon who introduced the personal touch at troop reviews, the "what's-your-name, old-war-horse, we've-seen-a-lot-together" brand of condescending camaraderie that could allegedly cheer even a weeping, bleeding young amputee. "Why are you crying?" came the comforting blast of ironic sympathy. "Now you only have one boot to polish!"

The soldier's pigtail did not vanish until 1802, more than a decade after its abandonment by the man in the street. Nor did the troops any longer lavishly lard and flour their hair. According to the author of *A Journal of a Party of Pleasure to Paris in the Month of August 1802*, Napoleon himself, glimpsed in a box at the theater, had trimmed the unkempt shoulder-length hair he affected at the time of his meeting with Josephine. "He is a little man, but with an intelligent spirited countenance . . . he wears his lank hair out of powder, very short, and was dressed in a blue coat most richly embroidered." Embroidered coats of his own invention might suffice for a First Consul, but for the climactic vault to emperor only a correspondingly spectacular professionally designed wardrobe would do. And who but the David could rise to the occasion?

Isabey, the painter, had been directed to augment David's contributions by plotting detailed pictures of the coronation's most crucial phases. Within eight days hundreds of figures had to be represented in seven formal compositions. Hysterical, Isabey turned Paris upside down in search of toy figures that could be dressed in various ceremonial costumes and endlessly regrouped in a sprawling model of Notre Dame. David was occupied with the transformation of the actual cathedral, brightening the walls with gold-fringed crimson velvet and silk, enormous gilded sconces and winged victories, carpeting the glacial floors and dangling two dozen mammoth crystal chandeliers from the vaulted ceilings. Nothing, unfortunately, seemed to dull the keenness of the cold in which many participants had to shiver for more than eight hours.

The imperial couple were two hours late for their coronation. Not only Isabey but also Josephine had become hysterical, thanks to the sabotaging of plans by spiteful in-laws. First, Napoleon's two brothers had refused to allow their wives to bear Josephine's train unless they themselves were made "princes." His sisters behaved with equal Bonaparte rancor and demanded that they be dubbed "princesses" in payment for their supporting performance. Familiar infighting was temporarily halted by a silly semantic compromise. The "princesses" were apparently mollified to learn that their rarefied function would be to *soutenir le manteau* (hold up the robe) rather than *porter le queue* (carry the train) of the empress.

On the morning of the momentous day Josephine's hair was being cajoled into a helmet of miniature curls, while Napoleon clucked about his bedroom half clad in a lace Henri IV ruff, white velvet pantaloons embroidered with golden bees, a cavalry tunic ("the only dressing gown he ever had"), and bare feet. Josephine's bee-strewn silver brocade dress had long sleeves but bared her throat and shoulders. Completely waistless, it was marked beneath the bosom by a thin encircling ribbon of jeweled gold. Here was David's immortal gift to fashion, the "Empire" silhouette at its most grand. For the coronation its lilylike line was gilded by a train, a fragile gold-

Top: Napoleon in the relatively modest though brilliant garb of First Consul. Painting by Ingres. 1804.
Above: The Empress Josephine in coronation robes. By François Gérard. 1804.
Lower right: One of Josephine's classically inspired jewels, a spray of laurel consisting of twenty-two diamond leaves set with Burma rubies.

Left: One of history's most pretentious pageants—the coronation of Napoleon in 1804, choreographed by the emperor himself and designed and recorded by his metteur en scene, David.
Below right: Napoleon's sisters and sisters-in-law consented to give their supporting performances only after they were dubbed "princesses."
Details from The Consecration of the Emperor Napoleon I and the Coronation of the Empress Josephine by Jacque-Louis David. 1807.

spangled lace ruff, golden brooches, bracelets and necklace set with ancient cameos and jewels, and a pearl tiara intertwined with diamond leaves. Napoleon, once he had assembled the eclectic components of his costume, presented, as did his male attendants, a rather more bizarre image. His unusual sartorial mélange, evoking the Renaissance, troubadours, and François I, embraced a crimson velvet doublet, a short satin-lined cloak, silk stockings, golden buckle, a ruff, a velvet cap, an aigrette sprouting from a diamond clasp, a sword and sash, white velvet breeches, and half boots.

The man who had sired the ambitious Bonaparte brood, Charles-Marie Buonaparte, a member of the Corsican nobility, had habitually dressed in velvets, ruffs, and gold braid, unlike the majority of his peers. As Napoleon was about to leave for his appointment with imperial glory, he turned to his brother and cried, "Ah, Joseph, if only Father could see us now!"

Having spent an inordinate amount of time getting themselves into these amazing outfits, Napoleon and Josephine set off hurriedly in a glass coach to the cathedral, where they once more proceeded to change their clothes.

It pleased Napoleon to consider himself the true descendant of the Holy Roman Emperor Charlemagne. To make this historical connection inescapably clear, he now arrayed himself in vestments recalling imperial Rome: an ankle-length, gold-embroidered satin gown, a crimson velvet mantle lined with eighty pounds of ermine and patterned in gleaming bees (the Bonaparte insignia) and foliage, and a flattering gold laurel wreath that, as the jeweler had been permitted to display it in his windows prior to the coronation, had been marked down considerably in price. Josephine's violet mantle was exchanged for a bee-encrusted crimson velvet robe, born with viperish contention by her jealous sisters-in-law. At one point, when their grating sotto voce altercations threatened utterly to disrupt the pontifical proceedings, Napoleon had to bark at them to behave. He too was having troubles and almost pitched backward off a dais when his brothers bungled their job of keeping in motion his cumbersome train.

The crowning ceremony permitted the emperor to display his own lack of grace. So palpable was his lust for the crown that he snatched it from the Pope's faltering hand and thrust it on his anointed head. Josephine, as can be seen in David's fraudulent "documentation," also received the imperial headgear from her megalomaniacal mate.

"When Bonaparte seized power, then truth disappeared." So writes Chateaubriand, stalwart defender of the freedom of the press. Even during the Revolution and the inexorable censorship of its guillotine, clamorous voices had left to history a disorderly mass of opinionated material from which

Joachim Napoléon, *Roi de Naples.*   Frédéric Auguste, *Roi de Saxe.*   Jérome Napoléon, *Roi de Westphalie.*   Frédéric, *Roi de Wurtemberg.*   Louis Nap *Roi de Holla*

Esquisse représentant la réunion   *au Bal donné*

the truth could be sifted. Napoleon and his police now imposed paralyzing controls, permitting only fabricated facts and false maxims to be printed. Furthermore, as Chateaubriand perceived, a monstrous pride and affectation spoiled the emperor's character. "At once a model and a copy, a real person and an actor playing that person, Napoleon was his own mime; he would not have believed himself a hero if he had not dressed himself up in a hero's costume. . . . It was not enough to lie to the ears; it was necessary to lie to the eyes as well." David's "Coronation," a travesty of commemorative accuracy, typifies the tyranny of imperial censorship. "*Madame Mère,*" Napoleon's formidable mother, flatly refused to attend the ceremony. In David's painting she is presented as a benign onlooker, as are her daughters, for whom the painter has dismissed the odious task of carrying Josephine's train.

Soon Napoleon's case of galloping grandeur would lead him to chide publicly generals' wives who dared to appear before him twice in the same dress. Forgotten was "the abyss" to which he had been brought by "the moral spectacle of this country." Yet he could still be repelled by the extravagance of those whom, ironically, he had pushed into international prominence—his siblings, in particular, who plagued him without mercy.

Jerome set about plunging his toy kingdom of Westphalia into the depth of debt and ridicule. Of the two million francs he borrowed from Hessian moneylenders, almost half was squandered on his own coronation robes. In 1812 he was obliged by his brother to assist in the invasion of Russia. An abbreviated inventory of the twenty-seven-year-old's battle gear reflects his entire family's neurotic susceptibility to the reckless, overweening flourish.

Seven wagons creaked into Russia beneath the weight of Jerome's personal wardrobe, including 200 shirts, 60 pairs of boots, and 318 silk handkerchiefs (the scenting of which had been anticipated by a provision of several cases of eau de Cologne). Dressing gowns, bathrobes, deerskin bed drapes, silver saucepans and chamberpots, bedding, and boxes of toilet articles were piled high on one another. One wagon was set aside exclusively for military and civil decorations and ornamental swords. A staff of chefs, secretaries, physician, and auxiliary mistresses rattled along in their own caravans. Napoleon, disregarding his own flights of sumptuary excess, was beside himself. "I said to him," he fumed, "if you want to go to the army as a king you had better remain at home!"

206

NAPOLÉON. Josephine. Madame. Marie Julie. Hortense Eugénie. Marie Caroline. Frédérique Catherine. Marie Pauline.
Empereur des Français Roi d'Italie Impératrice Reine Couronnée Mère de l'Empereur Reine des Espagnes Reine de Hollande Reine de Naples Reine de Westphalie Princesse de Borghèse

ouverains accompagnans Sa Majesté l'Empereur et Roi
Ville de Paris le 4.e Décembre 1809.

Almost all of Napoleon's political and military dreams are enshrined in the annals of dress and accessories. In Josephine's Egyptian brooches we see a bicorned figure bullying his troops toward an Oriental mirage. "You are like the Roman legions," he raves, "blinded in the desert by the dust of time." The fur-lined "Russian" hoods so popular with smart Parisians after the disaster at Moscow suggest to us the creak of freezing men, the dull footfall of a giant's catastrophic retreat. And finally, in the caftan and the madras turban affected by Napoleon during the final torpor at Saint Helena, we see the general without a country, the convict without hope, the once mighty conqueror sipping defeat in the costume of the Romantics he despised.

Opposite left: Napoleon crowned in the laurel wreath of a Roman emperor. He preferred the title and acoutrements of "Emperor" to "King." Engraving after a painting by Stephan Tofanelli. 1804.
Opposite right: Napoleon and the rulers of Europe–most of them Bonapartes, including Joachim Murat, Jerome Napoleon, and Louis Napoleon. Napoleon and Josephine are in the center, and to their right is Madame Mère with the emperor's sisters and in-laws. Engraving. 1809.
Top: Hortense, daughter of

Josephine and wife of Napoleon's brother, Louis, King of Holland, and her son. Portrait by François Gérard. c. 1807.
Above: Princess Pauline Borghese, Napoleon's favorite sister. Rapacious and a nymphomaniac, she was also touchingly loyal to her brother, whom she comforted on the Island of Elba. She dressed for her death in her most spectacular clothing and jewels, covering her face with a handkerchief lest a death spasm be visible. Portrait by Robert Lefèvre. 1808.

The 19th Century:
Romantics and Philistines

Money, as far as the nobility of the 18th century had been concerned, represented a means rather than an end. Money was something to enjoy rather than enshrine, to spend rather than earn. Revolutions and dashed dreams of imperial glory changed all of that. For the moment the curtains fell on these disruptive political melodramas and social tragedies, the bourgeoisie, brandishing their mortgage on the Industrial Age, charged out of the wings and began to commandeer the prestige and power for themselves. Money, great quantities of it, would sustain their position indefinitely, serving variously as their weapon or collective scepter, as the situation demanded. Money could now determine precise social position. A fat bank statement might obscure a faulty pedigree; money, it was found, could often purchase a passport to the xenophobic lands of the old aristocracy. Failing that, money could buy civic power or, at the very least, the social indifference of one's comparatively poorer social superiors. Respectability was valued as highly as money by the middle classes. A heightened sensitivity to occupation and material worth once and for all splintered the old monolithic structure of the middle class. The new stratification inspired palpable social goals; everybody scrambled to rise to the echelon above them, while never forgetting to trample the grasping hands of those below. A respectable appearance was helpful but not failproof. As students of Jane Austen will confirm, degrees of gentility, not to mention personal charm, were now to be conferred in strict ratio to one's specific annual income ("Mr. Darcy soon drew the attention of the room by his fine, tall person, handsome features, noble mien, and the report which was in general circulation within five minutes after his entrance, of his having ten thousand a year").

As a moving force, the cult of respectability inflicted itself not only on the British Isles and anglophilic America but also on most of the Western world. The cult worshiped propriety, industry, chastity, comfort, utility, caution, and unswerving conformity in thought and appearance. Innovative ideas were welcome only if voiced by the cult's two gods—Science and Technology. Respectable people bowed to unfamiliar inventions, statistics, and facts if they thought that Progress was being served. Progress was synonymous with industrial advancement, which in turn was synonymous with prosperity. And what could be more respectable than prosperity?

"When the Party entered"

Left above: Enter Darcy and company, fastidiously dressed, the advance guard of the 19th-century cult of respectability. By George Allen in the 1894 London edition of Jane Austen's Pride and Prejudice.
Left: A somewhat uncharitable view of English nouveaux riches aping the late-Georgian beau monde, including its fetishes for feathers and chinoiserie. Le Moulinet by Cruikshank. 1817.

Above: Coffeehouses had long provided a stage on which the socially ambitious could parade their finery. The hero in a novel by Smollet frequented one such stylish establishment in order to meet the right people. He reported: "My appearance procured all the civilities and advances I could desire." Le Café by J. J. Chalon. Early 19th century.

"Prinny"

Still, it was a royal taste for frivolity that stamped its name on the Regency period. In 1762 George, Prince of Wales and future Regent and King of England, was born to George III and his wife, Charlotte Sophia of Mecklenburg-Strelitz. Both parents, as we have seen, veered puritanically to the sparse, the frugal, and the plain. Their palaces were freezing, their diet meager, their demeanor cool and reserved. In other words, they provided an ideal ambience for flamboyant filial reaction. Bishop Richard Hurd, their son's tutor, had an early inkling of things to come; the boy, he prophesied, would grow to be "either the most polished gentleman or the most accomplished blackguard in Europe—possible both."

"Prinny," as the Prince of Wales came to be known, would, until his death at the age of sixty-eight, dependably behave like a gross, superannuated baby, abandoning piles of opulent toys to gurgle over new ones. He sulked and wheedled, simpered and threw tantrums. He was not without talents, however, being a brilliant, albeit too easily distracted conversationalist, an articulate connoisseur and impassioned patron of the arts. Yet at the same time he was fat, florid, and foolish, a capricious spendthrift, a compulsive womanizer and party-giver, lazy, vain—in short, a vintage Rowlandson cartoon of bloated self-indulgence.

"Prinny's" lingering image is that of an overblown fop. His sartorially restrained parents might have guessed what lay in store for them when first they allowed him to attend a court ball at the age of eighteen. Frizzed, powdered, and curled, the prince appeared in radiant pink satin with a waistcoat bedizened with gems of pink paste and a mosaic of colored foils and a hat blazing with five thousand metallic beads. The young bucks practically swooned with gratitude and admiration. They now had a royal model as an excuse to devote themselves to dress. Nor did he let them down; immediately following this particular success, young George devised a new style of shoe buckle, five inches in width, which became an overnight rage. Innovations of this order were to follow one after the other. The future Regent's tastes would set a tone of stylish license for an entire era. The fastidious Beau Brummel, when it came to clothes, eventually subdued "Prinny's" tendency to decorative excess, but happily not at Brighton, where the prince's dream pavilion still stands in all its "Regency" splendor

The Banqueting Room at Brighton. Chinese "neverland decor" illuminated by a miraculously modern gas-fueled chandelier. Master Chef Carême often concocted nine-course eating bouts with as many as 120 dishes to bolster Regency spirits and maintain voluptuous silhouettes. To recover, Prinny sometimes had himself bled. By John Cash. c. 1838.

A VOLUPTUARY under the horrors of Digestion.

WEDDING NIGHT or the FASHONABLE FROLIC;

as a fitting monument to a trend-setting urban voluptuary's need for romantic escape.

But by the 1830s such was the power of the respectable bourgeoisie that even monarchies capitulated to their dull, materialistic standards. The code of conventional behavior and appearance that their system imposed bred a virulent strain of hypocrisy, but this was overlooked by almost everyone but the sworn enemies of the cult of respectability—the Romantics.

The Dandy

One of the most highly visible and self-conscious of Romantic types was the 19th-century dandy. A dandy, as defined in *Sartor Resartus* by Thomas Carlyle, is "a Poet of Cloth . . . a Clothes-wearing Man, a Man whose trade, office and existence consists in the wearing of Clothes." One must understand the dandy's mystic significance or altogether misinterpret it, for he is "heroically consecrated to this one object, the wearing of clothes wisely and well: so that others dress to live, he lives to dress."

The Sportive Dandy had been the prodigal child of Regency England. Devotion to sport was emblematic of moneyed virility and aristocratic leisure. Sir Thomas Hoby in his perennially influential English adaptation of *Il Cortegiano* had arbitrarily defined *sprezzatura* as "recklessness," and to this the sports- and gambling-minded aristocracy dedicated themselves with ardor. Whether one's fortunes permitted or not, a reckless, conspicuous spending spree must never end. As it was tacitly agreed that the practice of economy would make one appear gauche, a high-handed attitude had to be taken to keep up appearances. Besieged by unpaid tailors, bootmakers, jewelers, wine dealers,

Opposite left top: Prince of Wales, Regent and King. A 1792 caricature of the fashion-conscious Regent's belly. In 1818, Lord Folkestone reported, it "now reaches his knees." By James Gillray.
Opposite left bottom: Still inclined to frizz and frill, the Prince of Wales–"Prinny"–wed the pious and buxom Mrs. Fitzhugh in her drawing room. His crony George Hanger fiddles them to bed in this comic engraving. 1786.
Opposite right: An expert horseman, the youthful Prinny rides in Hyde Park in faultless attire. By George Stubbs. 1791.

Left: The Prince Regent, in full Order of the Garter rig, by Sir Thomas Lawrence, 1819. His hair is now cropped and clean in the Brummell mode.
Below: French sportive dandies: men's hunting costumes from Le Petit Courier. 1833.

Far left: "Beau" Brummell: dressed to walk abroad and receive the mute adulation of his public. Drawing by Scotson Clark.
Left: A Regency buck promenades in The Cut Celestial, a drawing by M. E. 1827.
Below: George Beau Brummell

deigns to smile upon the Duchess of Rutland in Almack's Assembly Rooms. The whirling Czar of Russia enshrined a shocking new dance there: "The seductive waltz," crooned Byron, "the voluptuous waltz." Exclusivity was the keynote: "One can

and countless others, a man of fashion often barricaded himself at home behind paneled doors until nightfall, when frustrated creditors would traipse away in weary defeat. For many English gentlemen it remained a point of honor never to pay up one's tailor in full.

But with the coming of the Industrial Revolution and with the appearance of new fortunes, candidates for official dandydom, once the exclusive preserve of the aristocrat, now applied from the lower classes. Precedence in this, as in many other vital areas of 19th-century dandydom, had been set by the most intransigent arbiter of them all— that supreme poseur, that Parthenon of tailoring, the glacial and gorgeous Beau Brummell, grandson of a valet.

Impatiently Carlyle lumps all acolytes of dress into one "Dandiacal Body," whereas they should be grouped into three schools—the Classical-Purist, the Artistic-Romantic, initiated by Byron, and the Sportive. Brummell was the founder of the first school. His aversion to rococo fussiness and flash plus his insistence on immaculate understatement and purity of line established him, in matters of dress, as a major neoclassical force. But, as we shall see, in his role-playing flight from reality, in his naive belief that life could be transformed into an eternal charade with himself as the star, Brummell was the epitome of the doomed Romantic.

George Bryan Brummell was born in 1778. His father's obsequiousness had boosted the family's fortunes to the point where he was able to negotiate young George's enrollment at Eton, an institution that, according to Harold Nicolson, "has always been unequalled in the production of boys possessing self-assurance, adaptability, tidy hair and clothes, *sprezzatura*, and outward appearance of refine-

ment." George, or "Buck" as he was known at the time, immediately distinguished himself by the elegant and unusual way in which he adjusted his collar and cravat. From Eton, Brummell moved on to Oxford. A skilled flatterer and sarcastic wit, he maneuvered himself into the most desirable circles. Soon fortune smiled in the spreading form of the foppish Prince Regent.

The Prince invited Brummell to join the royal regiment. Such a commission assured a splendid career. In gratitude, Brummell sank to his knees before his benefactor, a position he would shortly resume to beg release from the post, because the regiment, he sulked, was to be sent to the north to put down riots in the cotton mills. As the Prince could graciously understand, this would seriously curtail Brummell's London social rounds. The Prince, much amused, gave his consent.

Now began the Beau's amazing tenure as England's prime minister of taste. Reading of his insupportable insolence, one wonders why he was not shown the first fashionable front door he ever entered. Instead, beauty, power, and nobility toadied

hardly conceive the importance attached to getting into
Almack's, the seventh heaven
of the fashion world," a mem-
oirist recalled. 1815.

to him. When the rear view of a duchess offended
him, Brummell ordered her to leave the ballroom—
backward. A merciless snob (the kind whose snobbery is constructed with much care because it rests
on the quicksand of an insignificant pedigree),
Brummell apparently was endowed with the kind
of magnetic conceit that, under suitable social
conditions, can strike a perverse, masochistic chord
in almost everyone.

Above all else, Brummell was fearlessly and truly
original, a combination to make faint hearts quake.
To fashion, he introduced not merely specific articles
of dress but a totally realized concept of masculine
elegance, the guidelines of which are still followed
today. First, we must acknowledge the Beau's
contribution to modern "good grooming." It was
he who made clean, cropped, unpowdered hair and
smooth-shaven chins fashionable. It was he who
insisted on faultless personal hygiene (his own
ablutions included a daily rinsing in milk) and
spotless linen. To men's clothes he brought a smooth,
tight, flawlessly tailored fit. It was his intention to
appear conspicuously inconspicuous. To the unlucky

*Above: Beau Brummell, the
Parthenon of Tailoring: milk-
rinsed, starched, Hessian boots
burnished with champagne.
He boasted a different snuff
box for each day of the year
and gloves for which the
thumbs were cut by one firm
and the fingers by another to
ensure perfect fit. Watercolor
by Richard Dighton. 1805.*

young man who, at Ascot, had the temerity to compliment Brummell on the elegance of his attire came the testy reply, "I cannot be elegant since you have noticed me!"

Perfection of line and texture was the Beau's goal. He persuaded the Regent to give up floppy ruffles and diamond buttons. Brummell himself eschewed all ornate jewelry, limiting his cache primarily to snuffboxes, monocles, gold-headed canes, and matched fobs. The fob dangled symmetrically at the tops of the skintight "trowsers" that he had made *de rigueur;* buff buck or doeskin was deemed suitable for morning, a closely knitted black fabric for afternoon and evening. Depending on whether he was going for a stroll or to a ball, with these trowsers (or "inexpressibles," as they were often coyly called) he wore either laced boots or light pumps, the last revealing a brief expanse of embroidered silk stocking. The extraordinary gleam of his boots, he let it be known, was achieved by applications of the froth of champagne.

But it was the formidable cut of the Brummell coat that transfixed all. Even Lord Byron, caught off guard, remarked on its uniqueness: "You might almost say the body thought." The Beau's tailcoats were invariably dark blue or black. Beneath the coat was worn a short colored waistcoat, a lightly frilled shirt, a stock or cravat, and a high, stiff, upturned collar that produced the same helplessly haughty effect as an orthopedic neck brace. The cravat, a large square of material, usually of snowy starched muslin, was wrapped around the collar with consummate care and knotted or bowtied at the front. Brummell, who was known to squander as many as six hours preparing for the public, gave an inkling of his future derangement in the fanaticism with which he approached the folding of a cravat. A morning visitor, perplexed by a heap of crushed muslin littering the floor of the Beau's dressing room, was informed by a valet that "these are our failures."

One suspects that Brummell, like most furtive publicity hounds, periodically fed the gullible Beauwatchers little tidbits of outrageousness in order to keep their appetites sharp. A perfect gentleman, he fatuously intoned, must change his gloves at least six times a day. The rupture of his engagement, he declared, had been provoked by the young lady's enjoyment of cabbage. Brummell enthroned himself in the bow window of his club, peering down maliciously at the fashionable passersby in St. James Street, insults dribbling from his curled lips. He grew bolder and dared to bully the Prince, who, Thomas Moore recalled in his memoirs, "began to blubber when told that Brummell did not like the cut of his coat." Finally he overreached himself. Having already offended the Prince over some silly trifle, Brummell encountered the vain and cruelly corseted Regent at a party. With unforgivable spite he inquired loudly of a royal companion, "Who's your fat friend?" Not even his smart clothes could disguise the shabbiness of this particular thrust. Stupidly, he had stabbed the golden goose. His creditors began to press, and at the age of thirty-eight the brilliant Beau was forced to flee to France, "leaving half of the tradesmen in the West End in lamentation." Abandoned by all his former friends and sycophants, he lived on for another quarter of a century in sordid poverty. Toward the end, ragged and incontinent, he nightly received imaginary guests in a narrow back room of a lodginghouse in Caen. A candle burned, a whist

216

table was set out, and the lodginghouse lackey would scrape at the door. Famous phantoms were announced and ushered in, to be greeted by their paralytic host. Eerie conversational monologues were keened until ten o'clock, when the servant would reappear to announce the visitors' carriages. Shrieking that he would not be taken to debtor's prison, Brummell was finally borne bodily to an asylum, where in 1840 he died unmourned.

Yet there were those who said that the Beau's life-work had been accomplished. For a given time he had installed himself as the leader of the male society of his day. Paradoxically, he had exerted a sobering influence despite his glittering reputation. To gain his approval, men of all ages had vied with each other in the subdued perfection of their dress. The art of tailoring was raised to new heights by the craftsmen of London. Brummell's subtle standards never grew obsolete, although following his abrupt departure many young English dandies began to broadly exaggerate the established Regency line.

Romantics and Philistines

No sooner had the fury of the Napoleonic wars subsided than the battle between the Romantics and the Industrial Age Philistines commenced. Almost immediately allegiances could be recognized by the antagonists' dress, particularly in the case of the Romantics, who flaunted their costumes before their stolid enemies like so many dropped gauntlets or matador capes.

The seeds of the Romantic movement had been sown in the 18th century, notably in England and Germany. The ideas of the Enlightenment were unacceptable to the early Romantics, as were the measured cadences of the Classical style. Life, they felt, was not meant to obey academic rules; it could not be shoved conveniently into cramped philosophical pigeonholes or trimmed into tidy scientific formulae. The Romantics accepted the disconcerting fact that they could never know whether the world could truly be understood or not. Cutting themselves metaphysically adrift, they proceeded to suffer the first great modern identity crisis. Small wonder that the hero of Goethe's *Sorrows of Werther*, a seminal Romantic work, ultimately commits suicide.

Having first rejected classicism, the Romantics went on to loathe the hypocrisy and humdrum realities of money-grubbing bourgeois life. By now they had isolated themselves not only metaphysically but socially. Backs turned defiantly to the world, they burrowed inward and founded the restless, rebellious cult of the Self. Down with materialism, up with the spirit. Down with bankers and sordid business schemes, up with poets and visionary dreams, "sincerity," creativity, sentiment, and courage. Dragged to the brink of the technological age, they refused to take the plunge. Cornered, they fought to escape. And escape they did—into

Below: Trend-setting Lord Byron, founder of Artistic-Romantic Dandyism and a model for the role of visionary poet, wanderer, bohemian and revolutionary—trousered, tousled, unbuttoned, starchless and pale. After a painting by Sanders. 1830.

the historic past (as long as it was either imaginatively redecorated or in mossy ruins), into political idealism, satanism, nature or despair, into hashish, costume parties, Bohemian cafés, into Oriental travel, love affairs, and other people's revolutions. Each was in search of an owl-haunted, bat-infested, Gothic ivory tower of his own: "And so you'll write your odes to the moon?" sneers the Philistine Durandin in the opening act of *La Vie de Bohème*, "And curse the selfish century which will not support you while you're idle?" Precisely. Could the soulless Durandin not appreciate the cardinal Romantic commandment—Thou shalt express thyself?

As the Romantics were quick to discover, one of the easiest ways to express oneself, especially when in a rebellious mood, is to adopt a pose, to cast oneself in a picturesque role, and, costumed to perfection, play it to the hilt. Banding together loosely, their movement was like an international repertory company whose resident players, as in the *commedia dell'arte*, could choose from a vivid, if limited, number of easily identifiable stock Romantic roles. These included the Visionary Poet, the

Wanderer, the Historian, the Revolutionary, the Satanist, the Virtuoso (whose wizardry might find an outlet in such diverse fields as music, mountain climbing, or love), the Bohemian, the Aesthete, and the Dandy. It was permissible to play several simultaneously. Women's roles were less plentiful; the company's all-purpose Columbine, until the stunning entrance of George Sand, was expected to play a supporting role to the male principals. Her costumes corresponded more closely to bourgeois dress, although she could alter her appearance cosmetically by sucking on lead pencils, sipping vinegar, oiling her hair, and half blinding herself with belladonna to achieve the desired effect of pining mystery and shattered health. Such was the impression cultivated by the pale and bony Princess Belgiojoso, a Bohemian *salonière* who contrived for guests to surprise her at her *prie-dieu* in the company of a fashionable priest, according to one intruder "under the orange ray of a Gothic window, among her dusty folios, with a skull at her feet. . . ." Lady Caroline Lamb, on the other hand, preferred to flee into the past by decking herself out as a Renaissance page boy. Adopting a more revolutionary stance on other occasions, it amused her to send Lord Byron clippings of her pubic hair.

For the Visionary Poet, the physical ideal had been set, somewhat dauntingly, by Lord Byron (and, sartorially speaking, his wardrobe embraced costumes for the Wanderer, the Revolutionary, the Bohemian, and the Aesthete as well). Clear-eyed and marble-throated, his full-sleeved shirt thrown open at the collar, in defiance of stormy elements and the swaddled bourgeoisie, Byron bounded in velvet jackets and midget slippers from passionate bed to passionate cause. To the discerning Roman-tic, not even the moonstruck Nile could compare in glory to Byron's translucent pallor. If one had not been blessed with the poet's prettily heroic profile, fortunately sallowness still lay within one's reach.

In England Byron was credited with the invention of loose trousers, regardless of the fact that they had been worn by the lower classes for decades. Byron had several reasons for affecting them: In the spirit of the *sans-culottes*, they bore bold testimony to democratic ideals; they suggested a tenuous affiliation with the Near East; and they disguised his limp. For all his liberated transports, Byron was vain and self-conscious. When the boyish waistline, after bouts of dissipation, began to bulge, he dieted on soda water and dry biscuits. Should it

La Vie Bohème

The fashion-setting influence of both Brummell
and Lord Byron was by no means confined to their
native land. For years after his death Byron's fashionable pallor continued to glow like a holy lamp,
illuminating even the Latin Quarter in Paris. But
in bourgeois circles under the regimes of Charles X
and Louis Philippe, conservative prosperity set in
like a bloating disease; its symptoms could be detected in the swelling proportions of both feminine
and masculine fashions. In retaliation the French
Romantics, later to be christened the "Bohemians"
by the novelist Henri Murger, thrust themselves
upon the public consciousness at a climactic encounter between staid age and flamboyant youth
subsequently known to history as the Battle of Hernani. The setting for this historic head-on clash
between Classicists and Romantics, between restriction and liberty, the Old Guard and the New, was
the premiere of Victor Hugo's poetic drama *Hernani*,
which departed radically from all literary and
dramatic conventions. Its hero was a brigand, and
weeks before opening night the play had become
the threatening symbol of Romantic ideals. Hugo,
in an earlier manifesto, had demanded "a verse
which is free, honest and straightforward, that dares
in all things to avoid prudery and affectation. . . ."
His young followers were determined to extend
his literary code to personal behavior and appearance. Early on the afternoon of the premiere, supplied with copious picnics of sausage and beer, they
occupied all the less expensive seats and waited
for their quarry. When the spruce and shaven

go limp, the cropped springiness of his windblown
curls was restored by a bristling nightcap of
butterfly curlers. Byron helped revive a flagging
interest in hair fetishism; it is a wonder that his in-
cessant sentimental exchanges of locks did not leave
him baldheaded.

Byron cast the physical and spiritual mold for
unborn generations of Romantics. In the roles of
wandering Childe Harold, virtuoso lover and
political idealist, he fanned a fondness for exotic
trappings and moral anarchy. Escapists thrilled
to the poet's defiant lyricism, Macedonian head
draperies, and final hours at Missolonghi. Consciously or not, he had made himself the eternal
matinee idol of the Romantic dream.

219

Establishment arrived, they found the theater a pungent mess populated by a hostile and extraordinarily dressed crowd, which in its rush to be "free, honest and straightforward" had clearly been unable to avoid affectation. Hugo later recalled "wild whimsical characters, bearded, long-haired, dressed in every fashion except the reigning one, in pea-jackets, in Spanish cloaks, in waistcoats à la Robespierre, in Henri III bonnets, carrying on their heads and backs articles of costume from every century and clime, and this in the middle of Paris and in broad daylight!" One young artist wore a jutting, diabolically pointed beard and waxed mustache and, in veneration of the Renaissance, introduced a tailcoat with velvet facings and a waistcoat modeled on a doublet. Another cut his fair hair like a medieval student, parted it to one side, and swathed himself in a long blue coat buttoned to the chin. But most resplendent of all was the fledgling eighteen-year-old author Théophile Gautier, who was claimed in later years to have worn a flaming red waistcoat at the premiere. Not at all, he contradicted. Along with pearl-gray trousers, their outer seams vertically banded in black velvet, a flat, broad-brimmed hat, and streaming shoulder-length brown hair he had worn a bright pink satin doublet. "That's very important! The red waistcoat would have had a political, republican shade of meaning. There was nothing like that about it. We were just medieval!"

The Romantics' escape into history, as exemplified by the Gothic Revival, the novels of Sir Walter Scott, and later the Pre-Raphaelite movement and other similarly backward-gazing phenomena, not only fired the sartorial imaginations of incipient eccentrics and fancy-dress-ball enthusiasts but filtered into the consciousness of bourgeois fashion—that is to say, feminine bourgeois fashion. The earlier neoclassical Empire style had had a resolute intellectual and political base that in no way might be described as sentimental. The Romantics' retreat into history, however, introduced to fashion the concept of the nostalgic daydream, which could be relived through one's wardrobe. Witness the return of "Tudor" ruffs, Highland tartans, "Renaissance" puffed sleeves, and, eventually, the ersatz medieval costumes of the Pre-Raphaelites. Furthermore, the romanticized female image coincided with the patriarchal bias of the men at the time. Only in their attitudes toward women were the Philistines and Romantics united, conspiring as it were to keep them submissively confined in the cloying seraglio of Victorian sentiment. Byron had confessed that it made him sick to see a woman eat, Tennyson rhapsodized on the merits of the "meek unconscious dove," and even Keats betrayed his true feelings by burbling about "the milk-white lamb that bleats for man's protection."

In the 1820s feminine fashions began to mirror Romantic attitudes. The waistline gradually began to drop toward its natural level and, with the aid of corsets (some of which were even equipped with pulleys), shrank fetchingly. Skirts belled, shoulders sloped, sleeves puffed, ringlets bounced. Bonnets began to supplant hats and bloomed into large topiary shapes bright with ribbons, feathers, flowers, and bows. Ethereal colors, stolen from pastel flowers beds—heliotrope, lilac, tender rose—helped ladies look like fugitives from a fairy bower, spirited sprites who skipped about in frail flat-soled silken slippers, their wide girlish skirts bobbing a handsbreadth above fragile hued ankles.

Moralists readied their attack. Frivolous impulses must be curbed. Respectability would be served by manual and tract. In 1824 nice girls were briskly warned by *The Female Instructor or Young Woman's Companion* that, to command respect, they must dress simply and never imitate "the fluttering votaries of that capricious dame called Fashion." Modesty must be their "principal beauty," and while an English miss might take "moderate exercise in the open air," she must never forget that her primary function was "to smooth the bed of sickness and cheer the decline of age." One wonders to what degree the relentless circulation of this kind of dispiriting prose was responsible for the despondent shapes of fashion in the late 1830s. The fashion silhouette, like a melting wax doll, started to drip downward; hair was plastered into drooping wings and spaniel ears beneath chaste bonnets; sleeves deflated and sank over wrists; defeated shoulders slid forlornly lower. In sympathy, skirts sank to the ground, where they huddled, sheltered by voluminous capes and cashmere shawls. All in all, just the outfit for Tennyson's meek unconscious dove.

Meanwhile, a lady's male protectors would usually dress in a simple blue or brown frock coat, which might be cut away in front, leaving tails to descend behind; a waistcoat; and trousers of a lighter shade, which might be held straight by straps at the instep (sometimes causing kneecap ailments). Trousers, like skirts, were becoming wider. A plain or flowered silk or madras cravat enveloped the neck, and a tall and flaring "stovepipe" hat, called a Bolivar, helped further elongate the line. Feet in flat slippers or boots could not have been as diminutive as they were usually portrayed. The 19th century seems to have had an almost Oriental fetish for tiny feet in both sexes.

221

Petit Courrier des Dames.

Modes de Paris. Nº 85.

Petit Courrier des Dames.
Boulevard des Italiens Nº 2 près le passage de l'Opéra
1re fig Habit à Collet de Velours. Pantalon de Coutil fig 2me. Redingote croisée. Gillet à col ouvert. Coupe de Cheveux de Mr. Bouché Palais Royal Nº 7.

Morni.

*Far left: The Sportive Dandy.
Dressed for the races, with the
checked trousers and fancy
waistcoat that would identify
a "sport" well into the following century. 1832.
Left above: The ultrafeminine
fashions of 1830—the bell-
skirted, embowered, bare-*

Parisian Fashions.

2   3   4   5

Walking Dresses.   Royal Lady's Magazine.

shouldered look—the last, something of an erotic novelty. From Petit Courier des Dames. *Left below:* Parisian gentleman's fashions, 1835. The hippy, cinch-waisted silhouette and the tiny hands and feet suggest a certain feminization.

Above: Morning and walking dresses from Royal Ladies Magazine, 1830. These "Parisian fashions," with their aprons, bonnets and trimmings, corroborate an aged French grande dame's recollection that in her time a Parisienne "insisted on having pretty shoes, pretty gloves, and pretty ribbons—the dress in those days was just an accessory."

Despite increasing social uniformity in dress, a man's interests as well as position might often be deduced from the type of clothes he wore. In *The Pickwick Papers*, Charles Dickens deftly introduces us to his central characters by using an established literary device—a description of the habitual dress of each. Together the members of the Pickwick travel society present a composite sartorial caricature of middle-class English society. Four principal modes of dress are displayed at the club's uproarious first gathering. Here we meet the pink and eloquent Pickwick, the very image of the worthy, supremely respectable bourgeois gentleman, his cherubic profile reproduced in cameo on the association's official brass buttons, "one hand gracefully concealed behind his coat-tails . . . his elevated position revealing those tights and gaiters, which, had they clothed an ordinary man, might have passed without observation." We are next introduced in turn to the overweight shadow of the Regency dandy, Mr. Tracy Tupman, overly susceptible to ladies, wine, and food, his once romantic form expanded by time and feeding, the black silk waistcoat more and more strained, his gold watch chain receding from his range of vision, "the capacious chin encroached upon the borders of his white cravat." Next to him stands the quintessential militaristic sportsman, "communicating additional lustre to a new green shooting coat, plaid neckerchief, and closely fitted drabs," and, lastly, Snodgrass, the ultimate poet, who maintains his reputation by never writing poetry and by shrouding himself in "a mysterious blue coat with a canine collar."

Dedicated to scientific observation and broadening travel, the Pickwickians on their first eventful journey fall into the scruffy clutches of a "lively stranger," whose improvised wardrobe tells us much about the typical dress of the period's poor. The stranger, long black hair escaping from a beaten old hat and wrists unfashionably bare between glove tops and sleeve cuffs, appears in a once smart green coat which, at an earlier date, "evidently had adorned a much shorter man," an old stock without vestige of shirt collar, and scanty black trousers that "displayed here and there shiny patches which bespeak long service, strapped very tightly over a pair of patched and mended shoes, as if to conceal dirty white stockings which were nevertheless distinctly visible."

Cast-off clothing had long been the major source of dress for the poor, but during the French Revolution isolated ready-to-wear shops began to appear. Ironically, it was the old-clothes dealers of the Marché Saint-Jacques who began selling new clothes ready-made by tailors eager to use up their leftover cloth. These were followed by more important ready-to-wear shops, such as the Belle Jardinière, founded in 1824. But the final step in modern garment merchandising came in 1838, when the Galeries du Commerce et de l'Industrie and later the Palais

Left: The new temples of materialism: a Paris department store in the 1850s. From L'Atlas Daquerrier.
Below: The carriage trade pulls up to Maison du Bon Marché. 1885.

Bonne-Nouvelle paved the way for the development of department stores. At first these were casual, bazaarlike affiliations of shopkeepers sharing a single premise, but they speedily developed into unified stores selling, among other things, ready-made clothing and accessories for both sexes and all ages. These items were bought or commissioned by the store, and they supplied the needs not only of the wealthy bourgeoise who could otherwise well afford to have her clothing made to order but also of a new class of customer, first seen in the 19th century. The mid-nineteenth century was still a period when the "peasant" and the "laborer" were easily distinguished by dress, and the blue smocks that manned the barricades of 1848 could not be mistaken for frock coats. But there were those who, with growing prosperity, might hope to rise in both appearance and in fact. And so a new, less extravagant and simplified middle-class dress slowly began to evolve.

Mr. Poole of Savile Row

Considerable fortunes began to be banked by certain tailors and dressmakers endowed with uncommon flair for both business and fashion. A few even managed to crash society. "The most beautiful horses I remember," the Duke of Portland was to write in his memoirs, "were Lord Calthorpe's and those of Mr. Poole, the Savile Row tailor." Had this nostalgic observation been made but fifty years before, His Grace would have been judged either senile or insane. What, then, had happened in the interim to allow a lowly tailor such a noble accolade?

The saga of London's Henry Poole and Company rightfully begins with the mobilization of his father's militia regiment after Napoleon's escape from Elba. James Poole was by occupation a linen draper, not a tailor, but in his patriotic zeal to join the ranks he hastily cut out a tunic for his wife to stitch up for him. The trimness of this garment made a deep impression on one of the commanding officers. James's fate was sealed, and, following Waterloo, he announced his services as a military tailor.

Henry, born in 1814, entered the family company as an apprentice, learning how to flat-braid a coat, face a lapel, and converse knowledgeably with the sporting crowd that his brother had lured to the premises. In 1846 Henry inherited the business and joined other fashionable tailors in moving to Savile Row, a street that until then had been the sacred preserve of surgeons. Into his Italianate new quarters the "swells" and "young bloods" soon crowded to sample Henry's matchless port and cigars while being measured for hunting clothes or the firm's court costume of mulberry velvet—innovative except for the formal knee breeches of the pre-Revolutionary era.

In addition, Henry Poole extended limitless credit to those special clients whose promise, he astutely guessed, might provide him in the future with negotiable social gold. His cultivated manners were beyond reproach; in the novel *Endymion*, Benjamin Disraeli would give him the fictitious name Mr. Vigo, "the most fashionable tailor in London . . . consummate in his art . . . neither pretentious nor servile, but simple, and with becoming respect for others and for himself." Soon Henry could be

spotted tooling his own superb horses in Rotten Row and watching races on the Thames from the deck of his own stylish steamboat. In concert with Baron Meyer de Rothschild, Poole took a long shot, advancing $50,000 for the exiled Prince Louis Napoleon's campaign to foist himself upon the throne of France. When to nearly everyone's surprise the Prince succeeded, who else but Poole should be named official tailor to the Court of the Second Empire?

The reign of Napoleon III and his Empress Eugénie, which established Paris once and for all as the international capital of giddily high fashion and deliciously low morals, was costumed, somewhat ironically, by two Englishmen—Poole and the despotic dressmaker, Charles Frederick Worth. According to that eminent 20th-century dandy-journalist, Lucius Beebe, "The celebrated stag hunts of the Imperial Court at Compiègne became largely a dress parade of Poole's wares. From the rifle-green jacket with gold lace, gold-laced tricorn hat, doe-

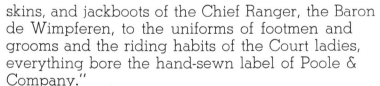

skins, and jackboots of the Chief Ranger, the Baron
de Wimpferen, to the uniforms of footmen and
grooms and the riding habits of the Court ladies,
everything bore the hand-sewn label of Poole &
Company."

Back on home ground, Poole penetrated London's
houses of power by allowing the perpetually in-
solvent Prince of Wales and his spendthrift Marlborough House set to order vanloads of personal
clothes and servants' uniforms on credit. Victoria
strongly disapproved of her son's hedonistic lifestyle and undignified companions and cut his
allowance to a miserly minimum. With his friends
the Rothschilds, Poole once more stepped in to
rescue a royal candidate from the reefs of debt. The
future Edward VII (who had first noticed the incom-
parable cut in a Poole dress coat worn by an actor
in the play Ruy Blas) gratefully responded by
admitting Henry to his aristocratic circle.

"Old Pooley," as he became known affectionately
to the Prince and other luminaries, died in 1876,
and it is said that his obituary would have aroused
the envy of an earl. Before his death he had taken
on a first cousin named Cundey to help direct the
business of outfitting the privileged world of emperors, rajahs, archdukes, and kings. The Poole
dynasty was carried into the 20th century through
the Cundey line. "If you were to go through the
pages of Burke's Peerage and the Almanach de
Gotha," said an incumbent Cundey a century after
old Pooley hit the jackpot on Napoleon III, "from
1850 to the end of civilization in 1914, I think we
could match you page by page with our old ledgers."

Below: "Tremendous Sacrifice." Savage satire on the "sweating system." By George Cruikshank, in Our Own Times, 1842.

Right: Child laborers spinning yarn in a textile factory, 1820. Five years earlier, reformers considered it a major victory when a bill forbidding employment of children under nine was barely passed. Marx and Engels, in retrospect, were not impressed.

The Needle Trade

As an industry, the garment, or "needle," trade as the manufacture of wearing apparel was collectively known, did not gather significant momentum until favored by technical innovations toward the middle of the 19th century. The most important of these was the invention of the sewing machine in 1846, followed by the use of steam power as early as 1865. In quick succession were introduced the standard pattern as well as button-sewing, buttonhole and pressing machines. Improved transportation facilities and higher standards of urban living gave impetus to the proliferation of garment factories. Once the public accepted the inevitable standardization of the finished products—in this, women would hold out much longer than men—these factories began to drive village and small-town tailors and dressmakers out of business, just as in this century mammoth "shopping centers" have forced many small-town retailers of ready-made clothes to shut their shops.

With the advent of garment factories, a new set of intolerable working conditions was substituted for the old. In England, prior to industrialization of apparel manufacture, the exploitation of needleworkers, working alone or in squalid little attic and cellar communes, had provoked writers to investigate and courageously damn social injustice. Dickens's outrage is well known, and it is also worth recalling that it was the wretched working conditions in the Manchester textile mills (where, due to the introduction of gaslight, seventeen-hour days were common) that led Marx and Engels to deplore in print the antagonism between the factory proletariat and the lords of industrial feudalism.

More germane to the history of dress are the writings of the reformer-journalist Henry Mayhew. Mayhew was a pioneer in the field of door-to-door surveys. Among the dire conclusions he dared draw from his exhaustive interviews were that the factory system tended to destroy the family, that a corrupt middleman system had sprung up, that masters were infringing on an established law regulating the time of labor for tailors at twelve hours a day, that the best remedy was a "combina-

tion of working men in trades' unions," that England was infected by "rabies" for cheapness, and that in consequence thousands of free-lance needlewomen were so atrociously overworked and underpaid that they were impelled to take up prostitution on the side.

Frequently dressmaking and millinery were pursued beneath the same roof, the dressmaker's work being confined to the production of ladies' dresses, including every kind of outer robe or gown. Bonnets, hats, scarves, and other ladies' accessories were created by the milliner, who was considered a more highly skilled worker than the dressmaker.

As in most other trades of the day, the milliners and dressmakers fell into two distinct classes— the adequately paid and the poorly paid, or those belonging to the "honorable" and those belonging to the "dishonorable" or "slop" part of the trade. Those lucky enough to be included in the first category were putatively employed on a regular basis at fixed wages and hours, whereas the "slop" workers were forced to compete with each other for piecework assigned with increasing frequency by "sweaters," middlemen who drove down the pay scale to below subsistence standards. It was the "slop" workers, for example, who, for a miserable pittance, outfitted the Empire's armies through the unofficial agencies of Her Majesty's "sweaters." It was the "slop" workers, both male and female, who made it possible for Victorians of even modest means to dress like perfect ladies and gentlemen.

An etiquette manual of the 1840s, *The Habits of Good Society*, decreed that a well-dressed man must possess, among other prerequisites, a minimum of four morning coats, an overcoat, a dress coat, and a frock coat, plus seven pairs of trousers and five waistcoats for morning and evening wear. Unless he was a spendthrift dandy, for these alone he should budget no more than a modest thirty pounds per annum. The Industrial Revolution did in fact eventually succeed in democratizing Western dress, but only with the exploitation of "slop" workers— the project was launched by human machines.

Here we should pause to study the professional pecking order both before and behind the scenes of what Mayhew terms a first-rate house of dressmaking business. The workers consist of apprentices, improvers, assistants (including day workers), "third, second and first hands." The business of the "first hand" was to wait on the customers, take orders and measurements, cut out the material and present it to the workwomen. A "second hand," or "superintendent," would oversee the actual labor while instructing and working alongside the "improvers" and "apprentices." The "third hand" assisted the "second hand." Farther down the ladder toiled the "assistant," a workwoman engaged by the week, month, quarter, year, or for the social "season," which ran its course from February into July.

We descend next to the self-indentured individual known as the "improver." Improvers, Mayhew explains, "are a very numerous class. When a girl has completed her apprenticeship or other term of engagement in a country town, or even Edinburgh, or Dublin, she comes to London to *improve*. If she has an intention of establishing herself in business in the town where her parents and friends reside, she and they feel that it would be hopeless to attain the 'patronage' of the neighboring ladies unless she have the *prestige* of having been trained to the perfect exercise of London taste and skill—a *prestige* which must be duly maintained, when in business, by at least one annual visit to London 'for the fashions.' "

Apprentices were sentenced to serve a two- to five-year term of instruction in the "art and mystery" of their calling. Like the improver, an apprentice was usually boarded in the house of her employer. Her work was considered the equivalent of her tuition. The pace was grinding due both to the greed of management and the quixotic arrogance of the carriage trade, whose demands would have taxed a firm of Rumpelstiltskins. Translated into commercial jargon, what they expected of tailors and dressmakers was custom-made ready-to-wear. It was not uncommon for a client to order in the afternoon a gown to wear to a ball the following evening.

"Empress Crinoline"

When in 1848 a landslide electoral victory returned Prince Louis Napoleon to France, he rose to the occasion uniformed in Poole's epauletted interpretation of neo-Napoleonic grandeur. "The success of Louis Napoleon," wrote a pensive Queen Victoria, who thought him a parvenu, "is an extraordinary event. It will, however, perhaps be more difficult to get rid of him than one at *first* may imagine." Her doubts were well founded. By 1852 Louis Napoleon was no longer a prince but, again by popular vote, Napoleon III, Emperor of the French. The way was finally cleared for the rebirth of imperial glory as conceived by the first reigning Bonaparte. But where Napoleon I had shown a flair for strutting about in neoclassical pageants, Napoleon III's talents seemed better suited to operetta. Corseted and twirling his waxed mustachios, he tripped out of the wings of exile and waltzed to the tunes of Offenbach through the tinsel-trimmed extravaganza known as the Second Empire. His co-star for this production was the clothes-mad Eugénie. Worth costumed the supporting cast of international beauties. The posters were designed by the painter F. X. Winterhalter.

It was during the Second Empire that the reputation of Paris for unquenchable gaiety, extravagant fashions, spectacular women, glittering parties, and Bacchanalian menus was launched. Visitors then, as now, came from every part of the globe to buy new clothes, take a fling at romance, and giggle into champagne glasses.

Encouraged by Napoleon III's example, *nouvelle riche* France sank into an orgy of ostentation. To the old bourgeois motto "enrich thyself" a second dictum was appended—"and put it all on display." Accordingly, society set to work bedizening itself with a passion. The new architecture bristled with capitals, columns, and caryatids; it was gilded, sculpted, and marbled, festooned with plaster flora, veiled in black iron lace. Varnished carriages careened about the Bois de Boulogne. Sidewalk cafés were jammed. Everyone wanted to see and be seen.

As usual, clothes offered one of the easiest ways for social exhibitionists to eclipse each other while exciting the envy of the ordinary public. But for a man to dedicate himself to competitive fashion required the single-minded application of the dandy. Consequently the prosperous drone, the top-hatted, frock-coated man of modern commerce must be forgiven his discreet anonymity in the name of progress. In 1860 Burckhardt, the eminent historian, mourned the style and expressive individuality of the Italian Renaissance, comparing it to "our own age which, in men's dress at any rate, treats uniformity as the supreme law and gives up by this far more than it is aware of. But it saves itself much time, and this (according to our notions of business) outweighs all other disadvantages."

Above: Napoleon III, corseted into a semblance of military fitness, poses in a welter of medals and gold braid. His code of etiquette encouraged heavy embroidery on civic dress and uniforms according to each dignitary's "passion for splendor."
Right: Empress Eugénie, settling into maturity, notwithstanding Princess Mathilde Bonaparte's description of her as a clothes-mad coquette.

Opposite "Empress Crinoline," mother of the international set, in full glory. Portrait by Edouard Dubufé. 1854.

Under the Second Empire, men's dress took the form it was to retain into this century. The frock coat, no longer cut away, was simplified. In the city it was worn in black, blue, or brown, accompanied by striped or patterned trousers. The cutaway, now well out of fashion, was retained in black for evening wear, accompanied by black trousers and waistcoat, a top hat, and a bow tie rather than a cravat. About 1850 the skirtless, one-piece, "short" jacket appeared, imported from England. Called by various names according to the cloth of which it was made, it was generally black and worn with striped or patterned trousers, but only for morning or for informal indoor wear. It was not until 1868 that the first modern "suit," like the one we identify as such today, appeared, with jacket, trousers, and waistcoat of matching fabric. Again, these were acceptable only on the most informal occasions, or for travel and country wear.

While the Second Empire had a more than adequate population of fops—some of whom were known as *les petits crevés*, the little exhausted ones—the burden of fashionable dress had to be shouldered by women. They more than met the challenge. Technology offered an assist with the invention of aniline dyes, chemically produced colors of unnatural intensity. Certain shades, such as coral and electric blue, were of great beauty. But like most abrupt departures from the past these hues failed to please everybody. In 1898 Octave Uzanne, looking back on the fashions of the Second Empire, decreed that era "the most hideous period in female dress that has ever vexed the artistic eye." In his *Fashion in Paris*, Uzanne had particularly harsh words for the dressmaker's palette: "How," he raved, "can such overwhelming violets, such cruel pinks, such glaring greens, such shabby cockchafer browns, such dirty grays, such blinding yellows, ever have left the dyer's hands? But all these cheap oleograph tints were received with acclamation, and reds of every kind—solferino, marengo, sang de boeuf, etc.—were constantly invented, and greedily purchased." The shades called solferino and the even more garish magenta were geographically inspired by Napoleon III's military triumphs in the Italian campaigns. The fashion for giddily named colors had gathered steam in the 1830s with Nile-water and mignonette seed making their debuts alongside frightened mouse, amorous toad, and spider-meditating-crime. By the late 1860s the point had been reached where a single fashionable color, Bismarck brown, had been subdivided and categorized, like the Humours of medieval science, as shades presumably corresponding to the future Iron Chancellor's mercurial moods: "content," "ill," "enraged," and "icy."

Accompanying the cacophony of chemical color was a plethora of false hair, dahlia-size parasols, tiny hats, fans, shawls, and slag heaps of jewelry.

Et David dess Paris   Napoléon III   Pce Impérial   Cte Benedetti   Imp Lemercier & Cie Paris

Presiding over all was the beautiful Spanish-born Eugénie, "Empress Crinoline" and mother of the International Set. It is said she introduced to France the Spanish bolero, the felt hat, and the tartans of her raffish mother's native Scotland. Perhaps this is so. It is also said that she was the first to abandon the genteel custom of wearing a lace-and-ribbon-trimmed cap while indoors. Again, this is possibly so. What is known for a fact is that Eugénie was a shallow, calculating adventuress for whom affection was a form of currency to be doled out to her husband, friends, ladies-in-waiting, and long-suffering son, the Prince Imperial, with thrift.

Eugénie's own monument is the crinoline, the billowing symbol of conspicuous consumption. When worn with a precariously low evening décolletage, the crinoline became a particularly perverse fashion, offering sexual promise from the waist up, but from the waist down setting a mountain squarely in the path of romance. This arrangement could not possibly have been better designed to costume Eugénie's spurious morality. According to Princess Mathilde, patroness of the arts and the emperor's first cousin, the empress, over the years of her reign, had acquired neither maturity, poise, nor respectability but remained "a trollop without any sentiment . . . still as mad about clothes as she was on her wedding day. Yes, she talks of nothing else. The last time I was at St. Cloud, she showed me all her dresses for the trip to Suez. And that was all!! The whole journey is nothing to her but an opportunity to make eyes at some Eastern prince from her steamboat. Because she always needs men around her to pay court to her and talk smut to her without rumpling her dress. You see, she carries flirtation as far as it will go. Why, the other day she actually said to me that a woman could yield almost anything, except the *main thing*."

Indeed, for the untouchable trollop, the recalcitrant tease, the crinoline had been made to order.

The crinoline outdid in sheer volume its ancestors, the farthingale of the 16th century and the panniers of the 18th century. In silhouette it differed, being round at first and then, by the 1880s, bell-shaped and widening toward the back to allow the train to be added to its excesses. The crinoline was best suited to the resources of the wealthy: It required a great deal of cubic air space and a generously proportioned architectural setting. The crinoline seems to have first appeared in embryonic form sometime around 1842. It grew steadily both in girth and popularity and soon necessitated the

Top: "Ornamentation and decoration," an Englishwoman
reported, "is the ne plus ultra
of a Frenchwoman's life."
Three elaborately garnished
coiffures, each with a fanciful
name. From Les Modes Parisiennes 1851.

Above: Ladies day dresses in
aniline colors. The carefully
arranged, assymmetric coiffures of the gentlemen retained
their line better when glossy
hats were held in the hand as
a fashion accessory.

Below: Contessa Castiglione, Italian mistress of Napoleon III, a schemer and paid informer who masked her shady deals behind a theatrical façade. Photographed by Adolphe Braun. 1858.

Lower left: Mocking the crinoline: She: "Oh, my goodness! How shall I get past?" He: "Holloa there, my good fellow! Open the turnpike gate." Satirical engraving of the 1860s.

most elaborate underpinnings ever devised for general use. By the late 1840s a young woman's lower underwear, from the skin out, consisted of pantalettes; a stiff wool and horsehair petticoat (hence the term "crinoline"—*crin* being the French word for horsehair), which might easily measure four yards around; another petticoat boned to the knee and padded from the knee down; a starched white petticoat with flounces; a muslin underskirt; and, finally, the gown, which was lowered onto the superstructure by servants armed with a polelike apparatus. However, the breadth of skirt thus achieved was considered barely sufficent. In 1850 a hooped structure replaced stiffened petticoats.

Later in the decade crinoline wearers were rescued from their prisons by the humane invention of one August Person, who devised a collapsible steel cage made of lightweight hoops attached by flexible metal tapes. One might well wonder at the effort required to produce a gown of such size, but as the railroad had enabled travelers of the 19th century to cover vast distances quickly, so the sewing machine enabled seamstresses to cover areas previously too huge to contemplate. Women of the *ancien régime* had been discommoded by their enormous coiffures; 19th-century women were again unable to sit on the seats of carriages. Now they kneeled or sat on the floor. A journalist writes, "Every woman today is a tempest. She cannot enter or leave a room without knocking over everything in her path . . . it sounds like rain or hail, according to the stuff her dress is made of." When Eugénie sent a Worth gown and crinoline to Queen Ranavalona of Madagascar that dignitary wore the dress but, very sensibly thinking that its crinoline was a coordinated canopy, had it hoisted over her head in a tree.

Left above: The arduous toilette of the Second Empire: lowering a dress over the crinoline. c. 1860.
Left: Armies of seamstresses served the fashion show known as the Second Empire. Other workers toiled furiously, too; here laundresses ply their *poorly paid trade. Zola's heroine, Gervaise, the mother of Nana, was trapped in a less picturesque version of this place. 1865.*
Above: Dresses by Fauret in a Les Modes Parisiennes. From July 1858.

Maison Worth

The gross ostentation of Second Empire fashion was tempered, however, by the taste of the masterly Charles Frederick Worth. So many ideas of French fashion originated in England that it should not be surprising that Worth, the founder of Parisian *haute couture*, should have been a pink-faced Englishman with wispy blond whiskers who spoke little French and that with an atrocious accent.

Worth was born in Lincolnshire in 1825, son of a ruined solicitor. Taken out of school, he was a cashier in a London dress-goods firm by the age of thirteen. When not yet twenty he set out for Paris, with five pounds given him by his mother, and found work at the Maison Gagelin, a silk mercer specializing in ready-made coats and shawls. There he met a pretty young shopgirl whom he married and who served as model for his first designs. These appealed to the Gagelin's customers, and in 1858 Worth set up his own *maison de couture* at Number 7, rue de la Paix. It became Paris's first true *haute couture* house.

Worth was certainly not France's first major dress designer. We have already noted the fatal career of Marie Antoinette's Rose Bertin. She in turn had been followed by the waspish Louis Hippolyte Leroy, the Talleyrand of fashion, who began his career under Marie Antoinette and proceeded in turn to dress the court of Napoleon and the restored Bourbons. But by the 1840s most of the fashionable women of Paris had fallen back into the hands of the "little dressmaker." Worth brought éclat to *couture*. He was an innovative merchandiser and the first designer to present a collection of dresses that could be ordered by his customers. He was also the first to make use of mannequins, called "doubles" because Worth deliberately chose girls who resembled his principal customers.

These were not Worth's only innovations. In a world dominated by taffeta, faille, moire, grosgrain, and velvet he repopularized satins, which he had loomed to his specifications. When he induced the empress to wear a brocade dress that looked to her "like a curtain," he breathed life back into the Lyons silk industry. Worth used lace lavishly, along with jet and a variety of other decorations. Above all, he brought his own taste and order to the welter of jewels, embroideries, posies, fringes, ruches, roulettes, flounces, and feathers that would otherwise have been permitted to run out of control.

Members of the international upper classes collided daily in Worth's salon on the rue de la Paix, which was drenched in the perfume of massed camellias. Through this setting flitted a bevy of *jolies demoiselles* in the master's latest styles, all of them executed in black so that the client could choose a sleeve here, a flounce there. Social harmony was orchestrated by a group of young men with curled hair, pearl tiepins, and English accents, like so many embassy attaches. In the *salon de lumière* the windows were sealed from the light of day, the walls were lined with mirrors, and one hundred gas jets burned so that a lady might observe exactly how her gown would appear at a ball. In another mirrored room the finished products were exhibited before delivery.

Such was the palace of the emperor of fashion, as highly respected as any artist of his period. He, in fact, never doubted that his art was as august as that of sculpture, painting, or musical composition. He composed reclining on a sofa, a cigar in his mouth, while a *demoiselle* of the *maison* played selections from Verdi operas. His most favored clients were allowed no more choice in what he created for them than a canvas has in choosing its paints. "I am a great artist," he claimed. "I have the color sense of a Delacroix, and I create. A dress is the equal of a painting." He would go so far as to expostulate, "In every artist there is a Napoleon. Art is God; the bourgeoisie are made to take our orders."

On the subject of the crinoline, the bourgeoisie was indeed "made to take orders." The master finally designed a crinolineless dress with a deflated, gored skirt, its fullness swept to the back. Eugénie refused to wear it, but it found other takers. The women at Longchamp began to discard their crinolines. Before his death Worth declared with megalomanic glee, "The 1870 Revolution is not much compared with my revolution: I dethroned the crinoline."

Opposite: Charles Frederick Worth, in luxurious "artistic" attire. "I am a great artist," he announced, "I have the color sense of a Delacroix, and I create. A dress is the equal of a painting." Such was his fame that women on other continents impatiently awaited replicas of his clothes.

Below: New York's Lord and Taylor presented this copy of his separate "Basque" and "full-trained trimmed skirt"; the first could also be "combined with a demi-trained or walking skirt for street wear or plainer costumes." As this plate attests, Worth had indeed dethroned the crinoline. December, 1874.

Avant-garde ephemera on view in London at the Great Exhibition of 1851.
Far left: "Cosmic electric telegraph" by G. R. Smith and, left, a clock of tortured complexity by Jacob Loudan.
Below: The sun pours into the Crystal Palace. Thackeray

was overwhelmed: "It was a noble awful great love-inspiring gooseflesh-bringing sight . . . the general effect, the multitude, the riches, the peace, the splendour, the security, the sunshine great to see—much grander than a coronation—the vastest and

Excursions into Modernity

Worth's revolution had come earlier, in 1867, the same year in which the apotheosis of Second Empire carnival gaiety was reached at the great Paris International Exhibition. Its international flavor and technical scope supported Emerson's theory that where London had been built for the English, Paris had been built for the world. The spiritual and social gulf which now separated the two cities had never been illuminated so glaringly as when mid-Victorian England's contribution to the fair was unveiled to the public. Venturing into a world more strange to them than Outer Mongolia, the sophisticated French gazed bemusedly upon Her Majesty's presentation of a model farm, agricultural machinery, a school, a Protestant church, and a Bible Society kiosk. Not surprisingly, the French had taken a more hedonistic approach. Included in their many displays were mounds of magnificent food, the products of each of their wine districts, a miraculous jeweled lilac blossom owned by the empress, along with demonstrations of glass blowing and diamond cutting. Clamorous machinery of French design spewed out torrents of shoes and hats and perfumed soap. In fact, the only inventions his countrymen had failed to devise, complained Offenbach's librettist, were those that could turn out plays and novels.

The race for international expositions—which presented millions of visitors with a panoramic survey of arts, sciences, skills, and styles, both past and present, including those of previously remote countries and civilizations—had, in fact, started in England. The Victorians worshiped science, and in 1851 they thronged to Prince Albert's signal achievement, the Crystal Palace Exhibition. Among the many machines and artifacts to be admired were America's McCormick reaper and Colt revolver,

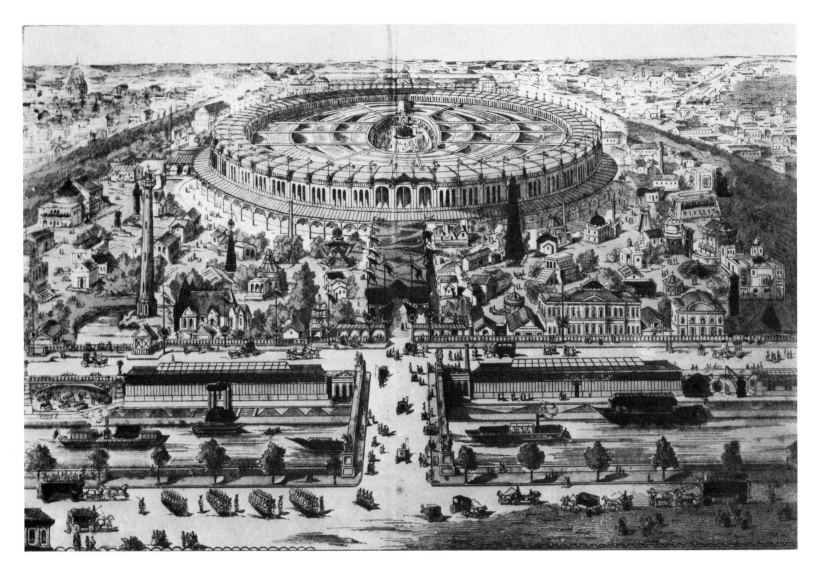

beards and mustaches sported by Continental gentlemen, a shirt "cut on mathematical principles," and a "Patent Ventilating Hat" through which air was admitted to the overheated head by channels cut in thin cork and "fastened to a valve in the top of the crown, which may be open or shut at pleasure." The aesthetic standards of the English during this phase of Victoria's reign can be gauged by the extreme popularity of an exhibit in which a party of stuffed cats was shown seated in chairs and taking tea.

For the taste-making middle classes in the 19th century, science and technology, by extending the boundaries of general knowledge and the physical world, offered a kind of spiritual escape. Whereas in Paris a mania for pleasure usually took precedence over the test tube, the English and Americans were consumed by a passion for new "contrivances." There seemed to be no aspect of life that science could not improve. What would they think of next?

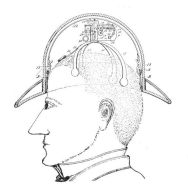

Street lighting, speedy transport, boiled germs, Darwin's monkey-ridden family tree. Not even clothes could hide from innovative genius. As early as 1820 the detachable collar had been awarded a patent. In 1823 Mr. Macintosh perfected a technique for molding rubber between two layers of cloth, bringing the world revolutionary waterproof rainwear, including the poncho made by Poole to protect Henry M. Stanley against tropical deluge in his search for Dr. Livingston. In rapid succession came the sewing machine (the eventual democratizer of dress), the development of standardized paper patterns in graduated sizes, and the Jaeger Sanitary Woolen System.

In the 1870s Dr. Gustav Jaeger, a messianic German physician, advanced the theory that wearing vegetable fibers such as cotton or linen poisoned the health. Wool, he explained, absorbed the exhalations of the body far more effectively. Therefore it behooved a woman not only to wear woolen stockings, drawers, petticoats, chemise, corset, dress, and shoes but to sniffle into woolen handkerchiefs and slumber between heavy woolen sheets. Men must adopt a tight-fitting Jaeger suit (the young George Bernard Shaw would follow this advice) that allowed the minimum passage of air along the skin. The public had already been conditioned to sweltering year round in odoriferous second skins by their belief in the salubrious properties of brushed flannel, which had been invented in England in 1786. In 1855 Francis Galton, in his perennial best seller *Art of Travel*, sounded an authoritative trumpet: "The importance of flannel next to the skin can hardly be overrated: it is now a matter of statistics; for, during the progress of expeditions, notes have been made of the number of names of those in them who had provided themselves with flannel, and of those who had not. The list of sick and dead always included names from the latter list in a very great proportion." Not until the end of the century when overheated American houses drove their male occupants to the relief of "B.V.D.'s," the brand name of a loose, sleeveless, knee-length cotton "union suit," did men dare endanger their health by discarding long-sleeved, ankle-length, drop-seated woolen underwear, the mass manufacture of which had been made possible by the perfection in 1863 of a power-driven knitting machine that could shape fabric as it was knitted. Its inventor's name, ironically, was Cotton.

Ingenuity unleashed:
Above left: An automatic hat-tipper or "saluting device," registered in 1896, several decades after the "Patent Ventilating Hat."
Above center: Elias Howe's pioneer sewing machine. c. 1845.

Top: Lady's waterproof cloak from an 1870 pattern book.
Above: The Tomkins Upright Rotary Knitting Machine, an 1875 improved design of a standard apparatus in use for nearly twenty years.

No number of doctors' endorsements, however, could appease public outrage over the bifurcated garment attributed by history to Mrs. Amelia Bloomer, the editor of a feminist paper called *The Lily*. The costume, which overnight became the hated symbol of women's rights' adherents, consisted of a tunic dress worn over loose trousers gathered harem fashion at the ankle. Its origins have been traced back to the first quarter of the century when, at Robert Owens' cooperative colony at New Harmony, Indiana, the women wore such an outfit for riding.

A decade later George Sand would create the feminist ideal of *la lionne* in Paris. Mme. d'Agoult, one of Lizst's mistresses, writes in her *Souvenirs* that *la lionne* perpetrated the first women's attempts in France "at *clubs* and *sport*, and [coincided] with the invasion of the cigar." *La lionne* "affected to disdain the feminine graces. She did not want to please by her beauty, or charm by her wit; she wanted to surprise and astonish by her audacity. Horsewoman and huntress, whip in hand, spurs on boots, gun across her shoulder, cigar in mouth, glass in hand, all impertinence and rowdiness, *la lionne* delighted in defying and disconcerting the peaceful elegance of the *salons*." Strong, heady stuff—until one studies the actual costume of this emancipated Amazon. Above the hips she wears a wasp-waisted, drop-shouldered, puff-sleeved travesty of a man's riding coat, minus the tails, a soft cravat, and a gauzily veiled top hat; from the waist down she wears a voluminous skirt, its train long enough to be draped over one arm. George Sand, to exaggerate her romantic independence, liked to confront Parisians in authentic men's clothes, but only on relatively rare occasions. The effect must have been one of ambiguity, for according to a puzzled restaurateur, "It's a funny thing, but when she's dressed like a man I call her Madame, and when she's dressed as a woman I call her Monsieur."

The middle classes were not the only ones to rail against certain excursions into modernity. In England William Morris was the leading exponent of a school of design that called for a return to the guild of the romantically viewed Middle Ages. Henry James was entranced by Morris as a leading Pre-Raphaelite visionary, craftsman, poet, and creator of fanciful personal patterns and designs. James wrote many pages to his sister describing the charm of both Morris's Bloomsbury studio and his wife, Jane. James's portrait of Mrs. Morris—"This dark silent medieval woman with her medieval toothache"—preserves for us in prose the ultimate Pre-Raphaelite fashion plate, the symbolic nemesis of Victorian technology and conformity. In the bric-a-brac–strewn studio Morris designs

with his own head and hands all the figures and patterns used in his glass and tapestry, and furthermore works the latter stitch by stitch, with his own fingers—aided by those of his wife and

Above: The cycling craze prompted Mrs. Bloomer's "rational costume," which immediately became the butt of crude music-hall jokes. In England, Queen editorialized in her favor: "The wheel women of today and tomorrow are sharp, wide-awake, aggressive, self-assertive. They know no fear and what sense of shame they have wears a different aspect from their ancestors." Fashion plate of the 1850s.
Right: French cartoon: "Bluestocking is an amphibious being, half man, half woman." Late 19th century.

Left: The haunting figure of Jane Morris, whose Pre-Raphaelite beauty and idiosyncrasies of dress melted Henry James. Photographed by Dante Gabriel Rossetti in July 1856.

Below: "Brother Rabbit," a Morris design for chintz, recalling the charming flora and fauna of medieval decorative arts.
Bottom: "Wreath," a Morris wallpaper pattern, anticipating Art Nouveau motifs.

little girls. Oh, ma chere, such a wife! *Je n'en reviens pas*—out of one of Rossetti's or Hunt's pictures—to say this gives but a faint idea of her. . . . Imagine a tall lean woman in a long dress of some dead purple stuff, guiltless of hoops (or of anything else, I should say), with a mass of crisp black hair heaped into wavy projections on each of her temples, a thin, pale face, a pair of strange sad, deep, dark Swinburnian eyes, with great thick black oblique brows, joined in the middle and tucking themselves away under her hair, a mouth like the "Oriana" in our illustrated Tennyson, a long neck, without any collar, and in lieu thereof some dozen strings of outlandish beads—in fine complete.

Ironically, the letter is dated 1869, the year in which that miracle of advanced engineering and fettered bourgeois taste, the "bustle," was trundled into the marketplace of fashion.

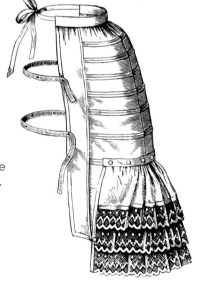

Above: The bustle: a sway, a flick, a discreet "follow me" slither and rustle. From Gazette de la Famille, *September 1874.*
Right: Dimity bustle back. From Harper's Bazaar, *February 1881.*
Far right: Bustles for evening and day. From Revue des Modes Parisiennes, *February 1888.*

The bustle, which probably evolved to facilitate "walking abroad," gave a woman the general appearance of a deformed creature, a music-hall centaur designed by Worth. Where the back of the crinoline had once protruded, the dress was now swept up over a boned half cage. To achieve this sweep successfully, a two-part dress appeared, with a "polonaise" or "tunic" drawn up and back to expose an underskirt. The bustle itself varied yearly in size. The underskirt was often plain when worn with a striped or printed tunic and of a darker color when accompanying a plain tunic. A tightly corseted waist and hair drawn to a fullness at the back completed the silhouette; small but flirtatious hats perched on top of the head. Slippers were reserved for balls or the home. Otherwise, high-top boots were worn (a tasseled version and a low cloth boot with patent-leather toes were fashionable).

Another Englishman working in Paris, the tailor Redfern, had devised a neat "tailor-made" suit with a short jacket for women, but despite his efforts to simplify women's daytime clothes the usual effect was as heavily draped and fringed, and as stuffily claustrophobic, as the gewgaw-cluttered interiors associated with Victorian English taste. Moreover, it was apparent even at a casual glance that dress reflected to an extraordinary degree the stuffiness and rigidity of bourgeois society toward the end of the 19th century, a rigidity sanctified by the widowed Queen Victoria's repressive persona.

This rigidity was exemplified not only by the painfully boned waists of the era but also by the conformity of dress demanded of all "respectable" men and women. That word "respectable" had taken on the connotation of a class division, the line being drawn at the bottom of the middle class. This conformity dictated the precise type of outfit to be worn for any occasion, be it a dinner party, the theater, the opera, a visit (depending on the time of day), a picnic, a boating party, or whatever. Suitability according to age and physical endowments was also prescribed.

Left: Lightweight woolen gowns, "suitable for summer or autumn," designed by the Messrs. Redfern as part of the trousseau of Victoria's daughter, Princess Beatrice. The two models at left are for travel and yachting. From Harper's Bazaar, May 1885.

Above: The scientific bustles of the 1880s: When a woman stood up, a "Langtry" collapsible bustle would spring back to its original shape. The "Health Bustle" was touted for its "lightness, cleanliness and flexibility."

Below: Edward VII's daughter-in-law, the future Queen Mary, smartly dressed for a sportive dash in a barouche drawn by a thoroughbred.

Bottom: Appropriate dress: Harper's Bazaar sport clothes for the moderately energetic. Left to right: For modern travel. April 1868. For taking the mountain airs. August 1870. For lawn tennis. August 1881. For promenading. June 1869.

tation one by her style of dress. Vulgarity is readily seen even under a costly garment," and "no woman should overdress in her own house; it is the worst taste." Mrs. Sherwood prescribes: for church, reading, walks, a morning concert, or a call on foot—a tailor-made costume; for picnics, excursions or journeys—tweed, serge, or piqué; but for a late breakfast—a morning dress as luxurious as one pleases; and a handsome, high-necked gown for a country tea. Light-colored silks, sweeping trains, and gay bonnets are suitable for carriage wear at the races but not permissible for walking in the streets. The list is endless, and the author is as heartless in criticizing the aged and out of shape as those with pretensions above their station: "An elderly, stout woman never looks so badly as in low-necked, light-colored silks or satins."

A sense of exaggerated social propriety is taken for granted in the pages of Mrs. Sherwood, as is that obsessive prudery that led to the discovery of neurosis. Mrs. Sherwood has an Anglo-Saxon contempt and distrust of Worth and his orange, blue, pink, and lilac Parisian dresses trimmed with lace flounces and disapproves of women who wear them in public "without a mantle."

Mrs. Sherwood also disapproves of the tightly corseted waist, not entirely on grounds of health, although she admits that two or three women "well known in society" had killed themselves by tight lacing. (Not all medical authorities agreed. In 1888 a paper extolling the physiological benefits derived from corseting of the abdomen was read to a congress of British scholars.) It is the sexual attraction of the "hourglass" shape, however, that really rattles Mrs. Sherwood: "But if a woman laces herself into a sixteen inch belt, and then clothes herself in brocade, satin and bright colors, and makes herself conspicuous, she should not object to the fact that men, seeing her throw aside her mantle, comment upon her charms in no measured terms. *She has no one to blame but herself.*"

"Manners and Social Usage"

In any society in which class distinctions are drawn by those enjoying the higher rung, the excluded become desperate. This desperation in Victorian society invited a plethora of manuals on deportment. Never in Western history have so many dicta on the niceties of behavior and appearance been promulgated. They all seethe with the very snobbery the intimidated reader is attempting to vanquish. *Manners and Social Usages*, by Mrs. John Sherwood (author of *A Transplanted Rose*), is a volume to crush the sensibilities of a Castiglione. To set the timid mind at ease, Mrs. Sherwood proclaims ". . . one can always tell a real lady from an imi-

Left top: A sense of occasion: Harper's Bazaar recommended this elaborate gown of apricot and sky-blue faille, white silk and lace as appropriate for both opera and concert. December 1871.

Left bottom: "Ladies and children's bathing suits." From left, a serge dress and a leather dressing cape; a costume for child of six or seven; two flannel ensembles. From Harper's Bazaar.

Demi-monde and decadence: Victorian siren songs.
Top: Oscar Wilde, 1894.
Above: La Goulue, "The Glutton," a teen-aged laundress who raucously can-canned her way to fame in Montmartre dance halls. 1898.
Right above: Cora Pearl, whose bejeweled figure made her one of the highest-paid courtesans of the age. 1870.
Right below: Rejane, a great actress with a flair for the ladylike. Photographed by Reutlinger. c. 1905.

Curiously, the bustle and tightly boned torsos of Victorian women had another, subconscious implication. The costume was not only as rigidly confining as the society it represented but, seen through the telescope of present-day psychology, almost aggressively erotic. "Follow me," the heaving bosoms, flicking trains and swaying buttocks seemed to coax in the silken whisper of a diamond-spattered *grande cocotte*.

By the closing decades of the 19th century, both the *grandes cocottes*, queens of Paris's amoral demimonde, and the dandified Aesthetes visually bore out two of Oscar Wilde's most insouciant credos. The *cocottes*, stylish whores with hearts of golden strongboxes, proved his notion that "nothing succeeds like excess," while the Aesthetes devoted themselves to his principle that "the first duty in life is to be as artificial as possible. What the second duty is no one has yet discovered."

When in 1855 Alexandre Dumas *fils* created the term "Le Demi-Monde" for the title of a play about Second Empire morality and manners, he defined a *demimondaine* as a woman whose marital infidelity or careless behavior had cast her outside the boundaries of respectable society. She did not necessarily demand money from men. But by the time such prominent harlots as La Paiva, Caroline Otero, the cockney Cora Pearl (who commanded up to ten thousand francs a night, in the days when the average worker received three francs a day) set themselves up in Paris, prostitution had been raised to a commercial art form.

The sordid truths of these women's careers were more than the sensibilities of decadent poets and painters were prepared to take, so to protect themselves from the squalid reality of merchandised sex they invented the myth of the jeweled succubus, the man-devouring orchid, the heartless Salome in a lace-flounced peignoir. Nietzsche helped to propagate this menacing illusion when he said that the two things a real man likes are danger and play, and for this reason he liked women, the most dangerous of playthings. Proust delivered the master stroke: "The kept woman," muses Swann, ". . . an amalgam of mysterious, diabolical elements, set like a Gustave Moreau apparition in poisonous flowers intertwined with precious stones." The transformation was now complete. The overdressed, bauble-laden prostitute of the Second Empire and Third Republic had become an artistic device, the fashion-setting model for the 20th-century "vamp."

Above: Le Moulin Rouge, the quintessential Parisian pleasure garden of the belle époque. 1885.
Far left: The wonderfully outrageous La Goulue, in her prime, demonstrates the erotic potency of black stockings and gartered thighs. 1898.
Left: Yvette Guilbert, the sophisticated diseuse, who understood the erotic grace of her trademark—long black gloves. By Toulouse-Lautrec.

YVETTE GUILBERT
dans « Linger, Longer, Loo ».

Top: The tyranny of the corset.
c. 1910.
Above: More than one determined woman achieved an
eighteen-inch waist by the sur-
gical removal of the lowest
ribs. 1900.

But the squandering of money on the decoration of the female species provoked more hardheaded men to a restless concern having nothing to do with titillating literary fantasies. Thorstein Veblen, the American sociologist, writing at the end of the century, used the clothing of his era as cogent proof of his theories of "conspicuous consumption" and "conspicuous waste." Dress he saw as the visual incarnation of the ideals and aspirations of the industrial society. That the expenditure on "respectable appearance" far outweighed that on mere protection, and the show of a decent amount of wasteful consumption indicated "*prima facie* evidence of the pecuniary success" of the individual went almost without saying. But Veblen saw further. The dress of the bourgeoisie was contrived to show in every detail the fact that the wearer could not possibly "put forth any useful effort," let alone manual work. What better proof of leisure than the "patent leather shoe, the stainless linen, the lustrous cylindrical hat and the walking stick." The evidence against women's clothing is even more explicit: the elegant feminine bonnet, the high-heeled shoe, the skirt that hampers its wearer at every turn, and above all the corset, which he saw as "substantially a mutilation, undergone for the purpose of lowering the subject's vitality and rendering her permanently and obviously unfit for work." Moreover, women's elaborate dress was the badge of her servitude, evidence that she was still man's chattel, ". . . servants to whom, in the differentiation of economic functions, has been delegated the office of putting in evidence their master's ability to pay." In short, women "consume vicariously for the head of the household."

We have already observed that men had loaded onto their wives and mistresses the jewels and silks that since the French Revolution had been unfashionable for their own use and cumbersome in the pursuit of business. It was as if a woman's function was to advertise a man's material success by parading about in a sandwich-board of finery. Moreover, Veblen's view of the woman as chief servant is in keeping with the legal and emotional position of women whom the Victorian ideal had relegated to complete servility. Cruikshank's *Comic Almanack* effectively skewers the frock-coated façade of the all too typical Victorian paterfamilias in satirical verse:

It is said he's a tyrant at home,
    That the jewels his Wife has for show,
Were all of them salves for some wound—
    That each diamond's heal'd up a blow;
That his Children, on hearing his knock,
    To the top of the house always ran—
But with ten thousand pounds at his Banker's
    He's of course a respectable Man.

Below: Veblen's "conspicuous consumption" on the rampage: Mrs. Jay Gould, trussed, chokered and betrained, provides a suitable background for her $500,000 pearl necklace.

Below right, top to bottom: Icing on the provocative hour-glass shape: Ostrich-ribbon- and rose-trimmed straw hat. A bonnet similarly adorned. From Harper's Bazaar. June 1889. Evening slippers of beaded bronze kid, left and right, and bowed and beaded black patent leather. From Harper's Bazaar. February 1887.

255

Left: The antiquated dress of one's servant might suggest a family connection with a vanished ancien régime. 1850. Below: Sarah Bernhardt in her salon: Conspicuous consumption, no matter how romantic, demanded the arduous attention of a staff. 1890.

The other servants of a "respectable man's" household were also utilized as vicarious consumers, according to their master's means. Someone suddenly set down on a London, Paris, or (much more rarely) New York street at any point in the Victorian era might well be confused as to whether he was in the 18th or the 19th century. This was because the wealthy bourgeois and aristocratic household abounded in servants; many of these, particularly the male, were kept busy running errands and attending their employers through the streets, and they were dressed in the fashion of the 18th, rather than the 19th century. The curious fossilization of servants' dress dates back to earlier eras, when servants actually wore their employers' cast-off clothes. At the court of Louis XIV pages were accoutered in the trunk hose of an earlier day. During the 19th century masters kept their male servants in the silk stockings, knee breeches, embroidered coat, and powdered hair of the court of the decapitated Louis XVI, perhaps out of the desire of the well placed to be related to the aristocracy of the *ancien régime* without themselves dressing unfashionably, as well as a kind of ostentation no longer condoned by fashion. Toward the end of the century, trousers and the square cutaway tailcoat, outmoded for a generation, replaced the knee breeches and the eternal *justaucorps*, but as late as 1892 a New York matron, quoted in *Vogue*, could rhapsodize on the livery worn by the servants of Mrs. Ogden Mills:

It's a lovely house for a dance, more like a London house than most in New York, one of the few where you find dressing-rooms on the ground floor as you enter. She has servants in knee-breeches, too, which I think looks very well. Mrs. Stuyvesant Fish says hers hate wearing powder, and that's a pity, because all that sort of ceremonious costuming of servants is part of the great social game, and I do think it's amusing to see it well played.

Right top: Protected from a wintry London downpour by furry thatching, a footman acts as a carriage groom. 1898.
Right bottom: Two German maids gossip about their employers. Their occupation is advertised by their aprons their caps, and their bows, once the garments of respectable middle-class housewives. 1906.

Below: "All Paris," meaning
all members of the fashionable
élite, at the Folies-Bergère. The
line between haut monde and
demimonde is less visible than
ever. Poster by Adrienne
Barrère, 1885.

Right: The "social game"
played well: a Proustian cast
of fin de siècle characters scin-
tillate at a fashionable soirée.
By Jean Beraud. c. 1880.

TOUT PARIS A LA REVUE DES FOLIES · BERGÈRE

La Belle Epoque

"The great social game" indeed. Here with mindless accuracy *Vogue's* confidante sums up not
only a tightly structured way of life but a whole
era in a single vacuous phrase. Actually the name
of the game itself was fashion, fashion in all its most
exacting forms, and it would continue to be played
with slavish allegiance until the abrupt finale of
the Edwardian period, *La Belle Epoque*—the last
of the so-called good old days.

The principal players of the game, the *beau
monde*, must always follow the rules. Of cardinal
importance was to take little seriously but the
superfluous. Here, for instance, is Clovis Sangrail,
Saki's insouciant, snobbish young Edwardian
aesthete-dandy, the forerunner of Noel Coward's
limp drawing-room tailor's dummies, being coaxed
to a garden party: "You can just wear your sweetest
clothes and a moderately amiable expression and
eat chocolate creams with the appetite of a blasé
parrot. Nothing else is expected of you." Saki has
an assassin's grasp of great social gamesmanship in

general, Clovis elsewhere observing that "all decent people live beyond their incomes nowadays
and those who aren't respectable live beyond other
people's."

A prime exponent of Clovis's philosophy was
the fashion-setting Edward VII himself. It is uncanny
in how many ways he closely resembled that other
sybaritic ex-Prince of Wales, the similarly debt-
ridden George IV. Of particularly interesting significance is the fact that both were reactionary offspring
of tight-fisted puritanical authoritarians. Their re-
bellions took almost identical forms, each devoting
himself to the pursuit of pretty women, rounds
of extravagant parties, fattening food, and fleeting
divertissements. Both spent fortunes on decorating
palaces. And, of course, on dressing up. King Edward, known as "the uncle of Europe" because
of his network of relatives reigning in foreign courts,
became the most influential male fashion image
of his time, both in England and abroad. Appropri-
ateness rather than splashy show was his tailors'

Left above: Lily Langtry, an early Edwardian professional beauty and a later Edwardian grande dame, of whom it was said that "ladies so far forgot their Society manners as to clamber on their chairs in their keenness to see 'the Jersey Lily.'" 1882.
Left: The indestructibly chic Queen Alexandra, Danish wife of Edward VII, and the fashion icon of the era. 1905.

Above: As Prince of Wales, Edward began to stamp his name on an age well before the end of his mother Victoria's reign. His tailor helped. Photographed by Bassano.

Right: A modern monarch mechanized. Edward VII, in appropriate driving dress, takes command of a 12-h.p. Daimler. Photo by Tugwell, 1899.

Right above: A pleated Parisian shirtwaist for an Edwardian rose. From L'art et la Mode, 1895.
Far right: The shirtwaist and separate skirt vanquish the hourglass silhouette. 1903.

guiding principle, and accordingly, whether outfitted for a ball, shoot, yachting party, or dress parade, he was always the portly acme of sartorial etiquette.

Queen Alexandra, Edward's chic and serenely lovely Danish wife, was equally endowed with flawless fashion sense. As previously mentioned, it was she who popularized the expertly tailored suit along with many other personal trademarks such as tall pearly dog collars and an upswept bird's-nest coiffure. Never did she appear ostentatious or outré—a stylish achievement in a period when many aristocratic women, particularly in France, still aspired to look like well-bred courtesans.

By the 1890s women's dress was finally beginning to evolve along somewhat more sensible lines. In 1885 a pleated skirt had appeared alongside the usual heavily draped version, and now dresses became somewhat—although only somewhat—simpler. A small bustle was retained, but fullness now moved to the sleeves, and in 1895 the leg-of-mutton and balloon sleeve became enormous. Later these were replaced by long sleeves with a smaller puff at the shoulder. By the turn of the century the belled skirt, corseted wasp waist, tight puffed sleeves, and high collar worn by the independent heroines of Charles Dana Gibson's sketches was balanced by piled-up hair or an enormous, heavily burdened hat. The bustle remained as a memory, but its spirit lingered on as an S-shaped matronly stance. Emancipation might be finally on its way, but not until the 1914 firing of guns would a simultaneous death knell be heard for incapacitating fashions. As a popular song of the period put it: "I'm only a bird in a gilded cage, a beautiful sight to see." However, not for long.

Overleaf: Descending the steps of a boulevard café or of an era? La Belle Epoque, the Edwardian Age—the Good Old Days—draw to a close. Painting by Abraham A. Anderson. c. 1885.

The 20th Century:
The Luxury of Freedom

World War I has long been considered a watershed of social revolution, one even more clearly marked by a change of dress than the French Revolution. It would seem, however, that the manners and mores of the 19th century had become obsolete well before 1914.

The telephone, the electric light, and the automobile are customarily evoked as causes of change. But if the steam engine had not already shaken 19th-century morality loose it is unlikely that the electric light would have done so. All were labor-saving devices and hence the instruments of freedom; all played their parts in the social change that became apparent after 1918.

The true "revolution" came well before the war, and it was more profound than any technological advance. It was not so much the product of the violence as a reaction to the suppression of the spirit inflicted by Victorian attitudes. By the turn of the century Frank Lloyd Wright had replaced the claustrophobic clutter of the Victorian world style."

During the first decade of the 20th century the Cubist experiments of the young Georges Braque and Pablo Picasso evolved into the pure abstractions of Kasimir Malevich; and Sigmund Freud, who had already delved into psychopathology and published *The Interpretation of Dreams*, undertook the onerous task of exposing the warped emotions of the Victorian psyche. But the mood of change was not confined to a small circle of advanced spirits. The world became modern in a thousand tiny, subtle ways. In 1906 French coiffeurs devised the permanent wave, and a year later Annette Kellerman shocked the world with her one-piece bathing suit.

When, in 1909, Parisian audiences greeted Sergei Diaghilev's Ballet Russe with wild enthusiasm, they were cheering the crystallization of their newfound liberation. *Vogue* captured its immediate effect:

> The art of the Russian Ballet is undeniably barbaric . . . a region of primitive emotions. Beauty, anger, lust, terror, jollity, timidity stalk the stage naked and unashamed. This art is the antithesis of what . . . has been labeled with the name "Victorian." The note of Victorian literature is a note of almost harrowing self-consciousness. Of this disease of super-civilization these Russians are emphatically free . . . they are pagan with the pure untroubled paganism of the healthy child. . . . The material may be barbaric; the craftsmanship, if anything, is super-civilized.

This was the "barbarism" of the sophisticated, of the avant-garde, of Bakst and Benois, Stravinsky and Rimsky-Korsakov. It summed up in one stroke the break with the Victorian past. In the words of J. B. Priestley, "The demure but ever-present sexuality of the musical comedies and Viennese operettas was blown wide open. Young men and girls who never set eyes on the orgiastic scene of sex and death in *Scheherazade* began to lead very different lives from their parents and grandparents." Three years later *Hello Ragtime* opened in London with blasts of Irving Berlin. Rupert Brooke went to see it ten times.

The depth of Victorian repression rendered the rebellion of women all the more vehement. It was said in horror that they had begun to paint their faces. The horror itself indicated how totally the dictates of the Marquise de Pompadour, who actually wrote an entry on "rouge" in Diderot's encyclopedia, had been obliterated from memory. Male "vices" were adopted with alacrity. When Mrs. Patrick Campbell lit up a cigarette in the tearoom of the Plaza Hotel in New York, the management requested that she put it out. "I have been given to

Opposite: Permanent wave. The technique of "marcelling" hair was developed in 1870 by Marcel Grateau. Then, in 1906, C. Nestle, a London coiffeur, announced a process for "waving to withstand water, shampoo and all atmospheric influences," and the permanent wave was here. These marcelled "waves" are permanent.

The photographer Lartigue's cousin Simone in a daringly mid-calf-length skirt, wins a prize in the skating championships at St. Moritz in 1913.

Left: Mrs. Patrick Campbell, the actress, who dared to light a cigarette at the Plaza. c. 1901. Left below: Poiret's revolution: a woman shedding her corset. At the turn of the century Paris manufactured fifty million such garments a year. Drawing by Borelli-Vranska, from Les Dessus du Panier. 1914. Below: The suffragettes' shy fury: at their 1913 prim and flower-bedecked "Summer Festival."

understand this is a free country," she replied. "I propose to do nothing to alter its status."

Mrs. Campbell's retort was a weak reflection of the despair of the Suffragettes, the members of the Women's Social and Political Union. They were perhaps the first to discover the use of the rapidly growing press as a weapon. For the purposes of publicity, they submitted to imprisonment and employed the tactic of illegal demonstration. Ironically, in England the Liberal government championed their cause but hung back from granting the vote to women precisely because they feared that most women would be conservative. The Suffragettes were driven to a shy fury. They wanted to blow up the world without hurting anyone. They broke shop windows, set fires in empty houses, and planted bombs to go off when they knew no one was present. Their agitation reached its height when

Emily Wilding Davison, an Oxford graduate, threw herself under the King's galloping horse on Derby Day at Epsom and endured a hideous martyrdom.

Emancipation was more than a disembodied concept; it took a highly physical form. Women covered their white complexions with cold cream and went out on the tennis courts. They skated, rowed, cycled in divided skirts, and took to ballooning. The Duchess d'Uzes, known as "The Amazon" and a lieutenant of the *louveterie* (the wolf-hunt), was said to have been the first woman in Europe to drive a car. For this highly messy and faintly dangerous occupation women wore a simple skirt and shirt with jabot, a gray dustcoat (derived from the coachman's coat), a large hat and veil. Certain women, moreover, struck a new note even in their daily dress. The Czarina Alix shocked the Austrian court by wearing a tailored black suit with a white shirt and tie like

266

Above: Liberation trussed: dancing the Turkey Trot in a hobble skirt. 1912.
Left: Poster advertising Tango Teas at the London Pavilion: the hobble skirt slit to the knee. 1913.
Far left: Irene and Vernon Castle doing the Castle Walk. Skirt slit and hair "shingled," Irene Castle was regarded as the respectable cousin of the tango-craze vamp and so epitomized an era. 1914.

a man's and appearing in the evening in a long-sleeved black crepe gown ornamented by a single Russian order. Clearly the "new woman" stood in need of comfort, freedom to move, and simplicity in dress. This need was given focus and form by one extraordinary individual.

The Revolution of Paul Poiret

In the summer of 1934 a heavy-set, bearded man, wearing a straw hat and superbly tailored white flannel suit, walked into a French provincial town hall and demanded unemployment relief. When the bewildered clerk asked the man's occupation he replied, "Couturier." The clerk announced that he was unable to find such a term under the official listing of trades and professions eligible for relief. The man replied, "Of course not. I pioneer everything."

The clerk could not have known that he was addressing the man who had singlehandedly created the visual ideal of early 20th-century womanhood. Paul Poiret was born in Paris in 1879, the son of a small but prosperous cloth merchant who owned a shop called, suitably, L'Espérance, in the area of Les Halles. The gawky toadlike boy, his head spinning with the art of Bonnard and Vuillard, the drama of Sarah Bernhardt and Eleonora Duse, and the exotic fantasies of Pierre Loti, was sent to work in an umbrella shop.

Young Poiret, who from the first had envisioned himself as the savior and embellisher of womanhood, knocked on the doors of Paris couturiers with the desperation of a condemned man. Several purchased his sketches, and he was finally accepted as a junior assistant by Jacques Doucet himself, at the moment the favorite couturier of the *grandes cocottes* and of the more adventurous and energetic young matrons of Paris. Doucet was a collector of Impressionist paintings and African sculpture, a man of the world, and young Poiret's idol. The paternal Doucet sent his young apprentice to a good tailor and advised him to find an attractive young woman to function as wife and model.

It was soon after following this last bit of advice that Poiret provoked his "revolution." He had by then parted from Doucet, worked briefly for Worth, and set up shop on his own with a small investment from his mother. In 1905 he became engaged to the daughter of a family friend from the provinces, a tall, gangly girl with handsomely carved "classical" features. Denise was not at all the rounded beauty

of the day, but Poiret saw in her the woman of the future and proceeded to "create" her as such.

In his salon Poiret paraded the new clothes of the new woman with unerring flamboyance. When the Countess Greffulhe (Proust's model for the Duchesse de Guermantes) wore one of his outrageous creations, a sheath, to her daughter's wedding, Poiret was launched. But the real reason for his success was not the momentary patronage of a famous woman of fashion, nor was it even the undeniable novelty of his concept. As Poiret saw it from the beginning, he succeeded because he gave women precisely what they had been wanting for some time. "I do not impose my will upon fashion. . . . I am merely the first to perceive women's secret desires and to fulfill them." Like the free-flowing tunics and expressive movements of the "divine" Isadora Duncan, Poiret's clothes were a cry of freedom.

Poiret's revolution was based on the ideal of liberation from the corset. The dress was no longer supported by a steel substructure radiating from the waist. Rather, the pinched waist disappeared and dresses flowed, in the manner of the Greek chiton, from two points of support at the shoulders. This robe was gently gathered beneath the breast and then fell in a narrow column to the floor. Thus Poiret created a classical or "Hellenic" silhouette, such as had not been seen since the Napoleonic Empire almost a century earlier. Moreover, his "line" was not encumbered by unnecessary ornamentation, that joy of the *fin de siècle* couturier. Poiret was one of the first 20th-century designers to call for simplification: "I strive for omission, not addition."

The new line necessitated new textiles "soft and brilliant as water reflecting the sun or the trees." These were frequently supple gauzes, chiffons, and crepe de Chine. But unlike Empire fashions Poiret's "Hellenic" dresses were not romantic recreations of the past. He also worked in heavier, less drapeable materials than were used in the Empire: gold and silver lamés, damasks and brocades of Byzantine and Renaissance design. He anticipated the orgiastic color of Bakst. As he saw it, in the creations of his

Opposite: Poiret's new line confronts the old, as seen in the German periodical Simplicissimus.

Above: A Poiret evening gown in purple and red ("Au Clair de la Lune"), drawn by Lepape and worn by the new feminine ideal, a humorous seductress, just a touch evil and a mite bored. From Gazette du Bon Ton, 1915.

Overleaf: Poiret's mannequins promenade through his own garden showing several of his designs, including the tunic and sack, as well as the bandeaued and turbaned head. Still from a film made to accompany Poiret's lectures, 1910.

contemporaries, "lilacs, sky blue hortensias, straw, anything that was cloying, washed out and dull to the eye, was held in the highest regard." The Fauves had just burst upon the public. Matisse wrote, "Color is liberation," and Poiret, "the Fauve of fashion," adopted this from liberation as well. The colors of Matisse, Marquette, Rouault, and Utrillo —reds, oranges, lemons, and burning blues—appear in his creations. He wrote: "My sunburst of pastels brought a new dawn."

To perfect his concept, Poiret decreed that heads must be small. His wife cropped her hair, and the confining "bandeau" became a basic part of Poiret's total vision. Moreover, Poiret's new line was so successful with younger and more adventurous women, despite the hoots of the more conservative, that it was immediately copied by Paquin, Lanvin, and others. Its influence may have dealt the death blow to the fast-declining popularity of the ten-course meal. Huge breakfast menus involving cutlets and grilled fish had already given way to flapjacks and eggs, and other overindulgences were soon to go. Moreover, Poiret did not merely inspire women to throw away their corsets and lighten their figures. His fertile imagination also provided them with new modern supportive garments. He devised a light rubber girdle to retract the hips, and, being an admirer of the small bosom of Botticelli's Venus, he invented the *soutien-gorge*, or brassiere, to achieve breasts "that rise forth from the bodice like an enchanting testimonial to youth."

Although it was Poiret who first applauded the "youthful" figure that was to be the ideal of this century, as opposed to those splendid but heavy curves usually achieved in middle years, he was a touch regretful. He later wrote: "Had I known that those charms were about to become extinct, I might have taken greater advantage of them." Some concept of the magnitude of his revolution may be grasped from the fact that Paris at that time was manufacturing roughly fifty million corsets a year.

Poiret's innovation was not limited to introducing a new line. He elaborated it. The smoothly falling drape of his narrow sheaths might be covered by one or two tunics of varying lengths. He then created a looser "sack" gown. Finally having freed women, Poiret chose to enslave them again with the hobble skirt, the dimension of its hem just large enough to allow tiny, mincing steps. In 1910 hobble skirts caused such a frenzy that the doors of his establishment were broken down by women trying to buy them. The fashion was soon denounced by the Pope. The Pope, however, need not have worried about this disablement of women, since Poiret had already devised a way to free them. He slit the skirt to the knee. He then publicized his innovation by taking a series of mannequins in their slit skirts to the Longchamps racecourse. The scene was one of slapstick outrage, and the publicity was entirely negative. However, like much negative publicity, it

achieved its end. Indubitably, the slit-skirted seductress of the "tango craze," her cheeks rice-
powdered, her eyes smeared with kohl, her cigarette holder clasped in vermilion lips, was a Poiret
product.

A growing Oriental mania, similar to that for chinoiserie in the 18th century, culminated in the
ecstatic success of the Ballet Russe. But the Orient
interpreted by Bakst and Benois, Golovine, Goncha-
rova and Derain, the Orient of *Scheherazade, Fire-
bird,* and *Le Coq d'Or,* was a mystic land in the
style of the then popular *arts décoratifs,* later called
"Art Deco." Europe was entranced by yet another
"Orient of the imagination," and it had a profound
effect on design for a generation. In the words of
one writer: "There are today lampshades in Scottish
boarding houses which owe their existence to
Scheherazade."

Where fashion was concerned, the cynosure of
inspiration was not the divine Anna Pavlova or
the dark and beautiful Tamara Karsavina but Ida

*Opposite above: "Petite robe
de compagne de Paquin" by
Georges Barbier: Paquin's
adaptation of Poiret's line.
From Gazette du Bon Ton, 1913.
Opposite below: "Au Jardin
des Hesperides," a drawing by
Georges Barbier of a simple
day dress by Poiret. From
Gazette du Bon Ton, 1913.*

*Above: "When yokels pester
us by following our troikas, we
cut off their heads and throw
them into sacks that look like
that thing."–Princess Bariatinsky. The revolutionary kimono cut and motifs of Poiret's
coats forecast the oriental
mania induced by Diaghilev's
Ballets Russes. From* Les
Choses de Paul Poiret *by Paul
Iribe, 1908.*

Top left: Ida Rubinstein, who danced "like Indian princesses, like Nubian women from the Cataracts, like Bacchantes from Lydia." Photograph by Otto, c. 1912.
Lower left: "How to Dress" in the slit hobble skirt. Fashion advertisement by Swan and Edgar, Costumes and Drapers, London. 1913.
Top right: The hobble skirt at its most crippling. Illustration by Georges Lepape in Gazette du Bon Ton, 1913.
Lower right: Serge suit with coral buttons. From Gazette du Bon Ton, 1913.

Rubinstein, the "Oriental Peri as dreamed by Moreau or Beardsley." This incarnation of the 19th-century decadent ideal, virtually worshiped by the arbiter of taste, Robert de Montesquiou, was a wealthy Russian Jewess who danced "like Indian princesses, like Nubian women from the Cataracts, like Bacchantes from Lydia." In *Prince of Aesthetes*, Philippe Jullien tells us, "This Balkis, this Salomé hurled at the society of *le Tout-Paris*, decapitated good taste as if it were the head of John the Baptist, and the blood from it spattered Poiret's dresses and lacquered Dunand's furniture."

Poiret had the right to claim that his own predisposition for Orientalia long predated the arrival of the Russians. As a boy he had a passion for Oriental rugs. When no more than a junior assistant designer at Worth, he offered the Princess Bariatinsky a new design for an overcoat in the style of a kimono. The Princess's opinion of it is worth recording. "In Russia," she said, "when yokels pester us running after our troikas, we cut off their heads and throw them into sacks that look like that thing."

When Parisian tastes turned violently "Oriental," Poiret was in a position to present a thousand and one inspired variations. Noticing that his shopgirls tied up their hair in scarves to keep it clean, he devised a simple turban that soon became the headdress of the era, often ornamented with an egret feather. For his wife Poiret created "Oriental" pantaloons to be worn under a short, hooped skirt, which enjoyed a brief but exceptional vogue as the "lampshade tunic." He foresaw that women, whose daily life was becoming "masculinized," would eventually wear trousers. The new pantaloons suited both walking and the tango perfectly, and *Vogue*'s correspondent gasped, "Excitement has raged in Paris unlike anything in my memory of gowning." Cocteau wrote, "The duchesses are ready to be dressed, undressed, costumed by Paul Poiret. They wish to be transformed into Egyptian dancing girls, silk and fur furniture covers, lampshades, cushions in the harem of the sultan à la mode." It was the decadence of Pierre Louys at couture prices.

Poiret possessed an uncanny ability to sight new trends and to find and utilize undiscovered talent. It could be claimed, for example, that he revolutionized fashion art, making it the record of social and aesthetic history that it is today. He achieved this when he commissioned Paul Iribe and Georges Lepape to illustrate, respectively, two volumes of his designs, *Les Robes* and *Les Choses de Paul Poiret*. Poiret's new fashions were interpreted in terms of contemporary art. Composition and line—the casual, telling line of the new century—were all-important. This style of fashion art and its practitioners, such as Lepape and Erté, who also worked for Poiret, were taken up by the fashion publications, which were enjoying their own evolution. *Vogue* had progressed from rather prim essays of interest to "ladies" to the droll cynicism and "throwaway" chic of a

Left: Poiret's wife Denise in a gown he made only for her. Called "Sagesse," it consisted of an ivory-colored brocaded silk top, trimmed in gold braid, over a skirt of chestnut panne velvet. 1911.
Above: Anne de Noailles peeks with kohl-smeared eyes from beneath her Poiret turban. Photograph by Otto, 1912.

Dorothy Parker. Lepape's kind of woman, Poiret's kind of woman, had a sense of humor and a touch of evil and worldly boredom as yet foreign to the fashion publication. Moreover, Poiret was the first to realize the possibilities of fashion photography. To photograph his collection he hired two unknowns, Edward Steichen and, later, Man Ray.

Poiret wished to assault all the senses with his unified aesthetic. For him, the heavy and mysterious scents of the Orient were quite as much a part of its heady allure as its silks and brocades. At that moment the science of scent manufacture was just developing, and Poiret was the first couturier to work with chemists to produce his own perfumes. These were to embody the mystique of the Poiret woman, and he was the first to replace the usual fragrances of rose and lavender with scents meant to invoke a specific image, an intriguing and mysterious one. They were aptly named: Le Fruit Défendu, Nuit de Chine, L'Etrange Fleur, or simply Borgia. Thus, even in the way she smelled, the Victorian lady of purity and sweetness was replaced by the seductress. Every woman could have the wickedness of an Ida Rubinstein at her fingertips.

Not the least of Poiret's inspirations was his deliberate use of the press for what was later to be called "public relations." Poiret never advertised. He preferred to spend his money (and a great deal of it) on costume parties that invariably netted him spectacular publicity as well as amusement. In June 1911 he gave a party of the "1002nd Night" to launch his Oriental models. The "sultan" himself, in white beard, pale gray, green, and ruby-red velvet, welcomed his guests into Ali Baba's cave, where glints of light emanated from carafes containing jewel-toned liquids. In the garden, luminous blue and violet fruits and berries hung on the branches of trees, and the buffet was sheltered beneath an awning painted by Dufy and Segonzac. Paths were covered with thick rugs, and white peacocks, pink ibises, flamingoes, herons, macaws, parrots, and monkeys played on the lawn and in the trees. The air, moaning with the music of flutes, pipes, and the zither, was scented by braziers of myrrh and incense. A white slave, dressed only in a mass of gauze, danced, and the sky dripped gold and silver fireworks. At the height of the festivities, Madame Poiret, the "sultan's favorite," burst out of a golden cage, turbaned and wearing chiffon harem pantaloons of ocher and white under a "lampshade tunic" of transparent cloth of gold, both fashions then totally new.

It was a great era for costume parties—for every kind of party. In the hazy retrospect of later, more highly taxed epochs, it could be said that "the rich were still rich," and manners were looser than they had been in over a century. At one party the Marchesa Casati, described as a "Medusa or tigress smiling as though she would bite," was accompanied by a macaw, an ape, and a leopard. Princess Radziwill may have alarmed guests at the Hotel Excelsior in Rome by arriving with a leopard and a lion. Meanwhile, in Paris, a muffled little hypochondriac nibbled on pastry, sipped hot chocolate, and observed everything; Marcel Proust had made an arrangement with a waiter at the Ritz who noted down for him everyone who entered its portals, what they ate, and what they wore.

The general populace in America felt that unreality had reached extremes when the works of Duchamp, Brancusi, and Matisse first appeared in New York's notorious 1913 Armory Show. In fact, the first great temple of true fantasy was raised in that same city the next year when the Strand Theater, the first

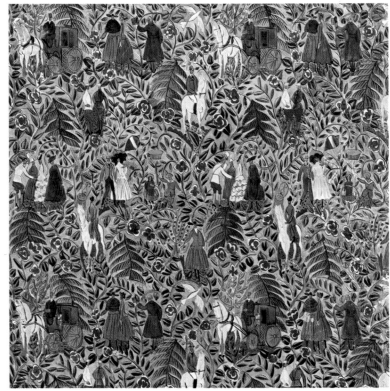

"motion picture palace," opened, offering Broadway audiences marble halls, Oriental rugs, gilt, crystal chandeliers, original works of art, and a thirty-piece symphony orchestra to accompany the feature.

In the escapist phantasmagoria of the moment, war came as if by an arbitrary act of nature. Paul Poiret, then thirty-four and at the height of his career, closed his salon, provided for his wife and children, and announced he was prepared to die for his country. Before leaving he designed a uniform for Jean Cocteau to wear as a driver in Misia Sert's private ambulance unit, which had been equipped with the vans of the major couturiers. For himself he designed a uniform consisting of a blue suit, a blue silk shirt, and a tie with a picture of a nude woman on it. He was discouraged from wearing this outfit, although he was invited to redesign the uniform of the French army along more practical lines.

277

Top: A World War I American auxiliary corps leaves for France to serve as "clerks, store-keepers or motor drivers." In mannish coats, sturdy boots and hair tucked into hats, they marched into a more liberated future. 1918. Above: British nurses in a transport carrying wounded soldiers. 1917.

World War I

It is useless in a way to discuss "fashions" during the Great War. Horrified by the disaster that had engulfed them, French women, for the first time perhaps in a thousand years, lost something of their interest in fashion. The decrease in social life left little inducement for it. A small group of couturiers, mosty women, banded together for a showing at the San Francisco Exhibition of 1915. Their dresses were quiet and conservative, with natural waists and wide skirts permitting the wearer to move freely. The war years produced one notable change in "line," however: For almost the first time since antiquity, something slightly more than the foot peeked out beneath ladies' skirts, which remained severe and quite demure nevertheless.

If the fashion in dress changed little, the fashion in women changed considerably. The life of the woman whose ample leisure was devoted to dress and the direction of a battery of servants—in short, the life of the comfortable bourgeoisie of every Western country since the 18th century—changed significantly. The fact that most servants were pressed into military service was an excellent rehearsal for the economic realities of the years to come. Moreover, women had new tasks to fill their leisure. No war, before or since, has effected such a drain on manpower. Women, especially in Europe, found themselves obliged to join or even manage their husbands' businesses, or simply to work because of financial necessity. The absence of male employees gave women considerable opportunity. Moreover, a life of leisure was considered nothing less than unpatriotic. A scrapbook of wartime *Vogue* pictures shows familiar faces very unfamiliarly dressed. Two shy young girls, looking like rumpled baker's assistants, are labeled "Miss Maude Kahn, daughter of Mr. Otto H. Kahn, and Miss Marianne McKeever, Red Cross nurse." In another a rather smarter figure, hands on hips, dangles a scalpel from the belt of her white skirt: "Miss Elsie de Wolfe, who served a nurse's apprenticeship in France, under Dr. Barthe de Santfort." A delicate young woman looking like someone's nervous little sister: "Miss Mary Hoyt Wiborg aided by Mrs. H. Squires and only two French nuns, cared for six hundred wounded men in a hospital behind the Marne." "English women, organized under the frivolous title 'Fannies,' run first-aid stations in France . . . the whole of the convoying of wounded for the enormous Calais district is done by these sturdy girls." Five round and girlish faces contrast with a landscape of ice and an endless cavalcade of Red Cross trucks the color of death. Glancing through the pictures at the mannish coats, Sam Brown belts, sturdy boots, and shapeless hair tucked in neat caps, one understands why when the war was over women were given the vote without a murmur.

It has frequently been assumed that the "flapper" appeared full-blown to throw off grim recollections of World War I. In fact, the vision of the dizzy 1920s

Below: American girls, their ankles just peeping from their tiered skirts, dance with uniformed young men during World War I. The new step is the Fox Trot. 1918.

emerged more slowly. In 1919 the fashion houses of France foundered in complete confusion. Crafts-men were lacking, and the textile industry had been dismantled. Shortages were drastic. There was no real notion of the direction fashion would take. Many hoped to return to prewar styles. Skirts were swathed or tiered, with panniers and even hoops.

Bodices were loose, although the bosom had disappeared. Bat sleeves, "Russian" or "Medici" collars appeared. Poiret organized a new collection. Skirts were at mid-calf for the day and to the floor at night. "Tailor-made" suits became popular, but women who were beginning to paint found few cosmetics available. Fashion was in a state of flux.

However, it was during the period of the war and subsequent recovery that the great weight of middle-aged fashion gave way to the youthful line for men as well as women. The man who escorted Poiret's slim and natural woman was himself a nattier vision. Unpadded shoulders became fashionable, along with narrower sleeves and trouser legs, which were now not only cuffed but also creased, an innovation credited to Edward VII. Jackets were shorter, lapels longer, and the body had been given the nipped "military high waist." To preserve cloth during the war, belts and pleating disappeared, and patch pockets were replaced by slash pockets.

Even before the war a few as yet unknown young designers were able to see beyond Poiret to what must be the ultimate movement in 20th-century fashion. Cubism and abstraction had already served as an inspiration to fashion. Sonia Delaunay, among the pioneers of abstract art, designed cubistic fabrics with trompe-l'oeil patterns that, as Cubist doctrine dictated, appeared to move in space. In 1914 she went further, designing dresses that were "no longer a piece of fabric draped according to current fashion, but coherent compositions, living paintings or sculpture using living forms." After the war she opened her own textile printing factory, working in embroideries, appliqués, and even furs. Her hats, bags, and belts, often embroidered in abstract designs with dully metallic thread, enjoyed immense success. But she was always primarily a painter. It was another woman who divined the true bent of postwar taste and who saw that wartime necessity in clothes had become desired comfort: Coco Chanel.

Below: The Arrow Collar man always wore a white tie in the evening before the war. Day and night his noble and therefore heavy chin was sliced with exquisite pain by his high, stiff collar. Arrow Collar advertisement, 1913.

ARROW COLLARS & SHIRTS FOR DRESS

Top and Center: The narrower, less padded suit, with shorter jacket and trouser legs cuffed and creased. Ready-to-wear styles by Brandegee Kincaid and Co., New York, 1914. Above: The Arrow Collar man embraces a slim and natural Poiret woman. Postcard, 1910.

Below: Coco Chanel: "... one was surprised by her small size. She was very thin, her black hair was thick, her eyebrows met, her mouth smiled and her eyes were hard. She almost always dressed in the same way, very simply and usually in black." 1936.

Right: Chanel wearing two of her "discoveries," jersey and costume jewelry—in this case, pearls of uniform size. 1929.

Overleaf: Against the back-drop of Chateau de Madrid is a "Fashion Promenade in the Bois, a modish Pageant: The models are wearing skirts slightly longer and waistline higher, polka dots, crepe de Chine, small handkerchief scarves, pleats.

Irregular side panels are fashionable, and imitation flowers have returned to hats, which are small and close-fitting." Fashion sketch by Hemjic of 1929.

sion: She would do neither. She would live independently and she would work.

Chanel had already undergone some training in millinery and couture, and she possessed strong opinions as to how women should dress. She began to refashion simple store-bought hats into neat little models that appealed to the women she met in the increasingly sophisticated circles in which she moved. By 1905 her stiff straw boaters and tight cloches were taken seriously by women tired of the masses of feathers and froufrou they were expected to wear on their heads. In 1910, with the assistance of Boy Capel, she opened a shop on the rue Cambron, where, ironically, her lease prohibited her from making dresses because there was another couturier in the building. It was by talking to women during the war, however, that she came to the conclusion that they yearned for more "sporty" clothes and for the comfort of silk or wool knitted outfits. In 1915 she discovered the use of jersey for high fashion and went into couture. No problems were presented by her lease; a jersey dress, by established standards, was not a dress.

Chanel was determined to "rid women of their frills from head to toe." "Each frill discarded," she said, "makes one look younger." There is a story, perhaps apocryphal, that Chanel borrowed a polo player's sweater one chilly day, belted it, and pushed up the sleeves. She was so entranced with her own appearance in this makeshift that she soon produced similar sweaters for women, and they sold immediately. In any case, it was Chanel who attended the races at Deauville, where other women appeared in silks and laces, wearing a Shetland sweater and pearls. In the words of fashion editor Diana Vreeland, she "cropped and edited" fashion, and her lean chic triumphed.

The bobbed hair of the 1920s has been attributed variously to Poiret, who certainly made the smaller head more fashionable; to the dancer Irene Castle, who shingled her hair for freedom in movement; and to Chanel herself. According to one account, Chanel was on her way to the opera when a heater exploded and almost singed the hair off her head. Always resourceful and never fainthearted, she chopped off the remainder of her lovely locks with a nail scissors. Shortly thereafter her friends, and soon the rest of le Tout-Paris, were busily clipping away. Even if she did not actually invent "bobbed hair," however, it is certain that Chanel accounted for a good many other innovations of the 1920s: the twin sweater set, crocheted lace, the leather belt,

Chanel and the "Little Black Dress"

Gabrielle Chanel was herself an exemplar of the new woman. Born in 1883, the illegitimate and soon orphaned daughter of a poor but respectable family of the Auvergne, she started her career as a cocotte —a sharp-tongued and amusing female companion— with dark hair, tiny features, and a perversely wide mouth. She was kept first by Etienne Balsan, then by his English polo-playing friend, Boy Capel. However, even in her unlikely role as "gentleman's plaything," Coco was an eccentric, dressing often in a simple navy-blue suit and white blouse when others of her ilk loaded themselves with furbelows. Faced squarely with the 19th-century prospect of a life as a successful courtesan, amassing jewels and possessions while still young to tide her comfortably over her later years, or possibly a marriage if it could be managed, she made a 20th-century deci-

Left: Chanel No. 5: the rebellion of simplicity against Poiret's perfume fantasies. Below: Chanel's little black jersey suit: proper for drinks before dinner. 1926.

Right: Chanel's sailor dress with white satin collar and pearl embroidery in Art Deco style. 1925.
Far right: Chanel's loose leather coat with deep pockets: epitome of the "deluxe poor" look. 1925.

sailor pants, the short evening dress, the small hat, the relaxed coat with useful pockets, and, perhaps, most revolutionary of all, costume jewelry.

The simplicity of Chanel's taste was symbolized by the plain square bottle of her Chanel No. 5. Five was her lucky number (she was born on the fifth of the month), but the name she chose for her perfume was also a rebellion against the overblown romanticism of Poiret's heady Oriental scents. In fact, she waged open war on Poiret. She claimed that during the intermission at an opera gala she observed the mass of women in the brilliant clashing colors of Poiret's "new dawn." Chanel, the champion of beige and neutrals, was repelled. "This can't go on," she announced. "I'm going to stick them all into black dresses."

Chanel was accused of invading haute couture with the style of the working girl, of creating the "deluxe poor look." She may have been simply the first couturier to understand one of the most profound changes of the century—the fact that it was no longer fitting or desirable for a woman, in the clothes she wore daily, to create the immediate impression of great wealth. Women now wanted elegance in line, cut and detail in clothes that did not, at first glance, appear obviously expensive. Chanel was the first to sense this and the first to respond with the neat chic of her sweaters, trimmed with crisp white collars, her "little" knitted suits and her "little" black dresses. She believed strongly that women should never overdress during the day. A trim tailored suit was fitting for drinks before dinner. Poiret, unwilling to accept any innovation that was not his own, fought her with richer silks and velvets, more extravagant motifs (one skirt was illuminated by little flashing light bulbs). And he failed. Later he wrote: "We should have been on our guard against this miss with the head of a young boy who was going to cause all hell to break loose and pull out dresses, hair styles, jewelry and sweaters from her magician's hat."

The Coco of "the deluxe poor look," however, was even more of a social lion than Poiret himself.

Her success and her fortune were her entrée, and she manipulated them brilliantly. The beguiling world of bohemia had tipped the scales against the comparatively staid milieu of the balls and receptions of prewar Paris. The Paris of the 1920s was the city of the artist and writer's café and bistro, where meals were served at all hours, of visits to artists' studios and surprise parties, a world of café society in which the aristocracy and upper echelons of the bourgeoisie felt lucky to rub shoulders with the latest success of the music halls or the creator of Diaghilev's most recent *mis en scène*. The new women, of whatever birth, had seized on the chic, the dash and glamour formerly the realm of the *grande cocotte*, who, in the busy world of busy women, ceased to exist. Chanel, in her mansion on the Faubourg St. Honoré, played hostess and muse to this new world, a friend to Picasso, Stravinsky, Cocteau, Satie, Hemingway, and many others. She was the epitome of woman, "a little black bull," as Colette saw her. She was shrewd, tough, infinitely charming. The ubiquitous French writer Maurice Sachs described her: "When she appeared, one was surprised by her small size. She was very thin. Her black hair was thick, her eyebrows met, her mouth smiled and her eyes were hard. She almost always dressed in the same way, very simply and usually in black. She would put her hands in her pockets and begin to talk. She spoke in a rapid, staccato voice. . . . She did not give the impression of wool-gathering, nor was she deflected from the main subject by incidental ideas which would prevent her from getting to the point."

Chanel's career was indicative. As women plunged into the business world, the number of couture houses founded or run by women soared, and in the decades following World War I the already thriving establishments of the Callot sisters and Madame Paquin were joined by those of Mesdames Lanvin, Vionnet, Grès, Carven, Schiaparelli, Ricci, and Rouff, who had trained as a doctor. During the 1920s, however, several of the older houses, such as those of Doucet and Paul Poiret himself, closed down, while Lelong, Molyneux and Patou emerged or thrived.

The designs of Coco Chanel.
Left: The ultimate "little black dress," with a touch of white at collar and cuffs. 1930.
Above: The little tweed suit. 1930.
Right: Suit with green jersey jacket. 1931.

Above: A mad melange of
Chanel designs in the surreal-
istic manner of the thirties.
"I made for Harper's Bazaar
these romantic sketches"
—Gabrielle Chanel, 1938.
Opposite: Chanel in 1936. "We
should have been on our guard
against this miss with the head
of a young boy...."—Paul
Poiret. Photograph by Cecil
Beaton.

Opposite left: Dresses and coats by Doucet, 1924 and 1925. Skirts are at mid-calf, but the eye is diverted by gores, pleats and handkerchief points.
Opposite right: Dress and coat by Lanvin, who emerged as a major designer. 1924-25.

Left above: Evening dress designed by Worth, 1921. Skirts were still long, but waists had dropped to the hip.
Left below: Garden-party dresses, 1921.
Above: Evening dress by Paul Poiret, 1921. Illustration from the Gazette du Bon Ton.

Extremism: The Fashion of the Twenties

Gradually the flat and angular line we associate with the 1920s was formulated. Laces, feathers, and flowers were no longer popular, but the new "casual" look did not mean merely the adoption of simple businesslike day wear around the clock. Rather, an aesthetic of the casual was needed, and the emergence of abstract values in art added inspiration to simple practicality. Paul Poiret's "up and down" line was now exaggerated and developed well past what the master might have planned.

By 1922, although the hem was at the ankle, waists settled down to the hip, a line championed by Chanel. Silver replaced gold as the favored form of glitter. A year later the deep cloche had appeared, an abstract form weirdly resembling a German helmet, covering foreheads and making the already popular bobbed and marcelled hair a necessity. Various more extreme hairdos became fashionable, including the exaggeratedly short Eton crop that would make the wearer appear mannish if she did not balance the effect with earrings to the shoulder, sometimes unmatched and of varying lengths. The small, rounded head of the *garçonne* cut was popularized by performers like the Dolly Sister, but suited few.

The hat itself was a necessity. At the popular *thé dansant* that characterized the decade, the debutante who had come to kick up her heels was distinguished from the hotel or restaurant's professional partners solely by the fact that she was wearing a hat. No one could capture the dizzy charm of the *thé dansant* years just after the war as well as the Scott Fitzgeralds. In "A Millionaire Girl" they wrote:

> Through the gloom people went to tea. On all the corners around the Plaza Hotel, girls in short squirrel coats and long flowing skirts and hats like babies' velvet bathtubs waited for the changing traffic to be suctioned up by the revolving doors of the fashionable grid . . . hundreds of girls with marcel waves, with colored shoes and orchids, girls with pretty faces, dangling powder boxes and bracelettes and lank young men from their wrists—all on their way to tea. . . . Under the somber, ironic parrots of the Biltmore the halo of golden bobs absorbed the light from heavy chandeliers, dark heads lost themselves in corner shadows, leaving only the rim of young faces against the winter windows. . . .

Above: Aline Berry, Olive Shea and Leba Vaughn. Three "flappers." 1929.
Above right: Brimmed variation on the cloche, which all but obstructs the view. Hat by Marthe Rivière, 1928. From Les Modes.
Right: Conspicuous consumption in the form of $500 silk stockings. 1924.

Opposite: The Rowe Sisters, ballroom and tap-dancing twins of the Café de Paris, twin cadets in the cloche-helmeted army of the 1920s, as photographed by Lartigue, 1929.

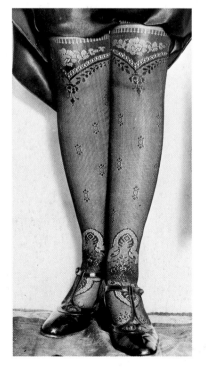

Below: "... hundreds of girls with marcel waves, with colored shoes and orchids, girls with pretty faces, dangling powder boxes and bracelets and lank young men from their wrists...."–F. Scott and Zelda Fitzgerald. Tea dance at the Atlanta-Biltmore, 1920.

Opposite left: "Joan Crawford is doubtless the best example of the flapper, the girl you see at smart night clubs, gowned to the apex of sophistication ... dancing deliciously, laughing a great deal, with wide, hurt eyes"–F. Scott Fitzgerald. Opposite right above: Clara

Bow, 1928. The "It" girl, shows what "It" is all about: bee-stung cupid's bow, spit-curled bob.
Opposite right below: Lindbergh's "Spirit of St. Louis" is the spirit of the Jazz Age, captured in a pen-and-ink drawing by John Held Jr.

It was not until 1924 that skirts really became shorter, reaching mid-calf. Dresses now fell straight from the shoulder, with a simple bateau neck and no evidence of bust or hips. Crepe de Chine had long since replaced linen and light wool for underclothing, and now even these were seeking a light, fine nonexistence. The brassiere was designed to flatten, and the cloche was brought down to cover the eyes themselves.

The skirts of 1926 and 1927 were the shortest of the decade. They stopped just under the knee. Pleats, flounces, circular gores from the hip or "handkerchief points" served to distract from the basic exhibitionism of the design. As dresses shortened, necklaces, particularly strings of pearls, which were universally worn, became longer. Evening dresses were as short as day dresses but were distinguished by fringe, lamé, silk, and an immense amount of

Overleaf: "Turned-up nose, rolled-down hose, Flapper–yah –she's one of those, Has anybody seen my gal. . . ." Flappers in a Charleston Endurance Contest at the Parody Club, New York.

intricate embroidery of beads and paillettes that reached the stature of art. The cocktail dress emerged. The Callot sisters produced one-of-a-kind embroideries, transforming dowagers into undines shimmering in panels of white, gold, jade, sea green, rose, peach, celadon or mauve silk, traced with flickering peonies and lilies, like Chinese watercolors. Vionnet's shades of oyster or pearl-gray satin contrasted with the extraordinary color combinations of other designers: dusty coral crepe de Chine and cocoa velvet, "pink toast" and midnight blue.

Women covered their exposed legs with flesh-colored silk stockings, evidence, in the view of the actress Yvonne Printemps, that they dress solely for fashion: "That women do not dress for men," she told the Paris paper *Candide*, "may be seen in the fact that although men prefer black silk stockings on women, yet women all wear tan and other light colors because they are fashionable, and in spite of the fact that they make the ankles look larger."

Mary Pickford, with her marcelled fluff and flirtatious laces, was replaced on the screen by another heroine, Clara Bow, the "flapper" with bee-stung lips, a headband only just controlling her tousled bob, and her soul emanating from the new erogenous zone, the legs. With stockings rolled at the rouged knee, a whole new kind of sex appeal had been created. The appearance of the legs necessitated a new way of standing and moving. The woman whose stance resembled, in the words of Poiret, "a pair of great semicircles towing a barge," was replaced by a creature who assumed "debutante slouch," with hips thrown forward. The loose, short dresses allowed the freedom of nudity itself. And these flappers were not necessarily the daughters of the serene and matronly maidens in the stays of 1910. They were often the same women.

Below: Artist and designer Sonia Delaunay greets a guest at the Greenwich Village Quill office.
Lower left: Cover of the Greenwich Village Quill.
Lower right: "What lips my lips have kissed, and whose and why, I have forgotten, and what arms have lain under my head til' morning;"—from Collected Sonnets, 1941. Edna St. Vincent Millay expressed the liberation of the Twenties intellectual womanhood by wearing a man's shirt and jacket more in the spirit of George Sand than of Paris' fashionable garçonnes.

Opposite left: Nancy Cunard, the first to appreciate the barbaric splendor of African jewelry, as photographed by Poiret's American discovery, Man Ray, 1927.

Opposite right: Greenwich Village in the 1920s, confirming the popular impression of carefree eccentricity, especially in the realm of dress. The thick stockings, the inkwell on the restaurant table, all suggest "Village" to staid uptowners.

The flapper, however, was only one of many incarnations of the new woman. Less publicized but perhaps more influential was the new "thinking woman," the antithesis of the mindless flapper. It was in the 1920s that a university education for women became more than a rare exception, and a female intelligentsia emerged in the bohemian cafés of the Left Bank and the Greenwich Village of Edna St. Vincent Millay. In the Café Brevoort, the Villager's haven north of the Washington Arch, the fashion ran to Dutch-boy hairdos, emancipated yet not extreme, berets, and asexual smocks of rebellious colors—puce, henna, chartreuse, magenta. Moreover, the Jazz Age had brought with it the African aesthetic. Nancy Cunard's arms supported the numerous bangles of a Watusi princess.

Deliberately "artsy-craftsy" jewelry of neolithic materials such as bone, wood, shell, or mock jade actually predated the opulent sham of Chanel's costume jewelry.

In 1923 it was calculated that two pounds of face powder were consumed yearly by every woman in Paris. The days of brows darkened crudely with burnt matches were definitely over. The new and crying need was filled by two women. Elizabeth Arden worked with chemists experimenting in the use of lanolin, benzoin, almond oil, and other lubricants to create moisturizers, tonics, and eventually the colored creams of rouge, eye shadow and lipsticks. Helena Rubinstein, a girl from Cracow, began her career selling protective cream to women in Australia.

Protection from the sun, however, ceased to be a factor in beauty care, as women uncovered their faces in attempts to acquire the newly fashionable sunburn. It is uncertain who first brought tan into vogue. It may have been Chanel, returning bronzed from a trip on board the Duke of Westminster's yacht, but there are a dozen other contenders for pride of place. In any case, the tan was a natural consequence of women's new athletic interest. What is certain is that sunburned skin became fashionable as the Riviera became the place to go in summer rather than in late winter months.

Resistance to the new style was strong, in predictable proportion to the violence of the change.

Women who had accepted Poiret's flowing silks with alacrity were not necessarily as ready to accept rouged knees. Many older women staunchly wore their skirts to the floor, causing one of those distinctions of fashion with reference to age that appear intermittently in history. Mrs. Claude Beddington, a London hostess of some repute, knew that her sentiments were reflected by most of her associates when in 1923 she castigated "the present young girls smoking cigarettes incessantly; drinking not only with their meals, but cocktails on an empty stomach; using latchkeys; driving motor cars without even a chauffeur on board to chaperone them; sitting crosslegged in skirts shorter than a Highlander's kilt and riding to hounds astride. . . . [In the past] a woman's greatest charm was her unattainability. Who ever enjoyed hitting a low-flying pheasant?" Mrs. Beddington lived into the 1960s, but she never raised her skirts from the floor.

On the other side of the Channel the cry was heard from the pulpit and duly reported in the press: "The Archbishop of Milan Refuses Communion to Women Who Offend." In consequence of the small heed paid to his past warnings against the prevailing feminine fashions, Cardinal Ferrari, Archbishop of Milan, in his Lenten Pastoral, ordered his clergy to refuse communion to women who presented themselves in unseemly garb.

Below: Five years before, the police would have arrested these men and women at the beach for indecent exposure. At this period a suntan also became fashionable. c. 1927.

Opposite left: Parisiennes seated on the bumper and fenders of an automobile, as photographed by Lartigue in 1928. For a brief period the coiffure de garçonne and men's smoking jackets were fashionable for women. Opposite right: Androgynous dress—the 1920s.

It would be difficult to guess precisely what the good Archbishop's reaction would be to the alternate to the tea gown (the traditional déshabillé that had not yet gone out of style) proposed by *Harper's Bazaar* in the mid-1920s. The fashion artists' drawings suggest epicene male figures, rouged and slouching on one hip, cigarette holders between their teeth. It is only after rather close study that we realize that these are women, their hair in the *coiffure de garçonne*. The captions read: "For the dusty Pullman journey the serviceable lounging robe of a man is the smartest thing a woman can wear; here of brocade in green, blue, and rose. When a feminine negligee will be rumpled, a masculine loung-

ing suit will come out of the trunk crisp and fresh. . . . The vogue of the masculine lounging robe has increased incalculably. . . . Women find them both comfortable and smart. . . . These purely masculine garments are smartest when bought at a men's shop where no compromise with the feminine angle is attempted.''

In fact, men's fashions for women enjoyed considerable popularity during these years. Blazers were worn with pleated skirts, shirts with ties and cuff links, and tailor-mades were constructed like men's suits and even dinner jackets. The copy-

writer's appeal seems to suggest practicality, but the suspicious might attribute the vogue to a burgeoning tendency toward lesbianism. Certainly in Colette's audacious circle lesbianism attained muffled cachet. But what appears a perverse, androgynous sexuality in dress is perhaps more accurately described as a final statement of emancipation. The fashion of ''women in men's dress'' never enjoyed a wide currency. It was only the fad of a few years, but its existence gave women the assurance that anything was possible and that their own fashions were not a matter of dictation but choice.

In fact, men's wear itself speedily evolved. The returning soldier, like his female counterpart, the lady war worker, demanded the comfort of his uniform. The soft shirt finally gained acceptance, and the butterfly bow tie and long tie with sailor's knot became standard wear. The oxford replaced the high-buttoned shoe and the wristwatch the pocket watch and fob. Moreover, the concept of a sports jacket, the belted and box-pleated Norfolk jacket (often accompanied by knickers), was imported from England to the United States and France. And while women displayed their liberation by donning harem pantaloons and shorter skirts, men were not without their fads. In 1912 it had been the purple suit. Six years later it was the jazz suit, with tight-nipped jacket and pipe-stem trousers.

The easily fitted suit that became popular in the teens of the century best pleased the flapper's boyfriend. "Flaming youth" asserted itself by the adoption of Oxford bags, hugely wide trousers (at times twenty-five inches around the knees) devised by Oxonians to cover the knickers they were not allowed to wear to class. Still, the line of the 1920s was not established by the Ivy Leaguer but by the 20th century's greatest arbiter of taste, the Prince of Wales. His fair and clean-cut good looks were sufficient to make him an idol, considering his position, but he possessed just that combination of conventional good taste and slight but never exaggerated whimsy to make him a fashion idol. He wore "working-class" brown suede shoes or an "effeminate" bright red tie, and both became de rigueur. He popularized "plus fours," the by then obsolete Panama hat, the tie with a broad "Windsor knot," the colored pocket handkerchief, and the white waistcoat worn with a tuxedo. It was the Prince of Wales who brought back padding, favoring a suit with wide shoulders and lapel narrowing to a tight fit around the hips over loose trousers. Prince of Wales hysteria reached such a peak that *Men's Wear* wrote: "The average young man in America is more interested in the clothes of the Prince of Wales than in the clothes of any other individual on earth." The prepossessing boldness of the new cut appealed in a very special way to captains of industry and to Wall Street men, many of whom already shopped on Savile Row in any case.

Opposite: "The average young man in America is more interested in the clothes of the Prince of Wales than in the clothes of any other individual on earth." The Prince of Wales is seen here in riding clothes; dressed for cycling; in golf clothes; in overcoat and flight helmet.

Above: American and British golfers playing for the Walker Cup at Garden City. They wear the "plus fours," loose knickers extending four inches below the break at the knee, popularized by the Prince of Wales.

The Thirties: Real and Surreal

It has often been taken as writ that in "hard times" skirts will be long. The lengthening of the skirt at the time of the 1929 Wall Street crash is considered proof positive of the dictum, but that coincidence is paralleled by Christian Dior's "new look," which in fact preceded "good times." Since women's skirts swept the ground in every century of the Christian era but this, such generalizations are difficult to uphold.

The short skirt of the mid-1920s lasted only a few seasons, and the tendency toward longer skirts began as early as 1927. By that year extremely short hair was no longer popular. The revolt against the boyish, angular look and the return to softer, more feminine fashions was spearheaded the next year by Chanel, with her easy pullovers and jerseys, Lanvin with her feminine embroidery, and above all by Madeleine Vionnet, the prim and matronly authoress of both the "cowl" and "halter" necklines, who had developed the technique of subtle "bias" cutting so that light fabrics could be made to cling and flow as they softly enveloped the body. There was a return to drapery and to dresses for evening that trailed to the ground in back or moved with floating panels. Waists were more natural and day skirts somewhat longer, although lengths varied from collection to collection. Moreover, hat brims were now folded back to display the forehead. It would appear that the exaggerated "flapper" line, although inspired by profound social change, had died a natural death, the revolution that was its impetus having been accomplished.

The new aesthetic was completely in keeping with the new interest in the "streamlined," whether expressed in Norman Bel Geddes' trains and kitchen equipment or in the "built-for-speed" curves of the Chrysler or Empire State buildings. The youth cult of the 1920s had collapsed, and the adult problems of the next decade were faced by a more adult image. This fact was curiously expressed by the return to popularity of white-tie-and-tails, however uncomfortable and inconvenient. There can be no doubt that security and maturity were equated in the public mind, almost piteously anxious to retreat to parental comfort. A poll of college students found the majority far more anxious for marriage than those of the Twenties. *Vogue* in 1932 proclaimed, "Spring styles say *Curves*," brassieres promised to uplift the bust, and Mae West reflected a turn-of-the-century ideal that was gaining popularity, even if it was not to *Vogue*'s taste.

Above: Powers' models in the early 1930s wearing brimmed hats, longer skirts and waists at "normal" level. Separates now became more important and the white skirt a summer necessity. Such an outfit would be perfect for observing the increasingly popular "spectator sports."

Right: Paquin dresses, 1933. The long evening skirt had returned, and gentle curves were emphasized with ruffles and ruching. As in the Gothic and Renaissance periods, the "line" of clothing reflected the lines of architecture—in this case the attenuated flow of the Art Deco skyscraper.

Top: The "built for speed"
curves of the Chrysler tower,
New York, designed by
William Van Allen in the style
known as "zigzag moderne."
1930.
Above: The "streamline"
shapes of Art Deco were
adapted to jewelry. Such
brooches and clips were logical accessories to the tidy,
draped symmetrics of the 1930s
dress. Brooch designed by
Raymond Templier. 1935.

Overleaf: Birds of a feather: A
migratory flight of American
tourists alights in Paris.

The English "drape" suit with its broad but un-padded shoulders, moderate lapels, tapered sleeves, and a nipped waist became fashionable for men. The high-waisted, double-pleated trousers were supported by suspenders hidden under a neatly cut waistcoat. This suit was to remain the standard wear of the well-to-do Englishman for the next thirty years, fortunately for those who preferred that their clothing possess the patina of several decades. The "drape" suit was adopted by those Americans still wealthy enough to aspire to "fashion." It was adult,

manly, and, in the words of Esquire, "the way to dress if you are so sure of yourself under the New Deal that you are unafraid of offering a striking similarity to a socialist cartoonist's conception of a capitalist. Since a good appearance is about all that is left to the capitalist anyway, why not go ahead and enjoy it?"

Going ahead and enjoying it was a philosophy that led to the development of "sport" clothes as never before. Women wore backless bathing suits and bared their legs on the tennis court as well as

Left, above: The sports jacket, first worn with non-matching pants in the 1920s, became increasingly popular. Drawing by A. Berretti from La Moda Maschile, 1936.

Far left: A drape-suited Gary Cooper in two-toned "spectator shoes" attends a prize fight in Los Angeles with his wife, Rocky. 1938.

Near left: The drape suit "for those unafraid of offering a striking similarity to a socialist cartoonist's conception of a capitalist." J. P. Morgan and son, 1938.

Above: Mr. and Mrs. John Astor, Jr., dressed for an evening at the opera. 1936.

Above: Flesh-baring "cruise and resort wear" for women: the halter top and leg-exposing "shorts." 1934.
Right: Gerald Murphy was voted "Best Dressed" by the Yale class of 1912. "His beautiful clothes," wrote Calvin Tomkins," would have seemed a trifle too elegant if anyone else had worn them." American trend-setter, aesthete, patron and painter, he was the first to adopt the French sailor's striped jersey and espadrilles. He is seen here with his wife, Sara, on the Riviera, 1923.

Below: Café Society. William R. Stewart and his wife, seen in one of the many night clubs that became a 1930s way of life. Few realized that the

Depression-pressed clubs often enlivened their tables by inviting young people to dine "free of charge, providing they were beautifully dressed." 1936.

at the beach. Summer finally became the "third season" for men only just freed from the flannels of the first two decades of the century. The playgrounds of the remaining rich supplied the fashion, and it was on the Riviera that the man's sport shirt was born. Its true father, perhaps, was the Fitzgeralds' friend, Gerald Murphy, among the first to enjoy the south of France in the summer and among the first to adopt the comfortable striped jersey of the French sailor. The white wool jersey with short sleeves and a turndown collar had been worn for polo since the turn of the century, but it was now joined by a white knitted tennis shirt. Then, in 1933, the "dishrag shirt," made of a loose woven print or solid, open at the chest and laced with string,

achieved popularity. Riviera styles quickly reappeared in America's golden sandbox, Palm Beach, which had already given its name to a white suit of cotton and mohair. New summer-weight suits in light fabrics also reappeared. Seersucker, long popular in the south of the United States, was still regarded as too rumpled in appearance for Northern tastes, but a variety of lighter fabrics came into use, often mixed with rayon.

During the 1930s a series of synthetic fabrics appeared like so many helpful *dei ex machina*. Rayon, the first of all synthetic fibers, was manufactured in 1889 by the Count Hilaire de Chardonnet from an extract of the silkworm's favored nourishment, the mulberry leaf. It appeared in the United

States as "artificial silk" in 1910, and in 1924 it was rechristened rayon—"ray" referring to its sheen, and "on," as in cotton, an ending suggesting fabric. Acetate, for shirts, sportswear, and linings, was first produced in the early 1920s, and the search for less expensive man-made fibers, spurred by the Depression, culminated in the presentation of nylon by the E. I. du Pont Corporation at the San Francisco Golden Gate Exposition in 1939.

The deepening Depression affected fashion in ways both superficial and profound. Basic changes in the structure of the fashion industry itself were under way. Improvements in machinery using the small electric motor had aided in the "mass production" of clothing. As early as the teens of the century Poiret was outraged to find his models pirated and "mass produced" in New York under his name. To the powered cutting knife were added new ironing and pressing machines. Moreover, from the 1880s on, free immigration had brought to the garment industry of New York and the textile mills of New England a plentiful labor supply. The relatively low investment in setting up shop encouraged both competition and enterprise. By the 1930s assembly-line techniques had streamlined the production of clothing itself, and industrial engineering and management specialization effected greater and greater efficiency. Clothing was sold in evergrowing numbers of department stores, which offered all prices and styles to customers of all ages and tastes. And the fat catalogues of mail-order houses brought fashion to every home, however isolated. The result was a great volume of ready-made clothing available in the United States. Now, for the first time, the follies of fashion were blamed on the "fashion industry."

America may have been in the lead, but England was not far behind. Only in France did couture remain a custom industry. The dressmaker satisfied her clients, and even larger clothing establishments preferred a system of subcontracting to home workers. This was in all probability done for two reasons: Less initial investment was involved, and the government had sponsored trade schools that turned out skilled workers ready for the haute couture industry, which itself was a major employer. Only men's shirts, blouses, and underwear were mass-produced.

Above: Winners of the Ohrbach Dress Design Competition, 1934. Their dresses are a potpourri of popular 1930s motifs: the sailor "middy," tennis stripes, the large bow, cap sleeves, the cummerbund sash and deep revers. "T"-strap shoes peep from skirts that again approach the ankle.

Left: Fetching shoe designs of 1932, including the latest "ankle strap."

Opposite: Dresses by Patou, 1933. "Zebra stripes were all over the Paris collections"–and all over international society from Patou to El Morocco, which opened its doors in 1931. The names of these dresses, "Casino" and "Diner au Cabaret," suggest the life they purportedly would entail.

Above: Escapism settled on the head. The "mad little hats" of 1933.
Above right: Dark lips and beribboned coquetry, the sophisticatedly innocent look of the era. Felt hat by Rose Descat, 1932. From Femina.

To the pinched world of the Depression, fashion itself reacted with a certain *folie*. Evening dresses appeared in lowly cotton fabrics, and Chanel's costume jewelry, her ungraded mock pearls and other beads, her confections of crystal and colored glass became a financial necessity, as did modish African and Cubist jewelry in gold and silver plate, enamel, and tortoise shell. It was in discussing costume jewelry that Chanel stated the basic premise that in the 20th century one no longer wore one's wealth on one's back: ". . . It is disgusting to wander around loaded down with millions around the neck just because one is rich. Jewelry isn't meant to make you look rich, it's meant to adorn you, and that's not the same thing at all."

Escapism settled on the head, in the form of a mad array of hats—fezzes, berets, stocking caps, wreaths, bird's nests, the birds themselves—tiny hats and enormous hats. A new Italian couturier, Elsa Schiaparelli, designed a hat in the form of an upside-down shoe and another in the form of a lamb cutlet in a frilled pantaloon. Surrealism, the sublime joke of the arts, amused people more in the desperate days of the 1930s than in the post–World War I years of its conception. In 1934 Marcel Rochas presented a full-skirted dress, its bodice covered with a stuffed seagull. But it was "Scap," a Roman woman with huge dark eyes and a taste for the "tasteless" shocking pink, whose surrealist fantasies most successfully succeeded in teasing and amusing the public.

319

After a brief period of selling skirts and sweaters in an attic, Elsa Schiaparelli opened her salon on the Place Vendôme in 1929. She had endless "nerve." She presented the zipper as a decorative ornament and "living Lastex" from America with the same panache with which she designed an evening gown with a lobster painted on its skirt and the bodice spattered with parsley. She reproduced the drawings of Jean Cocteau on her evening coats and designed gloves that ballooned out into enormous sleeves. Her dresses might be attached with buttons in the form of padlocks, butterflies, mermaids, hands, lips, or peanuts. Apart from the virtues of good line and intriguing fabric, she brought emphasis to the shoulder and introduced the use of "peasant" textures in rough and loose weaves. She was the first to base her collections on themes such as the circus or astrology. Moreover, she had the foresight to open the first ready-to-wear boutique on the premises of a house of haute couture. Amid gadgets, a wooden artist's dummy, and a life-size stuffed bear (dyed pink by Dali) she sold skirts, sweaters, and blouses. Her perfume Shocking appeared in a bottle designed in the form of a Victorian dressmaker's dummy by Leonor Fini. Schiaparelli's innovations were more in the tradition of Poiret's showmanship than Chanel's grasp of modern realities, but then the 1930s had had quite enough of realities.

Opposite above: Page of hats from Schiaparelli's sketchbook. The design on the extreme right suggests Dali's credo that surrealism is "concrete irrationality." 1937.
Opposite below: Schiaparelli, photographed by Horst, 1936.

Far left: Schiaparelli gown of red-and-white wool with blue coat, leather belt.
Left: Schiaparelli black gown with apron of jet shells had the iridescence of a Max Ernst reptile.
Above: A 1936 advertisement for Schiaparelli's "Shocking" perfume, with Leonore Fini's surreal dressmaker's dummy. "Shocking" was also her name for a certain shade of bright magenta pink.

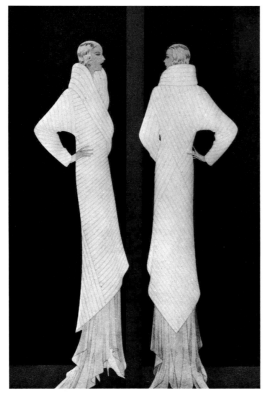

button.

The designs of Madeleine Vionnet: She devised the "bias cut" to enable fabric to fall into a smooth vertical drape and to cling subtly to the body. She adapted her "bias" principle to the seaming of furs, as in this ermine coat, far left, designed in 1930.
Left: Blouse of rose-colored crepe de chine. 1930.

Above left: The profile hat and three-quarter-length glove: Madame Martinez de Hoz, famous Parisienne hostess and beauty, dressed by Vionnet, photographed at Chantilly. 1935.
Above: Pink wool dress with silver buttons, 1930.
Right: Coat of tan cloth with lamb fur. 1930.

Right: Crowd in front of the Capitol Theater on Broadway, where the marquee advertises escape to the land of Oz. Below: King Kong, the ultimate romantic and noble savage, makes his last brave stand against technology atop New York's Empire State Building. Still from King Kong, 1933.

Opposite: Ginger Rogers and Fred Astaire, who, as the screen's gentleman dandy, sang of putting on his top hat, putting on his white tie and putting on his tails. Stills from The Gay Divorcee, 1936.

While surrealism "amused" the few, the mass of humanity, eighty-five million in America alone, sought their weekly escape in the movie houses. Hollywood manufactured larger-than-life confections: mountains of pretty girls who were like "melodies," monsters as tall as the Empire State Building, rich people enjoying solitary splendor in mansions the size of Versailles. The movies' influence on fash-

ion, however, was indirect. For the earliest films, the stars provided their own clothing. It was Cecil B. De Mille who first commissioned elaborate costumes, and many of them, especially those designed for musicals and historical dramas, bore little relation to any reality, past, present, or future. A film in contemporary dress might appear a full year after its costumes had been designed and was then ex-

Above: Greta Garbo, whose cheekbones set the standard for decades, wears a "slouch hat," that evolved from the cloche. 1932.

Above right: Garbo as Anna Christie, the virtuous prostitute driven by poverty to a life of shame. The beaten and defeated yet seductive "slouch" look.

Right: Marlene Dietrich, whose "natty men's suits" led the Chief of Police of Paris to try to evict her from the city. 1932.

pected to run for several more years. Fashions, although sufficiently exaggerated to be memorable, were of a classical nature, not likely to go out of style. Samuel Goldwyn may have had high hopes of attracting viewers when he invited Chanel to Hollywood in the mid-1930s to dress his stars both on and off screen, but little seems to have come of the venture. In certain subtle ways, however, the screen could not fail to exert influence. Since actresses invariably appeared ten pounds heavier on screen, they constantly sought a leaner line. Moreover, cameras picked up the glitter of sequins and the soft glow of satin more easily than other more understated stuffs.

Finally, it was the personal style of certain stars that influenced fashion most of all. Attention to actresses' offstage clothing probably reached its fever pitch with the ensembles created for Gloria Swanson's first trousseau. In the 1930s Garbo's slouch hat and gangling, waistless form affected notions of elegance, as did lean Katharine Hepburn's loose trousers and craggy cheekbones and, later, Joan Crawford's ankle-strap shoes. But few actresses were as eccentric or as influential in their appearance as Marlene Dietrich. According to Janet Flanner, Paris correspondent of The New Yorker, Parisians of 1933 were as heartened by Dietrich's domesticity and her activities as a good wife and mother as they were bewildered by her practice of going about in men's clothing. Although asked to leave town by the Chief of Police when she persisted, she was the social success of the city, where she appeared regularly, albeit skirted, in a man's hat, collar and tie and a boy's jacket from Lucien Lelong.

Toward the end of the 1930s high fashion fell into one of its interludes of flux. The "period revivalism" that had replaced "moderne" in interior decor was reflected in Edwardian upswept hair, bouffant skirts, and the Goyaesque black braided constructions of a new couturier from Spain, Cristobal Balenciaga. Shoulders were becoming even broader—they had never been narrow during the 1930s—and now skirts were shortened. Veils and elbow-length gloves were important, and hats, as eccentric as ever, might be slapped on the forehead like a flung custard pie. This new line was frozen in place by the chill of coming events.

"I believe in the future transmutation of those two seemingly contradictory states, dream and reality, into a sort of absolute reality, of surreality, so to speak."—André Breton for the First Surrealist Manifesto. Busby Berkeley's "You Stepped Out of a Dream" sequence from Ziegfeld Girl, starring Hedy Lamarr, Lana Turner and Judy Garland, 1941.

Wartime: The Tightened Belt

During World War II the Paris fashion world functioned in a curious limbo. Before the occupation the impending catastrophe was awaited with the grim levity that characterized the period of the French Revolution. Couturiers presented models with flippant names such as "False Alarm," a three-quarter length ermine coat, and "Offensive," which consisted of a silk blouse, long woolen skirt, jacket with silk lapels, and a gas mask bag of the same fabric. Balmain's "Occupation Evening Gown" and "Subway Gown" were to come later. The Paris of World War I had kept in contact with the Western world, but "occupied" Paris lost touch completely. Its populace, however, was at home, and most of the great couturiers, with the exception of Chanel and Vionnet, remained in operation. Two talented young men, Pierre Balmain and Christian Dior, prepared collections for the house of Lucien Lelong. Their public enjoyed a sham social life on the razor's edge between normalcy and an abyss so horrifying that most Parisians continued to survive by the expedient of not looking into it. For this hollow performance in the company of their invaders, the fashion houses, often suffering extreme shortages, created sham fashions—shoes with hinged wood or cork soles, hats made of pieces of newspaper, scraps of ribbon, and bits of tulle.

Meanwhile, in the desperate kinship of the "Bundles for Britain" era, England and the United States drew closer, and for a brief time British styles replaced French models in American stores. British fashion photographs of the period display a certain pathetic courage. Girls with frankly ridiculous hats perched on their brows cling to the arm of escorts who are always in uniform. Magazine copy exhorts women to assume the "uniform" look. Shoulder-length hair and deep eyeshadow are pronounced démodé. Both would seem messy and unsuitable if worn with uniform. Factory labor makes long tapering nails impossible. A fur-lined coat is more "fashionable" than a mink, and all show of wealth or dressiness is in poor taste. As a quote from *Fashion Illustrated* suggests, "The woman who could change instantly into service clothes or munitions overalls and look charming, soignée and *right* is the smart woman of today."

In both Britain and the United States, women did change into pants pure and simple as they went to work in heavy industry. "Rosy the Riveter" may have buried once and for all the notion that women could wear trousers or "slacks," as they were now called, only for sport. Expensive and unavailable stockings were not required under pants. Snoods kept women workers' hair out of their eyes, and shoulder bags were designed to cope with the wartime need to carry various emergency supplies. Finally, the "Eisenhower jacket" provided a sense of "uniformed" participation.

Above: "Rosy the Riveter," her hair wrapped in a snood, puts the finishing touches on a bomber nose section. 1942. Right: Saturday Evening Post *cover showing Norman Rockwell's jug-eared G.I. "Willie Gillis" being tended by two women, one in uniform and the other in civilian dress, including the requisite "silly hat." 1942.*

Left: General Dwight D. Eisenhower in the waist-length battle jacket that made fashion history. The style, with roomy shoulders and pockets, was adapted to civilian use, as was the waist-length leather jacket with windproof knit wristlets (based on the Air Corps flying coat) and the alpaca-lined gabardine coat. 1944.

Below: During World War II, skirts were shorter than they had been since the mid-1920s. Legs, such as Betty Grable's "million-dollar gams," were the favored erogenous zone, and exhibiting them was considered almost a patriotic duty —"something for the boys." Servicemen and girls at amusement park, Glen Echo, Maryland, 1943.

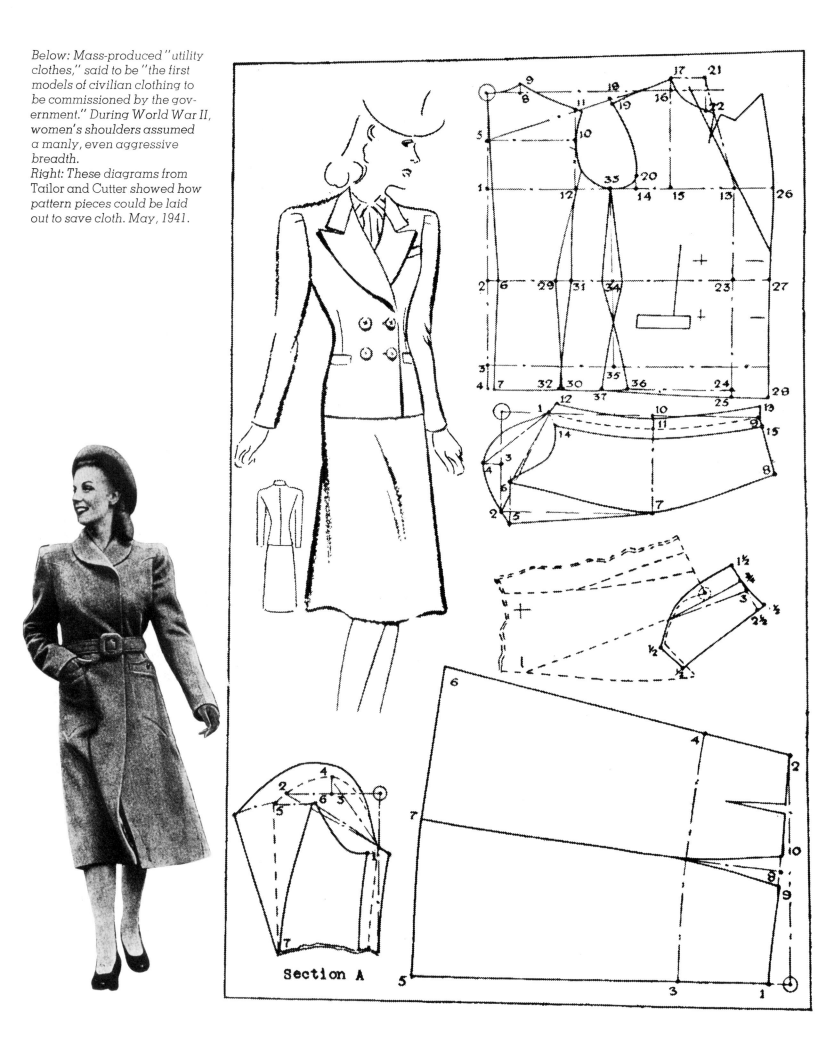

Section A

Designers, meanwhile, coped with shortages in various and ingenious ways. Milliners were obliged to design hats that would remain in place without elastic, with the result that berets became fashionable. Because straw was unavailable, crocheted headgear replaced bonnets. The wooden-soled "wedgie" shoe came to the English-speaking world, and gabardine replaced leather for both footwear and handbags, which might also be made of felt. Various synthetics called "Victory Fabrics," in colors such as "Flag Red" and "Victory Blue," were developed to replace wool. The Incorporated Society of London Fashion Designers, under the chairmanship of Captain Molyneux, devised blueprints for mass-produced "Utility Clothes." These stern, square-shouldered suits for women in sensible tweeds were touted to be, for better or worse, "the first models of civilian clothing to be commissioned by the Government." As part of English history, samples of these garments were accepted by the Victoria and Albert Museum; there the best-selling "battledress suit" was put to rest with remnants of Crusader chain mail.

Such men as remained at home in England and America sought a taller, more broad-shouldered and manly appearance, so that all clothing exuded a brash virility. The exaggerations of the "zoot suit" might be seen as the whimsical jazz man's underworld response to the same spirit of *machismo* that moved the *Incroyables* of an earlier century. It was curtailed, as were all men's fashions, by America's War Productions Board's regulations, which did away with trouser cuffs, vests, suits with two pairs of pants, most evening clothes, and, as in World War I, patch pockets, cloth belts, pleats, and complicated backs. The fact that the regulations of both wars focused on the same details of dress is a strong indication of 20th-century man's conservatism, his prevailing, almost century-old conviction that "fashion" was a matter for women.

Above left: Ever-smiling women in uniform: Kay Francis and Mitzi Mayfair return from a tour of American troop bases in Britain and North Africa, 1943.
Above: The 20th-century Incroyable, a young man in a zoot suit. Many such youths eventually exchanged their exaggerated fashions for army and navy uniforms but not before the pathetic "zoot suit riots" between servicemen and civilians. 1943.

Below: Simple, almost severe diamond-checked straight coat, typical of the designs of Pauline Trigère, known for styles that rarely go out of fashion. 1950.
Right: Black and white reversible coat by Trigère, 1956.

The war made an American designer of Pauline Trigère, a Russian Jewish girl brought up in the couture world of Paris, where she would certainly have remained. It was in desperation, as refugees with children to support, that she and her brother scraped together a few thousand dollars and presented her first New York collection in January 1942. It also made an American designer of a Chicagoan, Mainbocher.

Main Rousseau Bocher was one of those Jamesian Americans by nature best suited to a European climate. As a young art student, Main traveled first to the New York of Beaux-Arts, Worth and the Four Hundred, and then on to Art Nouveau Paris and Munich of the Jugendstil. It was not until he had spent ten years as editor of French *Vogue* that he quite suddenly decided to elide his name and open a maison de couture.

Dale McConathy has described Mainbocher as "one of the last of the great snobs—an 18th-century French cardinal who somehow got himself born on the West Side of Chicago." He ruled his domain with a discretion "redolent of the confessional," shunning publicity and all association with mass

With no word coming out of Paris, American designers of women's clothing were on their own for the first time. *Harper's Bazaar* cooed, "We publish the New York Openings with pride in the achievements of our American Designers. We have learned from the greatest masters of fashion in the world. Learned, then added something of our own. Such clothes have never been made in America before."

manufacturers. An admirer of Vionnet but not of Poiret, Mainbocher was a master of twisted and draped fabric, producing dresses "full of good breeding." Preferring "the ladies and the *grandes cocottes*" to the "in-betweens who didn't know themselves," Mainbocher pleased a host of clients that included Barbara Paley, the quasi-mythical patroness of the arts Marie-Laure de Noailles, and the Duchess of Windsor, whose long crepe wedding suit he created in a shade he dubbed "Wallis blue." The winds of war blew this *rara avis* of fashion to his native shore and to a very successful salon on New York's East 57th Street. Once here, he joined a flock that included Norman Norell and Charles James,

a fellow Chicagoan, a friend of Cocteau, Colette, and Poiret, and the country's greatest master of cut and structure. James was a "designer's designer," and his models hung in the wardrobes of Schiaparelli and the great Chanel herself.

Pauline Trigère's designs try to transcend fashion to achieve a "timeless quality."
Left above: Black chiffon gown embroidered with plumes, under ankle-length fleece coat. 1966.
Left below: Mainbocher's white linen with apple-green checks–ideal for "dashing to
the country club." Designed in 1941.
Above: The Duchess of Windsor epitomized the perfectly groomed woman of distinction and strong character who was Mainbocher's ideal. She is seen here in his silver lamé gown. Photograph by Horst. 1937.

335

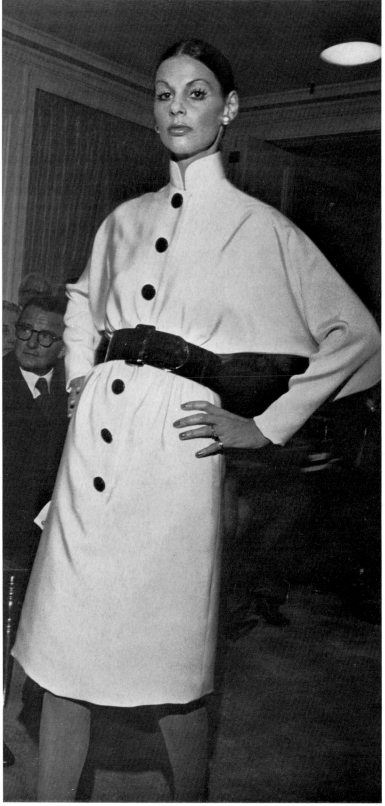

Left: The dazzling sparkle of
Norell sequins is teamed with
an elegant fleece coat for evening wear. Norell's designs
were as classic and as unlikely
to go out of style as Mainbocher's, Trigère's or James's.
Above: Norman Norell hallmarks: high neck, dolman
sleeves, black buttons, wide-
draped belt.

Opposite: Norell became
known for his paired paillette
"mermaid" sheaths, worn by
his models with heavy earrings and dramatic makeup
inspired by the women that
haunt the canvases of Kees
van Dongen. Norell's favorite
van Dongen painting is seen
here.

Antonio

Charles James designs—the sculptor's notebook: Clockwise, from the top: Mauve wool coat, 1947; Spiral dress, without center or side seam, called the "taxi" dress because it could be changed in a cab, 1929; Black velvet bell-sleeved jacket, 1952; Diagonal worsted pants and cupless bra, 1972. Opposite: The arc sleeve—a Charles James hallmark—on a suit. 1951.

Above: Roomful of ball gowns by Charles James, as photographed by Cecil Beaton in 1948. These dresses, created for such clients as Millicent Rogers and Mrs. William Randolph Hearst, Jr., suggest why James's designs have been regarded as works of sculpture.

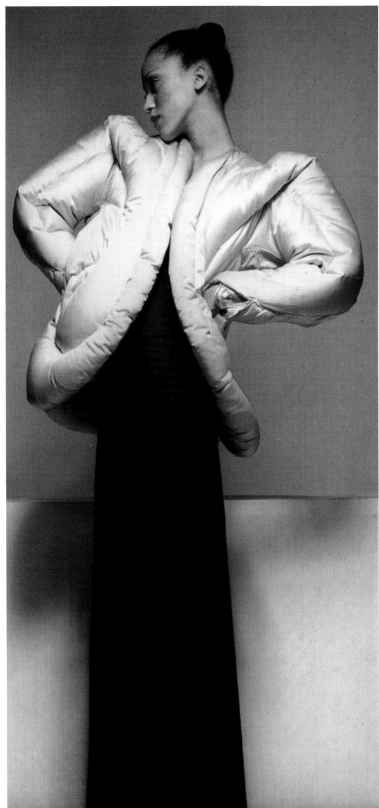

341

Above: "Drop everything . . . there's a girl up the street making a dress with no back, no front, no waistline, and, my God, no bust darts." "Mc-Cardell," by Sally Kirkland, in American Fashion. Claire McCardell's tent-shaped bias-cut, "monastic dress" was just one of many McCardell concepts that, like those of Chanel, has become basic to the vocabulary of fashion.

Right: McCardell's "baby dress" recalled the Napoleonic Empire line even more than did Poiret's sheaths. 1946. Far right: McCardell was the first to bring the dancer's leotard to the public and thus developed the "ballerina look" as early as 1943.

Opposite: Claire McCardell contemplates a wall of press clippings about herself.

But, perhaps most important, four years of isolation gave American designers of mass-produced clothes, such as Claire McCardell, the opportunity to create an "American Look." McCardell, daughter of a small-town Southern banker, spent virtually her entire working life in the hurly-burly of Seventh Avenue. A career woman herself, she saw the growing numbers of "American Career Women" as her archetypical clients. McCardell created the easy-fitting bias-cut dress with adjustable waistline, comfortable side pockets, and deep armholes. Her designs were practical, problem-solving: a tweed wrap for chilly evenings, a cozy hood for a warm street suit, easily packed "mix and match" separates. She used fabrics in new ways: wool jersey or "lingerie nylon" for a cocktail dress, mattress ticking for a suit. The list of McCardell's innovations is endless: double stitching, visible hardware closings (including her favorite brass hooks), the strapless elasticized "tube" top, the dirndl, the diaper bathing suit, the wrap-around coverall dress, and a variety of winter play clothes. Her inspiration was always America: "It's freedom, it's democracy, it's casualness, it's good health. Clothes can say all that."

Opposite: "Merely two huge triangles that tie at the neck, front and back." This particular model, worn here by McCardell herself, was designed as a "future" dress in 1945 and has in fact never gone out of style.

Above: Look magazine's retrospective of McCardell designs, photographed in 1953. Among them we recognize the hood, black jersey bathing suit, the wrap-around dress, pedal-pushers and her own adaptation of the dancer's maillot.

Left: American wartime summer fashions: simple shirtwaist cotton dresses, skirts with dungaree bibs, wedgies and shoulder-length hair. 1942. Below: The American Cadillac, 1946.

The American Look, however, took other forms than those devised by either the haute-couture or the mass-production designers. "A sweater, a sarong and a peek-a-boo bang" cooed three crimson-lipped girls in a wartime all-star musical devised to cheer up the boys at the front and the "folks back home." The first singer was Lana Turner, the second Dorothy Lamour, and the third Veronica Lake, and their triple image summed up the female ideal that the boys were fighting for. To the wartime mind, Hawaii and Mexico represented escape to unoccupied exotica, and the "strapless" freedom of the sarong, along with Mexican jewelry and huaraches, enjoyed brief but instantaneous vogue. Veronica Lake's bangs, curtaining half her face, aroused official warnings and was banned as hazardous in factories. But it was the tight sweater and the sweater girl who wore it, epitomized by Lana Turner, that characterized the "pin-up" wrapped in every soldier's duffel bag. The flat chest of the Twenties and low-breasted ideal of the Thirties had given way to the girl with the "uplift," and the brassiere industry obliged with a series of constructed and padded innovations. The "pin-up girl," while bosomy, had an otherwise boyish figure with narrow waist and hips and small buttocks. Her hair was vampishly long or swept up in flirtatious curls on top of her head. The sweater itself, however, completed a rather perverse image: It was the uniform not of the prostitute but of the college "coed."

The war world of padded shoulders, tight waists, and short skirts, of privation and makeshift, did not come to an end when the last shot was fired. Recovery, both economic and psychological, was slow. With the liberation of Paris, British fashion editors rushed to the French capital. They found shop windows looking like "dreams of the Arabian Nights," with elegantly ribbed pullovers, fragile, lace-covered or tucked blouses, and chapeaux to suit every fantasy—turbans, berets, and bonnets trimmed with organdy, tulle, ribbons, and flowers. But one mile from the Place de la Concorde they found that the city was, as one fashion writer put it, "heartbreakingly drab."

By 1946 a new aesthetic was emerging. It was noted that fashion in Paris, like the government of Britain, stood in need of a change. According to *Vogue,* "Skirts are lengthening . . . dipping, pointing, swaying a little, but longer and prophetic." These hints and tendencies were brilliantly brought into focus by one man.

1946 **1947**

Dior and the Counter-Revolution

A peace had been established secure enough for innovation in dress when, on the morning of February 12, 1947, a new fashion house and a new fashion were launched simultaneously by Christian Dior. The host of editors who had come to Paris more out of nostalgia than expectation gasped when presented with what Carmel Snow of *Harper's Bazaar* labeled a "New Look," although it was also a very "old look." The forty years' development of a square, mannish, waistless line for women, dating from Poiret's first revolutionary collection, had been relinquished in a moment. Dior presented models with natural, rounded shoulders and rounded, even padded, breasts, nipped waists, wide padded hips, and skirts sweeping to between eight and twelve inches off the floor.

Many explanations have been suggested for Dior's "New Look." It was noted that fashions were becoming more "romantic" before the war; some said that the Boussac textile interests, which had financed the House of Dior, wanted to see designs that consumed more fabric. It seems, however, to have been simply a return to the *fin de siècle* on the part of the creator. In his autobiography Dior wrote: "I thank heaven I lived in Paris in the last years of the Belle Epoque. They marked me for life. My mind retains a picture of a time full of happiness, exuberance, and peace, in which everything was directed towards the art of living. The general, carefree atmosphere derived from the illusion that the existence and capital of the rich as well as the thrifty lives of the poor were immune from any sudden reverse. . . ." Dior's New Look could not possibly have failed. It was soon repeated and developed in the salons of the newest designers to emerge in Paris's postwar fashion world—Pierre Balmain, Jacques Fath, and others. Who in the Europe or America of 1947 did not yearn for that idyllic past before the nightmare of two wars? Society embraced the turn-of-the-century image with the same innocent fuzzy-mindedness with which the survivors of the French Revolution embraced the image of ancient Rome. In the words of Pearson Phillips, they could not resist the temptation to interpret "hopes for the unknown in terms of memories of the known."

Economically, the world was far from ready for the New Look. The English, with fuel cuts and long queues, were suffering greater privations than they had known during the war itself. Rationing was still in force, prices rose steadily, and commodities such as soap were in shorter supply than they had been during the "blitz." Nylon stockings, the mainstay of the postwar woman's wardrobe, were as precious as silk to the Romans. A demoralized population waited in vain for the fruits of victory, while the press declared, "There's a good time coming. . . . One day you will be able to buy all the foundation garments you require." Naturally enough, the New Look was assailed as soon as it became known to the public. With clothing of any kind scarce due to the shortage of fabric, the new longer skirts seemed outrageous. Detractors claimed that a few inches added to the length of skirts would cut overall production by 800,000 garments. The government requested the British Guild of Creative Designers to boycott the Paris styles. The New Look was considered yet another act of irresponsibility on the part of France. Moreover, female politicians lashed out against the reactionary aspects of a New Look that would cost British women forty years of emancipation as well as endless footage of fabric.

Such rational arguments could not deal with the irrationality of desperation, however. British women could no longer face the drabness of a deprivation from which there was no escape—even travel abroad was curtailed or barred. They wanted, once again and before it was too late, to be young and seductive. *Vogue* and *Harper's Bazaar* had the spunk to disregard cruel reality in favor of the kind of dream that can inspire supreme effort: "If there is less food, all the more reason to cook it superlatively." The readers of these magazines were told, "Paris is marvelously elegant" and "Paris is more feminine than ever." The New Look was seen as the bearer of "the idea of one-world civilization," as unifying as the United Nations. British women responded by showing themselves willing to part with every last hoarded clothing coupon to possess one New Look skirt. When Dior himself visited London, and Princess Margaret, natural leader of the postwar younger set, endorsed the fashion, the Board of Trade gave up: "We cannot dictate to women the length of their skirts."

Opposite left: "I thank heaven I lived in Paris in the last years of the Belle Epoque"–Christian Dior in 1947.
Opposite right: "You can't be last year's girl": the transition. 1947.

Left: The "New Look": rounded shoulders, full bust, nipped waist, padded hips and long, sweeping skirt supported by petticoats, high heels and ankle straps. 1947.

Feast follows famine: Designs rush to obliterate the all too visible evidence of wartime privation.
Right: Elaborate construction of the "New Look," as disclosed in the pages of British Harpers Bazaar, 1947.
Far right: The New Look in Paris by: Christian Dior; Nina Ricci; Jacques Fath. 1948.
Above: The "New Look" suit with typical cinched waist and full skirt, by Christian Dior, 1947.

The British ambivalence toward French fashion at the time (or at any time) is perhaps best suggested by a scene from Nancy Mitford's *The Blessing* in which the English heroine is plunged into the wicked milieu of New Look Paris:

The first big occasion to which Grace went in Paris was a dinner given for her by the Duchesse de la Ferté. . . . She knew, or thought she knew, that French women were hideously ugly, but with an ugliness redeemed by great vivacity and perfect taste in dress. Perfect taste she took to mean quiet, unassuming taste—"better be under- than over-dressed" her English mentors such as Carolyn's mother used to say. . . . So all in all she was unprepared for the scene that met her eyes on entering the Ferté's big salon. The door opened upon a kaleidoscope of glitter. The women, nearly all beauties, were in huge crinolines, from which rose naked shoulders and almost naked bosoms, sparkling with jewels. They moved on warm waves of scent, their faces were gaily painted with no attempt at simulating nature, their hair looked cleaner and glossier than any hair she had ever seen. . . . Grace saw that these looks in the women were greatly enhanced by overdressing, always so much more becoming, whatever Carolyn's mother might say, than the reverse.

Top: French beauties wearing romantic hats more in tune with the "New Look," 1948. Above: Christian Dior's hotel picketed by the ladies of Chicago's "a-little-below-the-knee" club. The hated new length is worn by model on the left. 1947.

If the New Look kept the world of fashion agog, quite another "look" was evolving in postwar Paris, one not reported in *Harper's Bazaar* or *Vogue* yet destined to have a more profound effect than Dior's deliciously novel creation. Throughout the fifties, in the cafés and bistros, the dissatisfied young, a variegated pack of war orphans, street urchins, and intellectuals, had begun to attain an identity, a philosophy, and of course a uniform. Unlike the intellectuals of the years between the wars, this was an avant-garde that was in no way related to "high society." The new names were Camus, Sartre, Malraux, and de Beauvoir. The "Existentialists" existed for the sake of existing, seeing in the future a gaping void and assuming a deliberately disheveled appearance as an expectoration in the face of "fashion." The obvious descendants of a century of bohemians, they preferred a very "modern" déshabillé—a loose sweater and pants for men and women alike. Consciously or unconsciously, they exhibited a penchant for the dark eyes, pallid complexions, and black clothing favored by 19th-century romantics.

Opposite: The Parisian Existentialists of the 1940s were the spiritual ancestors of the 1950s "Beat Generation" American poets and writers. "To be Beat meant: leather jackets, jeans, workman's shirts—and black." New York café scene, 1958.

Left: Poet Gregory Corso wrote: "I make clothes! I don't need words,/ Actually our industry is not in jeopardy./ If it were, I'd another one to solve it!/ True. You rule the ruling products we wear./ Who says otherwise?/ He did./ He! What did he say?/ He asked: Is the body less than its raiment?"/ Allen Ginsberg, Gregory Corso, Peter Orlofsky and William Burroughs in San Francisco, 1957.
Top: Brigitte Bardot pioneered the tousled hair of the "Beat" ideal. Geneva, 1960.
Above: Real Beat: Poet Dick Woods with Eddy Slayton at a coffeehouse table. Their dress is prophetic. 1959.

353

The Fifties: The Man in the Gray Flannel Suit

Meanwhile, the New Look lumbered on into the Fifties and down into the most inexpensive ready-to-wear, translated into such formulas as "the Gibson Girl," favorite of the American high-school set and all too often worn with the traditional saddle shoes. But yet another aesthetic was developing: The ballet, already popular in England, slowly crept into the consciousness of the American public. Dance companies that had for a generation or more dryly repeated Diaghilev's triumphs were experimenting with new forms. In the late Forties Claire McCardell had seized on the idea of wearing reinforced ballet slippers for street wear, as well as the dancer's leotard. Eyes heavily made up as if for the stage now vied with lips for prominence. Hair swept back in a "pony tail" completed the "ballerina look." And the "ballerina look" suggested a changing feminine ideal—elongated, more leggy, and flatter chested. When Colette spied Audrey Hepburn, a young ballerina, in the lobby of the Hotel de Paris in Monte Carlo and said, "Ca, c'est Gigi," she was doing more than casting a new star. In her worldly way she indicated the return to a 20th-century feminine archetype—the slim, long-limbed, high-cheek-boned gamine.

If the feminine ideal was changing, it followed that fashions must change also. The curves of the aging New Look hung loose on the gamine figure. So it is hardly surprising that in the mid-1950s the more conventional square, waistless or natural line that had become characteristic of the Twenties returned. Some credit Coco Chanel with its reappearance. Moving listlessly from one Swiss hotel to another, sleeping late, dining early and frequenting her doctors, the old grizzly of fashion was licking her wounds in a state of mounting boredom. Seeing her own revolt against Edwardianism thrown into reverse by the New Look must have particularly piqued her. In February 1954, with the backing of her old friends and enemies in the perfume industry, she dusted the mirrors of her famous staircase and presented a new collection, which looked suspiciously like her old collections, with shorter skirts and dresses loosely following the line of the body. For the Paris press it was "a melancholy retrospective," a style "belonging to other days." But for the American buyer it looked new and easy to wear. (The fact that L'Humanité, the Communist daily, was at one point Chanel's fervent supporter may be a comment on the conservatism of Chanel, or of the French Communists, or both.) The matter is subject to dispute, but it may be that the heartening nature of Chanel's transatlantic success prompted the chemise of the shy and aloof Spanish designer, Balenciaga, and the sack dress and Dior's "A" and "H" lines. These led inevitably to the loose-flowing "trapeze," invention of the industry's child wonder, Yves St. Laurent—the bespectacled, gangling junior assistant who at the age of twenty-one inherited the

Leggy and lean, Audrey Hepburn personified the ideal woman of the mid 1950s. Here we see her, her hair pinned up and her ballerina slippers and stance curiously at variance with the "A"-line Givenchy gown she wears. She was regularly chosen one of the world's "10 Best Dressed Women." 1958.

House of Dior. For a second time in a century, the eye became accustomed to "clean lines" and the importance of the silhouette, one that was stiff, architecturally constructed, and still very definitely "couture."

Apart from the easily predictable and almost leisurely development of fashion during the 1950s, social changes of a rudimentary nature were taking

Left: Marilyn Monroe after signing her contract for Some Like It Hot: *1940s curves well disguised by the 1950s sack dress.*
Above: A Dior "A"-line suit worn by model Anne Gunning. This photograph suggests how the "line" was named. 1955.

place. These changes would come to fruition in the next decade, bringing about an extraordinary revolution in fashion and dress that would itself abet a social revolution.

After World War II the mass clothing industry so perfected its techniques, especially in the United States, that poverty began to disappear visually, if not in fact. When a boy's shirt, tolerably well made, could be bought for the price of three loaves of bread and the price of soap fell, it followed that rags and filth became the property of the inebriate or the deranged. Moreover, when factories provided lockers for their employees, work clothes were no longer seen on the streets of major cities. As a result, a presentable or possibly even stylish dress or suit might easily cover an empty stomach. In the words of Michael Harrington, "It almost seems as if the affluent society has given out costumes to the poor so that they would not offend the rest of society with the sight of rags." Democratization was such that it impressed even the Soviet Premier, Nikita Khrushchev. On meeting Nelson Rockefeller, he noted with some amazement: "The biggest capitalist in the world wasn't dressed in cheap clothes, but I wouldn't say he was dressed elegantly either. He was dressed more or less like other Americans."

Ironically, as industrialization brought affluence, and hence the ability to spend more on clothing, to broader sectors of society, the quality of mass-produced clothing improved only in terms of variety. The workers' affluence naturally meant mounting labor costs, which in turn left the manufacturer little temptation to indulge in fine craftsmanship. Heightening demand was met by more and cheaper clothing, while the quality of what the dollar bought decreased. Wealth was best expressed in garments, such as a mink coat, that could not be made cheaply or without skilled craftsmanship.

Meanwhile, the American concept of "the corporation man" had crystallized, and he soon acquired a uniform, or costume. By the 1950s the American executive had become "The Man in the Gray Flannel Suit." This outfit originated in the dress habits of the students at East Coast Ivy League colleges. On campus they had made a fetish of dirty white "bucks" or buckskin shoes with thick red rubber soles. New white shoes were "crass," and a "black shoe" was a greasy grind. When they graduated into the business world this generation shopped at Brooks Brothers, J. Press, and Chipp. The details of the uniform were very exact: a gray flannel three-piece, narrow-shouldered "sack" suit, loose at the

Above: Actress Susan Stras-
berg, right, and friend gossip.
Swept-back ballerina hair,
sweaters, modest jewelry and
ice-cream sodas. 1956.

Right: Gregory Peck in his star-
ring role as The Man *in the*
Gray Flannel Suit, *a film based*
on the novel by Sloan Wilson
from which the sartorial stereo-
type got its name. Gray sack
suit, narrow lapels and striped
tie, polished Oxfords and gray
fedora–all in place, 1956.

waist, with long jacket. A "natural" line was considered particularly aristocratic. It was accompanied
by a white shirt with buttoned-down collar, a
narrow tie of regimental stripes (infuriating those
Englishmen who were actually members of the regiment in question), and heavy-soled Oxford shoes.
A camel's-hair coat or black Chesterfield with velvet
collar completed the effect. This outfit, worn by Ivy
League graduates, hence the elite, was speedily
adopted by their corporate underlings. Meanwhile,
the old Ivy Leaguer, wherever he had settled, might

expect yearly visits from representatives of his favorite Eastern tailors.

The man in the gray flannel suit appears to have been attracted to a woman dressed with similar rigidity. His female counterpart modeled her ideals on the English rather than the French concept and chose always to be underdressed. She was a woman for whom "fashion" was a dirty word. She wore a cashmere twin sweater set by day, over a saggy-seated tweed skirt or pleated tartan kilt. Her jewelry was modest: a virginal string of pearls and gold

Above: A 1950s Miss America, on the beach in Atlantic City, still in some ways a well-fleshed Edwardian beauty.

Right: Coeds at Syracuse University, 1955: "Peter Pan" collars, sweater sets, tweed and plaid skirts, "bobby sox"—all prepared for marriage to the "man in the gray flannel suit."

circle pin (as unobtrusive and as status-bestowing as that of the Légion d'honneur). For summer she wore a madras skirt or Bermuda shorts, topped by a simple blouse with Peter Pan collar, preferably in Liberty of London fabric. She might, however, in a moment of madness, don a pair of red "ballet slippers" craftily produced for street wear by Capezio, the dance-shoe company. A timid "cocktail dress" completed a wardrobe exceptional only in its conformity. The 1950s, an era in the United States almost infamous for its complacency and lack of imagination, had evolved a fashion image almost perfectly in keeping with its traditionalist aspirations. Even the "Beats" and the "Brando" figures in T-shirts and black leather jackets expressed a macho ideal oddly in keeping with the time.

Left: White convertible with tail fins, with a woman in an aptly named "sack" dress. Late 1950s.
Below left: Between two worlds: During the 1950s women continued to wear the bouffant skirts of the 1940s, while hems climbed toward the heights they would achieve in the 1960s.
Below: Large-framed sunglasses, an Italian contribution, described as "a practical accessory for patio parties before the summer sun sets."

Overleaf left: Elvis "The Pelvis" Presley, rock-and-roll's baby-faced, bump-and-grind sex symbol in his trademark clothes: open collar, peg-top pants, oily "duck's tail" haircut and sacred "don't step on my blue suede" shoes. 1956.

Overleaf right: Leather-jacketed Marlon Brando as the idealized proletarian anti-dandy in On the Waterfront, displayed here along with a Checker cab, pop art and other Americana at the U.S. pavilion, Expo '67, Montreal.

Right: Haute couture at the House of Balmain, Paris. During the 1950s, the "bouffant" skirt remained high fashion for evening wear, accompanied by the boned strapless top. Short and full-length evening dresses were equally acceptable. 1959.

Far right: An Emilio Pucci shift dress for dinner at home. The Italian designer revived the interest in brilliant prints. Note that as fashions became narrower, toward the end of the decade, hair became more "bouffant." 1963.

The gray flannel suit remained in style throughout the decade. It was not until the 1960s approached that it met with competition, and then the challenge appeared from an unexpected quarter: Italy. The Italian tailoring establishments still provided exquisite workmanship, and for Americans with valuable dollars the price was right. The Italian line—a nipped, narrower, shorter jacket—was well proportioned for shorter men. Moreover, Italian couture had achieved considerable cachet. Fostered by the Marquese Giorgini, who staged a gala showing of Italian models for American buyers in his Florentine palazzo in 1950, the Italian fashion industry with designers such as Emilio Pucci, Simonetta Visconti, and Albert Fabiani, had gained international respect. Nor was their reputation based on tailoring alone. It was the Italians who gave to the men and women of the 1950s the look of people who live "in the sun." White, brilliant color, a sense of joie de vivre in dress were a Mediterranean contribution, as in the years before World War II. Now Italian sandals and sunglasses characterized fashionable summer dress for the decade.

If the man in the gray flannel suit and his consort were unable to withstand the attack—the sheer brio of Italian fashion as well as the entrenched glamour of the French couture industry—they were certainly ill prepared for the onslaught they were about to face: the youth rebellion.

The Great Masquerade

The "war babies," that vast crop of infants born immediately after 1945, were maturing. The word "teenager" had been coined innocently enough in America in the mid 1940s, and by the 1950s the "teen" had a well-established costume of his or her own: ankle-length or "bobby" sox, pony tails, duck tails, bangs. Junior sizes came into being to suit young figures.

By 1960 "teenagers" began to represent what had become a powerful class. The statistics speak for themselves. By the mid-1960s one third of the population of France was under the age of twenty, and in the United States fully half the population was under twenty-five. This energetic group had money to spend. During the boom period, children of the wealthy who continued their education were indulged by parents who remembered the deprivation of the Depression and the war. Jobs with sizable salaries were now available for those who left school early, in powerful contrast to former periods, when those who went to work at a young age became members of a "working class"—one that earned little even when mature and fully trained.

The young, moreover, were obsessed with certain material possessions but not with others. A *House Beautiful* poll showed that college girls who normally would be thinking of homemaking and home furnishings had little interest in the contents of their "hope chests." China and napery were far down on their lists. Instead, they preferred to spend their money on travel, education, records, high-fidelity equipment, and, above all, clothing. In 1965 American teenagers spent a whopping $3.5 billion on apparel. And Paris was not telling them what to wear.

The pants and jersey of the Existentialists of the 1940s and the "Beats" of the 1950s evolved into the basic wardrobe of the unbeat "hip" or "hippie" youth of the 1960s. For the young, influenced almost entirely by what became known as their "peer group," self-expression in dress became an article of faith in their code of rebellion. Charles Reich, in *The Greening of America*, found the rebellion itself best explained in terms of dress. The gray figure of authority, the new generation said, did not express in dress either his moods or the strength, shape, sensuality, and harmony of his body. The credo of the young—"Consciousness III," as Reich calls it— "starts with self": Their clothing expresses wholeness of self. There is no schizophrenic division between dress for the office and dress for play. No individual is limited by his clothing to a role. Because their garments are tightfitting, the young express rather than mask the body. Yet bell-bottoms give the freedom to dance. Finally Reich concludes, "If the individual wishes, he can add touches to his clothes that make them a costume . . . with the magic deftness of stage sorcery, a headband can produce an Indian, a black hat, a cowboy badman."

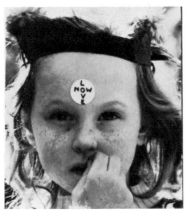

Opposite above: "The magic deftness of stage sorcery": hippie in top hat at a gathering to express "love for all mankind." Central Park, New York, 1967.
Opposite below: The "twain" meet in the reality of drugged mysticism: Hippies in the Nirvana of Katmandu find their dress in the bazaars. 1969.

Left: "Love child" in Central Park, New York, 1967.
Above: Group photographed in the drop-out mecca of the Haight-Ashbury section of San Francisco: jeans, hair, "love beads" and bare feet, which symbolize a return to the soil, even if it is a dirty sidewalk. 1968.

Right: Work pants of denim, the tough, durable, cheap and comfortable French workman's fabric "de Nimes," became in the 1960s and 1970s a means of self-expression. Here, studded jeans in imitation of those worn by "glitter" rock stars. New York, 1975.

"Denims" as a medium of self-expression.
Above: expensive, neatly folded-over boots accompanied by McGovern T-shirt–Britt Eklund, 1972; above right: cut off with scissors: shorts at Daytona Beach, 1974; right: trimmed to match Indian headband–antiwar protester, St. Louis, Missouri, 1970; far right: with Indian scarf, dark glasses–SoHo, New York, 1977.

The denim work pants devised out of tent canvas by the Bavarian, Levi Strauss, to clothe California's 49ers were embraced with almost religious zeal. The attentions of emblematic embroidery were given to every frazzled patch, and, as Peter Beagle observed in *American Denim*, junior-high kids sat on the stoop discussing the coolest way to shrink and fade new blue jeans. Levis became "the only garment, except for long red underwear, to enter American folklore." The symbolism was quite clear. In the words of Marshall McLuhan, "Jeans represent a ripoff and a rage against the establishment."

Above: Romantic escape into the past: 1960s model Twiggy achieves the "antique look" with dress and hair suggestive of the Pre-Raphaelites of a century ago.
Right: Blacks return to a more natural appearance: the "Afro" worn with army surplus shirt, 1973.

Opposite: Romantic escape into the past: Carnaby Street's, "mod" look, the return of the "artistic" dandy. The Beatles arrive for their American tour. Boston, 1966.

Politics were ever present in the mind of the revolutionary of the 1960s. Military surplus handily provided by Army–Navy stores could be used by pacifist youth to achieve a sense of membership in a guerrilla fraternity. But the young also rejected the reality of the present even more enthusiastically than did their spiritual ancestors, the romantic bohemians of the 19th century. And not since the French Revolution had the rejection of a way of life, of "established" authority, been so clearly marked in dress and appearance. Like rag pickers, the young dressed in scraps from any period and any society but their own. The bazaars of Casablanca and Katmandu were canvassed for everything from the ageless caftans of the Semites to those fitted skin coats and jackets with which the mountain tribesmen so impressed Darius the Great. Attics were scoured for Granny's stiff laces, crinolines, and even her wire-rimmed glasses, as well as Grandfather's army uniform. Ironically, in their choice of clothing the young were not as influenced by the films of their own day as by the televised classics of the 1920s, 1930s, and 1940s and by the mad vagaries of the rock stars, from the modestly long hair of the early Beatles to the androgynous glitter of Mick Jagger and the Rolling Stones. The liberated young also came to realize that "Black is beautiful."

Soho: "Street people" fashions
of the 1960s and '70s; democratizing denim and blue jeans
as universal modes of self-
expression.

Opposite: Return to the "sportive dandy." Fans arriving for the Muhammad Ali–Frazier fight, Madison Square Garden, New York, 1970.

Above: A black "classical" dandy.

Right: Hippie family: Sexual identity may be blurred, but oriental influence is as clear as in the days of La Pompadour. Opposite: The Arcadian dream reinterpreted, Woodstock, 1969.

Overleaf 1: In the 1960s the term "generation gap" was coined, and although the gap was ideological, it seemed most clearly expressed in dress: white-tie ball in New York.

Overleaf 2: Party in a SoHo loft, New York.

Finally, the sexual revolution expressed itself in the desire of the young to wear as little clothing and makeup as possible. Feminine undergarments were a particularly unwelcome encumbrance, not to be suffered by the nude bathers of Woodstock and elsewhere. The smash hit *Hair*, the first Broadway show to reveal avant-garde nudity to the general public, also presented the public with the favored garment of the "hip" generation—hair itself.

Various psychological interpretations have been offered for the blurred sexual identity of the clothing worn by the young. The concept of "unisex" has been regarded as part of the sexual revolution, but its relationship to a growing practice of promiscuity seems foggy. In fact, it was probably not true that the young chose to discard their sexual identity by dressing alike. Being on the closest terms with each other, boys and girls may have discovered that they shared the same tastes in clothes and therefore preferred to wear the same things. Girls wore pants not necessarily out of desire to be men but because they favored the long, clean, liberated line. Boys wore embroidered shirts and beads because peasant embroidery and bright colors offered a liberation from the notion of what had been masculine taste for a century and a half. The youths who wore their hair streaming to the shoulders and beyond may have envisioned themselves as Essenes in the desert but certainly not as girls.

The older generation greeted the extraordinary developments in dress among the adventurous young with reactions varying from bemused surprise to atavistic alarm. There is no question that hip youth appeared as invaders both alien and menacing to the "Establishment" men, the staid members of society. In the words of Peter Beagle:

Thinking about it now—about the "streaky, spotted, speckled, and spattered" costumes of the Celts; the horsehair plumes of the terrible Huns; the brilliantly dyed hide breeches of the Franks and the Visigoths; the stylized birds of prey ornamenting the shields of the Anglo-Saxons, and later the streaming red-blond hair, dragon helmets, and absurdly dainty trinkets of the Vikings—could it have been, even in the slightest, some deep turning of memories that had people so terrified of the hippies, and so disproportionately brutal toward them? The ghosts of ancient nightmares: grinning, shrieking, bearded faces, crazy clothes, and long, bloody axes under a freezing moon. The night of a thousand Charles Mansons.

Below: Twiggy, the model whose totally fleshless figure expressed the 1960s ideal of eternal, unisexual youth. 1967.

Opposite: The Space Age abstractions. Left, Ungaro designs, 1968. Right: Courrèges suit, 1968.

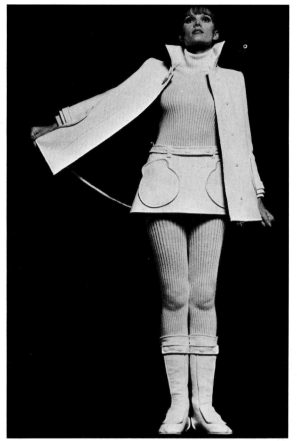

Fear, however, did not alter attitudes toward profit. It was inevitable that designers and the fashion industry should adapt themselves to the tastes of the massive youth market. The pop culture–couture revolution took place in London, however, rather than in New York or Paris. Among the poor in the working-class districts of Liverpool, Manchester, London, and the other cities of Great Britain there resided a good deal of creative talent isolated from the mainstream of the nation's culture. And in isolation it created the explosion of English "pop." The English "Mods" had been a late 1950s motor-scooter gang, but the now obscure origin of the term has far less to do with its prominence than a Welsh schoolteacher's daughter, Mary Quant. She and her husband, Alexander Plunket Green, had opened their first "Bazaar" shop in Chelsea in the mid

1950s. In a relaxed way they manufactured for and sold to the young. As early as 1955 Mary Quant saw the future of the shorter skirt. She is regarded as the mother of the "mini" and conceivably the first to introduce high boots, shoulder bags, the "poor boy" sweater, and the little-girl look that were to plague adult couture for several years. Mary Quant's sales, worldwide, skyrocketed to $12 million during the mid-1960s, by which time hundreds of other boutiques had opened in London, especially on the King's Road and Carnaby Street. Here ruffled shirts, glitter, jersey skintights, and Levi's were hawked to the "mod" of both sexes from shops such as "Hurry on You" or "Lord Kitchener's Valet."

Not all the revolutionary inspiration of the period issued from London, however. The bikini bathing suit, taking its name and date from the atomic atoll, was a widespread phenomenon in France by the mid-1950s. But it was in 1964 that the Vienna-born and California-bred Rudi Gernreich unleashed the topless bathing suit. The "topless" was created more as a preview of the future than as an article for immediate sale, and so it remained, but as a symbol its very existence was more powerful than its lack of sales would suggest. Banned in France and excoriated by *Izvestia*, the "monokini" gave heart to girls already attracted by the "braless" look. Pantyhose that covered the body from waist to toes with one stretch of transparent nylon had largely replaced the panties, stockings, girdles, and garter belts of times past. Now a little piece of elasticized nylon replaced the padded and wired brassiere, and the nipple returned as a recognized portion of anatomy.

Fashion magazines gave little or no space to

supportive garments. Rather, they published diets and exercises of every variety and made it quite clear that the new woman's girdle must be made of her own forever young muscle tissue. For those not gifted with eternal youth, the age of "body sculpture," of the plastic reconstruction of sagging breasts and "saddle" thighs as well as the face lift and hair transplant, dawned.

It was inevitable that the fashions of the youth cult would percolate upward. Paris had taken hints from abroad since the 18th century, especially from England, and it was only to be expected that a massive clamor would be heard. Perhaps the first Paris couturier effectively to come to grips with the "hip" look and to try to amalgamate it with Paris couture concepts was the young Spanish designer Courrèges. He carried it to new heights. His dresses had the intricate construction and the movement (or rigidity) of the best of Paris couture. As skirts became shorter, heels had become flatter. Now Courrèges balanced the mini with a pair of mid-calf high white boots to achieve a harmonious line. A kind of gold-plated, carefully seamed space-age goddess was created, a walking contradiction in terms. Courrèges also may claim to be the initiator of the pants suit for women. Ironically, his designs did not bring added physical freedom. Rather, he encased his devotees in stiff, armorlike suits and doll dresses that rode up and looked like a football player's shoulder guards when the wearer sat down.

Once Paris had ratified the "hip" look for those over twenty-five, abuses were sure to follow. Knees and thighs that had carried their possessors for well over half a century emerged, those selfsame knees that had peeked, when younger and better formed, from beneath flappers' dresses. Skirts that fell to the crotch and no farther were balanced by beehive hairdos that might have suited Versailles in its decadence. Women of mature years dressed not as young girls but as little girls, in flat "Mary Janes" and crisp white knee socks. Filthy white "Courrèges" boots were seen accompanying old-fashioned tweed suits worn to beneath the knee.

The hippies' search for garments "outside" established society influenced the society they meant to escape and turned it into a kind of costume party, with matrons appearing as everything from 19th-century dandies (yes, there was a "Beau Brummel" look) to inhabitants of an Eastern European *shtetl*. Women were exhorted to "do your own thing" regardless of the consequences, and Paris turned out designs in deliberately bad taste (although often with humor rare in couture) for the first time in its history. Yves St. Laurent's collection featuring a "forties" whore look complete with frizzy hair, clunky wedges, micro skirts, and puffed sleeves is a case in point.

Was Paris dead as the world's fashion capital? Far from it. Unless accepted by Paris, the new fashions reached no farther than the very young.

Opposite: Legally unacceptable: Rudi Gernreich's topless bathing suit, modeled by Peggy Moffitt.
Above: Legally acceptable: The bikini evolved into the "string." Italy, 1974.

Opposite: The peacock revolution, as waged by an extremist, 1972.

Below left: The Gray Flannel Suit, International: Japanese Emperor Hirohito is welcomed in 1975 by Vice President Nelson Rockefeller of whom

Nikita Khrushchev said, "The biggest capitalist in the world wasn't dressed in cheap clothes, but I wouldn't say he was dressed elegantly either. He was dressed more or less like other Americans."
Below right: Dinner party in Tokyo.

The connotations of Parisian approval, the result of centuries of what we now call public relations, could not be dispensed with so easily. The cachet of a Paris design remained necessary for the wide distribution of any fashion. Moreover, Paris is to the fashion world what New York and London stock exchanges are to the financial—a vast clearinghouse through which ideas must pass. Paris is the provider of designs and patterns to the world, a place where ten thousand craftsmen are equipped to design and execute the buckle of a shoe. In the words of Yves St. Laurent, "Paris is like an old grandmother who has a stock of recipes in her bag."

If women over thirty had become "baby dolls," it was inevitable that men should also be affected. As hair nestled around Wall Street collars, even the most conservative men abandoned their loose-fitting gray suits and narrow ties. The plunge into new ranges of color prompted the term "peacock revolution," as shirts with deep collars and wide ties in checks, stripes, and spots of every imaginable shade replaced the white, blue, brown, and black that had for a century suggested financial respectability. Colors formerly reserved for sport appeared in the board room and were applauded. What for the young was a rebellion against the Establishment and its "materialism" became for the core of that very group—the gray-suited businessman—a new "dandyism."

The gray suit had, however, found a home elsewhere. Ironically, while youths in the West were pleased to walk the streets in caftans, dashikis,

Mongolian shepherds' coats, and elephant-hair bracelets, young men of the upper and burgeoning middle classes throughout much of Asia, Africa, and the Near East were fitting themselves into approximations of the conservative Western business suit. Dress had finally become totally internationalized. The Jet Age and cheap travel had made it possible for the previously homebound to see the world and purchase its exoticisms, and the search for cheap production had led to the exploitation of labor markets in areas as far afield as India and the Philippines. American department stores now offered a dizzying variety of choices from every corner of the globe. Meanwhile, delegates at the United Nations, although they might don national dress for the General Assembly, were likely to buy their everyday wear off the rack at Barney's, New York's massive retailer, of everything from Cardin suits to budget socks.

In the 1960s and 1970s fashion and dress reached their highest level of social importance in centuries. This was in part due to the influence of the gossip columnists who, in attempting to interest a jaded public and discouraged by libel laws from reporting the juicier truth, fell back increasingly on reportage of what people wore. As a result, the celebrities of the fashion industries became the subject of curiosity—designers, manufacturers, photographers, and, especially, models. The poor "mannequins" (little men) who slaved for Chanel in return for a pittance in the 1920s (she had generously suggested that they supplement their pay by taking wealthy lovers) and who won the commiseration of Colette as little

387

soldiers putting a brave face on total exhaustion, had become figures of inestimable glamour in the imagination of the masses. The models of the 1950s possessed the allure of movie stars and the refinement of society women, who were meant to identify with them. The 1960s, however, provided the splashier talents of Jean Shrimpton, Twiggy, and Verushka. It is a commentary on the period's aesthetic of nudity that Verushka was perhaps the first "fashion" model known largely for photographs in which she wears little or no clothing at all.

With the emergence of the model as a social personality came the phenomenon of the woman who is known chiefly for her manner of dress and little else. The "clothes horse" as heroine is the natural product of a press that reports every detail of clothing for a public grown voracious for every such detail. The press's crowned queen, Jacqueline Kennedy Onassis, happened to be the widow of a President, but for a fashion-obsessed press she became much, much more—an ever reliable, peripatetic Big and Little Pandora.

If the rebellious hippie influenced the dress of men and women of established society, it was often at very close quarters. "Slumming" as a form of entertainment dated back to the 1920s and before, but now the habit was universal and compulsory. The Park Avenue matron who stepped out of her cab in front of the Electric Circus discotheque or one of its counterparts dressed in a little stretch of skintight nylon (or as a gypsy, or a Victorian girl, or whatever) was met by barefoot children in denims, or spangles, or love beads, or dressed as gypsies, or as Victorian girls or boys, or wearing nothing at all. Inside, strobe lights blinked, causing walls to pulse like a living heart and converting the dancers' motions to the jerky gait of early film. Music blasted; spotlights played on "performers." A girl might become an Indian temple dancer, performing the dance with her tongue. A boy on a platform might slowly, carefully consume a banana while a man in white-tie-and-tails grunts and howls for fully ten minutes: He is King Kong. There was a great deal of bare flesh in the audience, and in the adjoining "boutique" the naked could acquire a covering of "body paint" applied by an expert for a few dollars. Thus "dressed," the wearer might regard his attire as the essence of everything new. He probably did not realize that his "look" was so old that not even the most intrepid anthropologist would attempt to attach a date to it.

There is something almost awesome about the barbaric splendor of the late 1960s and early 1970s—the use of gold and silver, burning colors and lush if synthetic textures that suggest a society at the apex of its wealth and power and aware of it. It was a sort of ecstatic vision of Imperial Rome and Byzantium conceived by Moreau and Bakst and brashly adapted to the beat of rock-and-roll.

For those surviving the fashion *Walpurgisnacht* of the 1960s, it is not surprising that in the future there seemed to loom clouds of total anarchy, a complete break with all tradition, and most certainly all tradition in dress. The social forces that would shape the direction of fashion were, after all, unforeseen and to some extent unforeseeable. Who, in the giddy days of the novelty of the wear-once-and-throw-away paper dress, could have anticipated that the conservationists' attack on every aspect of the disposable society would make it seem a disgraceful waste and an affront to social conscience? As synthetic fabrics became increasingly inexpensive and elaborate, who could foresee an oil crisis that would inevitably affect their price? With some perception, however, one might have guessed that the growing sensibilities of the Women's Liberation movement would be unlikely to tolerate the dependent "little girl," let alone the "baby doll," look. For the liberated woman, pants and nudity would be permitted but not "teasing." The horde generated by the postwar "baby boom" had grown up and in their adulthood tired forever of being children. This generation would make maturity "fashionable." By 1969 Paris hems had dropped.

The concept of fashion as a mirror reflecting society is not a new one. Beginning with Isaiah, every critic of dress has in effect been a critic of his society. Looking back, it is not surprising that Charles Reich felt that he could best explain the 1960s rebellion of youth in terms of its dress, nor that our own most vivid recollections of the decade concern miniskirts, denims, naked breasts, and two-foot-high beehives. The togaed senators in their lambent draperies, the troubadours in tight hose and pointed shoes, the Shakespearean "Doll Tearsheets" in their lewd decolletage and hippie "bum rolls," the Puritans in their severe grays and blacks, the 18th-Century dandies smeared with cosmetics do more than epitomize their eras. Such indelible images implanted in our subconscious silently confirm our highest opinion or lowest suspicion. We cannot appraise history without these visual concepts. Art is a mirror clouded by idealization. Dress reflects not society at its best but at its most mundane, because it is devised to appease the vanity of the moment. And so when fashions of the past arouse our admiration, when we can say that a people of any era satisfied their vanity with a taste that appeals even to us, that is high praise. Henry Moore has said that "Art is evolution, not fashion." But it may be said, too, that fashion in dress is evolution, and on occasion it may also be art.

Left: Jacqueline Kennedy as the 1960s version of big and little Pandora dolls, combining an appearance of youth and health with one of polished grooming and precision.
Top: Jackie Kennedy doll, made by Lita Wilson of Lorraine, Ohio, and winner of first prize in the portrait class at the Dolls Club Convention, 1961.
Above: Souvenir heads representing Mrs. Jacqueline Kennedy, being made in West Germany for export to the United States. 1962.

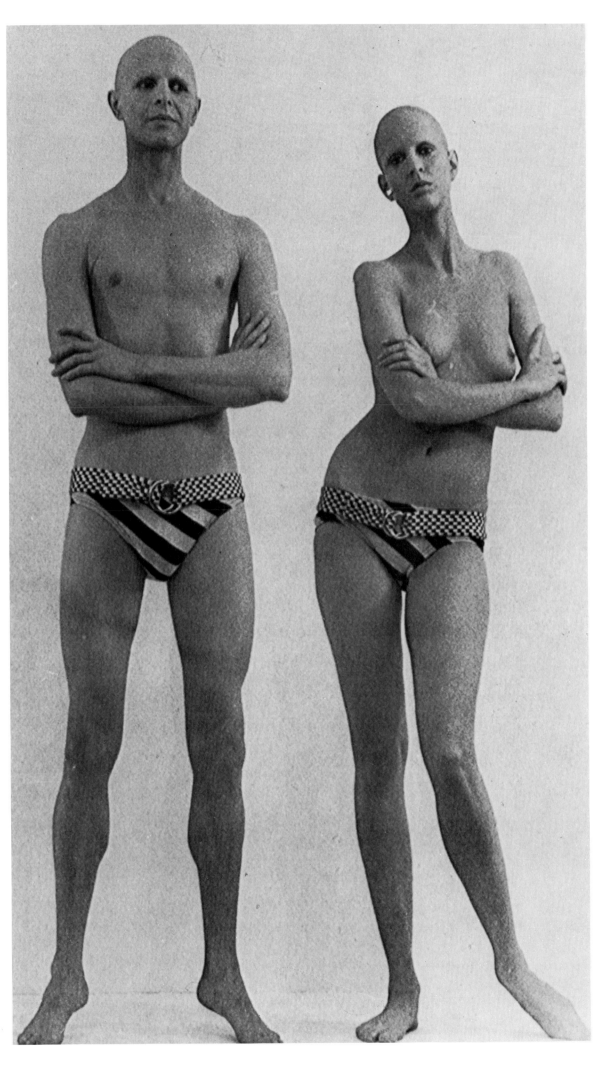

Top and right: The future as predicted: Models from "The Fashion Show of the Future," given by Rudi Gernreich in May, 1970. Gernreich foresaw, at least for those young in body, "a time for physical display, nudity and baldness." Above: Tweed dress with vinyl collar. Pierre Cardin, 1968.

The future as it happened: Left, Yves St. Laurent's "revival of folklore" or "peasant" look. A billowing taffeta skirt, embroidered blouse and turban suggesting a "turkish coffee server." 1976. Right, Yves St. Laurent's "19th century look" with ruffled skirt, lace blouse and picture hat. 1977.

Selected Bibliography

Abrahams, Ethel, and Lady Evans (edited by Marie Johnson), *Ancient Greek Dress*. Chicago: Argonaut Press, 1964.

Allen, Frederick Lewis, *Since Yesterday*. New York: Harper and Brothers, 1939.

Ariès, Philippe (translated by Robert Baldick), *Centuries of Childhood*. New York: Alfred A. Knopf, 1962.

Baldick, Robert (ed.), *Pages from the Goncourt Journal*. New York, Toronto: Oxford University Press, 1962.

Barber, Noel, *The Sultans*. New York: Simon and Schuster, 1973.

Barrow, R. H., *The Romans*. Middlesex: Penguin Books, Ltd., 1965.

Barzini, Luigi, *The Italians*. New York: Atheneum, 1964.

Battersby, Martin, *The Decorative Thirties*. New York: Walker and Co., 1971.

_____, *The Decorative Twenties*. New York: Walker and Co.,1969.

Bender, Marylin, *The Beautiful People*. New York: Coward-McCann, Inc., 1967.

Blunt, Wilfrid, *The Dream King*. New York: The Viking Press, 1970.

Bonnard, André (translated by A. Lytton Sells), *Greek Civilization*. London: George Allen and Unwin, 1957.

Boucher, François, *20,000 Years of Fashion*. New York: Harry N. Abrams, Inc.

Browning, Robert, *Justinian and Theodora*. New York, Washington: Praeger Publishers, 1971.

Burckhardt, Jacob, *Civilization of the Renaissance in Italy*. New York: Harper and Row, 1968.

Cameron, Nigel, *Barbarians and Mandarins, Thirteen Centuries of Western Travelers in China*. New York and Tokyo: A Weatherhill Book, Walker/Weatherhill, 1970.

Castiglione, Baldesar (translated by Charles S. Singleton), *The Book of the Courtier (Il Cortegiano)*. Garden City, N.Y.: Anchor Books, Doubleday, and Co., Inc., 1959.

Charles-Picard, Gilbert and Colette, *Daily Life in Carthage*. New York: The Macmillan Company, 1961.

Chesterfield, Earl of, *Letters to His Son*. New York: Tudor Publishing Co.

Clegg, Charles, and Emrich, Duncan (editors), *The Lucius Beebe Reader*. Garden City, N.Y.: Doubleday and Co., Inc., 1967.

Contini, Mila, *Fashion*. Milan: Arnoldo Mondadori, 1965.

Cooper, Wendy, *Hair*. New York: Stein and Day, 1971.

Corson, Richard, *Fashions in Makeup*. New York: Universe Books, 1973.

Cotterell, Geoffrey, *Amsterdam, The Life of a City*. Boston, Toronto: Little, Brown, 1972.

Cottrell, Leonard, *The Anvil of Civilization*. New York: New American Library, 1957.

_____, *The Bull of Minos*. London: Evans Brothers, 1953.

Cowles, Virginia, *The Romanovs*. New York: Harper & Row, 1971.

Crankshaw, Edward, *The Hapsburgs, Portrait of a Dynasty*. New York: The Viking Press, 1971.

Crespelle, J. P., *Montmartre Vivant*. Paris: Librairie Hachette, 1964.

Davenport, Millia, *The Book of Costume*. New York: Crown Publishers, 1972.

Davis, W. S., *A Day in Old Rome*. New York: Bilbo & Tannen, 1959.

Delort, Robert (translated by Robert Allen), *Life in the Middle Ages*. New York: Universe Books/Edita Lausanne, 1973.

Diesbach, Ghislain de, *Secrets of the Gotha*. London: Chapman & Hall, 1967.

Edwardes, Michael, *East-West Passage, the Travel of Ideas, Arts and Inventions between Asia and the Western World*. New York: Taplinger Publishing Co., 1971.

Eichler, Lillian, *Customs of Mankind*. New York: Nelson Doubleday, 1925.

Emery, W. B., *Archaic Egypt*. Harmondsworth, Middlesex: Penguin Books, Ltd., 1961.

Encyclopedia of Discovery and Exploration, "The Glorious Age of Exploration." Garden City, N.Y.: Doubleday and Co., 1973.

Erasmus, (translated by Betty Radice, introduction by A. H. T. Levi. *In Praise of Folly*. London: Penguin Books, Ltd., 1971.

Fairservis, Walter A., Jr., *Costumes of the East*. Riverside, Conn.: The Chatham Press, Inc., 1971.

Ferguson, George, *Signs and Symbols in Christian Art*. New York: Oxford University Press, 1966. A Galaxy Book.

Finley, M. I., *The Ancient Greeks*. London: Chatto & Windus, 1963.

_____,*The World of Odysseus*. London: Chatto & Windus, 1956.

Flanner, Janet, *Paris Was Yesterday*. New York: The Viking Press, 1972.

Flugel, J. C., *The Psychology of Clothes*. New York: International Universities Press, Inc., 1971.

Fregnac, Claude, *Jewelry, from the Renaissance to Art Noveau*. London: Octopus Books Ltd., 1965.

Galante, Pierre (translated by Eileen Geist and Jessie Wood), *Mademoiselle Chanel*. Chicago: Henry Regnery Company, 1973.

Galantiere, Lewis (translator and editor), *The Goncourt Journals 1851–1870*. New York: Greenwood Press, 1968.

Goethe, Johann Wolfgang von, *Goethe's Autobiography: Truth and Poetry; From My Own Life*. London: Harrison and Son.

_____, *Italian Journal* (translated by W. H. Auden and Elizabeth Mayer). New York: Pantheon Books, 1967.

Gorey, Edward, *The Listing Attic*. New York: Duell Sloan and Pierce—Little, Brown, 1954.

Gramont, Sanche de, *Epitaph for Kings*. New York: Dell Publishing Co., 1969.

_____, *The French, Portrait of a People*. New York: G. P. Putnam's Sons, 1969.

Grierson, Edward, *The Fatal Inheritance, an Historical Account of Philip II and the Revolt of the Spanish Netherlands*. Garden City, N.Y.: Doubleday and Co., 1969.

Hahn Emily, *Fractured Emerald: Ireland*. New York: Doubleday and Co., 1971.

Harper's Bazaar, J. Trahey (editor). New York: Random House, 1967.

Hawkes, Jacquetta, *The First Great Civilizations*. New York: Alfred A. Knopf, 1973.

Highet, Gilbert, *Juvenal the Satirist*. Oxford: The Clarendon Press, 1954.

Hodges, Henry, and Lane, Allen, *Technology in the Ancient World*. Harmondsworth, Middlesex: Penguin Books, Ltd., 1970.

Hurlock, Elizabeth B., *The Psychology of Dress, an Analysis of Fashion and Its Motives*. New York: Ronald Press, 1929.

Hutchinson, R. W., *Prehistoric Crete*. Harmondsworth, Middlesex: Penguin Books, Ltd., 1962.

Jullian, Philippe, *Prince of Aesthetes*. New York: The Viking Press, 1965.

_____, *Dreamers of Decadence*. London: Pall Mall Press. 1971.

Kantorowicz, Ernst H., *The King's Two Bodies, a Study in Mediaeval Political Theology*. Princeton: Princeton University Press, 1957.

Keller, Werner, *The Etruscans*. New York: Alfred A. Knopf, 1974.

Kelly, Amy, *Eleanor of Aquitaine and the Four Kings*. Cambridge, Mass.: Harvard University Press, 1950.

Kiefer, Otto, *Sexual Life in Ancient Rome*. London: The Abbey Library, 1934.

Knapton, Ernest John, *Empress Josephine*. Cambridge, Mass.: Harvard University Press, 1963.

Kochno, Boris, *Diaghilev and the Ballets Russes*. New York: Harper & Row, 1970.

Köhler, Carl (edited and augmented by Emma von Sichart), *A History of Costume*. New York: David McKay Co., 1963.

Koster, Joseph (editor), *Wings of the Falcon: Life and Thought in Ancient Egypt*. New York: Holt, Rinehart and Winston, 1968.

Lane, Frederic C., *Venice, a Maritime Republic*. Baltimore and London: The Johns Hopkins University Press, 1973.

Langner, Lawrence, *The Importance of Wearing Clothes*. New York: Hastings House, 1959.

Laver, James, *The Age of Illusion*. New York: David McKay Co., 1972.

_____, *The Concise History of Costume and Fashion*. New York: Harry N. Abrams, Inc., 1969.

_____, *Costume in the Theatre*. New York: Hill and Wang, 1965.

_____, *Manners and Morals in the Age of Optimism*. New York: Harper & Row, 1966.

_____, *Modesty in Dress*. Boston: Houghton Mifflin Co., 1969.

Lee Sarah Tomerliu, (editor). *American Fashion*. New York: Quadrangle Press, 1975.

Leloir, Maurice, *Dictionnaire du Costume*. Paris: Libraire Gründ.

Licht, Hans, *Sexual Life in Ancient Greece*. London: The Abbey Library, 1932.

Lloyd-Jones, Hugh (ed.), *The Greeks*. C. A. Watts and Co., Ltd., 1962.

Loomis, Stanley, *A Crime of Passion*. Philadelphia: J. B. Lippincott, 1967.

_____, *Du Barry*. Philadelphia: J. B. Lippincott, 1959.

_____, *The Fatal Friendship*. New York: Doubleday and Co., 1972.

_____, *Paris in the Terror*. Philadelphia: J. B. Lippincott, 1964.

McAllister, Ward, *Society as I Have Found It*. New York: Cassell Publishing Company, 1890.

McClellan, Elizabeth, *History of American Costume*. New York: Tudor Publishing Company, 1969.

Marks, Stephen S. (editor), *Fairchild's Dictionary of Textiles*. New York: Fairchild Publications, Inc., 1959.

Marriott, Alice, and Rachlin, Carol K., *American Epic, the Story of the American Indian*. New York: G. P. Putnam's Sons, 1969.

Meilsheim, David (translated by Grace Jackman), *The World of Ancient Israel*. New York: Tudor Publishing Company, 1973.

Mertz, Barbara, *Red Land, Black Land*. London: Hodder and Stoughton Ltd., 1967.

Mitford, Nancy, *Madame de Pompadour*. London: Hamish Hamilton, 1954.

Nicolson, Harold, *Good Behavior, Being a Study of Certain Types of Civility*. New York: Doubleday and Co., 1956.

Oldenbourg, Zoë (translated by Anne Carter), *The Crusades*. New York: Pantheon Books, 1966.

Owenden, Graham, *Pre-Raphaelite Photography*. New York: St. Martin's Press, 1972.

Parsons, Frank Alvah, *Psychology of Dress*. New York: Doubleday, Page and Co., 1920.

Payne, Robert, *The Christian Centuries*. New York: W. W. Norton, 1966.

Prestcott, William H., *Ferdinand and Isabella*, Vol. I. Philadelphia: J. B. Lippincott, 1837.

Priestley, J. B., *The Edwardians*. New York: Harper & Row, 1970.

_____, *The English*. London: Heinemann, 1973.

Pullar, Philippa, *Consuming Passions*. Boston, Toronto: Little, Brown, 1970.

Quennell, Margorie and C. H. B., *Everyday Things in Ancient Greece*. New York: G. P. Putnam's Sons, 1930.

Quinn, David Beers, *The Elizabethans and the Irish*. Ithaca Press, 1966.

Raitt, A. W., *Life and Letters in France in the 19th Century*. New York: Charles Scribner's Sons, 1965.

Reader, W. J., *Victorian England*. New York: G. P. Putnam's Sons, 1974.

Richardson, Joanna, *La Vie Parisienne 1852–1870*. New York: The Viking Press, 1974.

_____, *The Bohemians*. New York: A. S. Barnes and Co., 1971.

Saint Simon, Duc de (translated by Francis Arkwright), *Gossip and Glory of Versailles 1692-1701*. New York: Brentano's.

Schoeffler, O. E., and Gale, William, *Esquire's Encyclopedia of 20th Century Men's Fashions*. New York: McGraw-Hill, 1973.

Severin, Timothy, *The Horizon Book of Vanishing Primitive Man*. New York: American Heritage Publishing Co., 1973.

Sherwood, Mrs. John, *Manners and Social Usages*. Harper Brothers, 1888.

Sissons, Michael, and French, Philip, *The Age of Austerity*. London: Hodder and Stoughton, 1963.

Sitwell, Dame Edith, *The Queens and the Hive*. Boston, Toronto: Little, Brown, 1962.

Smith, Bradley, *Spain, a History in Art*. New York: Simon and Schuster, 1966.

Spiegel, Dr. Leo A., "The Child's Concept of Beauty: A Study in Concept Formation," in *Journal of Genetic Psychology*, 77, 1950.

Squire, Geoffrey, *Dress and Society 1560–1970*. New York: The Viking Press, 1974.

Steegmuller, Francis (translator and editor), *Flaubert in Egypt: A Sensibility on Tour*. Boston, Toronto: Little, Brown, 1972.

Steindorff, George, and Seele, Keith C., *When Egypt Ruled the East*. Chicago: University of Chicago Press, 1942.

Strong, Roy, *Splendor at Court*. Boston: Houghton Mifflin, 1973.

Symonds, John Addington, *Renaissance in Italy, the Catholic Reaction*, Vols. I and II. New York: Henry Holt and Co., 1887.

Tawney, R. H., *Religion and the Rise of Capitalism*. New York: Harcourt, Brace and Co., 1926.

Taylor, G. Rattray, *Sex in History*. New York: Vanguard Press, 1954.

Toffler, Alvin, *Future Shock*. New York: Random House, 1970.

Veblen, Thorstein, *The Theory of the Leisure Class*. New York: The Macmillan Company, 1899.

White, Palmer, *Poiret*. New York: Clarkson N. Potter, Inc., 1973.

Whittick, Arnold, *Symbols, Signs and Their Meaning and Uses in Design*. London: Leonard Hill Books, a division of International Textbook Co. Ltd., 1971.

Wilcox, R. Turner, *A Dictionary of Costume*. New York: Charles Scribner's Sons, 1969.

_____, *Folk and Festival Costume of the World*. New York: Charles Scribner's Sons, 1965.

Williams, Neville, *The Life and Times of Elizabeth I*. Garden City, N.Y.: Doubleday and Co., 1972.

Winston, Richard, *Charlemagne, from the Hammer to the Cross*. Indianapolis, New York: Bobbs-Merrill, 1954.

The World in Vogue. New York: The Viking Press, 1963.

Picture Credits

The page number is in bold face-type, followed by an identification and the location of the work. Photographers and photo agencies appear in parentheses. Two or more pictures on a single page are separated by a semicolon. The following abbreviations are used:

AM	Ampliaciones y Reproducciones Mas, Barcelona
AMH	Archaeology Museum, Heraklion
BL	British Library
BM	British Museum
BMFA	Boston Museum of Fine Arts
BN	Bibliotheque National
BR	Bibliotheque Royale Albert I, Brussels
CHM	Cooper-Hewitt Museum of Design
CHPL	Cooper-Hewitt Picture Library
FIT	Fashion Institute of Technology
HMQ	Her Majesty the Queen
KMV	Kunsthistorisches Museum, Vienna
MMA	Metropolitan Museum of Art
MOMA	Museum of Modern Art
NGAW	National Gallery of Art, Washington, D.C.
NGL	National Gallery, London
NPGL	National Portrait Gallery, London
NYPL	New York Public Library
OBV	Osterreichische Nationalbibliothek, Vienna
RTH	Radio Times Hulton Picture Library
UPI	United Press International
VA	Victoria and Albert Museum

Jacket, front and back: CHPL Title page: CHM:Holland Coll. Copyright page: Louvre: Coll. E. de Rothschild Contents page: BN

8 Clal-lum Indians. Royal Ontario Museum, Toronto; Hunt Ball. Courtesy Dr. Ludwig Glaeser **9** Indians, BM; Maori. NYPL; African Tribesmen. Musée de L'Homme, Paris (Haeberlin) **10** Flavian Lady. Capitoline Museum, Rome (Alinari); Portrait of a girl. Louvre **11** Bath attendant. Karl Marx University Library, Leipzig; Edwardian Belle, (Mander & Mitchenson) **12** Penitents. (George Holton); "Easy Rider". MOMA **13** Praetorian guards. Louvre (Giraudon); African Tribesmen. Musée de l'Homme, Paris; Edward VII. NYPL **14** Fresco. Coptic Museum, Cairo (George Holton) **16** (George Holton) **17** (Henri Lhote) **18** Lapis and shell plaque. University Museum, Philadelphia; Statues. Oriental Institute, University of Chicago **20** BM **21** Drawing by excavators, from *Ur Excavations: The Royal Cemetery*, London, 1934 by Sir Leonard Woolley; Helmet. (Thames and Hudson) **22** Palestine Museum, Jerusalem (George Holton); Wall relief. MMA **23** CHPL **24** MMA **25** MMA **26** Pectoral. Cairo Museum (Peter Clayton); Anklet and bracelet. Cairo Museum (Peter Clayton); Falcon collar. MMA (Peter Clayton) **27** MMA **29** Akhenaten and family. Egyptian Museum, Berlin; Akhenaten. Cairo Museum (Hirmer); Nefertiti. Egyptian Museum, Berlin (Bildarchiv Preussischer Kulturbesitz) **30** AMH **31** Fresco. Candia Museum (Leonard Von Matt); Seal ring. National Museum, Athens (Hirmer) **32** Pendant. BM; Snake Goddess. AMH; Design. Courtesy Adam and Charles Black Publishers **33** Fresco. Thebes Museum (Peter Clayton); Fresco. From Tiryns **35** Maidens. Glyptothek Museum, Munich; Gravestone. Staatliche Museum, Berlin; Drawing. Courtesy Adam and Charles Black Publishers **36** Drawings. Courtesy Adam and Charles Black Publishers; Hunter. BMFA; Chiton. Vatican Museum **37** Staatliche Museum, Berlin (Hirmer) **38** Details of red-figure vase paintings, left to right. "Dionysius and Bacchantes". Glyptothek, Munich; "Woman Playing a Flute to a Reclining Man". 6th century B.C. Louvre (Giraudon); "Crowning of Fiancee". 5th century B.C. National Museum, Athens; "Ganymede", attributed to the Pan Painter, c. 470-460 B.C. MMA **39** MMA **40** BM **41** Mother and child. ACL Brussels; Maenade. Palazzo Conservatori, Rome; Statuette. MMA: Rogers Fund **42** MMA **43** Vase painting Vatican Museum; Bracelet. MMA: Rogers Fund; Vase painting. Taranto National Museum **44** Museo Civico Archeologico, Bologna **45** Museo Villa Guilia, Rome (Leonard Von Matt) **46** Scabbard. BM; Necklace. BM; Facsimile paintings. (J.R. Freeman) **47** Museo Villa Guilia, Rome (George Holton) **48** Walters Art Gallery, Baltimore **49** Vatican Museum, Rome (Alinari) **50** Livia. Museo Nazionale, Naples (Alinari); Orator. Vatican Museum, Rome (Alinari) **51** Uffizi Gallery, Florence **52** Art and History Museum, Geneva (Alinari) **53** (Leonard Von Matt) **54** Livia. Vatican Museum (Giraudon); Augustus. Vatican Museum, Rome **55** Wall painting. MMA, Rogers Fund, 1903; Relief. Musée D'Epinal (Alinari); Octavia. Louvre (Giraudon) **56** Musée des Tissus, Lyon (Rene Basset) **57** CHPL **60** Louvre **61** Vatican Library **62** Constantine. Palazzo Conservatori, Rome (Hirmer); Bowl. MMA **63** Relief. Museo Civico, Brescia; Mosaic. (Leonard Von Matt) **64-65** (Leonard Von Matt) **66** Diptych. The Hermitage, Leningrad (Novosti); Theodora. Castello Sforzesco, Milan **67** Justinian. (Leonard Von Matt); Areobindus. Musée de Cluny, Paris **68** Silk. Vatican Library; Silk and wool. Musée de Valre, Sion (Heinz Presig) **69** Fibula and ring. MMA; Statuette. Dumbarton Oaks Coll.; Eagle.

Germanisches National Museum, Nuremberg **70** Helmet. Rheinisches Landesmuseum, Bonn; Crown. National Archives Museum, Madrid **71** Charlemagne. Louvre; Coin. BN **72** Ms. OBV **74** Ms. Roy. 16 6v, fol 56. BM **75** Ms. Fr. 2646. BN **76** Shield. BM; Ms. 9017, fol 240c. BR; Cotton Ms Nero D IX. f. 59v. BL **77** Redrawn from Strutt, *A compleate view of the Manners, Arms* etc. London 1775, Vol. 1, Plate 37. BM **78** Ms. 638, fol 28. BM; Drawing by J.P. Brooke-Little, in *Boutell's Heraldry*; Enamel. Le Mans Museum **79** Chart. MMA; Pigface helmet. HMQ: Tower of London; Milanese helmet. MMA **80** Ms. Lat. 17716, fol 91v. BN; Grandes Chroniques de France. BN; Queen Mary's Psalter. Roy. Ms10 EIV f.187. BM **81** BR; St. James. Louvre (Giraudon); Cockleshell. Museum of London **82** Ms 2A XXII fol 220. BM **83** Bath Attendants from Wenzelsbibel (Cod. 2759) OBV; Faites et Paroles Memorables de Valère Maxime. Municipal Library, Leipzig (Giraudon); Ms. Fr. 12559. p. 162. BN **85** Tomb relief. (Culver Pictures); Ms. Lat. 10532. BN; 19th century engraving. (Culver Pictures) **86-87** Ms. 5073. Bibliotheque de l'Arsenal, Paris; Musée Condé, Chantilly (Giraudon) **89** Loyset Leidet: Ms. 8, fol 33v. BR; Jacques de Guise's *Chroniques de Hainault* Ms. 9244c, fol. 213. BR; "Preaching the Crusades." Ms. 9242, fol. 1v. BR; Marguerite of York. Louvre **90** Ms. 5062, fol. 149v. Bibliotheque de l'Arsénal, Paris; Banners. NYPL **91** Historisches Museum, Basel **92** Prado (AM) **93** NYPL **94** Lorenzo de' Medici. Coll. Ira Spanierman, Inc.; Three Peasants. MMA; Soldier. (Marburg); Federigo Gonzaga. MMA **92** Armor. KMV; Boy. NGL; Triumph of Maximilian **96** Statue. Museo Verona; Textile. Musée des Arts Décoratifs, Paris; Altar cloth. Museo Poldi Pezzoli, Milan **97** Fashion plate. Queensboro Library Picture Coll. **98** Castiglione. Louvre (Giraudon); Title page. BL **99** Duke and Duchess of Urbino. Uffizi Gallery, Florence; Betrothal Scene. Staatliche Museum, Berlin; Panel. H. E. Huntington Library **100** Palazzo Medici-Riccardi, Florence (Scala) **101** Illus. from *Mores Italicae*. Yale University Library; Rector. Hospital of Santa Maria della Scala, Siena (Alinari) **102** Engraving. BMFA; Engraving. BMFA; Silver pomander. Parke-Bernet Galleries. Inc., N.Y. **103** MMA **104** Courtesan. Beinecke Rare Book Library, Yale University; Lady. MMA; *Diversarum Nationum Oenatus*, vol. 3. NYPL: Spencer Coll. **105** MMA: Bequest of Maitland F. Griggs, 1943 **106** Beatrice d'Este. Brera, Milan; Isabella d'Este. KMV **107** François I. Musée Condé, Chantilly (Giraudon); Diptych. Royal Museum, Antwerp **108** Brooch. KMV; François I. Musée Condé, Chantilly (Giraudon) **109** Diane de Poitiers. Musée de Dijon; Eleanor of Austria. Lisbon Museum; **111** Uffizi Gallery, Florence (Giraudon) **112** Henry VIII. HMQ **112-113** HMQ **114** Milwaukee Art Center: Gift of the Women's Exchange **114-115** Ball. Louvre (Giraudon) **116** Luther. Coll. Goudstikker; Savonarola. Museo di San Marco, Florence (Alinari) **117** Prado (AM) **118** Auto-da-fé. BN (Giraudon) **119** Prado (AM) **120** Princess Elizabeth. HMQ; Queen Elizabeth. HMQ **121** Coll. G. Tyrwhitt Drake, Bereleigh, Petersfield **123** Lord Darnley. HMQ; Sir Philip Sidney. NGPL **124** Dutch Caricature. NYPL; Elizabeth Throckmorton. Colonial Williamsburg **125** Courtesy of the Elizabethan Club of Yale University **126** Coll. Lord Methuen, Corsham Court, Wiltshire **126-127** Coll. Simon Wingfield-Digby **129** Kunsthalle, Bremen **130-131** NYPL **132** Musée Condé, Chantilly **133** Henri IV. Musée de Grenoble (IFOT); Equestrian portrait. Musée Condé, Chantilly **134** Miniature portraits. Uffizi Gallery, Florence **135** Gabrielle D'Estrées. BN; Marie de' Medici. Louvre (Giraudon) **136** Prado (AM) **137** Marchesa Doria. NGAW; Infanta. Coll. Parham Park, Sussex, England; Rogier Clarisse. M.H. de Young Memorial Museum, San Francisco; Modern Man. California Palace of the Legion of Honor, San Francisco **138** The Ball. MMA: Rogers Fund; Cobblers. NYPL **139** Hélène Fourment. Mauritshuis, The Hague **140** Calvin. Bibliotheque de Genève (Yves Arnaud) **141** Six Regents. Rijksmuseum; Family Group. NGL **142** Pepys. (RTH); William and Mary. Rijksmuseum **143** Queensboro Library Picture Coll. **144** Four Fashion Plates. BN **145** Courtiers. BN; Table. HMQ **146-147** Louis XIV and heirs. Wallace Coll.; Louis XIV. Versailles; Marie Thérèse. Prado (AM) **149** BN **150** French Indiennes. Top, CHM: Gift: W. & J. Sloane; Bottom, CHM: Gift of Alice B. Beer **151** French silk. Top, CHM: Gift of Mr. and Mrs. I. D. Einstein; Bottom, CHM: Gift of J. P. Morgan; Toile de Jouy. CHM: Purchase, Au Panier Fleuri Fund; English printed fabric. CHM: Purchase in memory of Mrs. John Innes Kane **152-153** MMA: Print Room **154** Watteau, Schloss Charlottenburg, Berlin; Sac dress. From *La Couturière* **155** Minuet. MMA: Print Room; Fashion plate. MMA: Print Room **156** The Mitre Tavern. (RTH); Bust. MMA **157** Fielding. NGL; Caricature. (J. R. Freeman) **158** Louvre **159** Bas-relief. Versailles; Console. Versailles **160** Boucher Print. CHM **161** MMA; Print Room **162** Maria Leszinska. Versailles; Vase. Courtesy of the Antique Co. of New York **163** National Gallery of Scotland (Tom Scott) **164** MMA: Print Room **165** Frick Coll. **167** MMA: Print Room **168** (Mansell) **169** Hogarth. MMA: Print Room; Caricature. NYPL **170-171** MMA: Print Room **172** Museo Lazaro Galdiano, Madrid (AM) **173** Ca' Rezzonico, Venice (Scala) **174** Smoking party. Staatliche Museum. Berlin (Bildarchiv Preussischer Kulturbesitz); Maria Theresa and family. Schloss Schonbrunn **175** Enamel portrait. Walters Art Gallery, Baltimore; Medallion. BN; Caricature. (RTH); Elizabeth. (RTH); Peter the Great. Coll. Count Bobrinskoy (Michael Holford) **176** Maximilian and Marie Antoinette. KMV; Copley portrait. NGAW **177** Wilhelmina and Frederick the Great. Schloss Charlottenburg (Jorg P. Anders);

Gainsborough portrait. Fitzwilliam Museum, Cambridge **178** MMA **179** Ink Silhouette. VA; George III. (RTH); Queen Charlotte. NPGL **180** Courtesy the Marquess of Cholmondeley **181** Mr. and Mrs. William Atherton. Walker Art Gallery, Liverpool; Lord Chesterfield. NPGL **182** MMA: Print Room **183** Museum of London **184** Costumes. BN; Marie Antoinette. KMV **185** Fashion plates. Louvre: Coll. E. de Rothschild **186** Yale University Library **187** Versailles **188** Rose Bertin (RTH); Fashion Plate. (RTH); Watercolor. Musée Carnavalet (Giraudon) **189** NYPL **190** BN (Roger-Viollet) **191** Portrait (Bulloz); Necklace. By Baszange, ancestor of Geneva's jeweler, Baszanger; Sketch. BN **192** BN **193** Caricature. BN; Fan. Musée Carnavalet (Bulloz) **194** Murat. Musée Carnavalet; Danton. (Wayland Picture Library); Robespierre. Musée Carnavalet **196** Mme. Elizabeth. (RTH); Execution. (Mansell); Temple. (Bulloz); Goddess of Reason. (Wayland Picture Library); Conciergerie. (Mansell) **198** Gillray. BN; Guillotine Dress. BN; Fashion Plates. CHPL **199** Incroyables. (Wayland Picture Library); Merveilleuse. CHPL **200** CHPL **201** Bosio Ball. BN; Dancers. BN **202** Barras. BN (Hachette) **203** Josephine. Musée Bonnat (Marburg) **204** Napoleon. Musée des Beaux Arts, Liege, Belgium; Josephine. Musée de Malmaison; Sacre. Louvre (Giraudon); Josephine's Burma ruby spray. Courtesy of Wartski Jewelers Ltd., London **205** Sacre. Louvre (Giraudon) **206** Napoleon. (Mansell); Napoleon and family. BN **207** Hortense de Beauharnais. Private Coll.; Pauline Borghese. British Embassy, Paris. (Both sold by Sotheby's) **208** Illus. from *Pride and Prejudice.* NYPL: Spencer Coll.; Le Moulinet (RTH) **210** CHM **212** "Prinny." (RTH); "Wedding Night." BM; "Prinny" riding. HMQ **213** George IV. Vatican; Fashion Plate. MMA **214** Beau Brummell. (RTH); "The Cut Celestial." (RTH) **214-215** At Almack's. (RTH) **215** Brummell. Coll. Sir Owen Morshead **216** Baron Alvanley. BM; Brummell. NPGL **217** (Mansell) **218** Marie Duplessis. Coll. of the Comédie Française (Foliot); Princess Belgiojoso. Petit Palais (Bulloz) **218-219** Salon of Princess Belgiojoso. (Rampazzi Ferrucci) **219** Hernani. Musée de Victor Hugo (Bulloz) **220** Pierre Loti. (Roger-Viollet); Literary Tea. Musée de Balzac. (Bulloz) **221** Brontës. NPGL; Trade Card. MMA **222-223** Fashion Plates. CHM: Holland Coll. **224** Snodgrass. NYPL: Berg Coll.; Pickwick. NYPL: Spencer Coll. **225** Store. (RTH); Bon Marche. Coll. Sirot **226-227** Courtesy Henry Poole and Co., Ltd. **228** (Mansell) **229** (RTH) **230** Louis Napoleon. MMA: Stieglitz Coll.; Eugénie. Musée de Compiègne **231** Versailles **232** Coll. Sirot **233** Court at Fontainebleau. MMA: McAlpin Fund; Fashion plate. Courtesy H. Poole & Co., Ltd. **234-235** CHM: Holland Collection **236** Countess Castiglione. MMA: McAlpin Fund; Crinoline. (RTH) **237** Photos. Coll. Sirot; Fashion plate. CHM: Holland Coll. **238** (RTH) **239** Harper's Bazaar **240-241** (RTH) **242** Exhibition. (Bulloz); Pavilion. (RTH) **243** NYPL **244** Mrs. Bloomer. (RTH); Blue Stocking. BN **245** Jane Morris. University of Texas at Austin: Gernsheim Coll.; Textile and wallpaper designs. VA **246** Fashion plate. CHM: Holland Coll.; Bustle. Harper's Bazaar **247** Redfern fashion plate. Harper's Bazaar; Bustles. (Mansell) **248** Princess Mary (UPI); Fashion plates. Harper's Bazaar **249** Harper's Bazaar **250-251** HMQ (A.C. Cooper) **252** Oscar Wilde (RTH); La Goulue. Coll. Sirot; Cora Pearl. Coll. Sirot; Réjané (Mander & Mitchenson) **253** Moulin Rouge. Coll Sirot; La Goulue. Musée de Vieux Montmartre (Hachette); Yvette Guilbert. NYPL **254** Top. (Brown Bros.); Bottom. (William Gordon Davis) **255** Mrs. Gould. (Brown Bros.); Hats & Shoes. Harper's Bazaar **256** Fashion plate. CHM: Holland Coll. **256-257** Sarah Bernhardt. (Roger-Viollet) **257** NYPL **258** Musée des Arts Décoratifs, Paris **259** Musée Carnavolet (Giraudon) **260** Lily Langtry. (RTH); Queen Alexandra. (RTH); Prince of Wales. (Bassano & Vandyck) **261** Edward VIII. (RTH); Fashion plate. CHM: Holland Coll.; Fashion plate. CHPL **262-263** Wadsworth Athenaeum, Hartford, Conn. **264** (Barnaby Picture Library) **265** (Lartigue: Photo Researchers) **266** Mrs. Campbell. (RTH); Corset. (Harlow Gallery); Suffragettes. (RTH) **267** Irene and Vernon Castle. (Brown Brothers); Turkey Trot. (Mander & Mitchenson); Tango Teas. (Mander & Mitchenson) **268** NYPL **269** CHPL **270-271** L'Illustration **272** Paquin dress. CHPL; Poiret Dress. CHPL **273** Poiret Coats. (Harlow Gallery); Grand Eunuch. Musée de Strasbourg (Harlow Gallery); Nijinski. NYPL **274** Ida Rubinstein. (Harlow Gallery); How to Dress. (Mander & Mitchenson); Hobble Skirt. CHPL; Suit. CHPL **275** "Sagesse." Collection of Mme. Poiret; Anna de Noailles. (Harlow Gallery) **276** (J. Guillot: Agence Top) **277** 1002nd Night. Collection of Mme. Poiret (DU Magazine); Fan. (Harlow Gallery) **278** (Brown Brothers) **279** (Brown Brothers) **280** Spring Men's Wear. NYPL; Arrow Collar Ad. Courtesy Cluett, Peabody & Co. **281** Arrow Collar Ad. Courtesy Cluett, Peabody & Co.; Spring Styles. NYPL; Postcard. Courtesy Mrs. Iwen Hsiao **282** (Horst) **283** (RTH) **284-285** CHPL **286** Courtesy of Chanel Inc. **286-287** Courtesy of Chanel, Paris. **288-289** FIT: Library Media Services, Davidow Coll. **290** British Harper's Bazaar **291** (Cecil Beaton: Camera Press) **292-293** FIT: Library Media Services, Davidow Coll. **294** Flappers. (UPI); Silk Stockings. (UPI); Hat. FIT: Library Media Services, **295** (Lartigue: Photo Researchers) **296** NYPL **297** Joan Crawford. (Brown Brothers); Clara Bow. (John Kobal); Drawing. Courtesy Graham Gallery **298-299** (UPI) **300** Sonia Delaunay. (Brown Brothers); Village Quill. NYPL; Edna St. Vincent Millay. (Brown Brothers) **301** Nancy Cunard. (Man Ray); Village, 20s. (Brown Brothers) **302** (Brown

Brothers) **303** Parisiennes. (Lartigue: Photo Researchers); Caricature. NYPL **304-305** (UPI) **306** (Culver Pictures) **307** (Culver Pictures) **308** (Culver Pictures) **309** Pacquin Dresses. CHPL; Chrysler Building. (UPI); Brooch. NYPL **310-311** Courtesy Mrs. Iwen Hsiao **312** (UPI) **313** Fashion plate. NYPL; Gary Cooper. (UPI); J. P. Morgan. (UPI); Mr. & Mrs. Astor. (UPI) **314** Resort Wear. (Culver Pictures); Gerald & Sara Murphy. Archives of the Cole Porter Musical and Literary Property Trusts, by permission of John F. Wharton, Trustee **315** (King Features Syndicate Library) **316** Bathing suit. (UPI); Shoes. (UPI) **317** Dress Competition. (UPI); Shoes. (UPI) **318** CHPL **319** Hats. CHPL; Felt hat. Femina **320** Hats. VA; Schiaparelli. (Horst) **321** Dresses. CHPL; Perfume. British Harper's Bazaar **322** Photo. (Seeberger Freres: BN); Fur Coats and blouse. FIT: Library Media Services, Davidow Coll. **323** FIT: Library Media Services, Davidow Coll. **324** (UPI) **325** (Culver) **326** Garbo. (Archivio Mondadori, Milan); Anna Christie. (MOMA); Dietrich. (Culver Pictures) **327** Crawford & Vanderbilt. (UPI); Mae West. (John Kobal) **328-329** (Cinemabilia) **330** Riveters. (Brown Brothers); Cover. Saturday Evening Post **331** Eisenhower. (Brown Brothers); Amusement Park. LC **332** Utility Clothes. NYPL; Tailor & Cutter. **333** Entertainers. LC; Zoot Suiter. (UPI) **334** Trigère Coat. (Maria Martel); Coat. Courtesy of Trigère, Inc. **335** Coat & Gown. Courtesy of Trigère, Inc.; Mainbocher Dress. CHPL; Duchess of Windsor. (Horst) **336** (Bill Cunningham) **337** (Milton Greene) **338** Courtesy Charles James. **339** Courtesy Charles James **340-341** Courtesy Charles James: Fashion sketches, drawn and signed by ANTONIO. 1929-1972. **342** Tent Dress. (Bill Cunningham); Baby Dress. From the Collections of the Design Laboratories at FIT: Courtesy Mrs. Adrian McCardell; Collections of the Design Laboratories at FIT: Courtesy Mrs. Adrian McCardell **344** (John Rawlings) Coll. of Design Laboratories at FIT **345** LC **346** (Culver Pictures) **347** 1942 Fashions. (RTH); Cadillac. LC **348** Dior. (Archivio Mondadori, Milan); Last Year's Girl. Harper's Bazaar 1947 **349** Harper's Bazaar 1947 **350** New Look. (Archivio Mondadori, Milan); Sketches. British Harper's Bazaar 1947; Drawings. La Femme Chic **351** Hats. La Femme Chic; Protesters. (UPI) **352** (Magnum) **353** Beat Poets. (Burt Glinn: Magnum); Bardot. (UPI); Coffee House. (UPI) **354** (UPI) **355** Monroe. (UPI); A-line. (John French Photo Library) **356-357** (Elliot Erwin: Magnum) **358-359** (Magnum) **359** Gregory Peck. (MOMA) **360** Miss America. (Magnum); Coeds. (UPI) **361** Convertible. (Bruce Davidson: Magnum); Skirts. (Culver); Glasses. (UPI) **362** (Brown Brothers) **363** Courtesy Mrs. Iwen Hsiao **364-365** (Camera Press); Pucci. British Harper's Bazaar **366** (UPI) **367** The Haight. (Elaine Mayes); Love Child. (UPI) **368** (Magnum) **369** Britt Eklund. (UPI); Daytona. (Magnum); St. Louis. (UPI); Soho. (Susan Weiley) **370** Twiggy. (WWD); Afro. (UPI) **371** (UPI) **372-373** (Susan Weiley) **374** (UPI) **375** (Bob Adelman: Magnum) **376** (Magnum) **377** (Magnum) **378-379** (Bruce Davidson: Magnum) **380-381** (Elliot Erwin: Magnum) **382** (David Steen: Camera Press) **383** Ungaro Dresses. (Marie France); Courreges Suit. (Elle: Harry Peccinotti) **384** (William Claxton) **385** (Elle: Roger Gain) **387** Hirohito. (UPI); Tokyo Dinner. (Magnum) **389** (UPI) **390** Gernreich designs. (UPI); Cardin. (Elle: Harry Peccinotti) **391** (UPI)

Index

Page numbers in italics indicate pictures

398

400